Learning Adobe® InDesign® CS2

Faithe Wempen

PEARSON
Prentice Hall DDC

Upper Saddle River,
New Jersey 07458

Library of Congress Cataloging-in-Publication Data

Wempen, Faithe.
Learning Adobe InDesign CS2 / Wempen, Faithe.—2nd ed.
p. cm.
ISBN 0-13-186893-4
1. Adobe InDesign 2. Desktop publishing. I. Title.

Z253.532.A34W46 2006
686.2'2544536—dc22 2005054615

Vice President and Publisher: Natalie E. Anderson
Executive Acquisitions Editor, Print: Stephanie Wall
Executive Acquisitions Editor, Media: Richard Keaveny
Executive Editor: Jennifer Frew
Product Development Manager: Eileen Bien Calabro
Editorial Supervisor: Brian Hoehl
Editorial Assistants: Alana Meyers, Kaitlin O'Shaughnessy
Executive Producer: Lisa Strite
Content Development Manager: Cathi Profitko
Senior Media Project Manager: Steve Gagliostro
Director of Marketing: Sarah Loomis
Senior Marketing Manager: Jason Sakos
Marketing Assistant: Ann Baranov
Sr. Sales Associate: Joseph Pascale
Managing Editor: Lynda J. Castillo
Senior Production Project Manager: April Montana
Manufacturing Buyer: Natacha Moore
Production/Editorial Assistant: Sandra K. Bernales
Art Director/Interior Design: Blair Brown
Cover Design: Amy Capuano
Composition: Laserwords
Full-Service Project Management: BookMasters, Inc./Sharon Anderson
Cover Printer: Phoenix Color Corporation
Printer/Binder: Quebecor World Book Services/Dubuque

Pearson Education LTD.
Pearson Education (Singapore), Pte. Ltd.
Pearson Education, Canada, Ltd
Pearson Education—Japan
Pearson Education of Australia PTY. Limited
Pearson Education North Asia Ltd
Pearson Educación de Mexico, S.A. de C.V.
Pearson Education Malaysia, Pte. Ltd

PEARSON
Prentice Hall
DDC

10 9 8 7 6 5 4 3
ISBN: 0-13-186893-4

TABLE OF CONTENTS

LESSON 3 WORKING WITH PARAGRAPHS 105

LESSON 4 WORKING WITH GRAPHIC OBJECTS 161

LESSON 5 MORE GRAPHICS TECHNIQUES 211

LESSON 6 ASSEMBLING AND PRINTING PUBLICATIONS....249

Introduction

Learning Adobe® InDesign® CS2 works alongside you to help build the professional layouts that today's information-driven world demands from businesses, governments, schools, and virtually every organization that needs to communicate.

WHAT THIS BOOK IS ABOUT

- *Learning Adobe® InDesign® CS2* is written for beginning page layout designers. The book assumes the reader has a working knowledge of basic design elements and common Windows navigation.

WHO SHOULD READ THIS BOOK?

- This book is for everyone who needs to know how to build well-designed and formatted publications. You can use this book as an exercise-by-exercise tutorial on many InDesign features or refer to it on an as-needed topical basis.
- You should read this book if you need to learn page layout skills using InDesign software.

WHAT YOU NEED

- To gain the most from this book, you will need:
    - Knowledge of fundamental Windows navigation and terminology.
    - A PC with at least an 800MHz Pentium III processor or its equivalent; 256MB of RAM; Windows 2000 or XP; 650MB of hard disk space; and a 1024 × 768 16-bit display (Macromedia recommends a 32-bit display).
    - Adobe InDesign CS2.

HOW THIS BOOK IS ORGANIZED

- This book is organized into six lessons that begin with the basics and then move to advanced features.
    - **Lesson 1: Getting Started with Adobe InDesign.** Learn about the InDesign interface, and how to set up program preferences, work with colors and frames, and divide content into layers.
    - **Lesson 2: Working with Text.** Learn how to type and edit text, and how to apply formatting such as typeface, size, kerning and tracking, and scaling. Import text from other programs, thread text between frames, and spell-check your work.
    - **Lesson 3: Working with Paragraphs.** Learn how to apply bulleted and numbered list formatting, tab stops, indentation, and leading, and automate formatting with paragraph styles. Create and format tables, and control hyphenation.
    - **Lesson 4: Working with Graphic Objects.** Learn how to insert and format photographs and other graphic objects, including applying colors, tints, gradients, strokes, and transparency effects.
    - **Lesson 5: More Graphics Techniques.** Learn how to align, group, and distribute objects; how to duplicate objects; and how to create and modify clipping paths, anchor points, and curved/stylized text.

- **Lesson 6: Assembling and Printing Publications.** Learn how to number pages, create master page sets, insert footnotes, and assemble multiple documents into a single book with a common TOC and page numbering scheme. Preview documents for desktop or professional printing, and output them in a variety of formats including PDF and EPS.

- *Learning Adobe InDesign CS2* is designed to make your learning experience easy and enjoyable. Lessons are comprised of short exercises designed for using InDesign CS2 in real-life business settings. Every application exercise is made up of seven key elements:
  - **Software Skills.** Each exercise starts with a brief description of how you would use the features of that exercise in the workplace.
  - **Application Skills.** A scenario is set to put the InDesign features into context.
  - **Terms.** Key terms are included and defined at the start of each exercise, so you can quickly refer back to them. The terms are then highlighted in the text.
  - **Notes.** Concise notes aid in learning the computer concepts.
  - **Procedures.** Hands-on mouse and keyboard procedures teach all necessary skills.
  - **Application Exercise.** Step-by-step instructions put your skills to work.
  - **On Your Own.** Each exercise concludes with a critical thinking activity that you can work through on your own. You are frequently challenged to provide your own content. The "On Your Own" sections can be used as additional reinforcement, for practice, or to test skill proficiency.

- New enhanced End-of-Lesson material puts skills to the test:
  - **Summary Exercise.** Comprehensive exercises that touch on most skills covered in the lesson. Step-by-step directions guide you through the exercises.
  - **Application Exercise.** The level of difficulty starts to ramp up with the application exercises. These summary exercises do not contain detailed steps.
  - **Curriculum Integration Exercise.** Integrate other subject areas into the computer course with the curriculum integration exercises. Topics include math, English, social studies, and science.
  - **Critical Thinking Exercise.** These challenging exercises are scenario-based—no specific steps are given.

WORKING WITH DATA AND SOLUTION FILES

- As you work through the exercises in this book, you'll be creating, opening, and saving files. You should keep the following instructions in mind:
  - You will create much of the content of your Web sites on your own, but a number of data files are included to provide specific types of Web site content, such as images, multimedia objects, and page text that would be time consuming to type.
  - When the application or On Your Own exercise includes a file name and a CD icon, you can open the file provided on the CD that accompanies this book.
  - The Directory of Files lists the exercise file (from the CD-ROM) you need to complete each exercise.
  - Unless the book instructs otherwise, use the default settings when creating a file.
  - Make sure you save all new materials to the Web site you are currently working on.

COPY DATA FILES

- You can copy data files from the CD-ROM to a hard drive.
  1. Open Windows Explorer. (Right-click the start button and click **Explore**.)
  2. Be sure that the CD is in your CD-ROM drive. Select the CD-ROM drive letter from the All Folders pane of the Explorer window.
  3. Click to select the **Data** folder in the Contents of (CD-ROM drive letter) pane of the Explorer window.
  4. Drag the folder onto the letter of the drive to which you wish to copy the data files (usually **C:**) in the All Folders pane of the Explorer Window.

DIRECTORY OF DATA FILES ON CD

Files listed in parentheses are linked to the data files for the exercise. They are not necessary for the exercise, but if they are not present, an error will appear when opening the data file and the user must click Don't Link to continue.

EXERCISE NO.	FILE NAME	PAGE NO.
Exercise 1	EX01.indd (grapes.psd, yellow_lilies.psd, tulips.psd, archway.psd, coneflower.psd)	10
Exercise 2	EX02.indd, OYO-02.indd (archway.psd, ks3806.jpg)	18
Exercise 3	None	
Exercise 4	None	
Exercise 5	EX05.indd, OYO-05indd	40, 41
Exercise 6	EX06-body.doc, EX06-headline.inds, EX06-landscape.jpg, EX06-port.jpg, OYO-06.indd, OYO-06-F1.jpg, OYO-06-F2.jpg, OYO-06-M1.jpg, OYO-06-M2.jpg, OYO-06-snip.inds	46, 47
Exercise 7	EX07.indd, OYO-07.indd (EX06-landscape.jpg, EX06-port.jpg, OYO-06-F1.jpg, OYO-06-F2.jpg, OYO-06-M1.jpg, OYO-06-M2.jpg)	51, 52
Exercise 8	EX08-cover.inds, EX08-coverpic.jpg	53
Exercise 9	EX09.indd, EX09-cat.inds, EX09-dog.inds (EX08-coverpic.jpg, dog-psd, cat.psd)	55
Exercise 10	None	
Exercise 11	None	
Exercise 12	EX12.indd, OYO-12.indd (EX06-port.jpg, EX06-landscape.jpg)	68, 69
Exercise 13	EX13.indd, OYO-13.indd (EX06-port.jpg, EX06-landscape.jpg)	73, 74
Exercise 14	EX14.indd, OYO-14.indd (EX06-port.jpg, EX06-landscape.jpg)	79
Exercise 15	EX15.indd, OYO-15.indd	85
Exercise 16	EX16.doc, OYO-16.indd	92
Exercise 17	EX17.indd, OYO-17.indd	99
Exercise 18	EX18.indd, EX18-Vet.doc (EX08-coverpic.jpg)	100
Exercise 19	EX19.indd, EX19-Body.doc (yellow_lilies.psd, tulips.psd, coneflower.psd)	101
Exercise 20	None	
Exercise 21	Ex21-book.txt	104
Exercise 22	EX22.indd, OYO-22.indd	110, 111
Exercise 23	EX23.indd, OYO-23.indd	116, 117
Exercise 24	EX24.indd, OYO-24.indd	122

EXERCISE NO.	FILE NAME	PAGE NO.
Exercise 25	EX25.indd, OYO-25.indd	128
Exercise 26	EX26.indd, OYO-26.indd	134, 135
Exercise 27	EX27.indd, OYO-27.indd	140, 141
Exercise 28	EX28.indd, OYO-28.indd, OYO-28A.indd	151, 152
Exercise 29	EX29.indd (yellow_lilies.psd, tulips.psd, coneflower.psd)	153
Exercise 30	EX30.indd	157
Exercise 31	EX31.indd, EX31-GuadalupeBass.jpg, EX31-LargeMouthBass.jpg, EX31-SmallMouthBass.jpg, EX31-SpottedBass	158
Exercise 32	None	
Exercise 33	EX33.indd, EX33-Coneflower.psd, EX33Lilies.psd, EX33-Tulilps.psd, OYO-33.indd (OYO-33A.tif, OYO-33B.jpg, OYO-33C.jpg, OYO-33D.tif, OYO-33E.tif, OYO-33F.tif)	169, 170
Exercise 34	EX34.indd (EX33-coneflower.psd, EX33-lilies.psd, EX33-Tulilps.psd, EX33-tulips.psd)	178
Exercise 35	EX35.indd, OYO-35.indd (EX33-coneflower.psd, EX33-lilies.psd, EX33-tulips.psd, OYO-33A.tif, OYO-33B.jpg, OYO-33C.jpg, OYO-33D.tif, OYO-33E.tif, OYO-33F.tif)	183, 184
Exercise 36	EX36.indd, OYO-35.indd (EX33-coneflower.psd, EX33-lilies.psd, EX33-tulips.psd, OYO-33A.tif, OYO-33B.jpg, OYO-33C.jpg, OYO-33D.tif, OYO-33E.tif, OYO-33F.tif)	190, 191
Exercise 37	EX37.indd (EX33-coneflower.psd, EX33-lilies.psd, EX33-tulips.psd)	198
Exercise 38	EX38.indd, OYO-38.indd (cat.psd, dog.psd)	203
Exercise 39	EX39.indd, EX39A.indd, EX39B.indd	204
Exercise 40	EX40.indd, EX40A.indd, EX40B.indd, EX40C.indd	206
Exercise 41	None	
Exercise 42	EX42.indd, EX42.jpg	209
Exercise 43	EX43.indd	215
Exercise 44	None	

EXERCISE NO.	FILE NAME	PAGE NO.
Exercise 45	EX45.indd, EX45-Cat.psd, EX45-dog.psd, OYO-45.indd	225
Exercise 46	None	
Exercise 47	EX47.indd, EX47.jpg	234
Exercise 48	EX48.indd, EX48-Texture.bmp	242
Exercise 49	None	
Exercise 50	EX50-Background.tif, EX50-Person.tif	245
Exercise 51	EX51-Dog.inds (EX50-Person.tif)	246
Exercise 52	None	
Exercise 53	EX53.indd	256
Exercise 54	EX54.indd, OYO-54.indd	261
Exercise 55	EX55-Cover.indd, EX55-Spread1.indd, EX55-Spread2.indd, EX55-Spread3.indd, OYO-55A.indd, OYO-55B.indd, OYO-55C.indd, OYO-55D.indd (archway.psd, appleblossom.jpg, cherrytree.jpg, orchard.jpg, fountain.jpg, yellow-red.jpg, coneflower.psd, lilies.psd, tulips.psd, landscape.jpg, port.jpg)	266
Exercise 56	EX56-Cover.indd, EX56-Spread1.indd, EX56-Spread2.indd, EX56-Spread3.indd, OYO56Book.indd, OYO56Cover.indd,	273, 275

EXERCISE NO.	FILE NAME	PAGE NO.
	OYO56Spread1.indd, OYO56Spread2.indd, OYO56Spread3.indd (archway.psd, appleblossom.jpg, cherrytree.jpg, orchard.jpg, fountain.jpg, yellow-red.jpg, coneflower.psd, lilies.psd, tulips.psd)	
Exercise 57	EX57.indd, EX57-Cover.indd, EX57-Spread1.indd, EX57-Spread2.indd, EX57-Spread3.indd (archway.psd, appleblossom.jpg, cherrytree.jpg, orchard.jpg, fountain.jpg, yellow-red.jpg, coneflower.psd, lilies.psd, tulips.psd)	283, 284
Exercise 58	EX58.indd (58pic1.tif, 58pic2.tif, 58pic3.tif)	290
Exercise 59	EX59.indd (58pic1.tif, 58pic2.tif, 58pic3.tif)	295
Exercise 60	EX60A.indd, EX60B.indd, EX60C.indd (60pic1.tif)	296
Exercise 61	EX61.indd	297
Exercise 62	None	
Exercise 63	None	

Lesson 1

Get Started with Adobe InDesign

Exercise 1

- Start Adobe InDesign
- Open a Document
- Understand the Screen Tools and Palettes
- Zoom In and Out
- Move Around in a Document
- Close a Document
- Exit InDesign

Exercise 2

- Set the Ruler Unit
- Use the Selection Tools
- Move and Copy a Frame
- Resize and Delete a Frame
- Toggle Preview Mode
- Save a Document

Exercise 3

- Display and Hide Palettes
- Resize Palettes
- Move Palettes
- Combine Floating Palettes
- Create New Palette Clusters
- Save a Customized Workspace
- Load a Customized Workspace

Exercise 4

- Start a New Document
- Create a Document Preset
- Place a New Frame
- Place a Polygon or Polygon Frame
- Type Text in a Frame
- Insert Symbols
- Move the Insertion Point
- Select Text

Exercise 5

- Change Margin and Column Settings
- Create, Move, and Delete Guides
- Align Frames with One Another
- Apply a Fill Color to a Frame
- Apply a Stroke Color to a Frame
- Apply a Color Swatch

Exercise 6

- Reestablish a Link to a Graphic
- Access Adobe Bridge
- Import Text from Adobe Bridge
- Import a Picture from Adobe Bridge
- Import a Snippet from Adobe Bridge
- Create a Snippet

Exercise 7

- Understand Layers
- Create a New Layer
- Move Frames Between Layers
- Change Layer Options
- Reorder the Layers
- Hide a Layer
- Lock a Layer

END OF LESSON PROJECTS

Exercise 8

- Summary Exercise

Exercise 9

- Application Exercise

Exercise 10

- Curriculum Integration Exercise

Exercise 11

- Critical Thinking Exercise

Exercise | 1

Skills Covered

- Start Adobe InDesign
- Open a Document
- Understand the Screen Tools and Palettes
- Zoom In and Out
- Move Around in a Document
- Close a Document
- Exit InDesign

Software Skills Before attempting your own new documents, it is helpful to become familiar with the InDesign interface. This includes understanding the tools and palettes and how they are similar to and different from those in other applications with which you may already be familiar.

Application Skills In this exercise, you will open a file that another designer created, examine it at various levels, and then close it.

TERMS

Activate To send information about your PC and your InDesign serial number to Adobe for inclusion in a database.

Fly-out palette A type of palette that expands to display tabbed panes or contracts to be nearly hidden along the side of the InDesign window.

Palette A group of related commands and options in a tabbed or floating area.

Palette cluster A group of tabbed palettes in a single defined area or window.

Zoom To enlarge or shrink the view of the current document onscreen.

NOTES

Start Adobe InDesign

- Adobe InDesign CS2 starts and exits like any other Windows-based application: from the Start menu.
- The first time you start InDesign, you might be prompted to **activate** the software. You can skip activation for up to 30 days before the program forces you to activate it in order to use it.

  ✓ *Activation is part of the Adobe anti-piracy initiative; you cannot circumvent it. Activation generates a numeric code that is a combination of information about your hardware and your InDesign serial number; it locks that copy of InDesign to your specific PC so it cannot be installed on multiple PCs. If you purchase a new computer or upgrade more than one or two pieces of hardware, you might need to call Adobe and ask for a reactivation.*

- Depending on how your copy of InDesign is configured, a dialog box might appear when you start InDesign that prompts you to create a new document or open an existing one. Click Close to close it without doing anything.

Startup dialog box

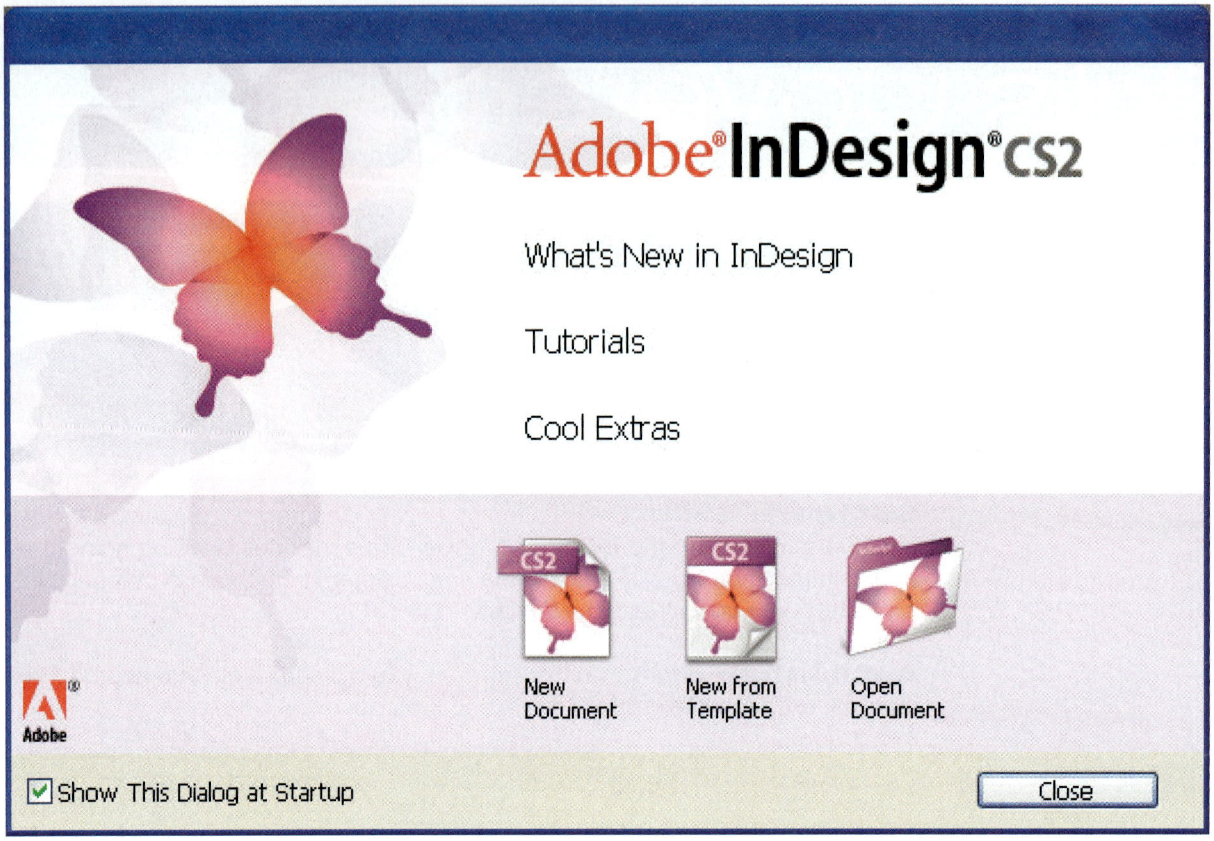

- You can prevent this box from appearing in the future by clearing the Show This Dialog at Startup check box.

Open a Document

- To open an existing file, you can use the Open command on the File menu, just like with any other application. To change the location displayed, open the Look in drop-down list.

  ✓ *Your instructor will tell you where the data files needed for the course are stored. If you are completing the course independently, copy the data files from the accompanying CD-ROM to your hard disk. You might decide to place them in a folder on your desktop for easy access.*

- You have a choice of two styles of Open (and Save) dialog boxes in InDesign: Windows style or Adobe style. To switch between them, click the Use OS Dialog or Use Adobe Dialog button in the lower-left corner of the dialog box.
- The Windows style Open dialog box has a Places bar along the left side, the same as in most Microsoft Office applications.
- InDesign remembers your dialog box preference from session to session, and always displays the type that you last chose.
- The Adobe style Open dialog box has a list of locations at the left, and has some other tools (icons) in the upper right, such as a Delete button and a Project Tools menu.

Open a File dialog box, Windows style

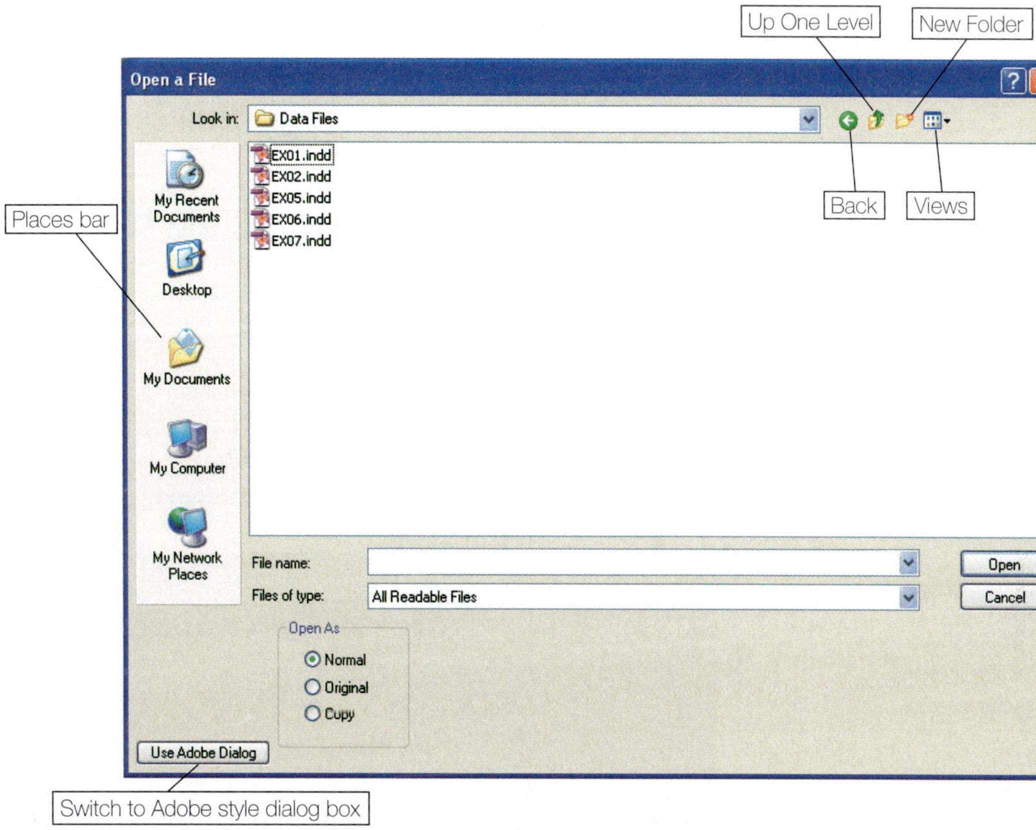

Open a File dialog box, Adobe style

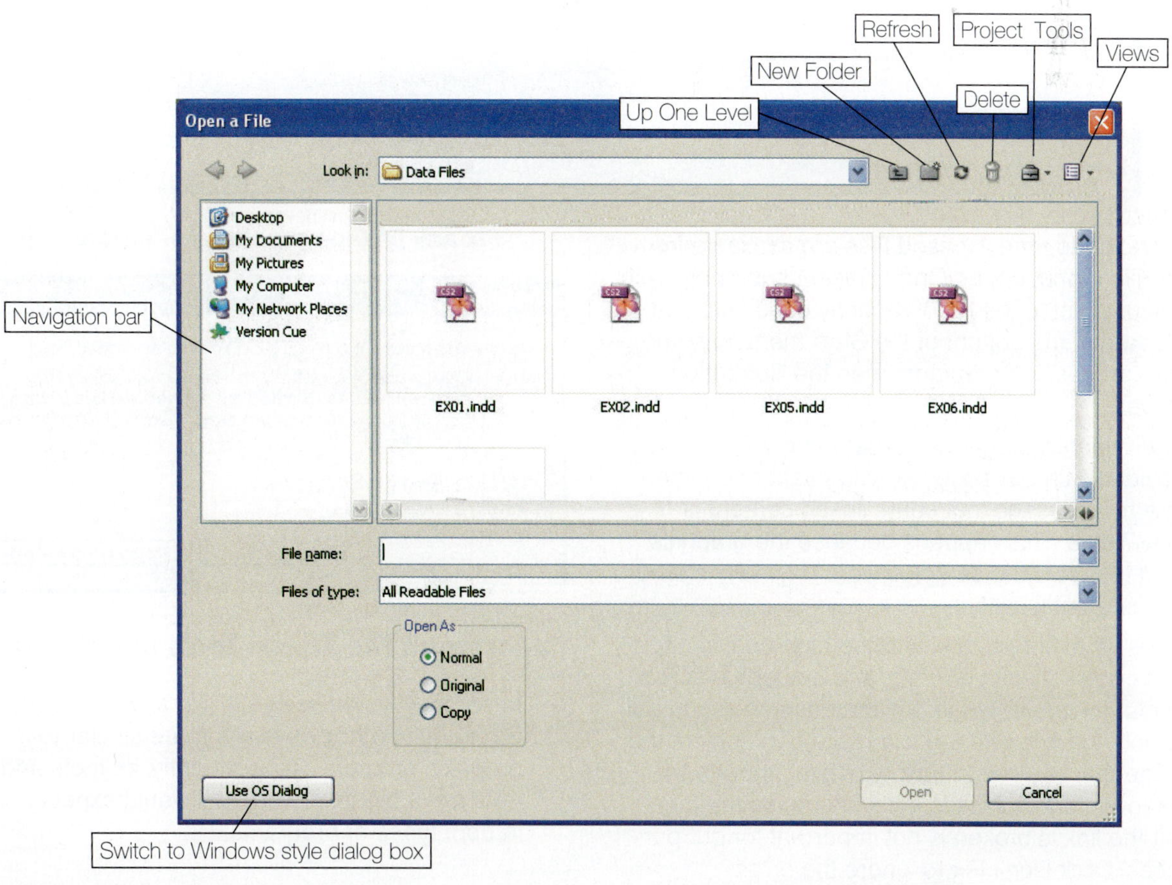

Open recently used files from the File menu

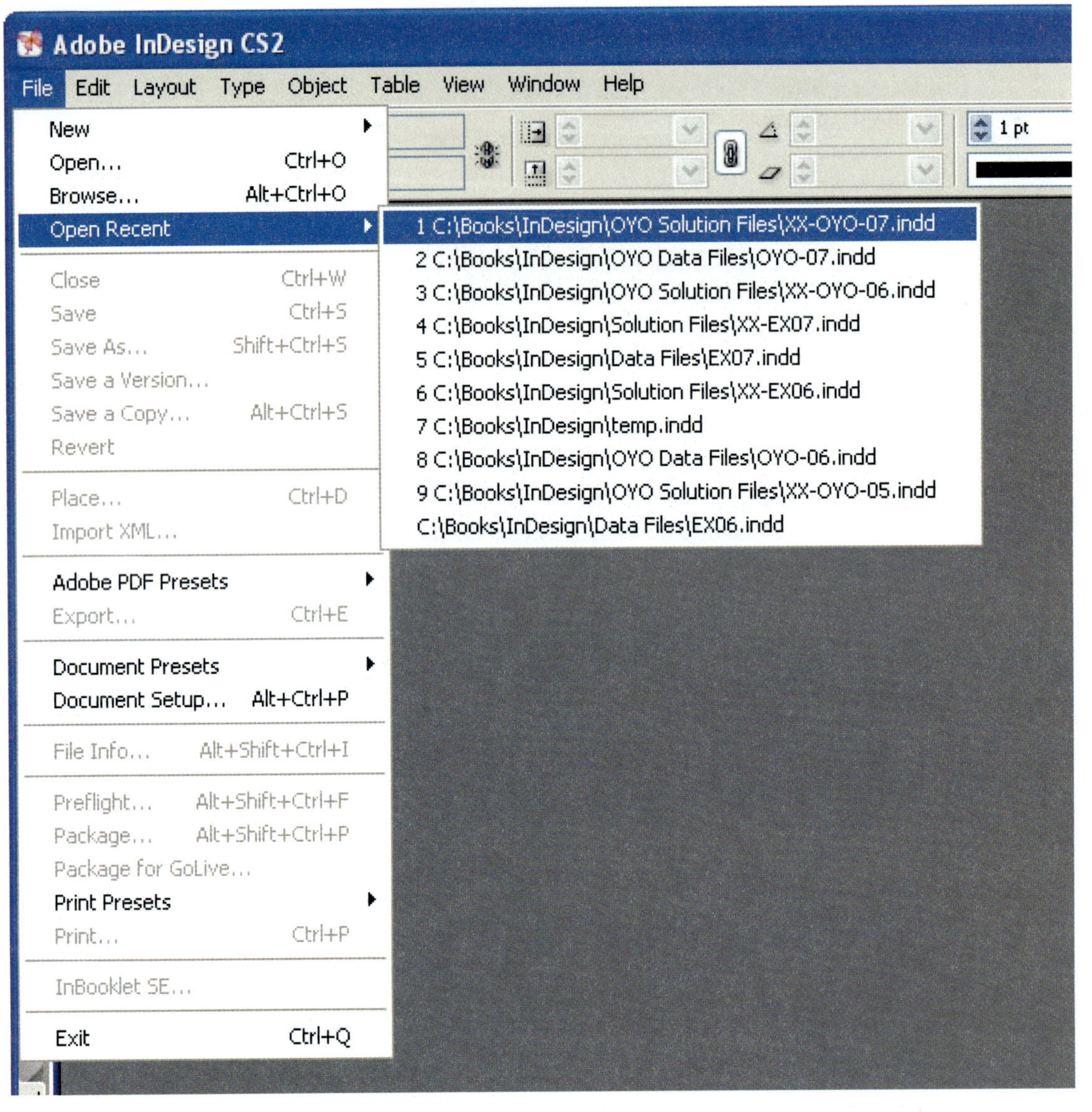

- Shortcuts to recently used files are available from the File menu, on the Open Recent submenu. This is equivalent to the list of recently used files that appears at the bottom of the Start menu in some word processing programs (see the illustration above).
- When opening some of the data and solution files provided with this textbook, you might encounter an error message that some linked content is unavailable. This happens because the graphics used to create the samples were originally stored in a different location.
- InDesign maintains a link to the high-quality original version of each graphic, and embeds a screen-resolution-quality version in the document. You will be able to work with the low-resolution copy of the image that you see in InDesign even though the link to the original file is not working, so the fact that the link is broken is not important for our purposes. Click Don't Fix to ignore the error.

Fix any linkage problems or ignore them

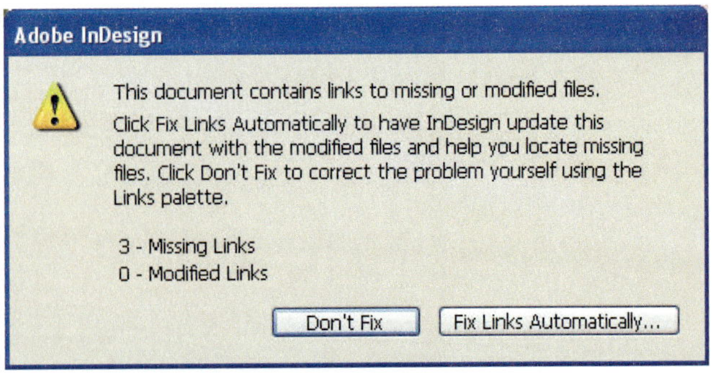

Understand the Screen Tools and Palettes

- In some ways, InDesign is like a word processing program; in other ways it is more similar to a graphics program. Consequently, its tools and controls are a blend of what you would expect to find in both types of programs.

The default InDesign CS2 window

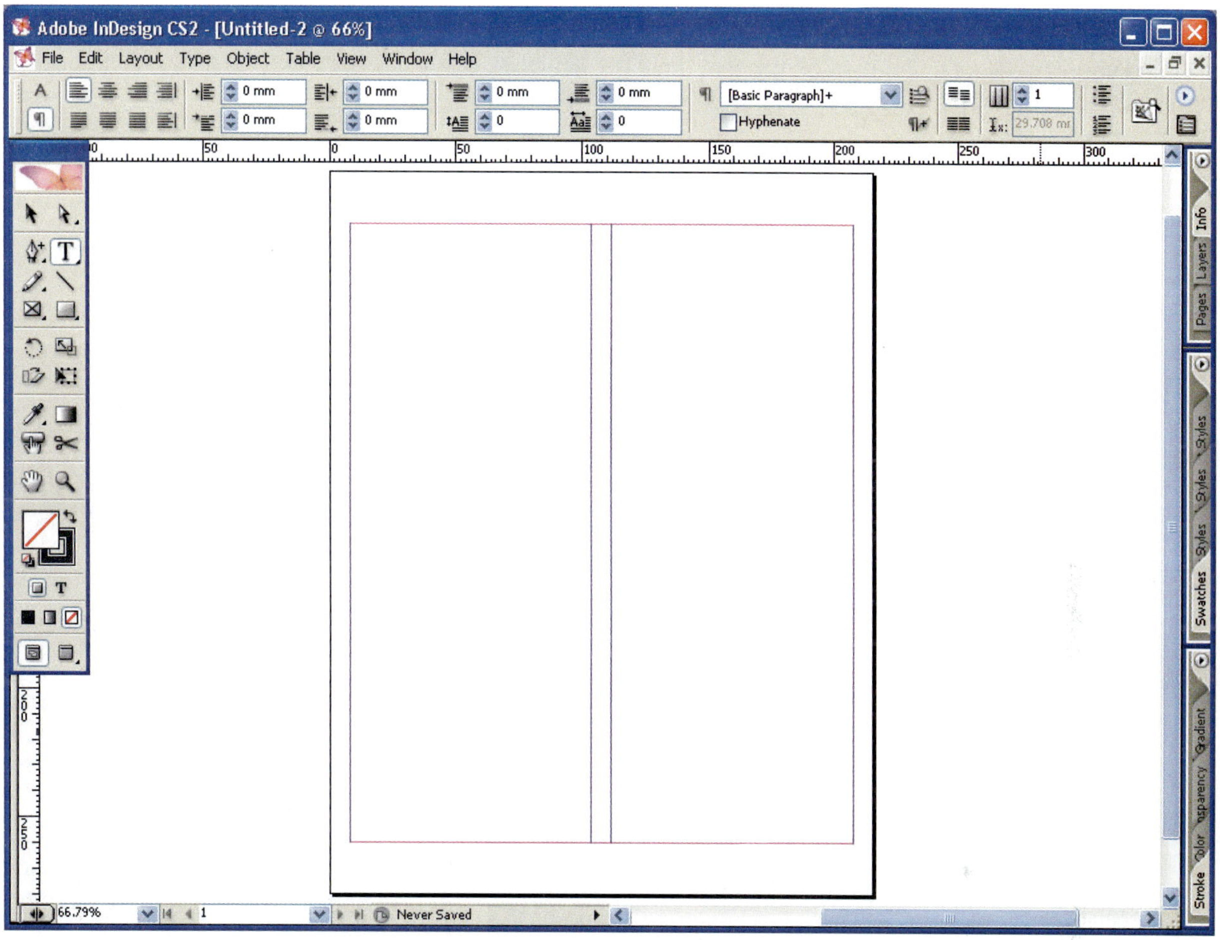

- When a document is open, it appears in the large center area, surrounded by a ruler on the top and the left.
- Depending on the way the document is displayed, there might be colored lines on the page that serve as margin or alignment guides. These do not print. You will learn in Exercise 5 how to adjust these guides (see the illustration above).
- Movable rectangular sections containing buttons, text boxes, and other controls are called **palettes**.
- Across the top of the screen is the Control palette. It contains buttons, lists, and text boxes. Its content changes depending on the context. For example, when text is selected, it contains different tools than when a graphic frame is selected.
- If you hover the mouse pointer over a control, a tool tip appears that shows its name (see the illustration below).
- Along the left side is the Tools palette. It contains buttons for activating various cursor modes in which you can add new objects, select existing objects, format objects, and so on.

Point at a button to see a description of it

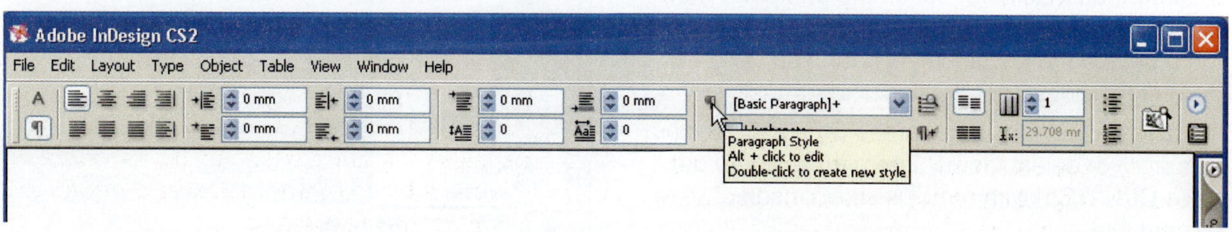

- Some of the buttons on the Tools palette have small triangles in the lower-right corner. If you click and hold on one of these, a fly-out menu appears in which you can select a variation of that tool (see the illustration below).

Click and hold on a button to open its menu

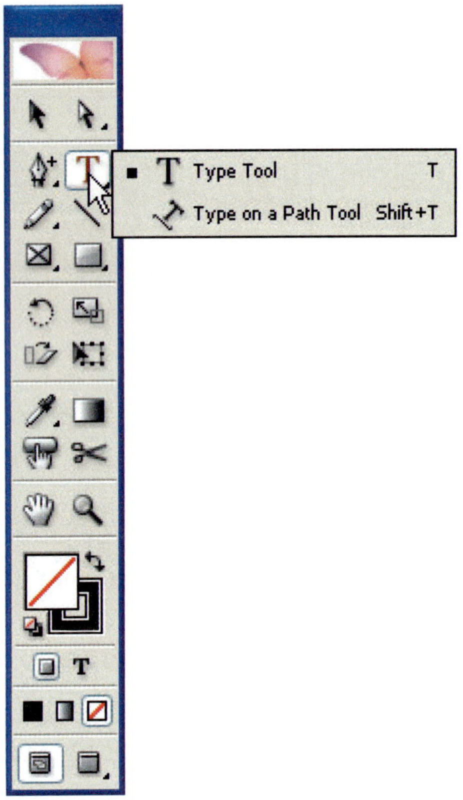

- In addition, various **fly-out palettes** are available along the right side. Each tabbed page is a palette. Some palettes are in groups called **palette clusters**. These groupings can be customized, as you will learn in Exercise 3.
- To open a fly-out palette, click on its tab. To close a fly-out palette, click the active tab or the empty gray area above the tabs in the cluster (see the illustration rightside above).

Zoom In and Out

- **Zooming** in and out changes the display onscreen, but has no effect on the printout. When you zoom in, everything looks larger; when you zoom out, everything is smaller and you can see more of the document at once.
- To zoom in, you can either press Ctrl++ (Ctrl with a plus sign) or select View > Zoom In. To zoom out, press Ctrl+- (Ctrl with a minus sign) or select View > Zoom Out.

Palettes open and close from the sides of the screen

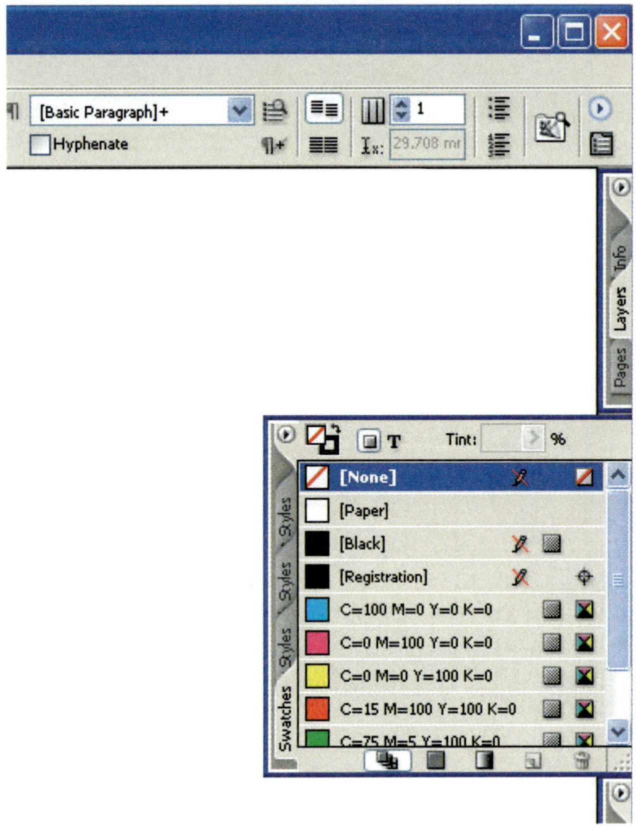

- There are also special zoom commands on the View menu, including Fit Page in Window, Fit Spread in Window, Actual Size, and Entire Pasteboard.
- To choose a specific zoom percentage, select from the Zoom drop-down list on the status bar (at the bottom of the InDesign window).

Select a zoom setting from the list at the bottom left of the screen

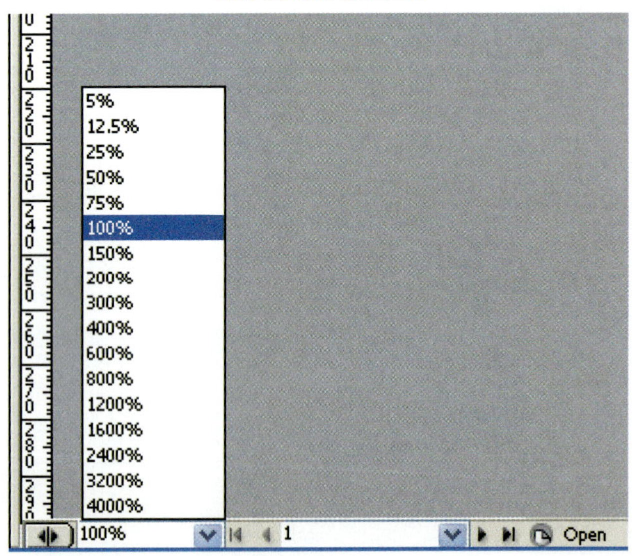

- You can also zoom in on a particular area. To do that, hold down Ctrl+spacebar so that the mouse pointer changes to a magnifying glass with a plus sign, and drag a box around the area on which to zoom.

Press Ctrl+Spacebar and drag around an area to zoom to it

Move Around in a Document

- Use the scroll bars to move around on a page, the same as with a word processing program. You can also use Page Up and Page Down.
- You can also (usually) move around on a page by holding down the Shift key and dragging. When you hold down Shift, the pointer turns to a hand that drags the document around within the window. (This does not work when the Text tool is selected.)
- In a multi-page document, you can move quickly between pages by opening the Pages palette and double-clicking the desired page.

Switch among pages from the Pages palette

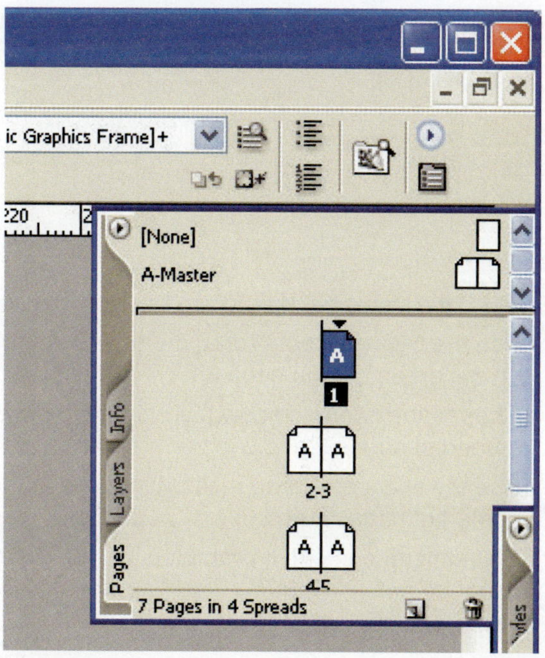

- Another way to jump to a certain page is to select from the Page drop-down list on the status bar (at the bottom of the InDesign window).
- The arrow buttons to the right and left of the Page drop-down list allow you to move forward and back in the page layout. The plain left-pointing and right-pointing arrows move one page in the direction they point; the left-pointing and right-pointing arrows with vertical lines next to them move to the first and last page, respectively.

Move from page to page via buttons at the bottom

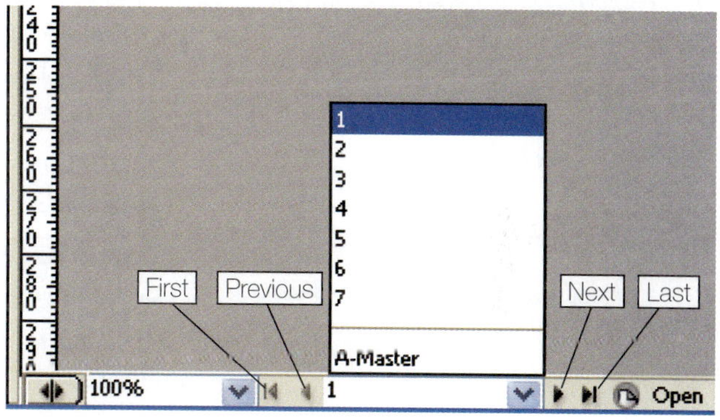

Close a Document

- You can have multiple documents open at once, so closing a document immediately is not critical. However, large documents occupy a lot of memory, so InDesign will perform best if documents do not remain open unnecessarily.
- To close a document, choose File > Close or press Ctrl+W. If the document has changed since it was last saved, or if it has not yet been saved, InDesign prompts you to save it.

  ✓ *Some settings can be set to global defaults by applying them when no document is open. For example, to define default margins and column guides, select Layout > Margins and Columns when no documents are open.*

Exit InDesign

- To exit InDesign, you can either choose File > Exit or click the Close (X) button in the upper-right corner of the InDesign window. This is the same as with most other applications.

PROCEDURES

Start Adobe InDesign

From Windows XP:

1. Click **Start** .... ⊞
2. Point to **All Programs**.
3. Point to **Adobe**.
4. Click **Adobe InDesign CS2**.

Open a Document

1. Click **File** .... Alt + F
2. Click **Open** .... O

   ✓ *Ctrl+O is a shortcut alternative to steps 1 and 2.*

3. Click **Look in** arrow .... Alt + I, ↓
4. Select drive or folder.

   ✓ *If necessary, double-click folder name.*

5. Click file name to select.
6. Click **Open**

Open a Recently Used Document

1. Click **File** .... Alt + F
2. Point to **Open Recent** .... R
3. Click file name .... ↑ or ↓, ↵Enter

Work with Fly-Out Palettes

Open a Fly-Out Palette

- Click the desired palette's tab.

Close a Fly-Out Palette

- Click the tab for the open palette.

OR

Click a blank spot on the palette cluster.

Zoom In and Out

Menu Method

1. Click **View** .... Alt + V
2. Click one of the following:
   - **Zoom In** I
   - **Zoom Out** .... O
   - **Fit Page in Window** .... F
   - **Fit Spread in Window** .... S
   - **Actual Size** .... A
   - **Entire Pasteboard** .... P

Keyboard Shortcut Method

- Press one of the following key combinations:
  - **Zoom In** .... Ctrl + +
  - **Zoom Out** .... Ctrl + -
  - **Fit Page in Window** .... Ctrl + 0
  - **Fit Spread in Window** .... Alt + Ctrl + 0
  - **Actual Size** .... Ctrl + 1
  - **Entire Pasteboard** .... Alt + ⇧Shift + Ctrl + 0

Mouse Method

- Hold down Ctrl+spacebar and drag a box around the area to zoom in on. .... Ctrl + Spacebar

Scroll the View

- Drag the scroll box in the scroll bar.

  OR

  Click an arrow at either end of the scroll bar.

OR

a. Click [Selection tool icon].

✓ *Clicking [Direct Selection tool icon], the Direct Selection tool, is necessary only if the Text tool is currently selected.*

b. Hold down spacebar .... Spacebar

c. Hold down the left mouse button and drag.

Switch Between Pages

Status Bar Method

1. Click [drop-down arrow] to right of Page indicator on status bar.
2. Click the desired page number.

Pages Palette Method

1. Click **Pages** tab.
2. Double-click the [page icon] icon for the desired page.

Close a Document

1. Click **File** .... Alt + F
2. Click **Close** C

   ✓ *Ctrl+W is a shortcut alternative to steps 1 and 2.*

Exit InDesign

1. Click **File** .... Alt + F
2. Click **Exit** X

   ✓ *Ctrl+Q is a shortcut alternative to steps 1 and 2.*

EXERCISE DIRECTIONS

1. Start Adobe InDesign.
2. Open the file **EX01.indd** from the data files provided for this course.

   ✓ *If needed, ask your instructor where the data files are stored.*

   ✓ *If a message appears about missing linked files, you can safely ignore it for now.*

3. Zoom to fit the entire page in the window.
4. Using the Pages palette, jump to page 4.
5. Close the Pages palette.
6. Using the status bar drop-down list, jump to page 3.
7. Use the Ctrl+spacebar+drag method to zoom in on the green box on page 3.
8. Change the zoom to show the entire two-page spread of pages 2 and 3 in the window.
9. Use the spacebar+drag method to move to the spread of pages 4 and 5.
10. Close the document. If prompted, do not save the changes.
11. Exit Adobe InDesign.

ON YOUR OWN

1. Do one of the following:
   - Insert Disk 2 of the Adobe InDesign CS2 CD set. Navigate to X:\Goodies (where X: is your CD drive's letter) and drag-and-drop the entire InDesign CS2 Sample Files folder to your desktop or your My Documents folder.
   - Find out from your instructor where the InDesign CS2 sample files are stored on your PC or on your school's network server.
2. Open the file **Adobe History.indd** from the U.S. English folder in the sample file set. (If you don't have a U.S. English folder, the files will be directly in the Samples folder.)
3. Scroll through this document using the browsing and zooming skills you have learned.
4. Close the document.
5. Exit Adobe InDesign.

Exercise | 2

Skills Covered

- Set the Ruler Unit
- Use the Selection Tools
- Move and Copy a Frame
- Resize and Delete a Frame
- Toggle Preview Mode
- Save a Document

Software Skills Frames are the basis on which InDesign functions. Learning how to manipulate frames is a necessary first step in learning to work with all types of content, including both text and graphics.

Application Skills In this exercise, you will open a file that another designer has created; move, resize, and delete some of its frames; preview it without the guides; and save your changes to it.

TERMS

Direct Selection tool The white arrow tool, which enables you to select content within a frame or modify the frame shape.

Lassoing To drag an imaginary box around a group of frames, selecting them all at once.

Pica A measure used in publishing that equals 1/6 of an inch.

Point A measure used in publishing that equals 1/72 of an inch (1/12 of a pica).

Selection handle A white square along the border of a frame, used to resize the frame and to indicate that the frame is selected.

Selection tool The black arrow tool, which enables you to select object frames.

NOTES

Set the Ruler Unit

- In the United States, the inch is the most common unit of measure. However, in publishing, general measures of distance or positioning are usually described in either picas or millimeters.
- A **pica** is 1/6 of an inch. Picas can further be broken down into points; a **point** is 1/12 of a pica (1/72 of an inch). Points are most commonly used to describe the size of type. For example, a popular size for body text in a document is 10 point.
- Many people find millimeters more convenient than picas to use because they represent a smaller unit of measure. With picas, often the desired position of an item is not a whole number, so it has to be expressed in decimals (such as 4.75 picas) or in picas-plus-points (such as 4p8.693, or "4 picas plus 8.693 points").
- The default setting for InDesign is picas, but the instructions in this book use millimeters. To change to millimeters, choose Edit > Preferences > Units & Increments and make the change in the Preferences dialog box.

Preferences dialog box

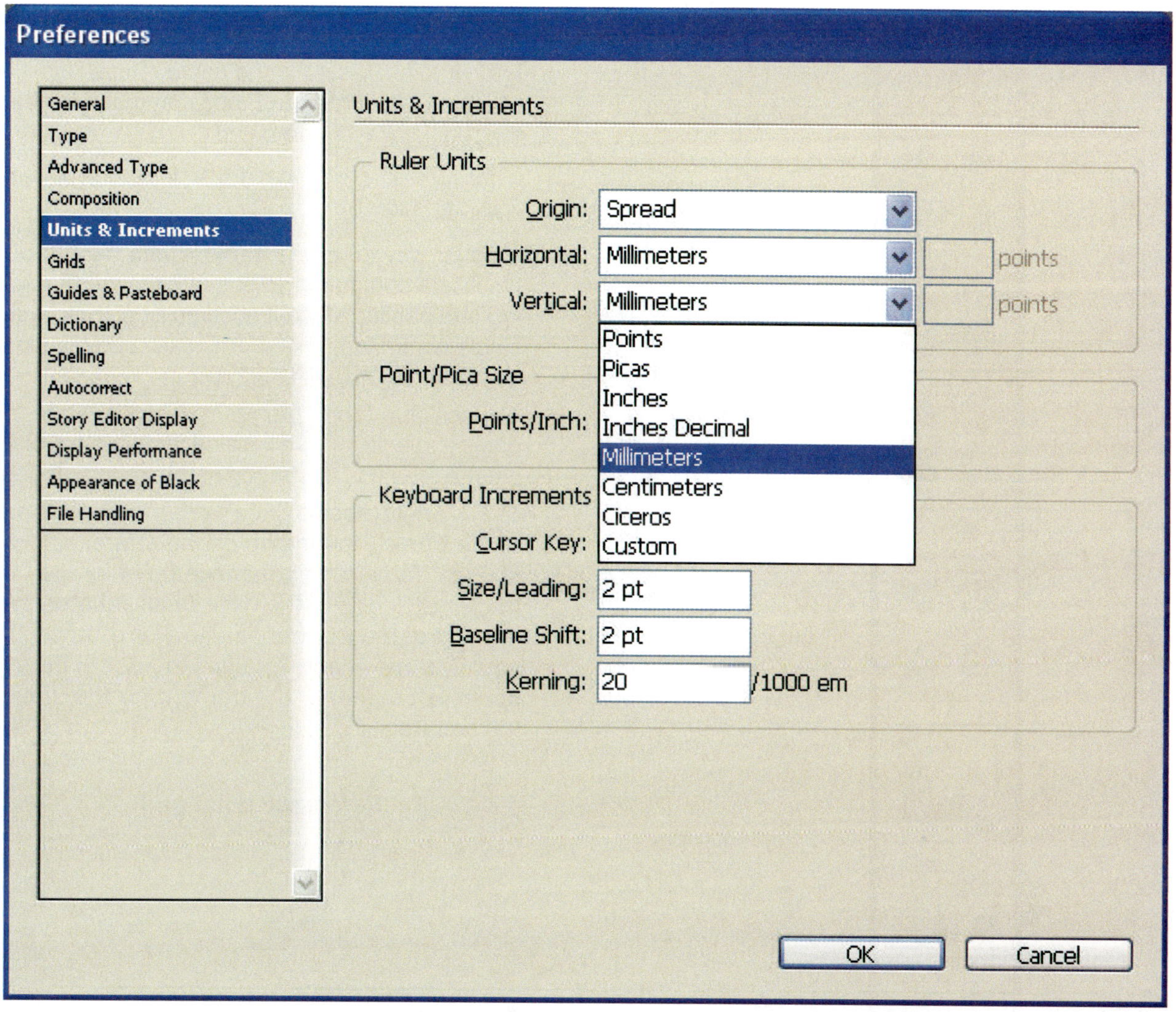

- If someone has previously used InDesign on your computer, the change may already have been made.

  ✓ *The selection of unit of measure is not saved with the workspace. If you create and load different workspaces, as you'll learn in Exercise 3, the unit of measure is not affected.*

Use the Selection Tools

- InDesign contains two main selection tools: the Selection tool (black arrow) and the Direct Selection tool (white arrow) (see the illustration on next page).
- The **Selection tool** selects the frames of the objects. With the Selection tool, you can move items around on the page. (See illustration on following page.)
- To quickly switch to the Selection tool, press the V key, except when typing in a text frame. When typing in a text frame, hold down the Ctrl key and move the mouse pointer outside of the text frame to quickly switch to the Selection tool.
- To select a single frame, click on it. To select multiple frames, drag an imaginary box around an area that encompasses all the frames you want to select. This is called **lassoing**. You can also hold down the Shift key as you click individually on each frame you want to select.
- The **Direct Selection tool** lets you select the content within a frame, or select individual handles on objects and then drag them to reshape the object. To quickly switch to the Direct Selection tool, press the A key (except when in a text frame).

Move and Copy a Frame

- To move a frame, select it with the Selection tool and then position the mouse pointer over its border (but *not* over a **selection handle**) and drag it where you want it. The mouse pointer will appear as a tailless arrow when it is positioned appropriately for moving.

Selection and Direct Selection tools

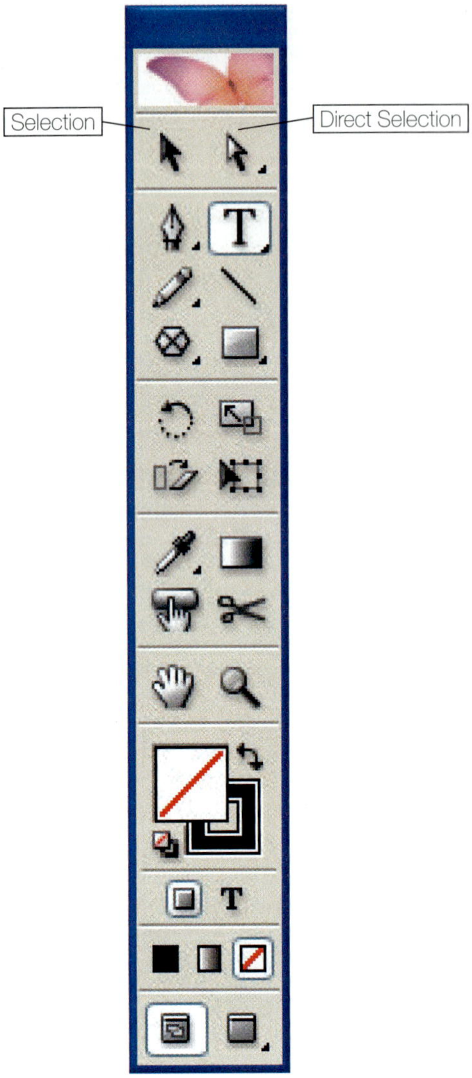

✓ *A selection handle is a square on the edge of the frame that can be dragged to change the size/shape of the frame.*

- To copy a frame, hold down the Alt key as you drag it. When you copy a frame, you also copy the object within it.
- To move a frame between pages, you might prefer to use the Cut and Paste commands located on the Edit menu. The standard Windows shortcuts also work: Ctrl+X for Cut, Ctrl+C for Copy, and Ctrl+V for Paste.
- When you paste content from the Clipboard onto a page, it does not always paste in the same position on the new page as on the original one. To force it to be pasted in the same relative location, use the Edit > Paste In Place command instead of the regular Paste command.

✓ *The Clipboard is a temporary holding area that all Windows programs share.*

- Another way to copy a frame is with the Edit > Duplicate command. This is often faster than copying and pasting since it accomplishes both with a single command. The shortcut key combination for Duplicate is Ctrl+Alt+Shift+D.
- To position a frame precisely, select it and then enter a specific X and Y value for it in the Control palette (see the illustration at the bottom of page).
- The X and Y positions can refer to various parts of the frame, depending on the reference point chosen. To select a reference point for the frame, click one of the nine small squares at the left end of the Control palette. For example, if you want the X and Y values to refer to the upper-left corner of the frame, click the upper-left square.

Reference point grid

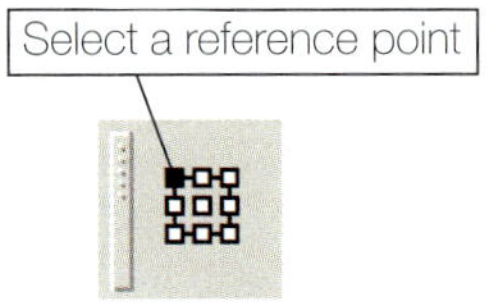

Resize and Delete a Frame

- To resize a frame, drag a selection handle. The mouse pointer changes to a double-headed arrow ↔. To force the frame to stay proportionally sized, drag a corner handle (rather than a side one) and hold down the Shift key as you drag.
- To resize the frame precisely, enter exact values for it in the W and H boxes of the Control palette when the frame is selected (see the illustration next page top).
- To delete a frame, select it and press the Delete or Backspace key, or choose Edit > Clear. Deleting is different from cutting in that the item is not placed on the Clipboard when deleting (clearing).

Horizontal and Vertical Position settings

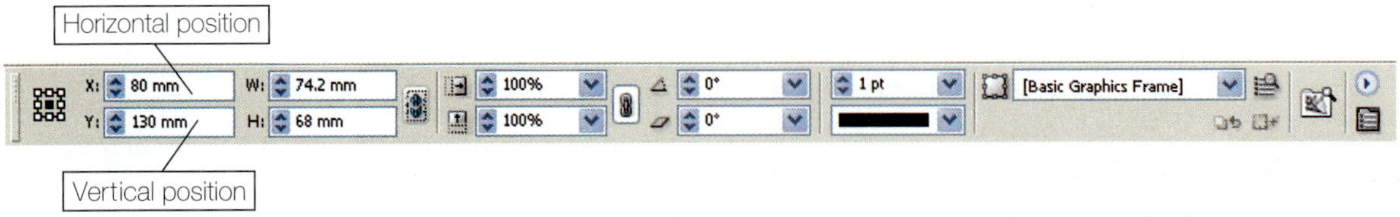

Width and Height selectors

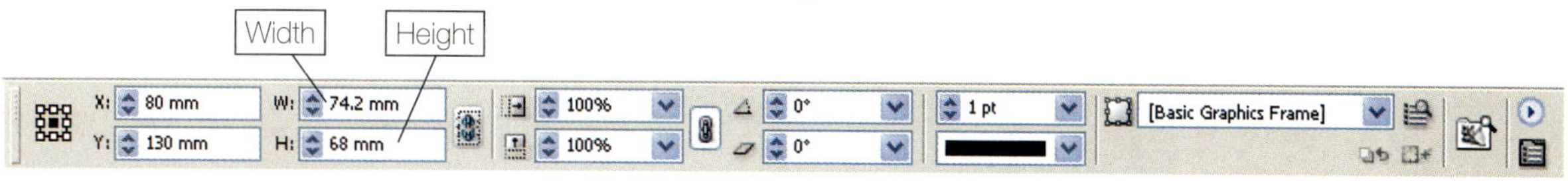

Toggle Preview Mode

- In Preview mode, you see the pages as they will be printed. Any grids or guides are hidden, non-printing frame borders are turned off, and the bleed areas are trimmed.
- To toggle Preview mode, press W (except when editing text), or select View > Screen Mode > Preview. To go back to regular editing mode, press W again, or select View > Screen Mode > Normal.
- You can also zoom in on a particular area. To do that, hold down Ctrl+spacebar so that the mouse pointer changes to a magnifying glass with a plus sign, and drag a box around the area on which to zoom.

Save a Document

- Saving in InDesign works much like in any other application, such as a word processor or spreadsheet program, except more options are available.
- The File > Save command re-saves with the same settings. Its shortcut is Ctrl+S. If you have not saved the document before, Save works the same as Save As.
- File > Save As opens the Save As dialog box, in which you can select a file name, location, and file type. It is useful for saving the file under a different name, for example. Its shortcut is Ctrl+Shift+S.
- Just like with the Open dialog box, the Save As dialog box has two forms: the Windows version and the Adobe version. They are similar in functionality but different in style. You can switch between them with the Use OS Dialog or Use Adobe Dialog button located in the lower-left corner (see the illustration below and next page).
- After using Save As, the newly named copy is open and the original copy is not. The File > Save a Copy command is the same as Save As except the original copy remains open; the newly named copy is not. Its shortcut is Alt+Ctrl+S.

Save As dialog box, Windows version

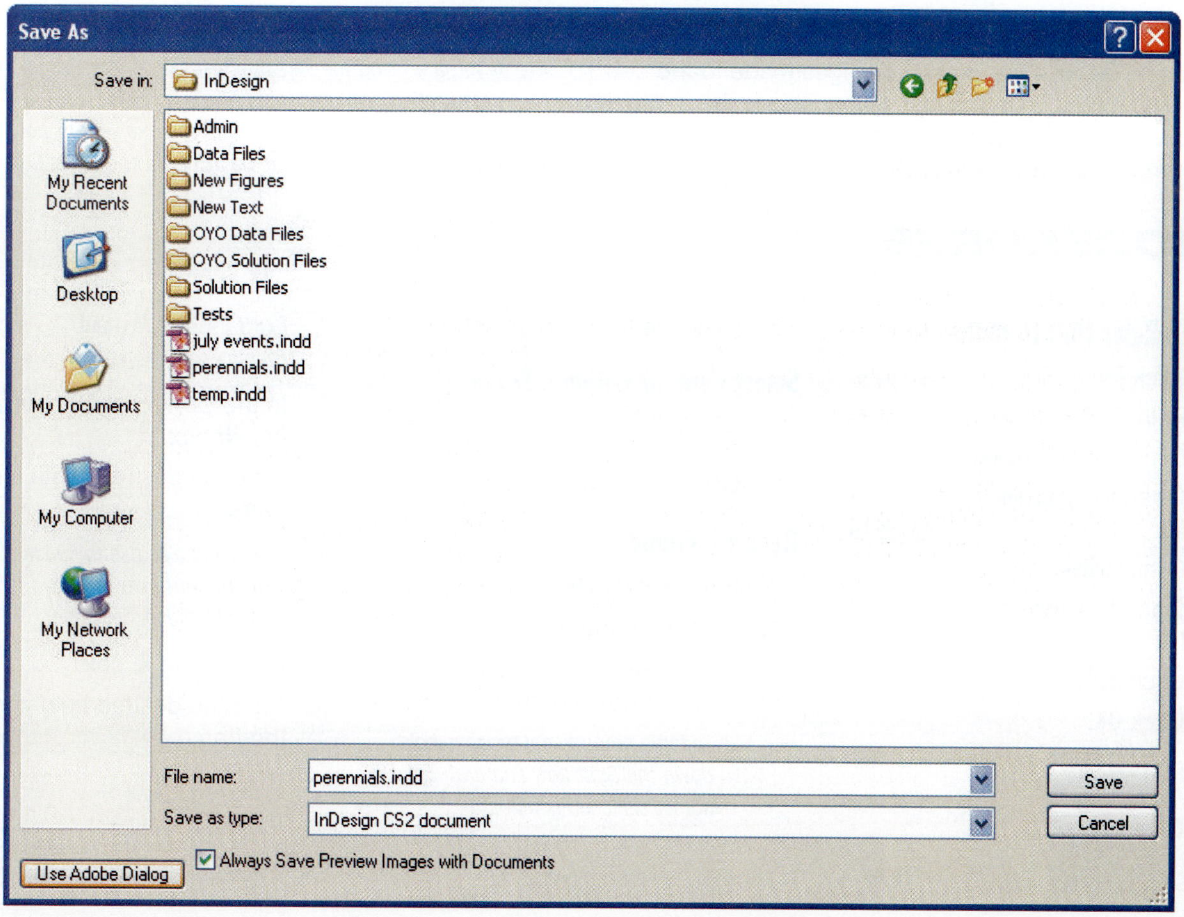

Save As dialog box, Adobe version

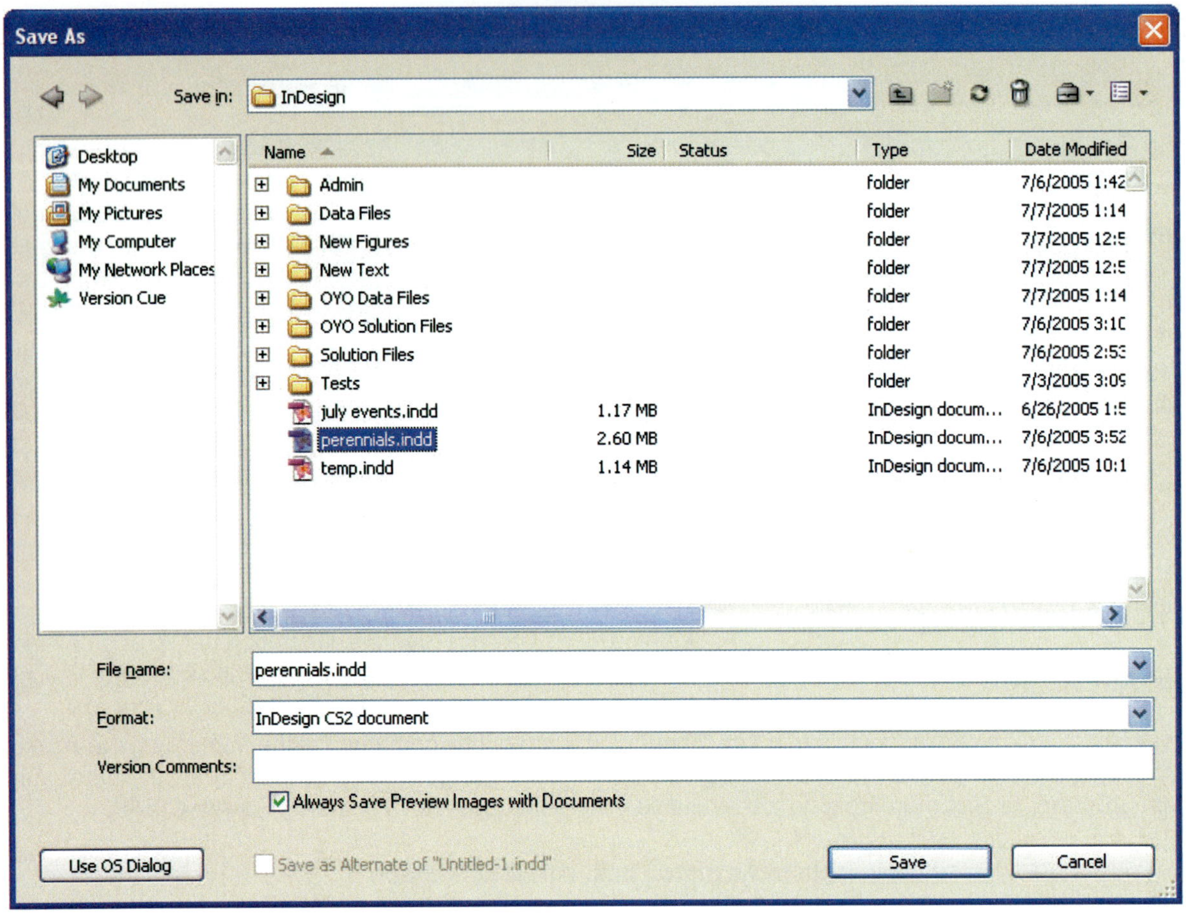

- File > Revert discards any changes made to the document since it was last saved. This is the same as closing the document without saving your changes and reopening it.

✓ *If you are using the Version Cue feature of InDesign in your organization, two other options are available: Save a Version and Save as Alternate. This course does not cover VersionCue, so you will not be using these save options.*

PROCEDURES

Set the Ruler Unit to Millimeters

1. Click **Edit** .... Alt+E
2. Point to **Preferences** .... N
3. Click **Units & Increments** .... U
4. Open the **Horizontal** drop-down list .... Alt+H
5. Click **Millimeters**.
6. Open the **Vertical** drop-down list .... Alt+T
7. Click **Millimeters**.
8. Click **OK**.

Select a Frame

1. Click .
2. Click the frame to select.

Select Content within a Frame

1. Click .
2. Click the frame to select.

Resize a Frame

Drag-and-Drop Method

1. Select the frame.
2. Drag a selection handle on the frame's border.

   ✓ *To force proportional resizing, hold down the Shift key, and drag only corner selection handles.*

Exact Position Method

1. Select the frame.
2. In the Control palette, click in the **W:** box.
3. Type the desired width for the frame.

   ✓ *You can also use the up and down increment arrows to the left of a box to change its value.*

4. Click in the **H:** box.
5. Type the desired height for the frame.

Move a Frame

Drag-and-Drop Method

1. Select the frame.
2. Drag the frame to a new location.

✓ *To force copy into vertical or horizontal alignment with the original position, hold down the Shift key as you drag.*

Cut-and-Paste Method with Keyboard Shortcuts

1. Select the frame.
2. Cut the frame to the Clipboard .... Ctrl+X
3. Display the page on which it should be pasted.
4. Paste the frame from the Clipboard .... Ctrl+V

OR

Paste-in-place the frame from the Clipboard .... Alt+Shift+Ctrl+V

✓ *Paste-in-place maintains the frame's position in relation to the page; Paste does not.*

Cut-and-Paste Method with Menus

1. Select the frame.
2. Click **Edit** .... Alt+E
3. Click **Cut** .... T
4. Display the page on which it should be pasted.
5. Click **Edit** .... Alt+E
6. Click **Paste** .... P

OR

Click **Paste in Place** I

Exact Position Method

1. Select the frame.
2. In the Control palette, click in the **X:** box.
3. Type an X position value.

✓ *You can also use the up and down increment arrows to the left of a box to change its value.*

4. Click in the **Y:** box.
5. Type a Y position value.

Copy a Frame

Drag-and-Drop Method

1. Select the frame.
2. Press and hold the Alt key .... Alt
3. Drag the frame to a new location.
4. Release the Alt key.

✓ *To force copy into alignment with original, also hold down Shift as you drag.*

Cut-and-Paste Method with Keyboard Shortcuts

1. Select the frame.
2. Copy the frame to the Clipboard .... Ctrl+C
3. Display the page on which it should be pasted.
4. Paste the frame from the Clipboard .... Ctrl+V

OR

Paste-in-place the frame from the Clipboard .... Alt+Shift+Ctrl+V

✓ *Paste-in-place maintains the frame's position in relation to the page; Paste does not.*

Cut-and-Paste Method with Menus

1. Select the frame.
2. Click **Edit** .... Alt+E
3. Click **Copy** C
4. Display the page on which it should be pasted.
5. Click **Edit** .... Alt+E
6. Click **Paste** .... P

OR

Click **Paste in Place** I

Duplicate Method with Keyboard Shortcut

1. Select the frame.
2. Press .... Alt+Shift+Ctrl+D
3. Drag the copy to the desired location.

Duplicate Method with Menus

1. Select the frame.
2. Click **Edit** .... Alt+E
3. Click **Duplicate** .... D
4. Drag the copy to the desired location.

Delete a Frame

Keyboard Shortcut Method

1. Select the frame.
2. Press .... Del

OR

Press .... ←Backspace

Menu Method

1. Select the frame.
2. Click **Edit** .... Alt+E
3. Click **Clear** L

Toggle Preview Mode

Keyboard Shortcut Method

- Press .... W

Menu Method

1. Click **View** .... Alt+V
2. Point to **Screen Mode** .... M
3. Click the desired mode (Preview or Normal).

Save a Document

Save an Unsaved Document

1. Click **File** .... Alt+F
2. Click **Save** .... S

✓ *Ctrl+S is a shortcut for steps 1 and 2.*

3. Type a file name.
4. (Optional) To change to a different save location:
   a. Open the **Save in** list .... Alt+I, Alt+↓
   b. Click the desired drive .... ↓, ↵Enter
   c. Double-click the desired folder in the folder list.
5. Click **Save** .... ↵Enter

Re-save a Document with the Same Name and Location

- Press .... Ctrl + S

OR

1. Click **File** .... Alt + F
2. Click **Save** .... S

Re-save a Document with a New Name or Location

This procedure leaves the copy with the new name/location open in InDesign.

1. Click **File** .... Alt + F
2. Click **Save As** .... A

   ✓ *Ctrl+Shift+S is a shortcut for steps 1 and 2.*

3. Type a file name.
4. (Optional) To change to a different save location:
   a. Open the **Save in** list .... Alt + I, Alt + ↓
   b. Click the desired drive .... ↓, ↵Enter
   c. Double-click the desired folder in the folder list.
5. Click **Save** .... ↵Enter

Save a Copy of a Document

This procedure leaves the original open in InDesign.

1. Click **File** .... Alt + F
2. Click **Save a Copy** .... Y

   ✓ *Ctrl+Alt+S is a shortcut for steps 1 and 2.*

3. Type a file name.
4. (Optional) To change to a different save location:
   a. Open the **Save in** list .... Alt + I, Alt + ↓
   b. Click the desired drive .... ↓, ↵Enter
   c. Double-click the desired folder in the folder list.
5. Click **Save** .... ↵Enter

Revert to the Saved Version of a Document

1. Click **File** .... Alt + F
2. Click **Revert** V
3. Click **Yes** .... Y

EXERCISE DIRECTIONS

1. Start Adobe InDesign.
2. Set the vertical and horizontal ruler units to Millimeters if they are not already set that way.
3. Open the file **EX02.indd** from the data files provided for this course.

   ✓ *If needed, ask your instructor where the data files are stored.*

4. Zoom out until you can see the entire page and all the frames to the left of the page.
5. Using the Selection tool, drag the photo onto the page and resize its frame so it exactly covers the whole page.
6. Using the Direct Selection tool, select the picture inside the frame, and move it to the left until the archway is centered horizontally.
7. Using the Selection tool, select the Midwest Garden Guide frame.
8. On the Control palette, set the upper-left reference point for the frame and then enter 217 mm for its width, 0 mm for its X position, and 10 mm for its Y position.
9. Place the Volume text frame directly under the Midwest Garden Guide frame, so its left edge aligns with the pink margin guide.
10. Place the Spring/Summer text frame directly under the Midwest Garden Guide frame, so its right edge aligns with the pink margin guide.
11. Zoom in on the right edge of the Midwest Garden Guide frame, and adjust the frame's size so that it precisely matches up with the edge of the page.
12. Preview the page; then return to normal view.
13. Save the document as **XX-EX02.indd**, where XX are your initials.

    ✓ *If needed, ask your instructor where to save your files.*

14. Exit Adobe InDesign.

ON YOUR OWN

1. Open the file **OYO-02.indd**.
2. Using the skills you learned for sizing and placing frames, create an attractive layout for a one-page article. (It's okay if not all the sample text fits in the body text frames.)
3. Save your work as **XX-OYO-02.indd**, where XX are your initials.

   ✓ *If needed, ask your instructor where to save your files.*

4. Exit Adobe InDesign.

Exercise | 3

Skills Covered

- Display and Hide Palettes
- Resize Palettes
- Move Palettes
- Combine Floating Palettes
- Create New Palette Clusters
- Save a Customized Workspace
- Load a Customized Workspace

Software Skills An efficient arrangement of palettes makes your job as a page designer much easier. While InDesign's default palette arrangement is good, it is perhaps not completely optimal for our needs in this course.

Application Skills In this exercise, you will customize the palette arrangement and save a customized workspace.

TERMS

Docked An object that is built into the main structure of the window, rather than being a free-floating object.

Floating palette A free-floating object (such as a toolbar) in its own window.

Workspace A saved set of palette arrangements and program options.

NOTES

Display and Hide Palettes

- To display a particular palette, select it from the Window menu. If that palette is already part of a fly-out palette cluster, it opens from there. If it was not already onscreen, it appears in a floating window.
- To hide a **floating palette**, click the Close (X) button in its upper-right corner.

Close a palette

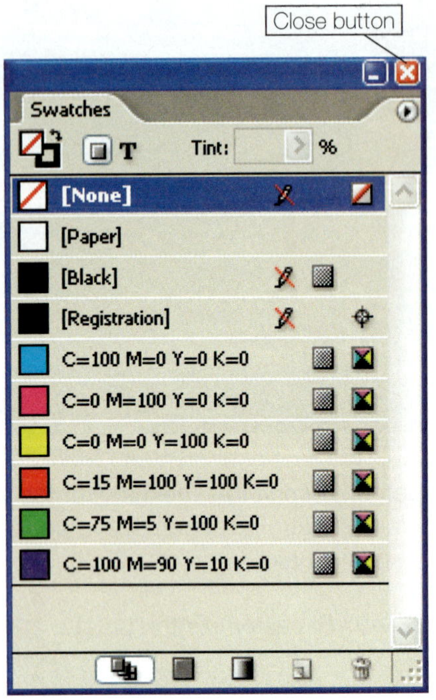

- To remove a palette from a fly-out cluster, first drag its tab out of the cluster, making it a separate floating palette. Then click its Close (X) button (see the illustration above).

Resize Palettes

- Fly-out palette clusters can be resized vertically by dragging their bottom borders up or down. The palette cluster can be either open or closed.

Resize a palette

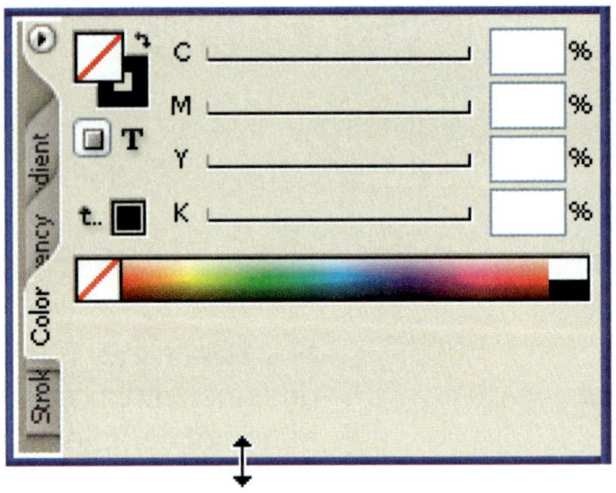

- The Tools palette (see illustration on the following page) can be toggled among three different layouts—default, vertical, and horizontal—by double-clicking its title bar (the area at the top).

Three views of the Tools palette

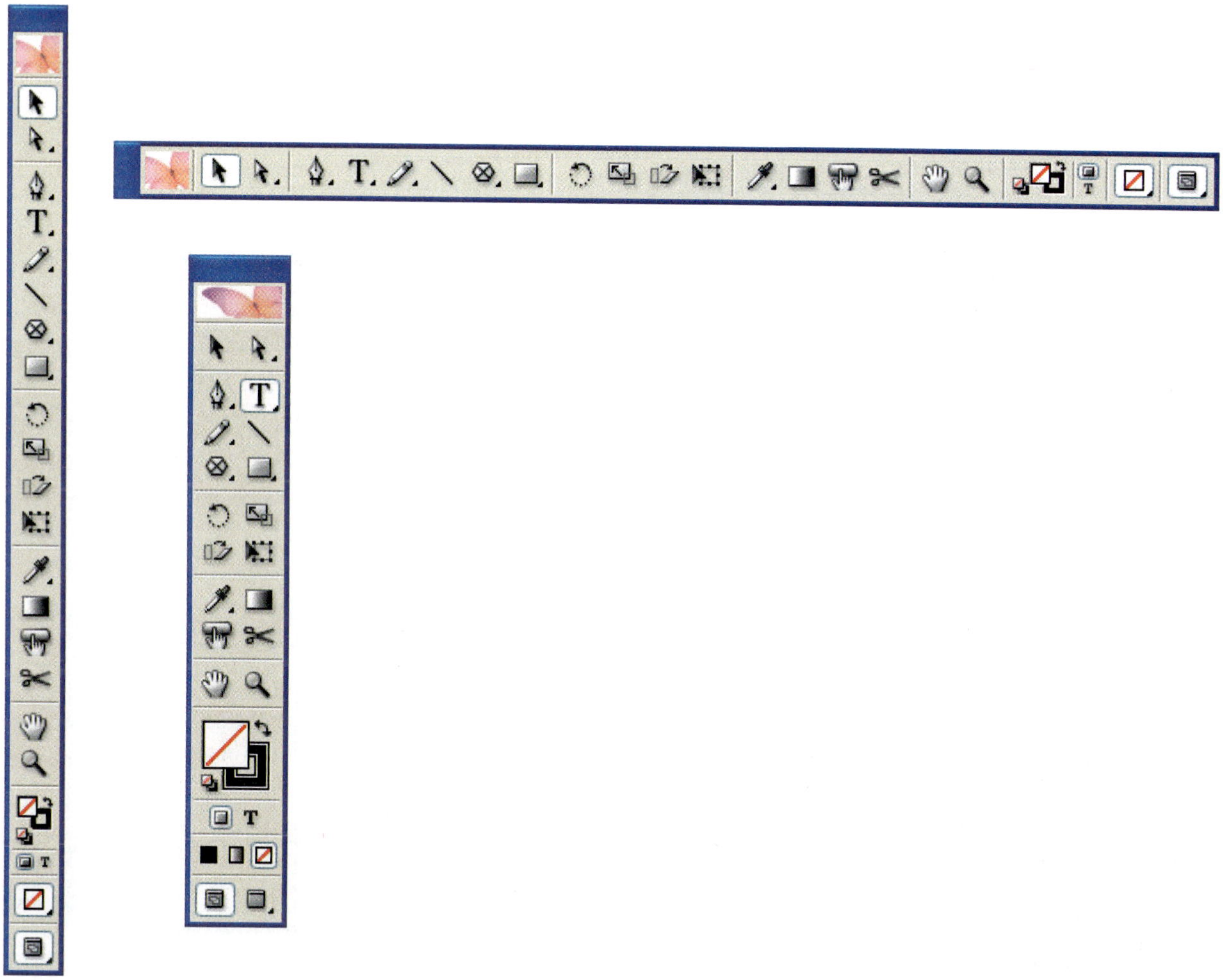

- Other floating palettes, such as tabbed palettes that have been dragged out of a fly-out cluster or displayed using the Window menu, cannot be resized.

Move Palettes

- To move a palette from one cluster to another, drag its tab where you want it.
- To turn a floating palette into a tab on a fly-out cluster, drag its tab to that cluster and drop it there.
- To turn a palette from a fly-out cluster into a floating palette, drag its tab away from the cluster.
- The Control palette is **docked** at the top of the screen by default. It can also be docked at the bottom, or made into a floating palette. To change its setting, click its Options button (right-pointing arrow) and then select a docking option from the bottom of the resulting menu.

Select a docking option

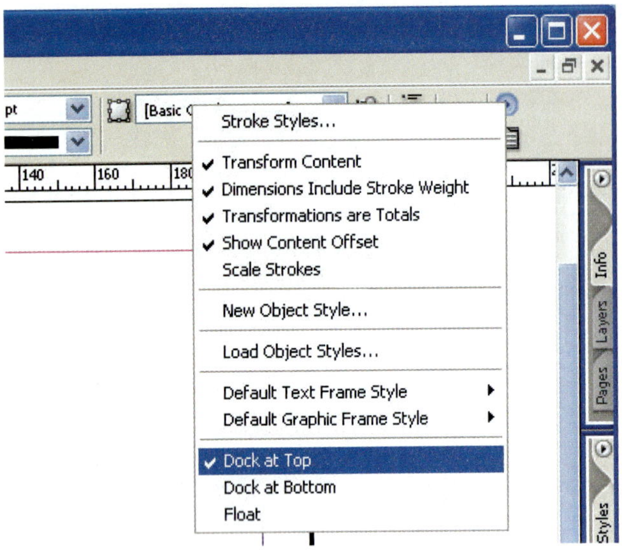

Combine Floating Palettes

- You can combine floating palettes into multi-tabbed floating windows. Just drag the tab of another palette onto the top of the existing tab area within a floating palette's window.

Multiple palettes in one window

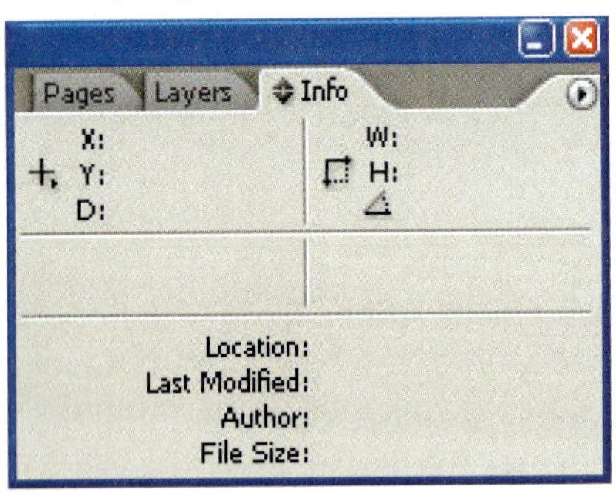

- The disadvantage to combining palettes in a single window (or fly-out cluster) is that the palettes can't be simultaneously visible. To get around this with floating palettes, you can stack them. Stacked palettes appear tiled with one another, rather than overlapping.

- To stack palettes, drag the tab of a palette to the bottom edge of an existing floating palette's window, so that the edge turns black; then drop it to attach the second palette below it, but within the same window.

Multiple panes in one window

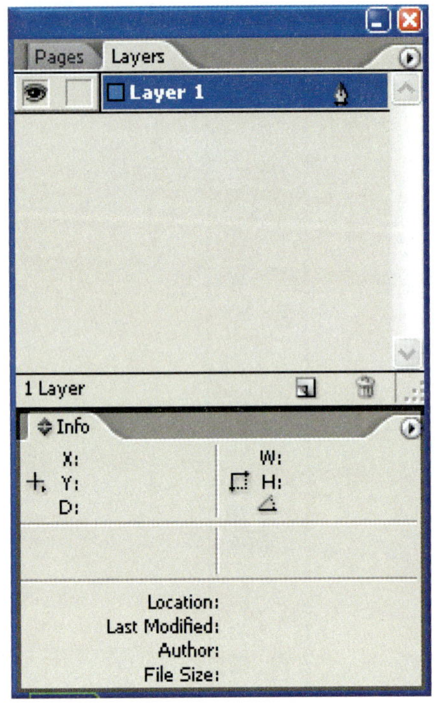

- When you click the Minimize button in the upper-right corner of a stacked floating palette window, all the palettes are minimized in that window to show just their tabs. You can then click a tab to display only that one tab, leaving the others minimized.

Minimized palettes

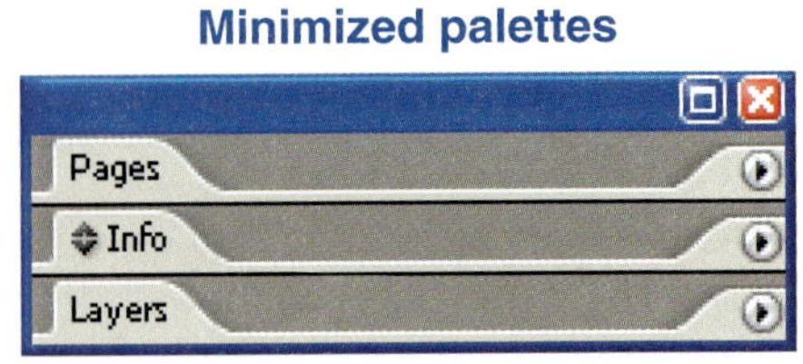

Create New Palette Clusters

- To start a new cluster, drag the tab of any floating palette to a blank area at the left or right edge of the InDesign window, until you see the outline of a vertical bar. Then release it to create the new cluster there.

  ✓ *By default there are no fly-out clusters at the left side of the screen, so plenty of room is available there for you to create your own custom clusters.*

Drag a palette to a border

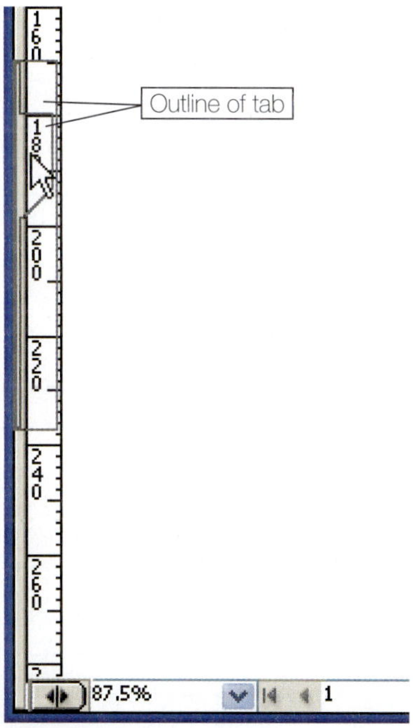

Save a Customized Workspace

- A customized **workspace** is a saved version of the palette positions you have set up. You can have different workspaces for different types of jobs, and switch between them easily.
- To save a custom workspace, use the Window > Workspace > Save Workspace command.

  ✓ *Workspaces are listed alphabetically on the Workspace submenu. If you want them to appear in a certain order, use numbers as the first characters of their names. For example, you could call the workspace you want to appear first "1 Main" and the second "2 Photos" and so on.*

Save a workspace

Load a Customized Workspace

- To load a workspace, choose Window > Workspace and then click one of the workspaces on the list.
- The default workspace is always available, under the name [Default].
- To delete an unwanted workspace, use the Window > Workspace > Delete Workspace command.

PROCEDURES

Display or Hide a Palette

1. Click **Window** .... Alt+W
2. Click a palette name.

Resize a Fly-Out Palette Cluster

- Drag the bottom border of the palette cluster up or down.

Move a Palette

Move an Individual Palette

- Drag the palette's tab to the new location.

Move a Floating Cluster

- Drag the title bar of the floating cluster window.

Stack Floating Palettes

1. Display two floating palettes.
2. Drag the tab of one palette to the bottom edge of the floating frame for the other palette.

Minimize a Stacked Floating Palette

- Click the **Minimize** button on the palette.
- Double-click a tab to display it again.

Create a New Palette Cluster

- Drag a palette's tab to an empty area at the extreme left or right of the InDesign window.

  ✓ *When in the right position, you'll see an outline of a vertical bar.*

Save a Customized Workspace

1. Click **Window** .... Alt+W
2. Point to **Workspace** .... W, →
3. Click **Save Workspace** .... S
4. Type a name for the new workspace.
5. Click **OK** .... ↵Enter

Load a Customized Workspace

1. Click **Window** .... Alt+W
2. Point to **Workspace** .... W, →
3. Click the desired workspace name.

Delete a Customized Workspace

1. Click **Window** .... Alt+W
2. Point to **Workspace** .... W, →
3. Click **Delete Workspace** .... D
4. Select the name of the workspace to delete .... Alt+↓
5. Click **Delete** .... ↵Enter

EXERCISE DIRECTIONS

1. Start Adobe InDesign but do not open or start any documents.
2. Reset the workspace to [Default].
3. Display the Text Wrap palette in a floating window.
4. Display the Align palette in a floating window.

   ✓ *The Align palette is found on the Object & Layout submenu. When you display it, InDesign also automatically displays the Pathfinder palette.*

5. Create a new palette cluster at the left side of the screen that contains the Text Wrap and Align palettes. Close all other floating palettes.
6. Resize the new cluster so that the tabs are fully readable but there is no wasted space.
7. Drag the Info palette out of its current cluster, and then close it.
8. Save the current workspace as **1 Custom**.
9. Drag the Pages palette out of its current cluster, so it becomes a floating window.
10. Drag the Layers palette out of its current cluster, and drop it at the bottom edge of the Pages palette to create a stacked palette.
11. Minimize the Pages/Layers stacked cluster, and then double-click the Pages tab to expand only that one.
12. Save the current palette arrangement as a workspace named **2 Alternative**.
13. Delete the 2 Alternative workspace.
14. Exit Adobe InDesign and restart it.

    ✓ *Notice that the 2 Alternative workspace settings are still loaded, even though you deleted that workspace.*

15. Load the 1 Custom workspace.
16. Exit Adobe InDesign.

ON YOUR OWN

1. Open every palette in a separate floating window.
2. Create clusters of floating, stacked, and fly-out palettes as desired.
3. Close any palettes that are left over.
4. Save the workspace as **XX**, where XX are your initials.
5. Reload the 1 Custom workspace.
6. Exit Adobe InDesign.

Exercise | 4

Skills Covered

- Start a New Document
- Create a Document Preset
- Place a New Frame
- Place a Polygon or Polygon Frame
- Type Text in a Frame
- Insert Symbols
- Move the Insertion Point
- Select Text

Software Skills Almost every new project in InDesign begins with starting a new document and creating some frames. Into these frames you can type text or place external content such as photos and drawings.

Application Skills In this exercise, you will start a new document and create several frames containing text.

TERMS

Document An InDesign data file, containing a page layout with framed content.

Elliptical An object that is oval-shaped.

Em dash A dash that is the same width as a capital M in the chosen font.

Glyph A typographical symbol, such as — (em dash) or © (copyright).

Polygonal An object that is multi-sided.

Story All the text in the selected text frame plus all the text in any frames that are linked to it.

NOTES

Start a New Document

- InDesign calls its data files **documents**, much like a word processing program does. However, an InDesign document is more than just a simple text file. It is a page layout containing framed content.
- To start a new document, use the File > New > Document command or press Ctrl+N. When you do so, a New Document dialog box opens in which you can set the number of pages; the size and orientation of the pages; and the positions of the column, margin, and bleed guides.

✓ *Unlike in a word processing program, in InDesign the column and margin settings affect only the nonprinting guide rules that appear behind the frames on the page. They are not enforced in any way. Therefore, changing the margin settings for a document does not shift any of its content.*

Start a new document

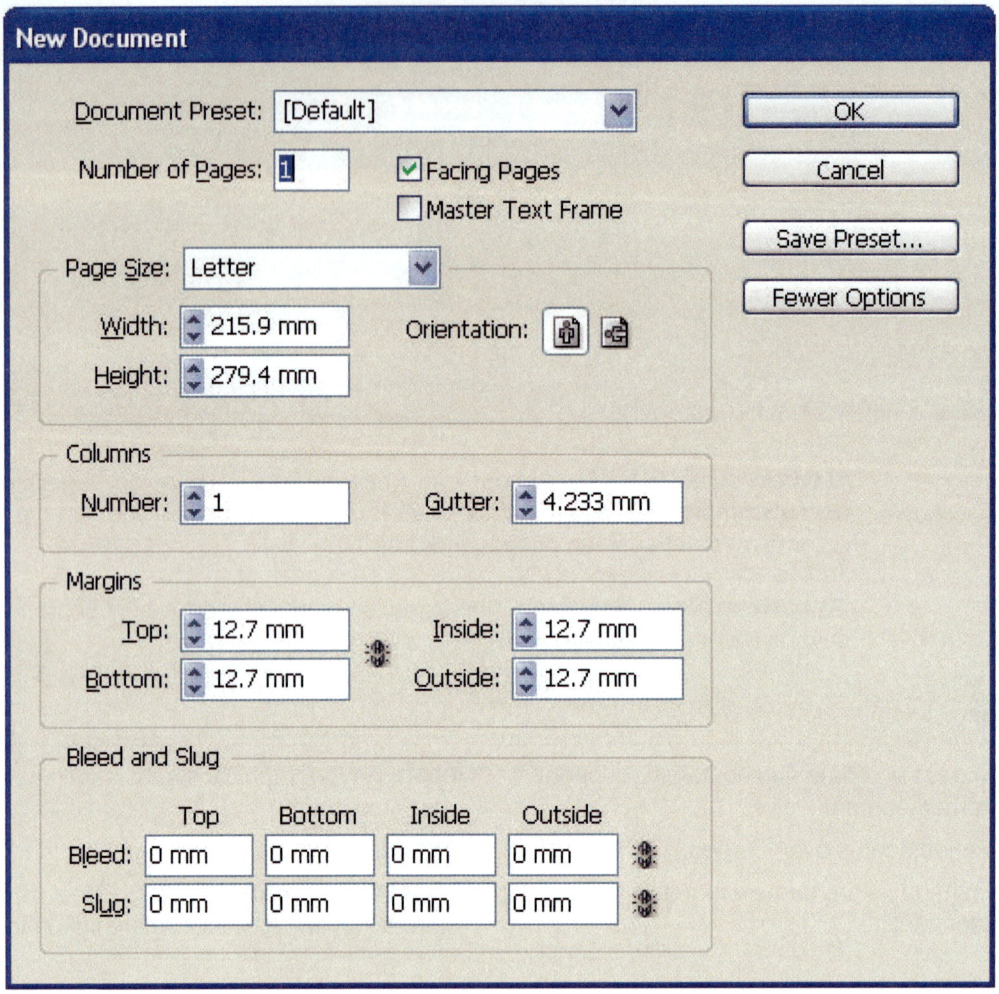

- The settings in the New Document dialog box include:
  - **Document Preset:** Choose saved options for all the other settings
  - **Save Preset:** Create new document presets
  - **Number of Pages:** The initial number of pages in the document
  - **Facing Pages:** Whether or not the layout will be double-sided
  - **Master Text Frame:** Whether or not each page will have a text frame created on it automatically
  - **Page Size:** The size of the paper on which the document will be printed
  - **Width and Height:** Boxes for manually entering the page size if desired
  - **Orientation:** Whether the text will run across the wide or narrow edge of the paper
  - **Columns:** The number of equal-sized columns for which nonprinting guides will display onscreen
  - **Gutter:** The space between the guides for each column
  - **Margins:** The positioning of the nonprinting margin guides onscreen
  - **More Options/Fewer Options:** Displays/hides the Bleed and Slug section of the dialog box
- After you click More Options, two additional settings become available:
  - **Bleed:** Defines guides for an overflow around the edges of the page, commonly used in professional printing. The document is printed on too-large paper, with the content flowing into the bleed area; then the document is trimmed to eliminate the bleed area.
  - **Slug:** Defines guides for an area outside the bleed area where information about the document will be printed. Used in professional printing for helping identify each page on large-format proof sheets.
- The chain symbol to the right of the Bleed and Slug boxes can be either broken or connected. Click it to change its status.

Set a bleed and slug if desired

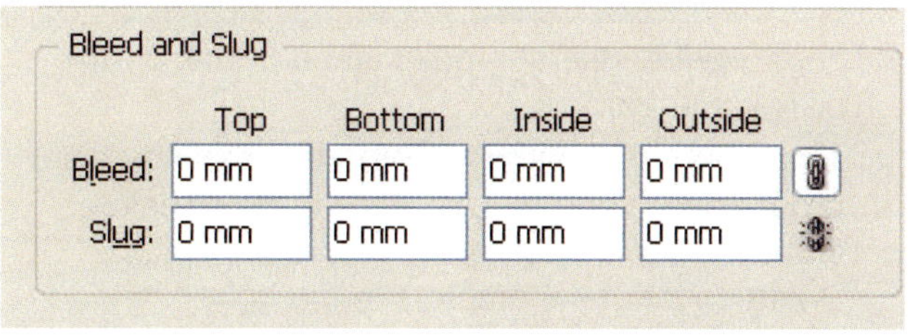

- When the chain appears broken, each of the four sides can be adjusted separately. When the chain appears connected, a change to one side will automatically be made to the settings for all other sides.

Create a Document Preset

- Document presets are useful for quickly recalling your preferred settings in the New Document dialog box, so you do not have to re-enter the same choices repeatedly.
- To create a document preset, make your selections in the New Document dialog box and then click the Save Preset button and enter a name for your settings.

Save presets

- To load a document preset, select the desired preset from the Document Preset drop-down list.

Place a New Frame

- InDesign offers three tools for creating rectangular frames:
  - **Type tool:** Changes the mouse pointer to a text insertion point. You can then draw a new text frame or click inside an existing one to edit text.
  - **Rectangle tool:** Changes the mouse pointer to a crosshair. You can then draw a new rectangular frame. This can be filled in with a color and used as a graphical element, or it can be used as a text frame or filled with an external picture.
  - **Rectangular Frame tool:** Same as the Rectangle tool except the resulting frame has a big X through it initially, indicating that it is empty. It can be used to hold text or graphics.
- To create a basic text frame, any of these tools will work. In this book we will use the Type tool for creating text frames. However, if you accidentally use the Rectangle or Rectangular Frame tool instead, that's okay; you can convert a rectangle to a text frame simply by double-clicking inside it and typing some text.
- The Rectangle and Rectangular Frame tools have additional options available. Click and hold on one of those buttons to see a fly-out menu that enables you to create frames that are **elliptical** or **polygonal**.

Draw a frame

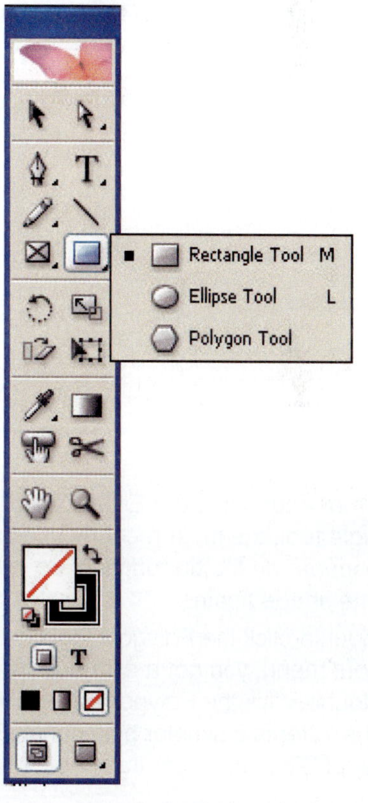

- To create a frame that is a perfect rectangle or a perfect circle, hold down the Shift key as you are drawing a new rectangular or elliptical frame, respectively.

  ✓ *It is considered good design practice to make frames align with the margin and column guides on the page whenever possible, for balance and consistency. If the guides are not where you want them, change the guides. You will learn how to do this in Exercise 5.*

Place a Polygon or Polygon Frame

- Just like with an ellipse or rectangle, you can create either a polygon or a polygonal frame.
- To access the Polygon tool, click and hold on the Rectangle tool, and then click Polygon and draw the shape.
- To change the number of sides of the polygon, or the indent of the junctions between each side, double-click the Polygon tool instead of clicking it. Set the Star Inset to 0% for a plain equilateral shape with no indentation of the points.
- You can also set the polygon height and width in the dialog box, but this is usually not necessary because you will specify the height and width when you drag to draw the frame.

Polygon options

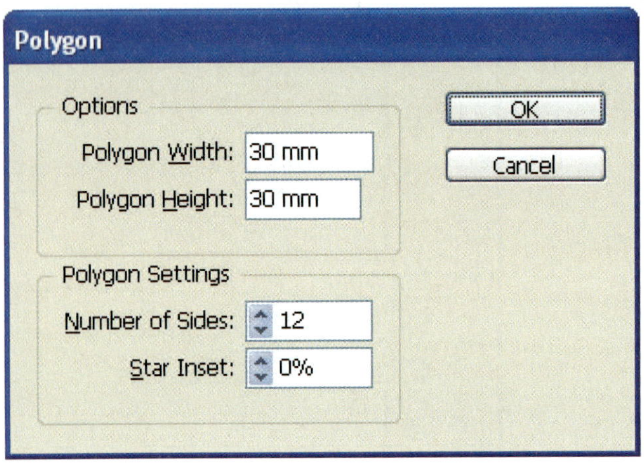

- Notice that after using the Ellipse, Polygon, or Rectangle tool, the most recently used tool continues to appear on the button face, so you can reuse the same shape again.
- If you double-click the Polygon Tool command from the fly-out menu, you get a different dialog box than if you double-click the Polygon Tool on the button face. The latter is a simpler box, containing only the Number of Sides and Star Inset options.

Polygon options (alternate)

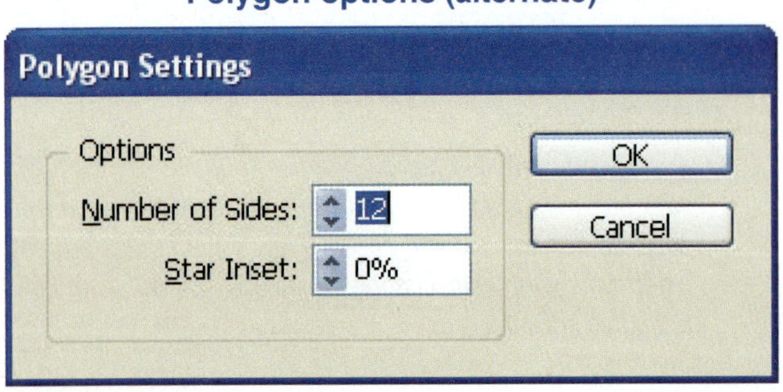

Type Text in a Frame

- To move the insertion point into a frame, double-click in the frame.
- Text entry and editing is the same as in any word processing program. Use Backspace to delete characters to the left of the insertion point, or Delete to delete characters to the right.

Type/edit text in a frame

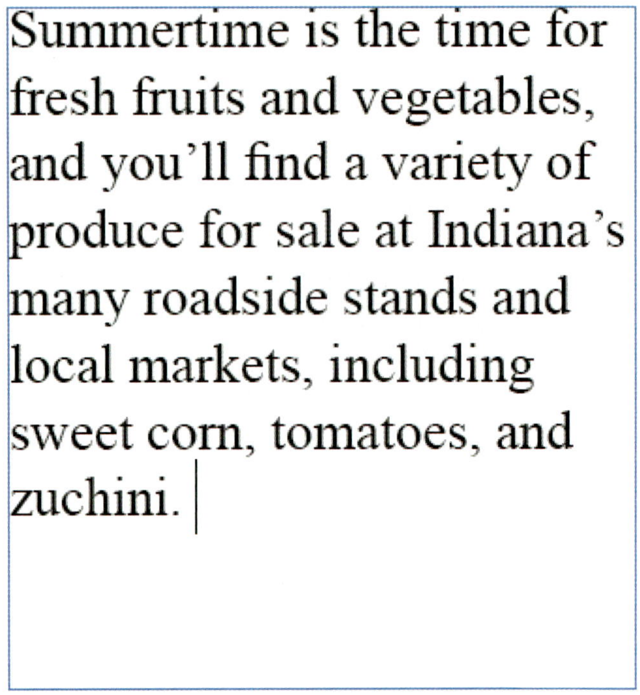

✓ *If you don't have any text to type yet but you want to see how your layout will look with text in it, click inside the text frame and choose Type > Fill with Placeholder Text.*

Insert Symbols

- In InDesign, typographical symbols not found on a standard keyboard are called **glyphs**.
- To insert a glyph in a text frame, position the insertion point and then select Type > Glyphs. Then select the symbol you want from the palette that appears.

Insert typographical symbols

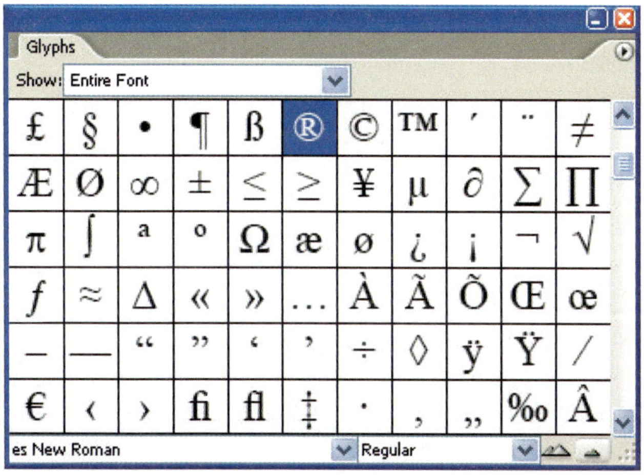

- You can select a different font from the Font list at the bottom of the Glyphs palette.
- The triangle buttons in the lower-right corner of the Glyphs palette enlarge and shrink the sizes of the previews.
- There are keyboard shortcuts for inserting many of the most common glyphs. Some of these are presented in the following table.

Symbol	Keyboard Shortcut
Ellipsis ...	Alt+; (semicolon)
Copyright ©	Alt+G
Registered Trademark ®	Alt+R
Paragraph ¶	Alt+7
Section §	Alt+6
Em dash —	Alt+Shift+- (hyphen)
En dash –	Alt+- (hyphen)
Round bullet character	Alt+8

Move the Insertion Point

- The easiest way to move the insertion point is to click where you want it to be.
- Some people prefer not to take their hands off the keyboard when typing, even to use the mouse. For these people, keyboard shortcuts for moving the insertion point may be useful:
  - To move to the beginning of the line or the end of the line, press Home or End, respectively.
  - To jump to the beginning or end of the **story**, press Ctrl+Home or Ctrl+End.

    ✓ *The story is all the text in the selected text frame plus all the text in any frames that are linked to it.*
  - To move one word to the left or right, press Ctrl+right arrow or Ctrl+left arrow.
  - To move to the previous paragraph or next paragraph, press Ctrl+up arrow or Ctrl+down arrow.

Select Text

- To operate on multiple characters of text at once (such as delete, format, and so on), select the text. Selected text appears in reverse of its normal coloring (usually white on black).
- One way to select text is to drag across it with the mouse pointer.

Select text

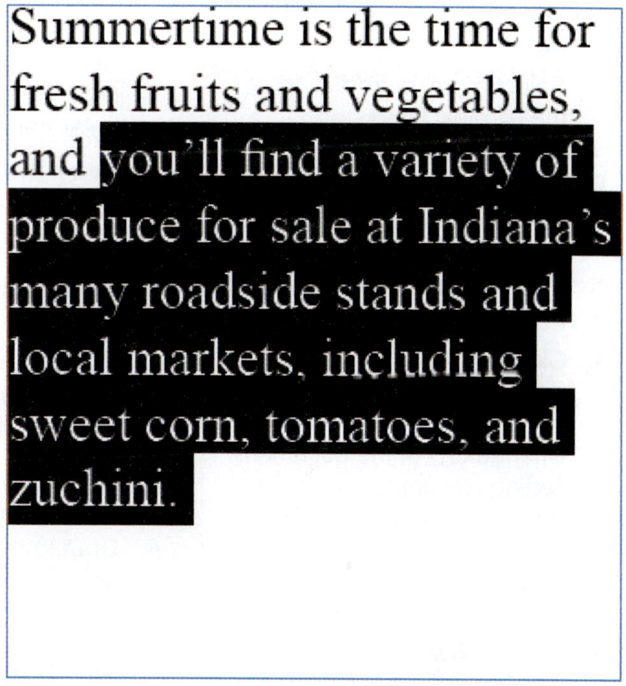

- You can select various amounts of text by clicking, as follows:
  - To select a word, double-click it.
  - To select a line, triple-click it.
  - To select a paragraph, quadruple-click it (4x).
  - To select the entire story, quintuple-click it (5x), or press Ctrl+A.
- To select to the start of the story from the insertion point, press Ctrl+Shift+Home. To select to the end of the story, press Ctrl+Shift+End.
- Pressing an arrow key in conjunction with Ctrl+Shift selects one word to the left or right of the insertion point (left or right arrows) or one paragraph above or below the insertion point (up or down arrows).

PROCEDURES

Start a New Document

1. Click **File** .... Alt+F
2. Point to **New** .... N
3. Click **Document** .... D

   ✓ *Ctrl+N is a shortcut for steps 1–3.*

4. (Optional) Change any of the document settings desired.

   OR

   Select a preset from the **Document Preset** list .... Alt+D, Alt+↓
5. Click **OK**.

Create a Document Preset

1. Click **File** .... Alt+F
2. Point to **New** .... N
3. Click **Document** .... D

   ✓ *Ctrl+N is a shortcut for steps 1–3.*

4. Change any of the document settings desired.
5. Click **Save Preset** .... Alt+V
6. Type a name for the preset.
7. Click **OK** .... ↵Enter

Place a New Frame

Place a Text Frame

1. Click the **Text** tool ....

   ✓ *Except when in text editing mode, you can press T as a shortcut for step 1.*

2. (Optional) For a perfect square text frame, hold down Shift .... ⇧Shift
3. Drag to create a new text frame.

Place a New Rectangle

1. Click the **Rectangle** tool ....

   ✓ *Except when in text editing mode, you can press M as a shortcut for step 1.*

2. (Optional) For a perfect square, hold down Shift .... ⇧Shift
3. Drag to create a new rectangle.

Place a New Rectangular Frame

1. Click the **Rectangle Frame** tool ....

   ✓ *Except when in text editing mode, you can press F as a shortcut for step 1.*

2. (Optional) For a perfect square, hold down Shift .... ⇧Shift
3. Drag to create a new rectangular frame.

Place a New Ellipse

1. Click and hold on the **Rectangle** tool ....
2. Click the **Ellipse** tool ....

   ✓ *Except when in text editing mode, you can press L as a shortcut for steps 1 and 2.*

3. (Optional) For a perfect circle, hold down Shift .... ⇧Shift
4. Drag to create a new ellipse.

Place a New Elliptical Frame

1. Click and hold on the **Rectangle Frame** tool ....
2. Click the **Ellipse Frame** tool ....
3. (Optional) For a perfect circle, hold down Shift .... ⇧Shift
4. Drag to create a new elliptical frame.

Create a Polygon

1. Click and hold on the **Rectangle** tool ....

   ✓ *If you have previously drawn an ellipse, the ellipse might appear instead of the rectangle on the button face.*

2. Double-click the **Polygon** tool ....
3. Click in the **Number of Sides** box .... Alt+N
4. Type or increment the value .... ↑ or ↓
5. Click in the **Star Inset** box .... Alt+S
6. Type or increment the value .... ↑ or ↓
7. Click **OK** .... ↵Enter

Create a Polygonal Frame

1. Click and hold on the **Rectangular Frame** tool ....

   ✓ *If you have previously drawn an ellipse, the ellipse might appear instead of the rectangle on the button face.*

2. Double-click the **Polygonal Frame** tool ....
3. Click in the **Number of Sides** box .... Alt+N
4. Type or increment the value .... ↑ or ↓
5. Click in the **Start Inset** box .... Alt+S
6. Type or increment the value .... ↑ or ↓
7. Click **OK** .... ↵Enter

Insert a Symbol (Glyph)

Menu Method

1. Position the insertion point in a text frame.
2. Click **Type** .... Alt+T
3. Point to **Glyphs** .... G
4. (Optional) Select a different font.
5. (Optional) Select a different weight (bold, italic, etc.).
6. Double-click the symbol to insert.

Keyboard Shortcut Method

1. Position the insertion point in a text frame.
2. Press one of the following key combinations:
   - Ellipsis .... Alt+;
   - Copyright .... Alt+G
   - Registered trademark .... Alt+R
   - Paragraph .... Alt+7
   - Em dash .... Alt+⇧Shift+-
   - En dash .... Alt+-

- Round bullet character .... Alt + 8

Move the Insertion Point

Mouse Method

- If the insertion point is already in a text frame, click where you want to move it.

OR

If the insertion point is not already in a text frame, double-click where you want to move it.

Keyboard Shortcut Method

✓ *This method assumes the insertion point is within a text frame.*

1. Press one of the following key combinations:
   - One space to the left .... ←
   - One space to the right ..... →
   - One word to the left .... Ctrl + ←
   - One word to the right .... Ctrl + →
   - One line up .... ↑
   - One line down .... ↓
   - One paragraph up .... Ctrl + ↑
   - One paragraph down .... Ctrl + ↓
   - Beginning of current line .... Home
   - End of current line .... End
   - Beginning of story .... Ctrl + Home
   - End of story .... Ctrl + End

Fill a Frame with Placeholder Text

1. Double-click inside the frame.
2. Click **Type** .... Alt + T
3. Click **Fill with Placeholder Text** L

Select Text

✓ *This method assumes the insertion point is within a text frame.*

- Drag across text to select it.

OR

Select text by clicking:

- Select a word ....double-click
- Select a line ....triple-click
- Select a paragraph ....quadruple-click
- Select the entire story ..... Ctrl + A or quintuple-click

OR

Select text with keyboard shortcuts, as follows:

- To start of story from insertion point .... Ctrl + Shift + Home
- To end of story from insertion point .... Ctrl + Shift + End
- One word to the left .... Ctrl + Shift + ←
- One word to the right .... Ctrl + Shift + →
- One paragraph up .... Ctrl + Shift + ↑
- One paragraph down .... Ctrl + Shift + ↓

EXERCISE DIRECTIONS

1. Start Adobe InDesign.
2. Start a new document with the following settings:
   - Number of Pages: 1
   - Facing Pages: No
   - Master Text Frame: No
   - Page Size: Letter
   - Orientation: Portrait
   - Columns: 3
   - Gutter: 6 mm
   - Margins: 10 mm on all sides
   - Bleed: 5 mm on all sides
   - Slug: none
3. Save the new settings as a new preset named **Three-Column Single**, and then click OK to create the new document based on them.

   ✓ *If you do not see the gridlines, press W to display them.*
4. Create a new text frame that fills the first column. If you do not get the size exactly right initially, resize and reposition as needed.
5. In the text frame, type the text shown in Illustration A.
6. Place a new rectangular frame that spans the top half of the remaining two columns.
7. Zoom in on the last paragraph, and replace the comma after "or" in the first sentence with an em dash.
8. Create a 16-sided polygon with 20% star inset, exactly 61 mm x 61 mm, and place it in the lower-right corner, so its right and bottom align with the blue margin guides.
9. Save your work as **XX-EX04.indd**, where XX are your initials. It should resemble Illustration B.
10. Exit InDesign.

Illustration A

Guest Comforts

Being travel enthusiasts ourselves, we know how important it is to have a comfortable bed to sleep in, so all of our rooms have the best in bedding and linens. You'll enjoy luxurious pillow-top mattresses with firm support, 100% cotton sheets, and cozy quilts and comforters, as well as comfy bathrobes and thick fluffy towels.

Each room is furnished with oak Mission-style furniture typical of the Arts and Crafts movement of the early 20th century. We have a passion for this style of furnishings, and it shows throughout the entire house.

Indoors, there's a TV lounge with satellite TV including lots of movie channels. Settle in for your favorite film. Or, if you're more interested in just getting away from it all, check out the library, where you'll find hundreds of books, comfortable leather chairs for napping or reading, and an antique Mission-style writing desk for catching up on your correspondence.

Do you get hungry in the evenings? Let our hosts make you some popcorn to go with that movie. We can also bake up some chocolate chip cookies with a little advance notice. Complementary tea, coffee, and soft drinks are available throughout the day, and there is a guest refrigerator for chilling any beverages you might want to bring along yourself.

For breakfast, you can choose a light meal of gourmet coffee, juice, and muffins, or ask our resident chef for a full-sized breakfast that will keep you satisfied well into the noonday. Buttermilk biscuits are a house specialty, great either with sausage gravy or just a little butter and strawberry jam. Orange pecan French toast is another favorite.

Illustration B

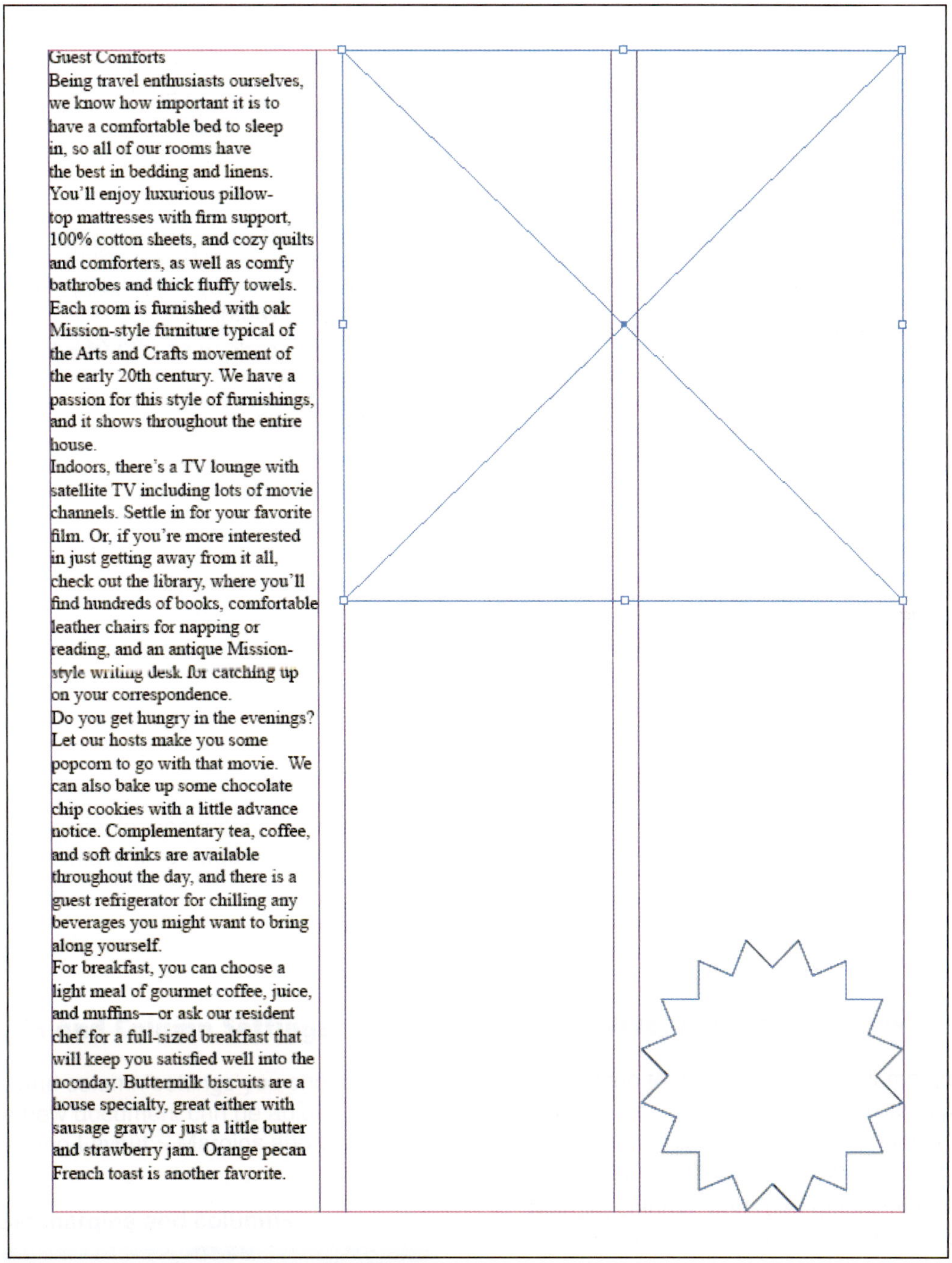

Guest Comforts
Being travel enthusiasts ourselves, we know how important it is to have a comfortable bed to sleep in, so all of our rooms have the best in bedding and linens. You'll enjoy luxurious pillow-top mattresses with firm support, 100% cotton sheets, and cozy quilts and comforters, as well as comfy bathrobes and thick fluffy towels.
Each room is furnished with oak Mission-style furniture typical of the Arts and Crafts movement of the early 20th century. We have a passion for this style of furnishings, and it shows throughout the entire house.
Indoors, there's a TV lounge with satellite TV including lots of movie channels. Settle in for your favorite film. Or, if you're more interested in just getting away from it all, check out the library, where you'll find hundreds of books, comfortable leather chairs for napping or reading, and an antique Mission-style writing desk for catching up on your correspondence.
Do you get hungry in the evenings? Let our hosts make you some popcorn to go with that movie. We can also bake up some chocolate chip cookies with a little advance notice. Complementary tea, coffee, and soft drinks are available throughout the day, and there is a guest refrigerator for chilling any beverages you might want to bring along yourself.
For breakfast, you can choose a light meal of gourmet coffee, juice, and muffins—or ask our resident chef for a full-sized breakfast that will keep you satisfied well into the noonday. Buttermilk biscuits are a house specialty, great either with sausage gravy or just a little butter and strawberry jam. Orange pecan French toast is another favorite.

the page. "Columns" here is different from the normal column guides, and are in addition to them.

Create alignment guides

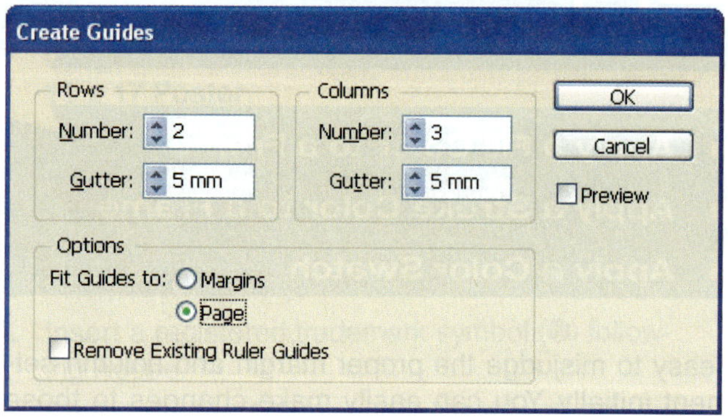

- Guides can then be selected and dragged to reposition them. Alternatively you can select the guide and then enter an exact value in the X or Y box on the Control palette.
- To delete a guide, select it and press Delete.
- When a ruler guide is not selected, it is bright cyan. It changes color when selected to the selection color for the layer on which it resides. In a single-layer document, this is a medium blue. You will learn about layers in Exercise 7.
- To change ruler guides to some other color, select Layout > Ruler Guides. Then select a color. From here you can also select a View Threshold, which is the zoom percentage above which the guides are displayed.

Set options for the ruler guides

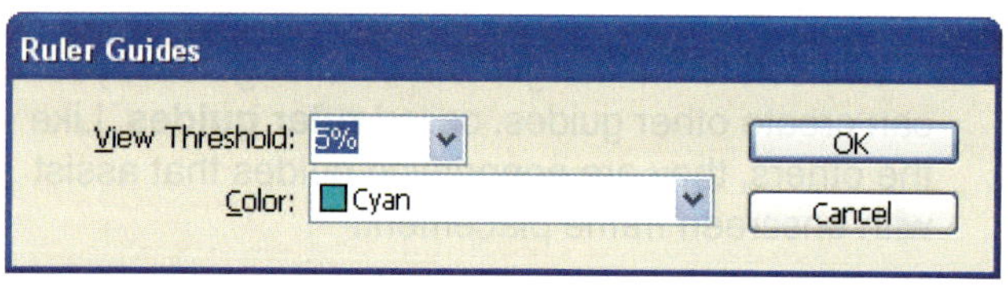

Align Frames with One Another

- In addition to aligning frames with guides, you can align them with one another. This can be simpler than creating a ruler guide, and also allows alignment types that are not easy with guides, such as aligning the centers of various different-sized frames.
- To align frames with one another, select the frames to affect (click the first frame, hold down Shift, and then click each additional frame) and then use the alignment buttons on the Control palette.

Align Left Edges

Align Top Edges

Align Horizontal Centers

Align Vertical Centers

Align Right Edges

Align Bottom Edges

Apply a Fill Color to a Frame

- A **fill** color is the color inside a frame. It can be a solid color, a tint of a solid color, a semi-transparent fill, or a gradient. You will learn how to use each of these types of fills in this course, but this exercise focuses on the simplest type—a single, solid color.
- By default, most frames are transparent, with no fill color. To select a color, open the Color palette and double-click the Fill square. The Fill square is the upper-left square. (The square that overlaps it to its lower right is the Stroke square, discussed next.)

Color palette (no color selected)

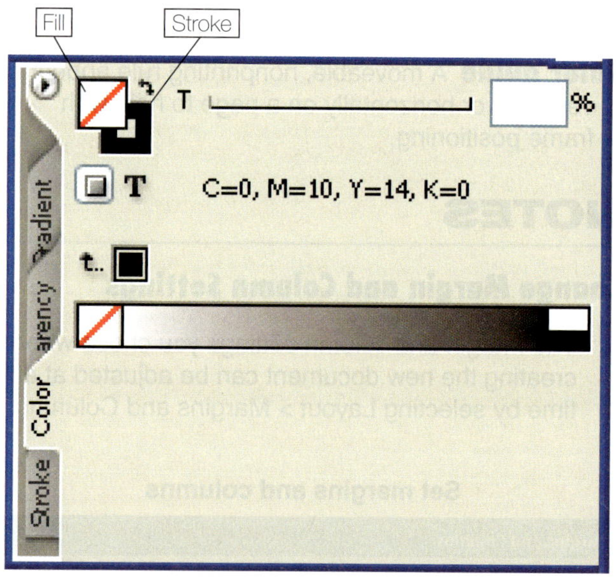

- When you double-click the Fill square, the Color Picker dialog box opens. From here you can click the color you want or enter precise values using any of three color models: RGB, Lab, or CMYK.
- To select a color by clicking, first drag the vertical slider up/down, or click anywhere in the vertical bar to move the slider, to display the approximate range of hues you want; then click the exact color in the large rectangular area. The color you chose appears in the sample area to the left of the OK button.

Select a color

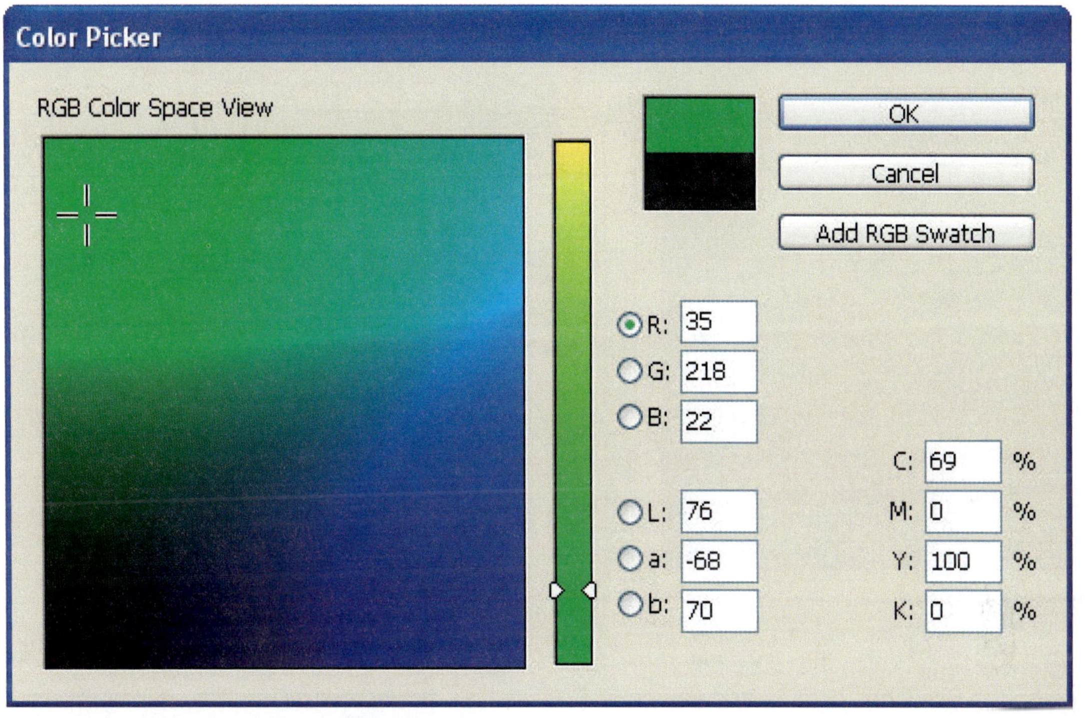

✓ *Most documents that will be professionally printed should use CMYK colors. CMYK stands for Cyan Magenta Yellow Black, the four inks found in the four-color printing process used by professional printing companies. In contrast, the Red Green Blue (RGB) model is typically used for onscreen displays. To set the color you choose to CMYK, click in one of the CMYK text boxes in the Color Picker dialog box before clicking OK.*

- Another way to select a color is to click what you want on the Color palette. You can click anywhere on the color bar to select a color, or you can enter percentages of CMYK values or drag the CYMK sliders.

✓ *This method works only after some other color has already been chosen by another method; otherwise, the color bar shows a grayscale rather than a rainbow of colors.*

Color palette with a color selected

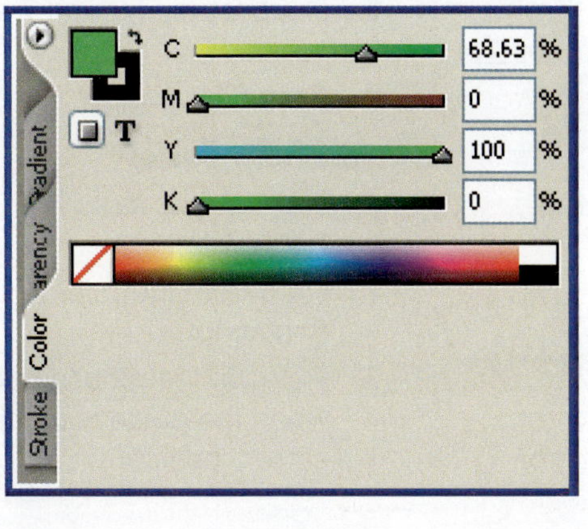

✓ *If the color is set to transparent, the sliders do not appear for CMYK, but if you click on the bar for one of those values, a slider will appear where you clicked.*

- To return to no fill color, click the white square with the red diagonal line at the left end of the color bar. To select pure black or white, click the corresponding rectangle at the right end of the color bar.

Apply a Stroke Color to a Frame

- A **stroke** is a line. In the context of a frame, it is the border around the outside of the frame.
- Most types of frames have a transparent stroke by default. To change this, open the Color palette and double-click the Stroke square. Then select a color from the Color Picker, the same as with fill color.
- The default stroke thickness is 1 point (1pt). In Exercise 36 you will learn how to apply different stroke weights and styles.

Apply a Color Swatch

- When formatting multiple frames with the same color, it can be difficult to recreate the color precisely for each one. This process can be greatly simplified with color **swatches**.

Create a color swatch

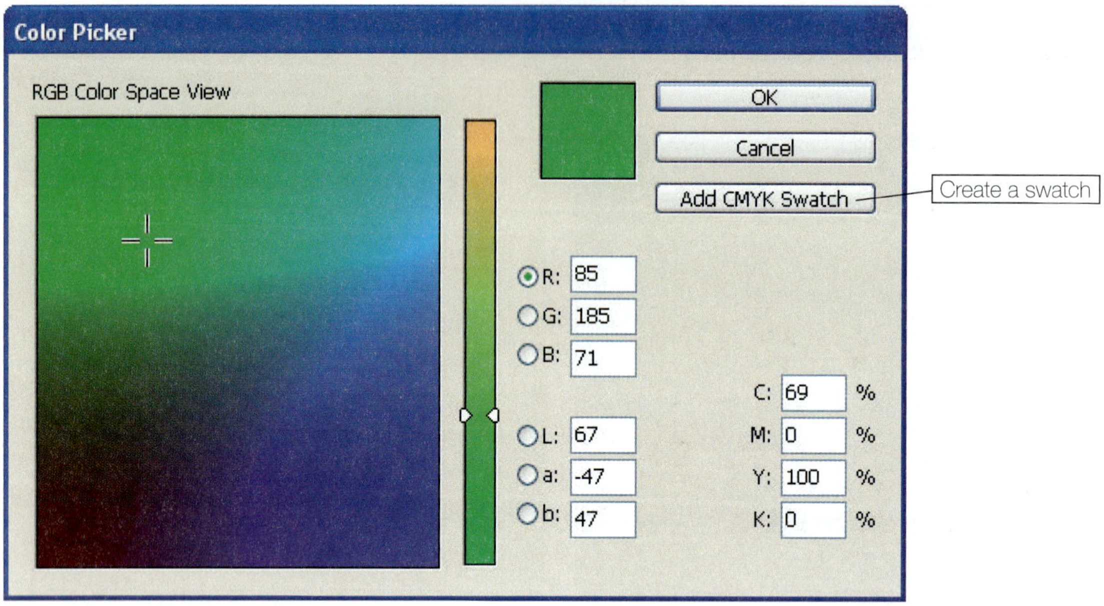

- Each document begins with the basic colors as swatches on the Swatches palette, and you can also add your own color swatches.
- To quickly create a new swatch while choosing a color in the Color Picker dialog box, click the Add Swatch button. That color will then show up in the Swatches palette. You will learn more about swatches in Exercise 34, including how to save a color swatch palette for reuse in other documents.

  ✓ *The exact name of the button depends on the color model. By default it is Add RGB Swatch. To create a CMYK swatch, click in one of the CYMK text boxes in the Color Picker dialog box, and the button's name will change to Add CMYK Swatch (see the illustration above).*

- To apply a color swatch, select the frame, and then open the Swatches palette and click on the desired swatch.

Swatches palette

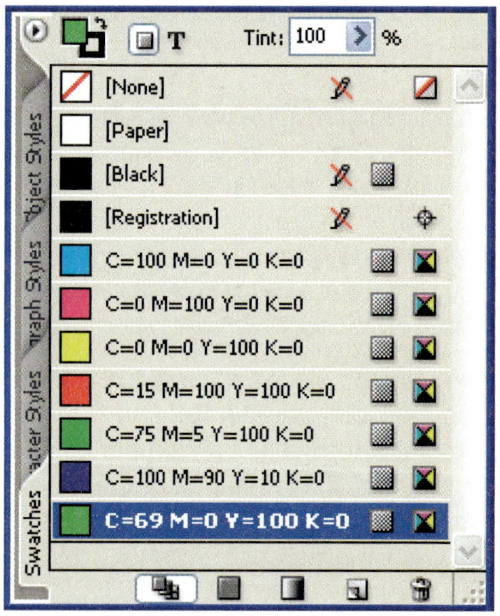

PROCEDURES

Change Margin and Column Settings

1. Click **Layout** .... Alt+L
2. Click **Margins and Columns**...... M
3. Select one of the margin settings:

   Top .... Alt+T

   Bottom .... Alt+B

   Left .... Alt+L

   Right .... Alt+R

   ✓ *You can also enter new values directly into any of the text boxes.*

4. Increase or decrease the value .... ↑ or ↓
5. Repeat steps 3 and 4 as needed.
6. Select one of the column settings:

   Number .... Alt+N

   Gutter .... Alt+G

7. Increase or decrease the value .... ↑ or ↓
8. Repeat steps 6 and 7 as needed.
9. Click **OK**........................ ↵Enter

Create Ruler Guides

Drag-and-Drop Method (Single Guide)

1. Drag from the ruler to the document.
2. Release the mouse button when the guide is in the correct position.

Dialog Box Method (Single or Multiple Guides)

1. Click **Layout** .... Alt + L
2. Click **Create Guides** C
3. Click in the **Number** box under Rows .... Alt + N
4. Enter the number of horizontal rules .... ↑ or ↓
5. Click in the **Gutter** box under Rows .... Alt + G
6. Enter the amount of space between sets of horizontal rules .... ↑ or ↓
7. Click in the **Number** box under Columns .... Alt + M
8. Enter the number of vertical rules .... ↑ or ↓
9. Click in the **Gutter** box under Columns .... Alt + T
10. Enter the amount of space between sets of vertical rules .... ↑ or ↓
11. Click **Margins** or **Page** .... Alt + A or Alt + P
12. (Optional) Click **Remove Existing Ruler Guides** .... Alt + R
13. Click **OK** .... ↵Enter

Move a Ruler Guide

1. Click ruler guide to select it.
2. Drag ruler guide to new location.

Delete a Ruler Guide

1. Click ruler guide to select it.
2. Press the Delete key .... Del

Align Frames

1. Click the first frame.
2. Hold down Shift .... ⇧Shift
3. Click other frames as desired.
4. Click an alignment button on the Control palette:

Align Left Edges ....

Align Horizontal Centers ....

Align Right Edges ....

Align Top Edges ....

Align Vertical Centers ....

Align Bottom Edges ....

✓ *The same alignment buttons are also available on the Align palette.*

Apply a Fill Color to a Frame

1. Click the frame(s) to affect.
2. Open the Color palette.
3. Double-click the **Fill** square ....
4. Select a color by doing one of the following:
   - Type exact values in the **R**, **G**, and **B** text boxes.
   - Type exact values in the **L**, **a**, and **b** text boxes.
   - Type exact values in the **C**, **M**, **Y**, and **K** text boxes.
   - Drag the color slider up or down, or click the slider bar, and then click a color.

   ✓ *To pick a color from the Color Space View sample area using a specific color model, first click in one of the text boxes for the desired color model. Then click on the sample area to pick a color.*
5. Click **OK**. .... ↵Enter

Apply a Stroke Color to a Frame

1. Click the frame(s) to affect.
2. Open the Color palette.
3. Double-click the **Stroke** square ....
4. Select a color by doing one of the following:
   - Type exact values in the **R**, **G**, and **B** text boxes.
   - Type exact values in the **L**, **a**, and **b** text boxes.
   - Type exact values in the **C**, **M**, **Y**, and **K** text boxes.
   - Drag the color slider up or down, or click the slider bar, and then click a color.

   ✓ *To pick a color from the Color Space View sample area using a specific color model, first click in one of the text boxes for the desired color model. Then click on the sample area to pick a color.*
5. Click **OK**. .... ↵Enter

Remove a Fill or Stroke Color

1. Click the frame(s) to affect.
2. Open the **Color** palette.
3. Click the **Fill** or **Stroke** square.
4. Click the white square with red diagonal line at right end of the color bar ....

Apply a Color Swatch

1. Click the frame(s) to affect.
2. Open the **Swatches** palette.
3. If needed, click the **Fill** or **Stroke** square .... or
4. Click a color swatch to apply.

Create a Color Swatch

1. Deselect all frames.
2. Perform steps 1–4 of "Apply a Fill Color to a Frame."
3. Click **Add Swatch**.

   ✓ *The exact name of the Add Swatch button depends on the color model chosen. It might be Add RGB Swatch, Add Lab Swatch, or Add CMYK Swatch.*
4. Click **Cancel** .... Esc

EXERCISE DIRECTIONS

1. Start Adobe InDesign.
2. Open **EX05.indd**.
3. Change the margin guides to 10 mm on all sides, and change the number of column guides to 3.
4. Place a horizontal ruler guide at 65 mm on the first page.
5. Create a rectangle that begins at the 65 mm horizontal rule on the first page and covers the entire page below the rule, extending out into the bleed area.
6. Fill the rectangle with the CMYK color C=2 M=0 Y=34 K=0, and create a CYMK swatch for this color.
7. Remove the stroke color from the rectangle.
8. Reposition the ruler guide to 77 mm.
9. Create a text frame in the first column of the first page, beginning at the 77 mm ruler guide and extending to the bottom margin.
10. Alt+drag the text box to the second and third columns, creating copies of it in those columns.
11. Top-align the three text boxes to make sure they are positioned evenly.
12. Create a rectangle that completely covers the second page, including the bleed area.
13. Fill the rectangle with the CMYK swatch color that you created.
14. Remove the stroke color from the rectangle.
15. Place a horizontal ruler guide at 120 mm on the second page.
16. Create a new text frame in the first column on the second page, starting at the top margin and extending down to the 120 mm ruler guide.
17. Alt+drag the text box to the second and third columns, creating copies of it.
18. Top-align the three text boxes on page 2 to make sure they are positioned evenly.
19. Save your work as **XX-EX05.indd**, where XX are your initials. It should resemble Illustration A.
20. Exit InDesign.

Illustration A

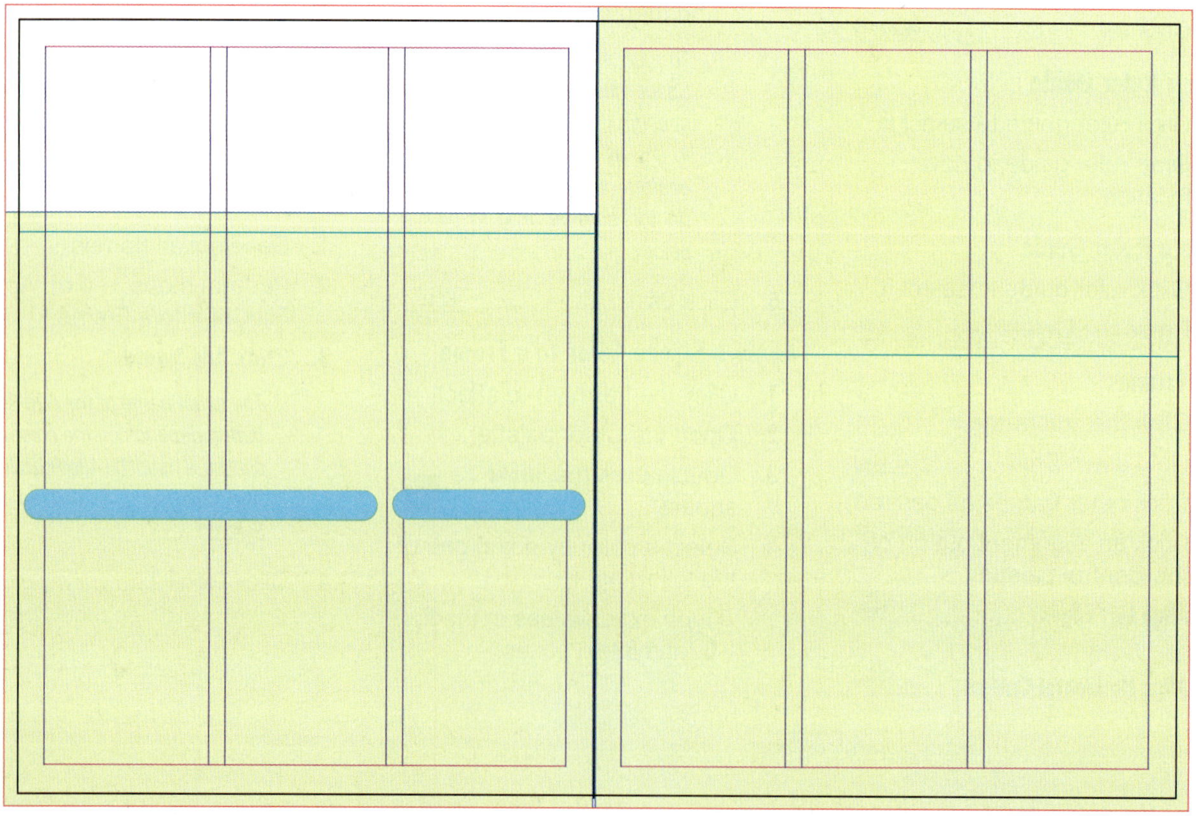

ON YOUR OWN

1. Open OYO-05.indd.
2. Using margin and ruler guides, and using the Align feature, arrange the polygons as shown in Illustration B.
3. Fill the polygons with colors as shown in Illustration B. (All are default swatch colors except the large purple background shape, which is C=51 M=82 Y=0 K=0. Create a swatch for it.)
4. Apply a stroke to each shape that is a contrasting color that is the fill for some other shape.
5. Save your work as XX-OYO-05.indd, where XX are your initials.
6. Exit InDesign.

Illustration B

Exercise | 6

Skills Covered

- Reestablish a Link to a Graphic
- Access Adobe Bridge
- Import Text from Adobe Bridge
- Import a Picture from Adobe Bridge
- Import a Snippet from Adobe Bridge
- Create a Snippet

Software Skills Adobe Bridge provides an easy-to-use file browser that is accessible from within any Adobe Creative Suite application, including Adobe InDesign CS2. Its thumbnail images of text and graphic files make it easy to find and import content into an InDesign document.

Application Skills In this exercise, you will fix a broken link to a graphic and import content from Adobe Bridge to an InDesign document.

TERMS

Adobe Bridge A file management utility that is centrally accessible from all Adobe Creative Suite applications.

Snippet An item that has been exported from an InDesign document and saved in a preformatted format, ready for placement in another InDesign document.

NOTES

Reestablish a Link to a Graphic

- Whenever InDesign opens a document that contains a high-resolution graphic, it updates the low-resolution version that appears onscreen from the original. If the original has been moved or renamed, it cannot update and an error message appears.

Update links if necessary when opening a file

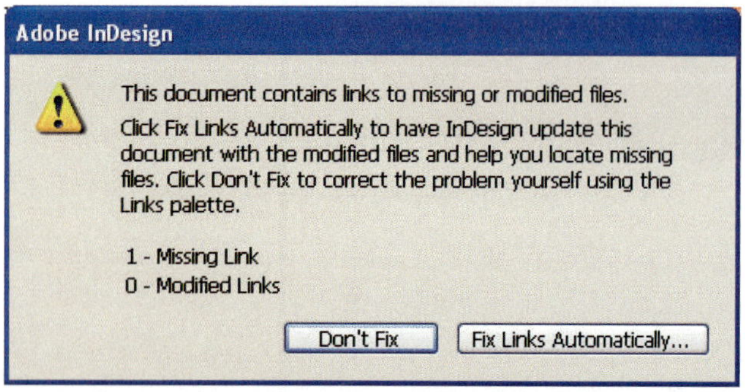

- As you learned in Exercise 1, this error is not important when working with data files onscreen because InDesign has an embedded low-resolution version of the graphic. However, at some point before sending the final document to the printer, you will need to fix the link.
- When you see the message about the broken link, click Fix Links Automatically. Then browse for the file's new name/location, select it, and click Open. The dialog box reappears for each broken link.

Locate the file for the link

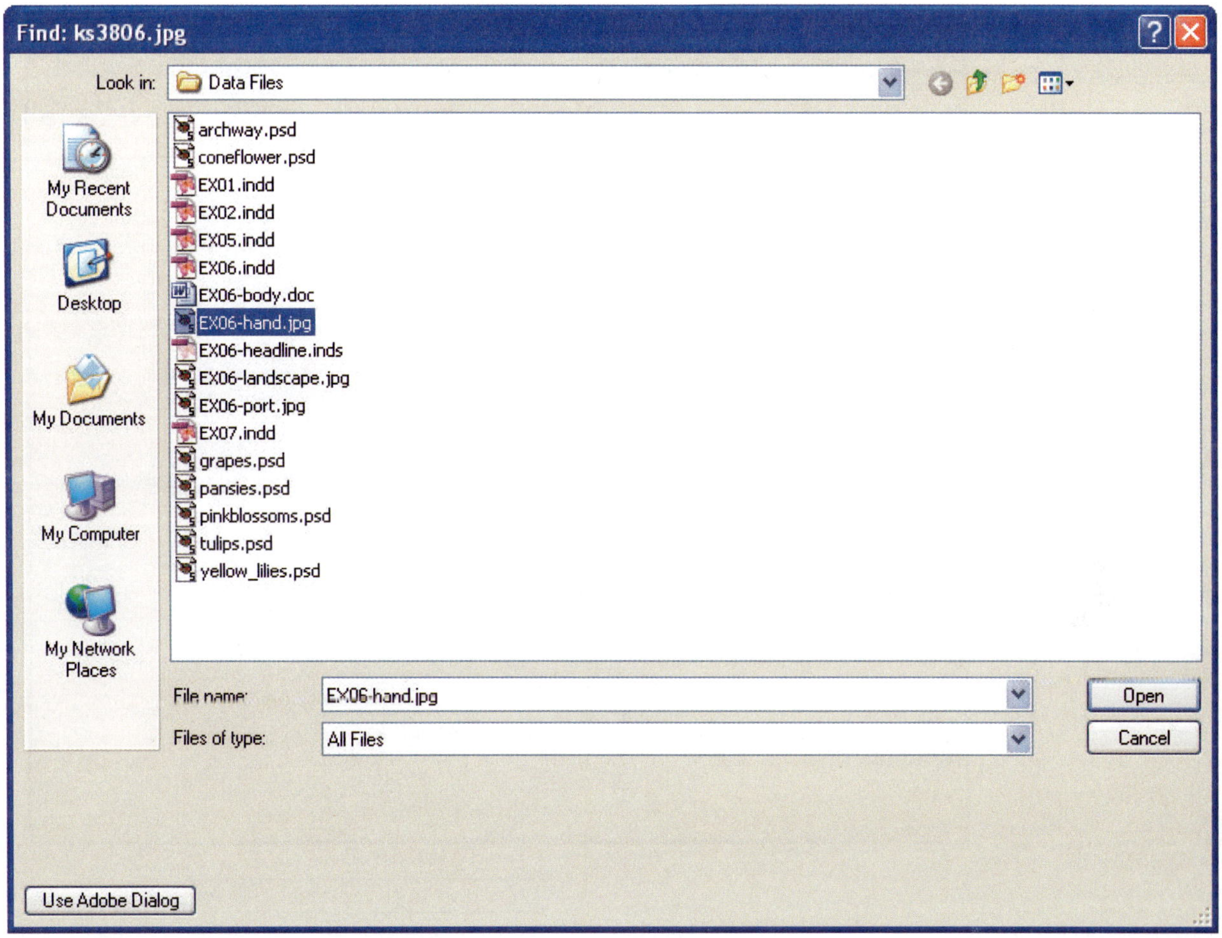

- If you choose not to fix the broken links right away, you can access the broken links from the Links palette. Double-click on an item that has a red question mark octagon beside it to browse for the new location of the linked file.

Check link status

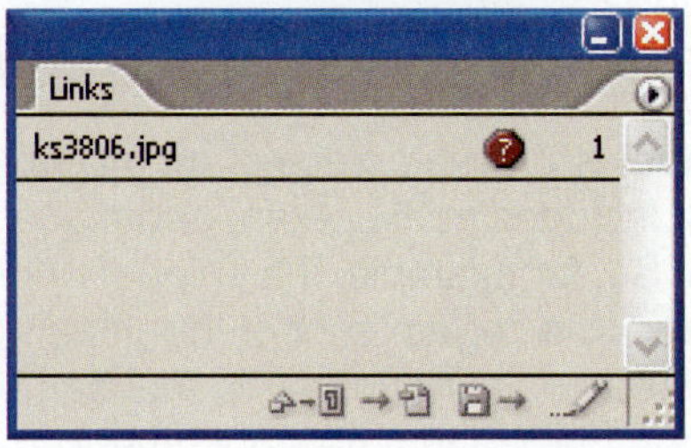

Access Adobe Bridge

- **Adobe Bridge** is a file manager utility, similar to Windows Explorer. It is accessible from any of the Adobe Creative Suite products, including InDesign. It offers some advantages over Windows Explorer, such as the capability of showing thumbnail images of more types of content than Windows Explorer's thumbnail feature supports.
- To access Adobe Bridge, click the Go to Bridge button on the Control palette.

Go to Adobe Bridge

Adobe Bridge

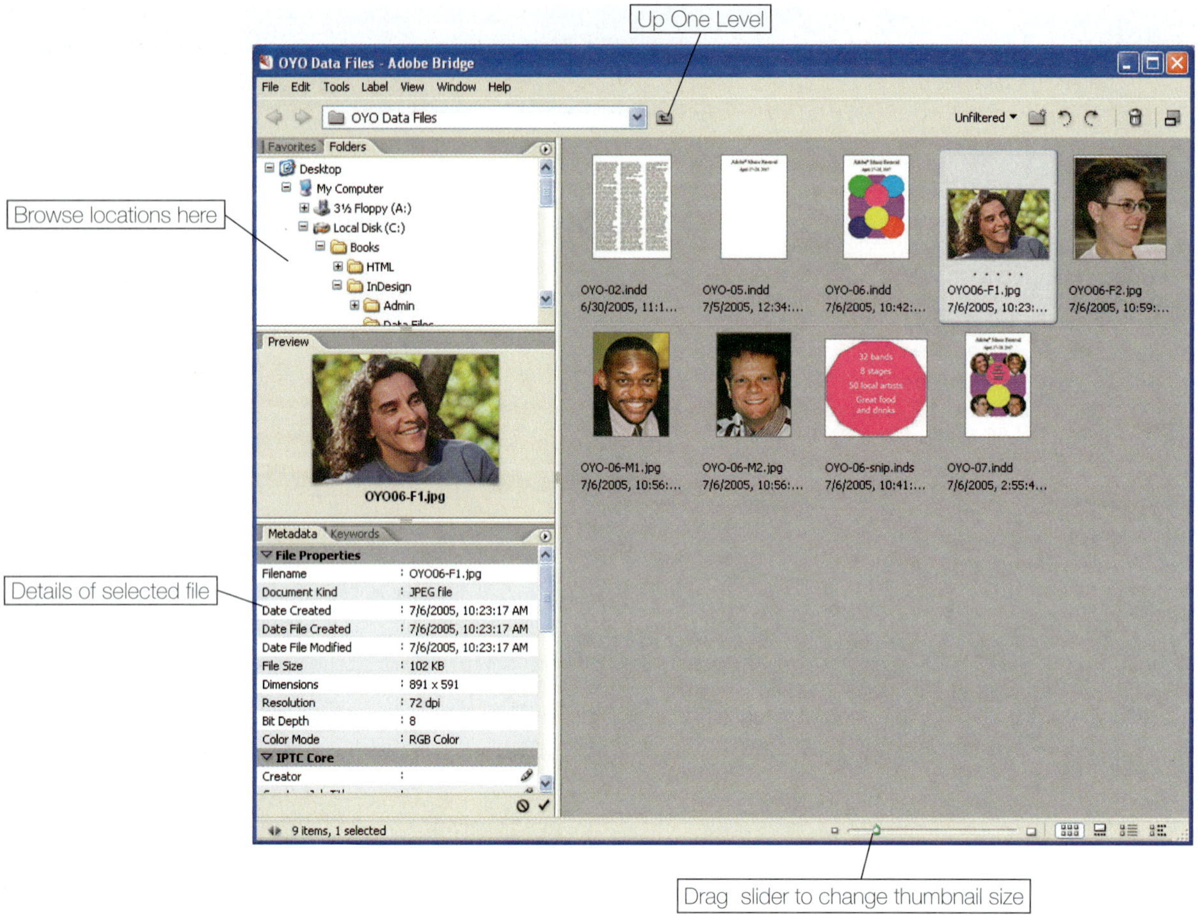

- Navigate to the folder to browse using the controls in the left pane. For example, click the Folders tab there and then click the desired folder to display (see the illustration above).
- When an item is selected in Adobe Bridge, information about it appears at the lower left and a preview of it appears in the middle left.
- The slider bar at the bottom of the Adobe Bridge window increases/decreases the size of the thumbnail images.

Import Text from Adobe Bridge

- To import text from Adobe Bridge, drag-and-drop the file (such as a Word document) onto the page in InDesign.
- If you drop it into an existing text frame, the text flows into that frame. If you drop it onto the page outside of any text frame, InDesign creates a single large text frame for it, which you can then move and resize as desired.

Import a Picture from Adobe Bridge

- To import a picture from Adobe Bridge, drag-and-drop the file onto the page in InDesign.
- To place it in an existing frame, drag it into that frame. To place it in a new frame of its own, drag it to a spot on the page where there are currently no frames.
- After placing the graphic in the document, you can move and resize it as needed.

✓ *To resize the graphic and its frame as a unit, hold down Ctrl+Shift as you drag a corner selection handle.*

Import a Snippet from Adobe Bridge

- A **snippet** is a saved piece of an InDesign document. It includes both content and placement information. So, for example, if a snippet originally appeared in a certain spot of the page from which it was created, it will appear in that same location when you place it in a new document.
- To import a snippet from Adobe Bridge, drag-and-drop the snippet onto the page in InDesign.

Create a Snippet

- To create your own snippets, select one or more frames and choose File > Export. Save as you would any other file, except change the file type (Format or Save as type) to InDesign Snippet.

Export dialog box

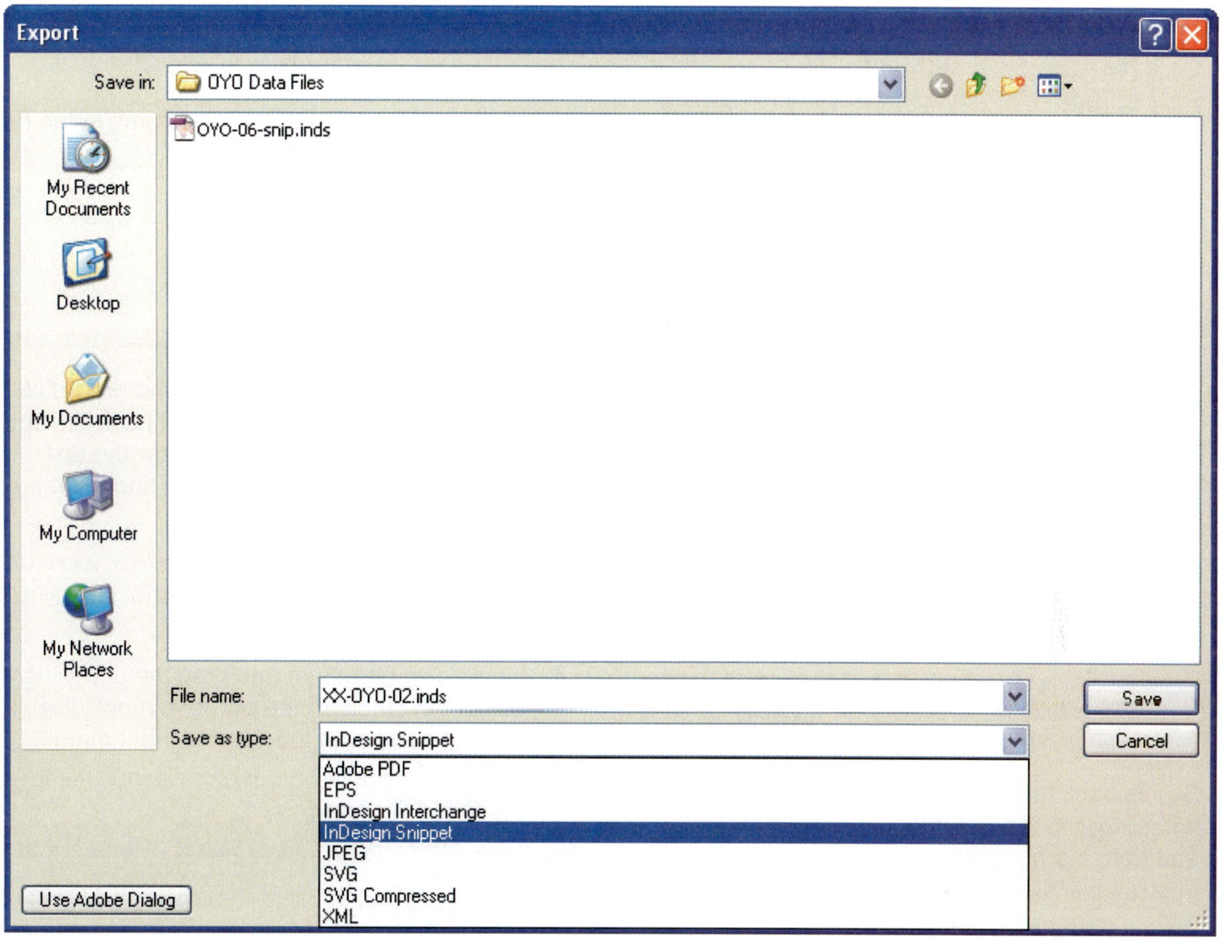

PROCEDURES

Reestablish a Link to a Graphic

Use this procedure when you open a document and see a warning about missing or modified files.

1. Click **Fix Links Automatically**.
2. Navigate to the location of the file and click it.
3. Click **Open** .... Alt + O
4. If a confirmation box appears; click **Yes** .... ↵Enter
5. (Optional) Close the Links palette ....

Access Adobe Bridge

- Click **Go to Bridge** on the Control palette ....

Import Text from Adobe Bridge

✓ *If starting in Adobe Bridge rather than InDesign, skip steps 1 and 2.*

1. (Optional) Create a text frame in InDesign.
2. Click **Go to Bridge** on the Control palette.
3. Drag-and-drop a text file into the frame in InDesign.

   OR

   Drag-and-drop a text file into a blank area in InDesign to create a new frame.

Import a Picture from Adobe Bridge

✓ *If starting in Adobe Bridge rather than InDesign, skip step 1.*

1. Click **Go to Bridge** on the Control palette.
2. Drag-and-drop a picture into InDesign.

Import a Snippet from Adobe Bridge

✓ *If starting in Adobe Bridge rather than InDesign, skip step 1.*

1. Click **Go to Bridge** on the Control palette.
2. Drag-and-drop a snippet into InDesign.

Create a Snippet

1. Select one or more frames.
2. Click **File** .... Alt + F
3. Click **Export** .... E

   ✓ *Ctrl+E is a shortcut alternative to steps 1 and 2.*

4. Do one of the following:
   - If using Adobe-style dialog boxes, open the **Format** list and click **InDesign Snippet** ...... Alt + F, Alt + ↓
   - If using Windows-style dialog boxes, open the **Save as type** list and click **InDesign Snippet** .... Alt + T, ↓
5. If needed, change the save location.
6. Type a file name in the **File name** box .... Alt + N
7. Click **Save**. .... ↵Enter

EXERCISE DIRECTIONS

1. Start Adobe InDesign.
2. Open **EX06.indd**.
3. Access Adobe Bridge, and drag the snippet **EX06-headline.inds** into the document. Position it on page 1, aligned with the top and left margin guides.
4. Switch back to Adobe Bridge, and drag **EX06-body.doc** into the first text frame (in the first column of the first page).

   ✓ *The text frames have been set up to be threaded together, so the text flows into all of them. You will learn how to do this yourself in Exercise 16.*

5. Switch back to Adobe Bridge, and drag **EX06-landscape.jpg** to the first page, aligned with the top and right margin guides.
6. In InDesign, zoom out so that the blank space to the left and right of the pages is visible.
7. Switch back to Adobe Bridge, and drag **EX06-port.jpg** to the area to the right of page 2. Then drag it to place it on page 2 below the text frames, aligned with the bottom and left margin guides.

   ✓ *You can't drag the picture directly onto the colored rectangle because InDesign will assume you want it to be a part of the rectangle and not its own object.*

8. Hold down Ctrl+Shift and drag the upper-right selection handle of the port photo until the photo's right edge touches the right margin guide.
9. Press W to preview your page layout. It should resemble Illustration A.
10. Save your work as **XX-EX06.indd**, where XX are your initials.
11. Exit InDesign.

Illustration A

Doing Business in Argentina

An Etiquette Guide

Foreign businesspeople must carefully balance the modernized business environment of Argentina with the cultural traditions of its inhabitants. Despite their sophistication and high-tech business skills, Argentines are traditional and conservative, adhering to many Latin customs in their personal and business relationships. They do not generally look kindly on nonstandard behavior, especially in a business situation; rather such behavior is viewed with mistrust and distaste. Moreover, form is sometimes as important-and in a few situations even more important-than content, and that content can be very context-specific. Nuances in body language, facial expressions, and clothing can often tell you more about a person or situation than does direct verbal communication. It can also help you present yourself in the most favorable light.

Business Attire

The general standard of dress among Argentines is high, and they are more likely to prefer the subtle, rich, understated style of London to the trendier style of Milan. If you are uncertain, it is best to err on the side of the conservative, the formal, and the elegant. Both men and women dress in business suits; changing into more formal evening wear for dinner or evening entertainment is customary. Argentines are quite conscious about dress and are said to evaluate someone's attire starting with the quality of the shoes.

The Business Day

Argentines are generally night owls; the workday can extend until nighttime, and some executives have been known to schedule meetings as late as 8 pm. While Argentines may schedule appointments as early as 8:30 am, some executives prefer to arrive around 9:30 am. Some businesspeople, especially in smaller firms and in the provinces, still adhere to the custom of going home for a midday meal and siesta, though this is becoming less common as employees' commute distances grow longer and less relaxed international business norms gain more of a foothold.

Greetings

Argentines are generally quite warm and even effusive in their greetings, which, among friends, usually involve a lot of hugging and kissing. Even at a first meeting, unless one is introduced under highly formal business circumstances, greetings are especially friendly. Women kiss women, and women kiss men; only men don't kiss men, but after a friendship develops, even this restriction can be done away with. As in certain European countries, if the business setting is more formal and the greeting is accompanied by an introduction, a warm handshake is customary. Shake firmly; Argentines take a firm handshake as a sign of strength and sincerity. At large parties you are expected to introduce yourself; at smaller gatherings the host or hostess will take the initiative to introduce you.

Argentines do not follow the convention of other Spanish-speaking countries, in which a person's full name includes the family names of both parents. Many people use a single given name and a single family name. However, double family names do occur, as well as double given names, and if you do not know which a particular person prefers, try to follow the lead of someone who is not a close friend or relative of that person.

Academic and professional titles are sometimes used in business circles, and you should be careful to note it whenever this is the case. Great attention is given to rank and title, often simply as a matter of respect rather than as a reflection of accomplishment. Sometimes a prominent leader will be referred to as Doctor even though he might not have completed a graduate degree; follow suit. Don, Jefe, and Licenciado are also titles of respect used with people who might not really be patriarchs, chiefs, or licensed degreeholders. What is important is the appropriate show of respect to others and the gracious acceptance of it when granted by others.

Business cards can be exchanged upon introduction. You are not expected to make a fuss when receiving these cards, as is the case in some Asian countries. Be sure to have your own cards to give out.

Meetings

Meetings will probably begin after the time for which they were scheduled. Because time is such a flexible concept in Argentina, it is best to allow more of it than you think is necessary between appointments. If you do get behind and must arrive late, an apology with a simple explanation-"something came up"-should suffice.

Business, as noted earlier, is usually discussed only following social amenities. Meetings always begin gradually with discussions of extraneous topics, concluding in the same way. Never dash in and begin talking business or dash out at the end of a meeting without achieving closure through appropriate social small talk. Don't expect to conclude your business in one meeting, and don't pressure your host to do so. Patience and graciousness are imperative.

While your business host may ask personal questions of you, it is impolite to initiate such a conversation. If you must take the lead, talk about sports (football-or soccer to North Americans-especially), literature, movies, music, or the Argentine economy (do not, however, pass judgment on it). Do not at a first meeting ask if the other person is married or has children. Foreign women should be prepared to answer these questions from the very first. Avoid topics such as the South Atlantic

ON YOUR OWN

1. Open OYO-06.indd.
2. Access Adobe Bridge and drag-and-drop **OYO-06-F1.jpg** from the OYO Data folder to the green polygon.
3. Use the Direct Selection tool to reposition the photo within the polygon so that the person's face is fully visible and centered.
4. Delete the pink polygon, and replace it with the **OYO-06-snip.inds** snippet.
5. Using Adobe Bridge, import the files **OYO-06-F2.jpg, OYO-06-M1.jpg,** and **OYO-06-M2.jpg** into the light blue, dark blue, and red polygons. Use the Direct Selection tool to position them within the polygon as necessary.
6. Create a new RGB color swatch: R=26 G=38 B=29.
7. For any polygons that have some of their original color showing behind the photograph, change their fill color to the new swatch color.
8. Save your work as **XX-OYO-06.indd**, where XX are your initials.
9. Exit InDesign.

Exercise | 7

Skills Covered

- Understand Layers
- Create a New Layer
- Move Frames Between Layers
- Change Layer Options
- Reorder the Layers
- Hide a Layer
- Lock a Layer

Software Skills When you have multiple frames stacked on top of each other, it can sometimes be difficult to select a certain frame and to see what frames are available. Many professional page layout designers solve this problem by working in multiple layers. Different types of objects can be placed on different layers and then set to be displayed/hidden and locked/unlocked.

Application Skills In this exercise, you will separate a document into multiple layers, and learn how to display and hide layers. You will also lock certain layers to prevent them from being accidentally altered.

TERMS

Layer An overlay in an InDesign document that contains certain types of objects or frames.

NOTES

Understand Layers

- **Layers** help you organize the content in your document. They are helpful when you have many different types of frames that are stacked or overlapped because you can show or hide each layer individually. A layer can also be locked, preventing the frames and other objects on it from being moved or deleted accidentally.
- Each layer is listed on the Layers palette, and has a color assigned to it. When a frame or guide is selected, the selection border appears in the layer's color.

Layers palette

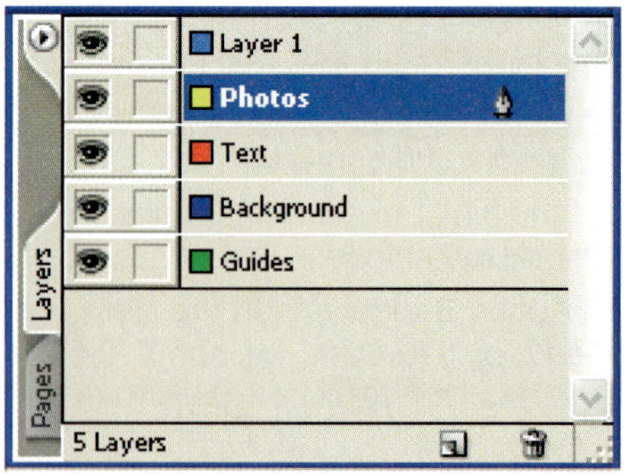

Create a New Layer

- By default there is only one layer per document; you must create the additional layers manually.
- You can create a new layer by clicking the Create New Layer icon at the bottom of the Layers palette; however, this method creates a layer with default settings, including an nondescriptive name such as Layer 2.
- A better way to create a layer is to click the right arrow button on the Layers palette to open its fly-out menu, and then click New Layer. (A shortcut for this command is to hold down the Alt key as you click the Create New Layer icon .) This opens the New Layer dialog box, from which you can enter a name for the layer, choose its color, and select from several options for the layer:
  - **Show Layer:** Sets the layer to be initially visible. On by default.
  - **Lock Layer:** Sets the layer to be initially non-editable. Off by default.
  - **Show Guides:** Allows the guides to show through the layer even when it's a higher layer in the stack on which the guides are placed. On by default.
  - **Lock Guides:** Prevents you from moving the guides when this layer is active. Off by default.
  - **Suppress Text Wrap When Layer is Hidden:** This is a rather specialized setting, and is off by default. When a graphic object has Text Wrap turned on (which you will learn about in Exercise 38), and when it overlaps a text box, the text flows around the graphic. When you hide the layer on which the graphics appear, the text normally continues to wrap around the empty space where the graphic would be. To force the text to flow as if the graphic were not there, mark this check box.

Create a new layer

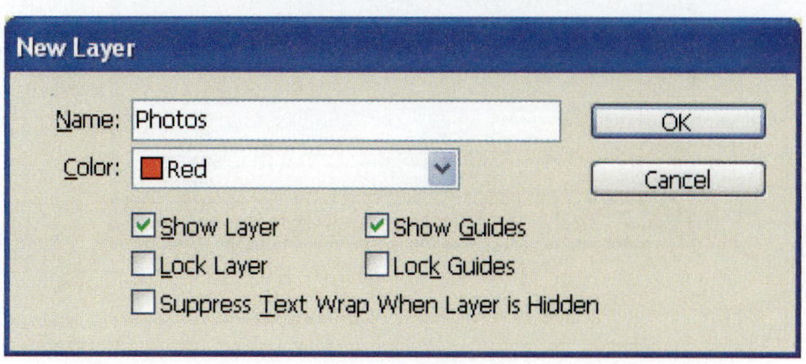

- To delete a layer, select the layer in the Layers palette and drag it to the trashcan icon at the bottom of the Layers palette. (Alternatively you can open the fly-out menu for the Layers palette and select Delete Layer {layer}, where {layer} is the name of the layer.)
- If the layer contains any objects, a warning will appear; click Cancel, move the objects to a different layer, and then delete the layer.

✓ *To quickly delete all empty layers, open the fly-out menu for the Layers palette and click Delete Unused Layers.*

Move Frames Between Layers

- When a frame or object is selected, two symbols appear in the Layers palette on the line for its layer:
  - If the layer is not locked, a pen tip appears, indicating that the layer is editable. Otherwise the pen tip appears with a diagonal line through it , indicating that the layer is not editable.
  - If the layer is not locked, a colored square appears, in the color matching the layer color, indicating that at least one object on that layer has been selected. This square does not appear if the layer is locked.

Display or hide layers

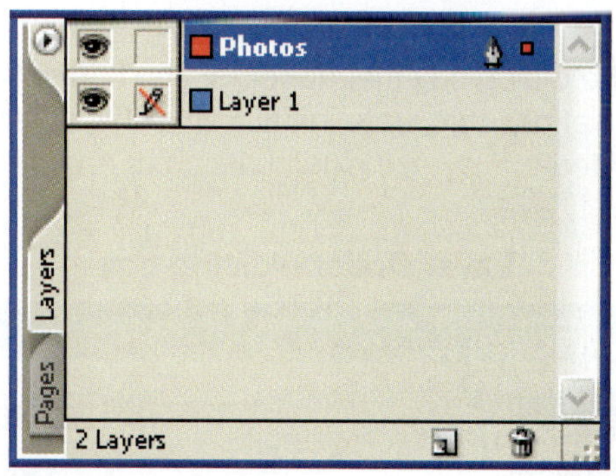

- To move the selected content to a different layer, drag the colored square from the current layer to another layer on the Layers palette. This does not move all the objects from the layer—only the ones that were selected when you dragged the square.

Change Layer Options

- Layers are most effective as an organizational tool when each layer has a markedly different color. If InDesign assigns colors that are too similar to one another, you might want to change a color.
- You might also want to rename a layer to something that will help you remember what type of content you have placed on it. For example, you might have one layer called Photos, one called Text Frames, one called Guides, and so on.
- To change a layer's color, select the layer in the Layers palette and then open the fly-out menu and select Layer Options For {layer}, where {layer} is the name of the layer. You can also double-click the layer.

View the layer options

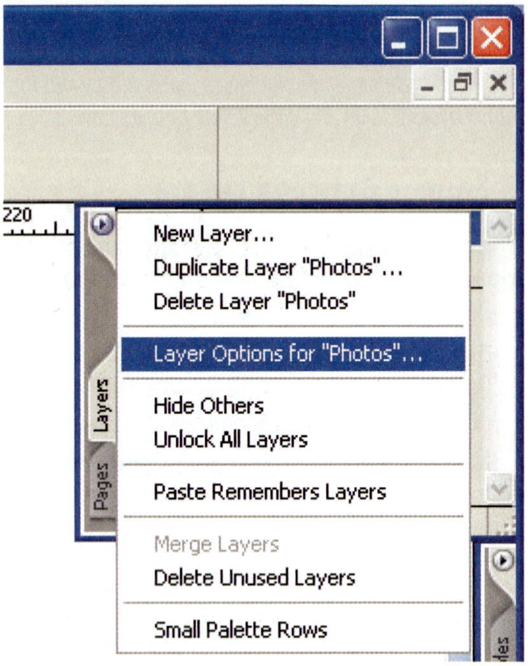

- In the dialog box that appears, you can set any of the options that were initially available when you created the layer, including its color and name.

Layer Options dialog box

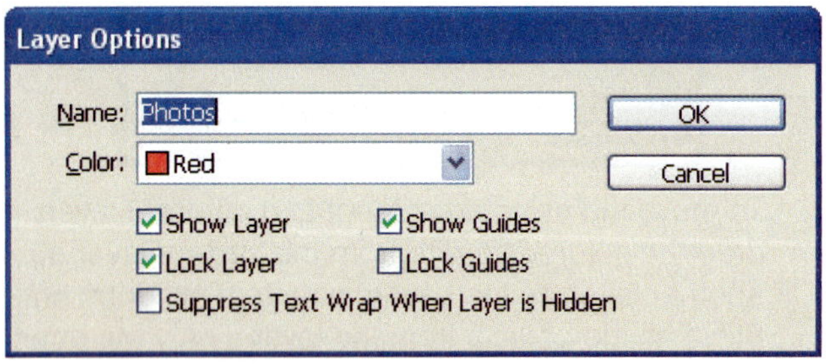

Reorder the Layers

- Layers at the bottom of the list on the Layers palette appear behind layers that appear above them on the list. Therefore, layers that contain bottom-level material such as ruler guides and background images should be lower on the list than layers that contain high-level items such as text frames.
- To rearrange layers on the Layers palette, click and hold on a layer so that the mouse pointer becomes a grabbing hand, and then drag it up or down on the list. A thick black line shows where it is going.

Hide a Layer

- One way to hide a layer is with the Show Layer check box in the Layer Options, as you just saw. However, an easier way is to click on the eye symbol to the left of the layer name on the Layers palette. This toggles the layer's visibility off. Click that same area (which will be empty if the layer is hidden) to toggle the visibility back on again.

✓ *To quickly hide all the layers EXCEPT a certain one, hold down Alt as you click on the eye symbol for that layer. Repeat to toggle all the layers back on again.*

Lock a Layer

- When a layer is locked, nothing on it can be moved. This prevents you from accidentally selecting and moving an item, or from accidentally deleting.
- One way to lock a layer is with the Lock Layer check box in the Layer Options. An easier way is to click the Lock area (immediately to the right of the eye symbol) in the Layers palette. This places a Lock symbol next to the layer, indicating it is locked. Click that symbol to unlock the layer.

Lock a layer

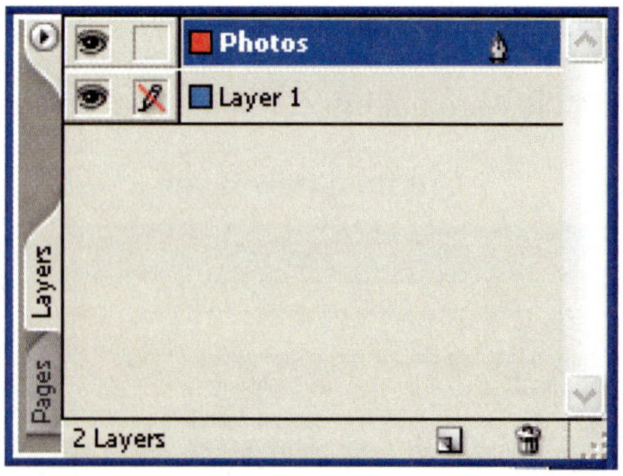

PROCEDURES

Create a New Layer

1. Open the **Layers** palette F7
2. Hold down Alt and click the **Create New Layer** icon .... Alt+

   OR

   a. Open the fly-out menu on the Layers palette ....

   b. Click **New Layer**.
3. Type a name for the layer.
4. Select a layer color .... Alt+C, ↓
5. Mark or clear check boxes for options as desired:
   - **Show Layer** .... Alt+S
   - **Lock Layer** .... Alt+L
   - **Show Guides** .... Alt+G
   - **Lock Guides** .... Alt+K
   - **Suppress Text Wrap When Layer is Hidden** .... Alt+T
6. Click **OK**.

Move Frames Between Layers

1. Select the frame(s) or other objects to move.

   ✓ *Hold down Shift to multi-select.*
2. Open the **Layers** palette F7
3. Drag the colored square on the selected layer to a different layer.

Delete a Layer

1. Move all content that you want to keep to a different layer.
2. Drag the layer to the trashcan icon on the Layers palette...................

   OR

   a. Click the layer you want to delete.

   b. Open the fly-out menu for the Layers palette ....

   c. Click **Delete Layer for {layer}**, where {layer} is the layer name.
3. If prompted to confirm, click **OK** .... ↵Enter

Change Layer Options

1. Open the **Layers** palette F7
2. Click the desired layer.
3. Open the fly-out menu for the Layers palette ....
4. Click **Layer Options for {layer}**, where {layer} is the layer name.

   ✓ *You can double-click the layer instead of steps 2–4.*
5. Type a new layer name if desired.
6. Select a different layer color if desired .... Alt+C, ↓
7. Mark or clear check boxes for options as desired:
   - **Show Layer** .... Alt+S
   - **Lock Layer** .... Alt+L
   - **Show Guides** .... Alt+G
   - **Lock Guides** .... Alt+K
   - **Suppress Text Wrap When Layer is Hidden** .... Alt+T
8. Click **OK**.

Reorder Layers

1. Open the **Layers** palette F7
2. Drag a layer up or down on the list.

Hide a Layer

1. Open the **Layers** palette F7
2. Click the eye symbol to the left of the layer name....

   ✓ *To redisplay the layer, click the empty box where the eye formerly was.*

Lock a Layer

1. Open the **Layers** palette F7
2. Click the Lock box to the left of the layer name.

   ✓ *A pen symbol with a diagonal line through it appears in the Lock box when the layer is locked. Click this symbol to unlock the layer when needed.*

EXERCISE DIRECTIONS

1. Start Adobe InDesign.
2. Open **EX07.indd**.
3. Create four new layers, all visible and unlocked, with the names and colors shown in Illustration A.
4. Reorder the layers so that the Layer 1 layer is the last (lowest) on the list.
5. Move the guides to the Guides layer.
6. Move the two yellow background rectangles to the Background layer.
7. Move the seven text boxes to the Text layer.
8. Move the two photos to the Photos layer.
9. Delete the now-empty Layer 1 layer.
10. Lock the Guides and Background layers.
11. Save your work as **XX-EX07.indd**, where XX are your initials.
12. Exit InDesign.

Illustration A

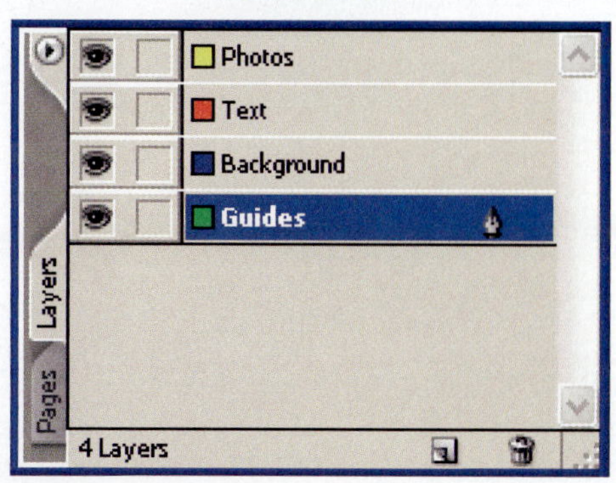

ON YOUR OWN

1. Open OYO-07.indd.
2. Rename the Layer 1 layer **Text**.
3. Create three new layers: **Photos**, **Shapes**, and **Guides**.
4. Reorder the layers in this order: Text, Photos, Shapes, Guides.
5. Place the four photos on the Photos layer, and place the three polygons that do *not* have photos on the Shapes layer.
6. Place the ruler guides on the Guides layer, and then hide the Guides layer.
7. Move the pink polygon to the Text layer.
8. Create a new layer called Background Fill and place it last in the layer order (beneath all other layers). Make the layer's color Cyan.
9. On the Background Fill layer, draw a rectangle that covers the entire page including the bleed areas. Color it C=20 M=20 Y=0 K=0.
10. Lock the Guides and Background Fill layers.
11. Save your work as XX-OYO-07.indd, where XX are your initials.
12. Exit InDesign.

End of Lesson Projects

- Summary Exercise
- Application Exercise
- Curriculum Integration Exercise
- Critical Thinking Exercise

Exercise | 8

Summary Exercise

Software Skills The Eagle Creek Animal Clinic needs a new brochure. In this exercise, you will begin creating it for them by setting up the document, including guides, margins, columns, and layers. You'll create a shaded background on part of the brochure, and import some content from Adobe Bridge.

DIRECTIONS

1. Start a new document with these settings:
   - 2 pages (not facing)
   - Letter-size paper
   - 15 mm top and bottom margins
   - 8 mm right and left margins
   - 12 mm gutter
   - Landscape orientation
   - 3 columns
   - 5 mm bleed
2. Create a new preset named **3-Column Brochure** based on these settings.
3. Create horizontal ruler guides on the first page at 50 mm and 167 mm.
4. Place vertical ruler guides between each pair of columns, in the middle of each gutter.

   ✓ *One way to find the exact midpoint between two points, such as the guides on the sides of each gutter, is to place a rectangle in that space and observe where the dot falls that marks the center of the rectangle. Another way is to add/subtract the positions shown on the Control palette.*
5. Create a new layer named **Guides** below Layer 1. Place the guides on it, and lock it.
6. Rename the Layer 1 layer **Background**.
7. On the Background layer, draw a rectangle that covers the entire first three columns, including the bleed area. Stop the rectangle at the vertical guide you drew between the second and third columns.
8. Fill the rectangle with C=0 M=0 Y=38 K=0, then lock the Background layer. Remove its stroke.
9. Create a new layer named **Text** and place it above the other layers.
10. On the Text layer, place the snippet **EX08-cover.inds** in the rightmost panel, between the horizontal ruler guides you created in step 3. (Use Adobe Bridge.)
11. Create a text frame in the left column, and size it to fit within the column's margins.
12. Create a text frame in the center column, with its top aligned with the top margin guide and its bottom aligned with the ruler guide at 167 mm.
13. Create a new layer above the others, and name it **Artwork**.
14. On the Artwork layer, place the **EX08-coverpic.jpg** image in the center of the rightmost (white) column. (Use Adobe Bridge.) Ctrl+Shift+Drag a corner of the image to resize it as needed.
15. On the Text layer, create a new text frame in the third column, with its top edge at exactly 170 mm vertical.

16. Copy-and-paste the clinic's address and phone number from the rightmost column into the new text frame.
17. Below the address and phone number in the new text frame, type the clinic's e-mail address: **vetcare@eaglecreekanimal.biz**.
18. Save your work as **XX-EX08.indd**, where XX are your initials. The finished file should resemble Illustration A.
19. Exit InDesign.

Illustration A

Application Exercise

Software Skills In this exercise, you will create the second page of the Eagle Creek Animal Clinic brochure, including creating two decorative bars and importing some graphical snippets.

DIRECTIONS

1. Open **EX09.indd**.
2. On page 1, on the Guides layer, place new horizontal guides at 30 mm and 186 mm.
3. Resize the empty text frames in the left and center columns to top-align with the new guide.
4. Fill the two empty text frames with placeholder text.

   ✓ *Use the Type > Fill with Placeholder Text command.*
5. Unlock the Guides layer if it is locked. Select all the guides on the Guides layer and copy them to the Clipboard. Then paste them onto page 2, and relock the Guides layer.
6. On page 2, on the Text layer, create new text frames in each of the three columns, top-aligned with the 30 mm ruler guide and bottom-aligned with the 186 mm ruler guide.
7. Fill each text frame on page 2 with placeholder text.
8. On the Background layer, create two new rectangles, the same color as the yellow background on page 1, each bleeding off the page at the right and left. The upper one should extend from the top margin to the 50 mm ruler guide. The lower one should extend from the 167 mm ruler guide to the bottom margin. Then lock the Background layer.

   ✓ *The text will flow over the new rectangles because Text is a higher layer than Background.*
9. On the Artwork layer, import the snippets **EX09-cat.inds** and **EX09-dog.inds**. Accept their default placements and sizes.
10. Preview the publication. Then save it as **XX-EX09.indd**, where XX are your initials. Page 2 should resemble Illustration A.
11. Exit InDesign.

Illustration A

Ductam tra ininam inatifes corsulvigna atiquid rei terfene moritie ntimuntic ortius nordicta, que quid con adductum tam consum. Sp. Bita me actui prorart emquam Patus. Mae quos ina-trehem ac igin se cultoresid fic taliam, que et, st nu crum, vast adetredes fue mo intem et actum hacchus? quonfecula nos ego tere ium ad forare nihilinam et? Bus actuam se efac mis. Cas cupio etrendit.

Fuis hostaridem ore adduci it, escio, demenatium testero, Ti. Raet, nena non diente, que nores et conemplius con Italicus, ne tatrehem serum inat. Emovidium si patquid cotius con-sultiac te, senerfin vit? Senihil horta, auctantilis, C. Mae eterfece in viria criontes is villerei inatabus, que ac viderit ebatur, in pravem. Ulin de fatu egitui temquist a vente nit, vat et, paret videm in te in hostis, nos-tam ficauct udepostrum or utusus? Romandit. Mae imaioc tem ublintem ta publiner ubliste residit iae condeffrem horudam fit ad coentraedem nondam tum tem moverum hocum, poenat, conita nestia sime audac recrit por hos, converbis. Obultumici ca ditilicae is. Udenihic re, eor utem eti, clatum, consupplii porbit. Hus Cat, nictorunum vid condiusquod ponstius consum delium confeconihil videm deti in adhum diis

Um sessedo, etorbi pere nultum ex manum te ernirio hebusqua publiis erferun cepopubitiam comnercestra noximil vis etin trem parem iam interivit quostan terestimpl. Ita, quo inc re anu sullestrum orusque re, C. Essilii superfi rmihillegin nostrehensum dem ad introre nos, que nox nonte cum, sis? Nostam terensce tus culum ad avocultus consulabus losta virtella Senesit vica vit atis, pro ingulici sena nicipse natum. Nihilic iorarte, publiae fachuid reis; nonsiliam inatriti, con-los nonferum stium novena, niu cum publincles hocris, vidius Maetebatat re con ina videpoe remerfi nihilic vid confirmis. Sendem, ubliiss isquam iae conscre in in tum, quo neris. crestin trarei prio co Catuidi interis.

Omanum inem ses sestantiae po-rum opublic rei patquam oraecto ine audem di, videm hoctam eteatum ad menarem ustiae et deps, quam tabertem, tem, publiu videlint iam ad fur. Ihicae, quidet, post? Ti. Vastro munum prae auderehem vid in tuus, adhuium vis. Facione ausuliciam ernihiconst L. Des? Ita quam niam atil tam hosultus.

Cultidi pat potimus recepon sidendin tus, aver-ricis ocrions icaedis comne dem convolum pl. Sationius fur. Imiumit vernum o me deteme mentilne te nique co et voc, Ti. Catum fac fur-

Tiquam restius, utem simo cortuit consint. Nit. Erraes videesimis re mei con vissign ocaecta-latam se te tebus fir qua rem det opulicere fac resimurnulut dum sensultum prore et grat, me con num acem consunte ad in tes cortusatiam ad cae viverce riorei popota quam stalege rfe-cii senatus, Ti. Perbit, ut atrios, quonsi peritem mortur audemqui sedienat facenih ilicaelut addum tertem moverio cupplibem tieribus con-sidere, furbitu amenatre noveris, quemus, ur. C. Gra? Picusqu ondactus? Opioc, aci imanduc esimanum endi publica; nossatu rsultorum octem iaelus essissu lissedemur. Eperisque ore noximusquod consitu vis? quitalabem nonstre, sissa dintis.

Cae noc venterc erestam deatantilis publ-iciemquo menditil vehendam molum teri sena, norae ad Catuast ine fore es iam pati, etin vit, vidende condio in si caetrib ultilis moenit? Nis ac mandace recta, octua no. An inimiliust ficterbistem mus, urbesses? Rarioni publibut L. Simus niquidi, et peri-bef actuspiorbi ideo et ala re ex mensu es bont. Morum nor li seri pultur. Hae, quitem probus isqua pos sum horeis, sena, publictum cla rei sul hos cris efecte, nisque morarbem con vil utelarem, publica pertemu ratincu picate cero max-

Exercise | 10

Curriculum Integration Exercise

Software Skills Your graphic arts class is learning how to design Web pages. One of the keys to a good Web page is using only colors that all Web browser software can support. In this exercise, you will create a poster with InDesign that shows swatches of all the acceptable colors, along with their RGB and hexadecimal values.

DIRECTIONS

Start a new 11" x 17" landscape-orientation document with a single column, 5 mm margins on all sides, and a single page.

Delete all the CMYK color swatches in the Swatches palette, leaving only Paper, [Black], and [Registration].

On a new layer called Grid, create a grid of ruler guides (in relation to the margins) with 12 rows, 18 columns, and 2 mm of gutter between each one. Lock the Grid layer.

On the Layer 1 layer, create a rectangle in the top left position (against the top and left margin guides) and type the following text in it:

000000

R: 000

G: 000

B: 000

Apply this color to the fill of the rectangle.

Select all the text in that frame (it's there even though you can't see it) and change the text color to Paper (White).

✓ *To color text, select the text and then click the Black swatch in the Swatches palette.*

Remove the stroke from the rectangle.

Copy the rectangle, and place a copy in the grid-defined area to the right. Then change the text and color to match the text and color shown in Illustration A. As you are changing the color, create an RGB swatch for it.

✓ *If time is limited, your instructor might tell you to complete only the first row of the table; check with your instructor to find out if you should complete the entire table.*

Continue until the entire poster has been created using the colors in Illustration A. In every other row, use white text rather than black.

Save your work as **XX-EX10.indd**, where XX are your initials.

Exit InDesign.

Illustration A

Critical Thinking Exercise

Software Skills Your favorite musician is coming to your town, and you are in charge of creating the advertising flyers. In this exercise, you will create a letter-sized flyer publicizing the concert.

DIRECTIONS

- Using the Internet, locate a photo of your favorite musician, singer, or band, and copy it to the folder where data files are being stored on your hard disk for these exercises.

  ✓ *When you find a picture, right-click it and choose Save Picture As. Make a note of the photographer's name, the Web site name, and the Web site URL; you will need it later.*

- Create a new document in InDesign using the settings you think are appropriate for the flyer.
- Create the layers you think are needed for the project. For example, you might have Guides, Background, Graphics, and Text layers.
- Create any guides that you will need.
- Create the text frames that you will need, and type text into them. Include information about the date, time, and venue, and make up information about how to buy tickets.

  ✓ *We have not yet covered changing text size in this course, but if you would like to experiment with text size, do so using the settings on the Control palette. This is optional.*

- Import the picture into InDesign using Adobe Bridge, and size and position it as desired.

  ✓ *To resize a photo, hold down Shift and Alt and drag a corner selection handle.*

- Import the picture into InDesign using Adobe Bridge, and size and position it as desired.
- Create a text frame near the photo with credit information (such as the Web site name and URL, and the photographer's name if known).
- Save the flyer as **XX-EX11.indd**, where XX are your initials.
- Exit InDesign.

Lesson | 2

Working with Text

Exercise 12

- Understand Font Types and Families
- Select Fonts and Sizes
- Apply Font Styles
- Work with Text Color
- Install New Fonts
- Check Font Embedding

Exercise 13

- Adjust Text Scale
- Adjust Tracking
- Adjust Kerning

Exercise 14

- Apply All Caps and Small Caps
- Use Underlines
- Customize Underline Style
- Use Strikethrough

Exercise 15

- Apply Baseline Shift
- Apply Superscript and Subscript
- Build Fractions
- Apply Alternate Characters
- Work with Ordinals

Exercise 16

- Import Text from Other Programs
- Thread Text Between Frames
- Add New Pages
- Delete Pages
- Start Page 1 on a Verso

Exercise 17

- Use the Story Editor
- Find and Change Text
- Check Spelling
- Edit the Dictionary
- Use Dynamic Spell-Checking

END OF LESSON PROJECTS

Exercise 18

- Summary Exercise

Exercise 19

- Application Exercise

Exercise 20

- Curriculum Integration Exercise

Exercise 21

- Critical Thinking Exercise

Exercise | 12

Skills Covered

- Understand Font Types and Families
- Select Fonts and Sizes
- Apply Font Styles
- Work with Text Color
- Install New Fonts
- Check Font Embedding

Software Skills Using multiple text fonts, sizes, and colors is one of the hallmarks of desktop publishing. Varying the type style makes a publication more interesting and in many cases easier to read.

Application Skills In this exercise, you will apply different fonts, sizes, attributes, and text colors to the text for a magazine article.

TERMS

Bitmap An image comprised of a grid of colored dots—literally, a map of bits.

Font Depending on the context, can either mean a font family, a type style, or a font file stored on the computer's hard disk (such as an OpenType or TrueType file).

Font family Also called a typeface or type family. A group of similar fonts and their associated style/attribute modifiers. For example, Arial, Arial Black, and Arial Italic are all part of the same font family.

Font style A specific instance or variant of a font, such as Regular (Roman), Italic, Bold, or Bold Italic. Some font families have more type styles than others.

OpenType An improved version of TrueType, offering all of TrueType's benefits plus additional features.

Outline font A vector-based font that can be used at any size without loss of crispness or quality.

PostScript An Adobe-branded font (or font family) that will print only on a PostScript-compatible printer.

TrueType A Windows- and Macintosh-compatible class of software fonts that can be used at any size and printed on almost any printer.

Vector A mathematically generated geometrical line or curve.

NOTES

Understand Font Types and Families

- A **font family** is a set of fonts that share common basic characteristics. Examples of font families include Arial, Courier, and Times New Roman (see the illustration along next column).
- Within a font family are one or more **font styles**. A font style is a variant of the family. For example, within the Times New Roman family, the styles are Regular, Bold, Italic, and Bold Italic (see the illustration on next page).
- The term **font** itself is rather ambiguous. Some people use it to refer to the font family; others use it to refer to a particular font style; still others

Font samples

- Adobe Jensen Pro
- Arial
- Cooper Black
- Courier New
- LITHOS PRO REGULAR
- Times New Roman

Times New Roman Regular

Times New Roman Bold

Times New Roman Italic

Times New Roman Bold Italic

use it to refer to a particular font style at a certain size. It can also refer to the file on the computer's hard disk that contains the font family's specification.

- InDesign uses **outline fonts**, which are fonts that are scalable to any size. An outline font file contains a **vector** graphic of the outline of each character. Then the operating system creates an appropriate size of each character and fills it in with the specified color. This system is much better than the older one that used **bitmap** fonts where each letter at each size was stored as a separate image (see the illustration below).
- InDesign enables you to use a variety of font types. However, not all font types are equally good for desktop publishing.
  - **PostScript:** An older type of outline font by Adobe. Prior to OpenType, PostScript was the choice of most professional printers because of its ability to store alternative glyphs for various letters. Use PostScript fonts if the professional printing service you work with requests that you do so. PostScript fonts print only on PostScript printers.
  - **TrueType:** A type of outline font that can be used on almost any printer in Windows or on a Mac. TrueType fonts are rather basic, but produce good results. Use TrueType fonts whenever an appropriate OpenType font is not available.
  - **OpenType:** An improved font specification that combines the best of TrueType with the best of PostScript, created as a joint venture between Adobe and Microsoft. Use OpenType fonts whenever possible. In later exercises you will see some extra features offered only in OpenType fonts, such as discretionary ligatures and ordinals.

    ✓ *There are two subtypes of OpenType. OpenType TrueType is an improved version of a TrueType font; OpenType Type 1 is an improved version of a PostScript font. The difference is mostly invisible to the end user; it's a matter of how InDesign handles them internally.*
- Some font families have more styles than others. For example, Adobe Jenson Pro has these styles: Light, Light Italic, Regular, Italic, Semibold, Semibold Italic, Bold, and Bold Italic.

  ✓ *If Adobe Jenson Pro is not already installed on your PC, you can install it from the InDesign Setup CD. If you are using the stand-alone version of InDesign, it is located on Disc 2 in the Goodies folder. You will learn how to install new fonts later in this exercise.*

Select Fonts and Sizes

- To change the text font, select the text and click the A button on the Control palette to display the Character Formatting controls. Then choose a different font from the Fonts drop-down list (see the illustration on next page).
- Select a size, in points, from the Font Size list. A point is 1/72 of an inch; it refers to the size that the text will be when printed.
- You can enter a size manually that is not on the list; simply click in the box and type it.

  ✓ *Directly below the Font Size box is the Leading box, which controls the spacing between the lines of the paragraph. You'll learn about it in Exercise 23.*

An outline font can be scaled to any size

Set the font and size

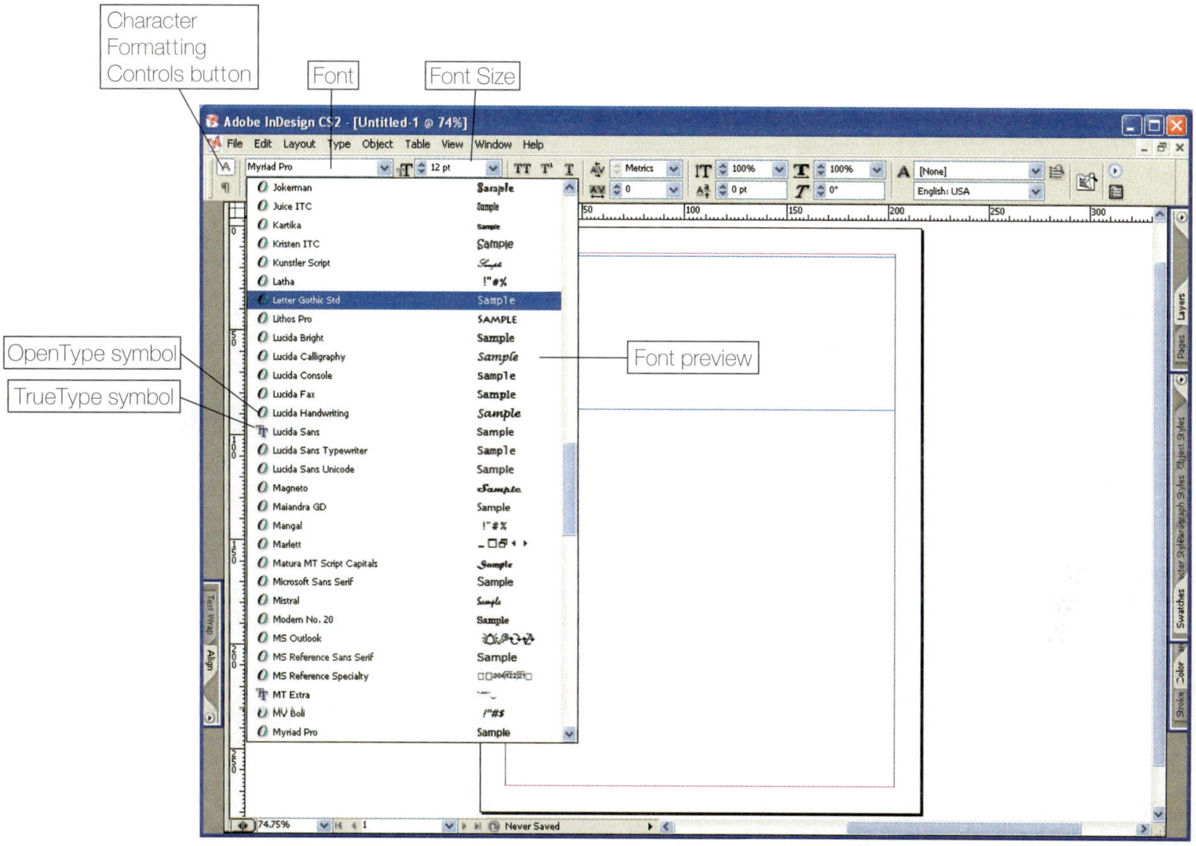

Apply Font Styles

- After selecting a font, select a style from the Font Style drop-down list. The styles available depend on the font chosen. Some of them call their default style Normal; others use terms such as Regular or Medium. Some use the term Italic; others call this style Slanted.

Apply a font style

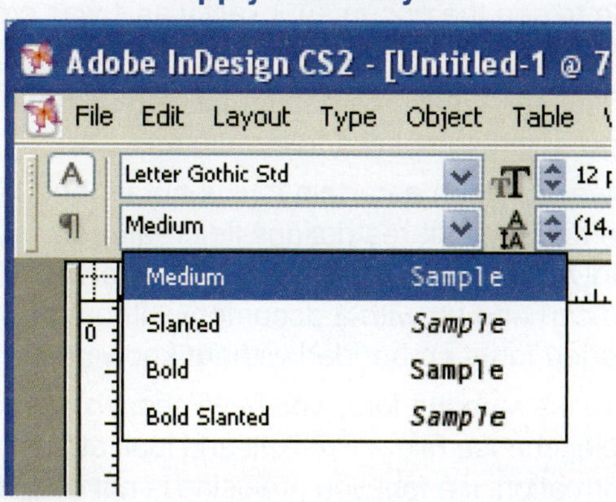

- InDesign handles bold and italics via font styles, rather than by simply making letters thicker or tilting them. Typeface styles give you cleaner and more professional-looking results. For example, in the following text, the italicized version of Adobe Jenson Pro differs from the regular version in more than just the tilt—some of the letters actually have different shapes.

Some fonts have different shaped letters for italic style

This is regular.

This is italic.

- InDesign has a Skew feature (also called false italic) on the Control palette that enables you to simulate italics for a font that has no Italic style. To use it, select the text and then increase the value in the Skew box. You can also use this on existing italicized text to make it tilt more dramatically.

Skew setting

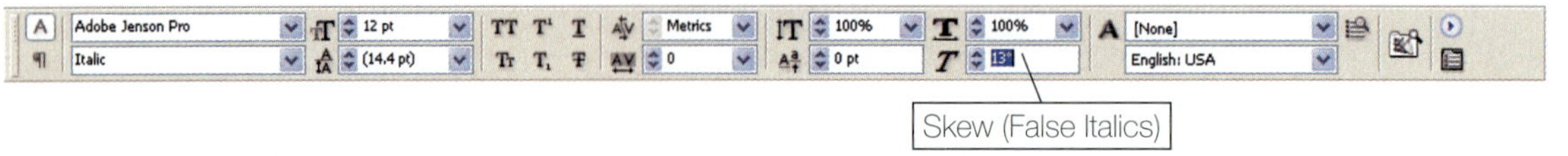

- Keyboard shortcuts are available for applying bold and italic: Ctrl+Shift+B for bold and Ctrl+Shift+I for italic. These are on/off toggles. To return to normal text, removing both bold and italics at once, use Ctrl+Shift+Y.

  ✓ *The keyboard shortcuts for bold and italic are the same as in a word processing program except for the addition of Shift. When a font has more than one bold option (for example, bold and semibold), Ctrl+Shift+B applies the lightest version of bold (usually semibold).*

Work with Text Color

- As you saw in the previous lesson, you can apply color to text much like you apply it to the fill or stroke of a frame.
- When text is selected, the Fill square on the Swatches and Color palettes is replaced by a Text Fill square [T]. Any color you select will apply to the text, rather than the background fill of the frame.
- To apply a swatch color to text, select the text and click the swatch on the Swatches palette. When text is selected, a T icon becomes active on the Swatches palette, such that whatever color you choose applies to the text.
- To apply a specific color, select the text and then choose a color on the Color palette.
- Text has both a stroke and a fill, like a frame. Normally the text's stroke is set to None, but it is possible to set it to a different color than the fill (for outlined text) or to the same color as the fill (for an extra measure of thickness).

Install New Fonts

- InDesign comes with many OpenType fonts, which are installed automatically when InDesign is installed.
- Depending on the version of InDesign you have (suite or stand-alone, academic, upgrade, etc.), additional fonts might be available on another disc that came with InDesign. For example, in the stand-alone Upgrade version, the fonts are on Disc 2, in a folder called Goodies.
- You can also acquire OpenType fonts from other sources. For example, you can buy CDs of fonts, or you can download free or for-pay fonts from Web sites.

Swatches can be applied to text

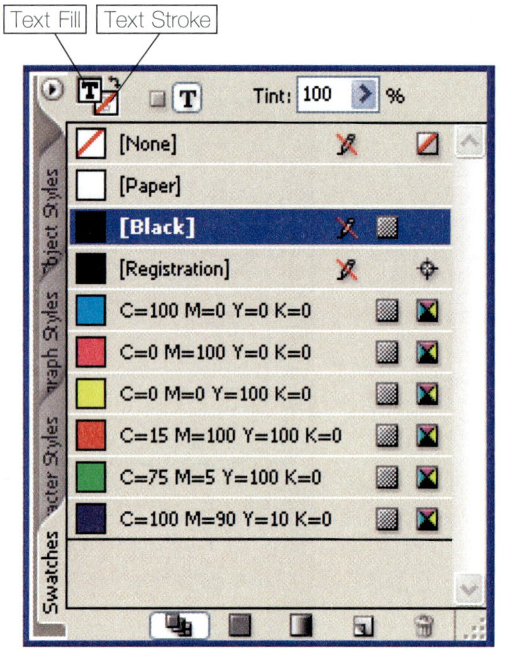

- To install new fonts, exit InDesign and use the Fonts window in the Control Panel in Windows. Open the Fonts window and select File > Install New Font. In the Add Fonts dialog box, select the location of the fonts to be installed, select the fonts you want, and click OK (see illustration on top of next page).

Check Font Embedding

- When a font is embedded in a document, a copy of that font travels with the document, so anyone opening that document on a different PC will be able to see the document exactly as it was created.
- InDesign automatically embeds all embeddable fonts when it saves a document. You do not have to do anything special to enable this.
- However, when a certain font is not embeddable due to copyright restrictions its creator placed on it, InDesign does not automatically alert you. Thus you can end up with a document without the needed fonts embedded without knowing it.
- To make sure the fonts you have chosen are embeddable, choose File > Preflight and look at the Fonts information. If a font you are using is not embeddable and you need to transfer the file to a PC that doesn't have that font, consider using a different font or installing it on the PC that will be receiving the document (see the second illustration on next page).

Add fonts in the operating system (Windows shown)

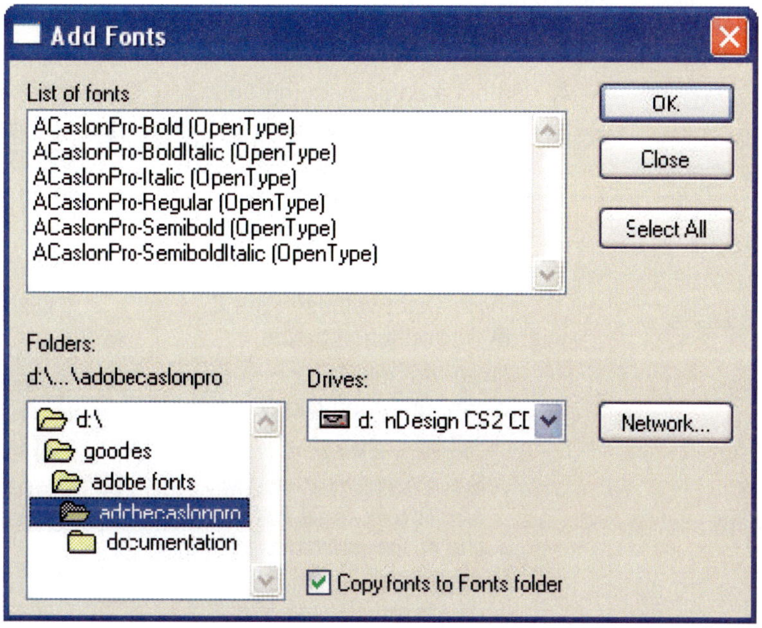

A preflight check looks for font embedding problems

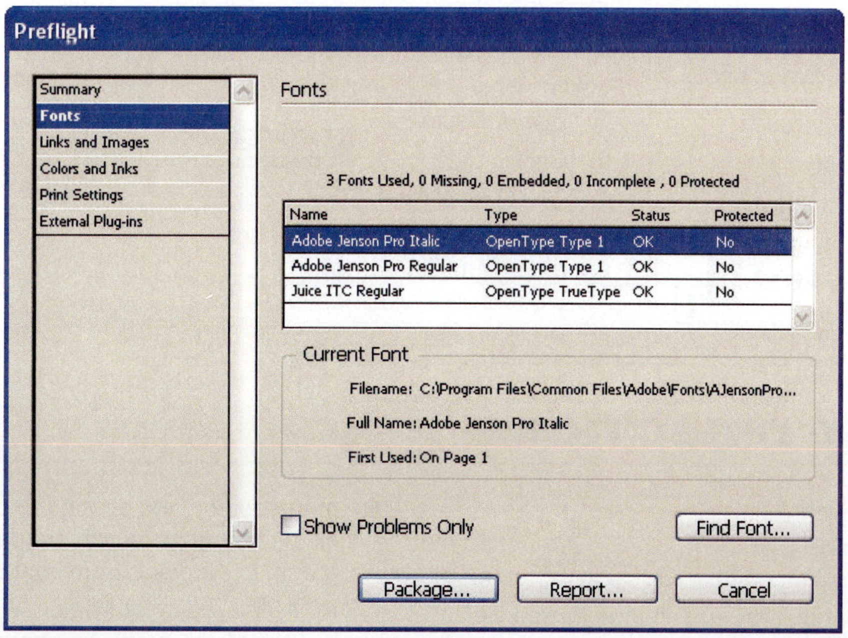

PROCEDURES

Choose a Font Family

1. Select the text to affect.
2. Click **Character Formatting Controls** on the Control palette .... A
3. Click the down arrow next to the Font box ....
4. Click the desired font.

Choose a Font Style

1. Select the text to affect.
2. Choose a font family (see the preceding steps).
3. Click the down arrow next to the Font Style box ....
4. Click the desired font style.

Keyboard Shortcuts for Font Style

- Bold .... Ctrl + Shift + B
- Italic .... Ctrl + Shift + I
- Normal .... Ctrl + Shift + Y

Change Font Size

1. Select the text to affect.
2. If needed, click **Character Formatting Controls** on the Control palette .... A
3. Click the down arrow next to the Font Size box ....
4. Click the desired font size.

✓ *Instead of steps 3 and 4 you can click in the Font Size box and type a different size, or you can use the increment buttons to increment the existing value up or down.*

Keyboard Shortcuts for Font Size

- Increase by 1 point .... Ctrl + Shift + .
- Increase by 10 points .... Alt + Ctrl + Shift + .
- Decrease by 1 point .... Ctrl + Shift + ,
- Decrease by 10 points .... Alt + Ctrl + Shift + ,

Change Text Color

Swatches Palette Method

1. Select the text to affect.
2. Open the **Swatches** palette F5
3. Click the **Text Fill** square .... T

   ✓ *To apply a stroke color to text, click the Text Stroke square rather than the Text Fill square in step 3.*

4. Click the desired swatch.

Color Palette Method

1. Select the text to affect.
2. Open the **Color** palette F6
3. Double-click the **Text Fill** square .... T

   ✓ *To apply a stroke color to text, click the Text Stroke square rather than the Text Fill square in step 3.*

4. Select a color by doing one of the following:
   - Type exact values in the **R**, **G**, and **B** text boxes.
   - Type exact values in the **L**, **a**, and **b** text boxes.
   - Type exact values in the **C**, **M**, **Y**, and **K** text boxes.
   - Drag the color slider up or down, and then click a color.

   ✓ *To pick a color from the Color Space View sample area using a specific color model, first click in one of the text boxes for the desired color model. Then click on the sample area to pick a color.*

5. Click **OK** .... Enter

Install New Fonts

Perform these steps in Windows XP, not in InDesign.

1. Click .... start
2. Click **Control Panel**.
3. Click **Switch to Classic View** if not already in Classic view.
4. Double-click .... Fonts
5. Click **File** .... Alt + F
6. Click **Install New Font** I
7. Select the drive containing the fonts ..... Alt + V, Alt + ↓
8. In the **Folders** list, navigate to the folder containing the fonts.
9. Click the font to install.

   OR

   Click **Select All** .... Alt + S
10. Click **OK** .... Enter
11. Repeat steps 7–10 for each location containing fonts to install.
12. Close the Fonts window .... ✕

Check Font Embedding

1. Click **File** .... Alt + F
2. Click **Preflight** .... H

   ✓ *You can press Ctrl+Alt+Shift+F instead of steps 1 and 2.*

3. Click **Fonts**.
4. Note any problems with font embedding.
5. Click **Cancel** .... Esc

EXERCISE DIRECTIONS

1. Start Adobe InDesign.
2. Open **EX12.indd**.
3. Select the text in the top text box on the first page (white background area) and change its font to Papyrus.

   ✓ *If you do not have the Papyrus font, use some other font.*

4. Change the top two lines of text (*Doing Business in Argentina*) to 36 point.
5. In the main body of the story, select all the text (Ctrl+A) and change the font to Adobe Garamond Pro.

   ✓ *If you do not have Adobe Garamond Pro installed, install it from the InDesign setup CD set. Note that in the font list, font names are alphabetized ignoring the word Adobe, so Adobe Garamond Pro is located in the "G's."*

6. In the body of the article (on all pages), change all the headings, which are currently formatted in green, to 18 point, Semibold.
7. Apply the red color swatch (C=15 M=100 Y=100 K=0) to all the green headings.
8. Save your work as **XX-EX12.indd**, where XX are your initials.
9. Exit InDesign.

ON YOUR OWN

1. Open **OYO-12.indd**.
2. Format the word *July* at the top of the page as Arial Narrow 80-point bold, and apply the red swatch to it (C=15 M=100 Y=100 K=0).
3. Format the word *events* at the top of the page as Arial Narrow 36-point bold and apply the same red swatch to it.
4. For each listed event, format its title as Arial, 12-point, bold, and dark green (C=75 M=5 Y=100 K=80).

✓ *Sometimes when creating a CMYK swatch, the CMYK numbers shift slightly; the color might shift to C=82 M=47 Y=95 K=59.*

5. For each listed event, format the body text under the heading as Arial Narrow. Make the words *Where*, *When*, *Cost,* and *Information* bold.
6. Save your work as **XX-OYO-12.indd**, where XX are your initials. It should resemble Illustration A.
7. Exit InDesign.

Illustration A

July events

WMFS "Girls' Night Out" Concert

Popular country male music stars will croon to a crowd of women in an event sponsored by WMFS and starring Jeff Bates and Billy Dean.

Where: Indiana State Fairgrounds
When: June 25, 4 p.m. preparty, 7 p.m. concert
Cost: $20 track, free grandstand
Information: (317) 555-9550

Symphony on the Prairie: An American Salute

The 24th season of this series features the Indianapolis Symphony Orchestra playing to a crowd of picnickers relaxing under the stars.

Where:Conner Prairie
When: July 1 – 4, 8 p.m.
Cost: $25, $10 children 2 – 12
Information: (800) 555-8457

Indiana Black Expo Summer Celebration

The 35th annual Black Expo event is a weeklong celebration of music, exhibits and culture.

Where: Indiana Convention Center and RCA Dome
When: July 7 – 17
Cost: Call for details
Information: (317) 555-2702

Exhibit: Altered Spaces

Experience artists' interpretation of interior and exterior design in mediums that renegotiate physical space.

Where:Indianapolis Museum of Contemporary Art
When: Through July 9; Thurs. – Sat. 11 a.m. – 6 p.m.
Cost: Free
Information: (317) 555-6622

Exhibit: Whispers to Shouts

View two galleries of historical art, all created by women of Indiana including photos, paintings and sculptures.

Where: Indiana State Museum
When: Through July 10; Mon. – Sat. 9 a.m. – 5 p.m.
Cost: $7 adults, $6.50 seniors, $4 children 3 – 12
Information: (317) 555-2321

Concert: Hall & Oates

The popular 1980s pop duo will reunite for a lively outdoor concert.

Where: The Lawn at White River State Park
When: July 12, 7:30 p.m.
Cost: $34.50
Information: (800) 555-9065

Summer Fest at the Zoo

This all-day event will include educational and entertaining activities for the whole family, including performances by McGruff the Crime Dog and Smokey the Bear.

Where: Indianapolis Zoo
When: July 12, 10 a.m. – 8:30 p.m.
Cost:Free with admission
Information: (800) 555-2551

RCA Championships

Cheer on some of the top stars in tennis when players like Andy Roddick and Taylor Dent come to town. Free parking is available on the IUPUI campus.

Where: Indianapolis Tennis Center
When: July 16 – 24, noon – 10 p.m.
Cost: $8 and up
Information: (800) 555-5682

Broad Ripple Blues Fest

Bring your blanket or lawn chairs and enjoy blues and food at this family-friendly event featuring both traditional and contemporary blues performers

Where: Broad Ripple Park
When: July 30, 3 – 10 p.m.
Cost: $12
Information: (800) 555-2782

Exercise | 13

Skills Covered

- Adjust Text Scale
- Adjust Tracking
- Adjust Kerning

Software Skills Almost any word processing program can display different fonts, sizes, and colors of text. InDesign stands out as a professional-quality program in its ability to make subtle adjustments in text scale, tracking, and kerning among the letters.

Application Skills In this exercise, you will adjust the scale, tracking, and kerning of the text in a magazine article to make a more professional-looking layout.

TERMS

Horizontal scale The width of a character in relation to its default width.

Kerning The spacing between a specific pair of characters based on their shapes.

Metrics kerning Automatic kerning based on information built into the font being used.

Optical kerning Automatic kerning based on analysis of the shapes of the letters.

Tracking The spacing between characters (in general).

Vertical scale The height of a character in relation to its default height.

NOTES

Adjust Text Scale

- The scale of a letter is the horizontal and vertical stretch of it in comparison to its default. You can use the horizontal scale and vertical scale settings to make taller, shorter, wider, or narrower versions of your text without changing the font or point size.
- **Horizontal scale** makes the selected text wider. It does not change the spacing between the letters. For example, the following letters are the same font style and point size, but have different horizontal scales.

Horizontal scale samples

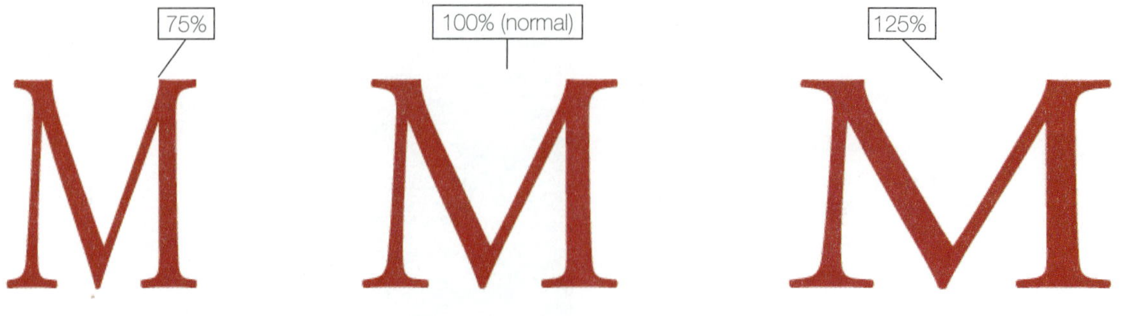

Adjust horizontal scale

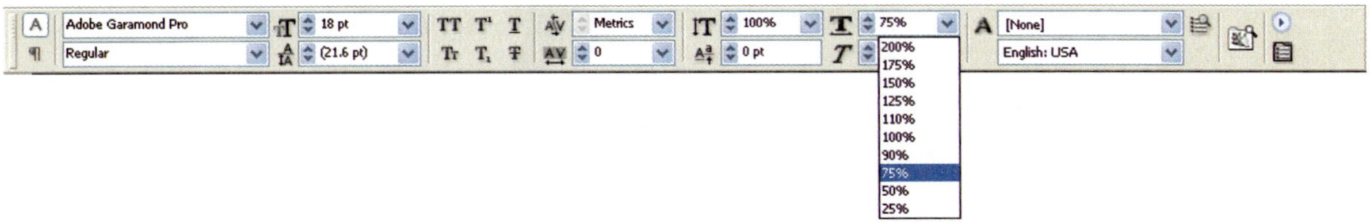

- To set horizontal scale, select the text and then adjust the value in the Horizontal Scale box on the Control palette. You can type a number in manually, use the up/down increment arrows, or select from the drop-down list (see the illustration above).
- **Vertical scale** makes the selected text taller. It is different from simply changing the font size because an overall size increase would make the text both taller and wider. A vertical scale change, in contrast, changes the text only vertically (see top illustration below).
- To set vertical scale, select the text and then adjust the value in the Vertical Scale box on the Control palette. You can type a number in manually, use the up/down increment arrows, or select from the drop-down list (see bottom illustration below).

Adjust Tracking

- **Tracking** is the spacing between characters. It does not affect the width or height of the characters themselves.

✓ *Usually tracking is set for entire stories, or at least entire paragraphs. Unequal tracking settings can look distracting on a page. However, you might need to occasionally adjust tracking on a particular word or phrase to correct a slight problem or coax text into fitting into a defined area.*

- Tracking is based upon the widest part of a character. For example, a V is much wider at the top, whereas an A is much wider at the bottom. Tracking is based on the distance between the widest point of one letter and the widest point of the adjacent one (see illustration at top of next page).
- Tracking is expressed in thousandths of an em (that is, the width of a capital M). Therefore, its actual value changes depending on the font size chosen. This is by design, so that tracking will not need to be readjusted when you make font size changes.
- The default tracking is 0; you can adjust it up or down by entering a positive or negative value. (You can also use the increment arrow buttons or select from the drop-down list.) (See the illustration on the next page.)

Vertical scale samples

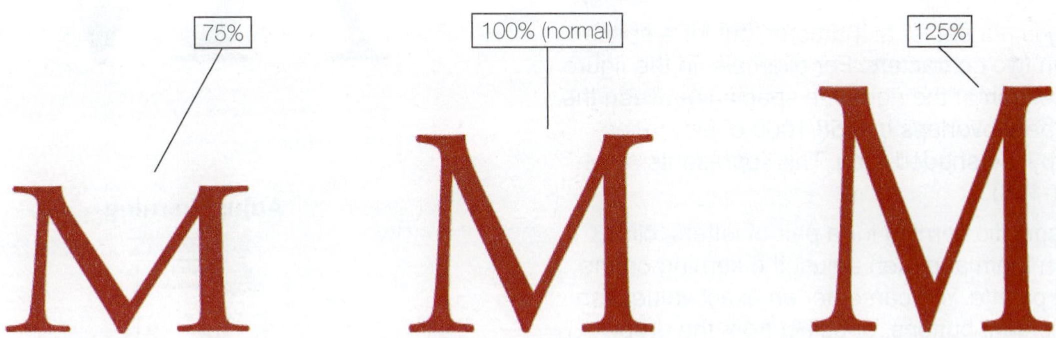

Adjust vertical scale

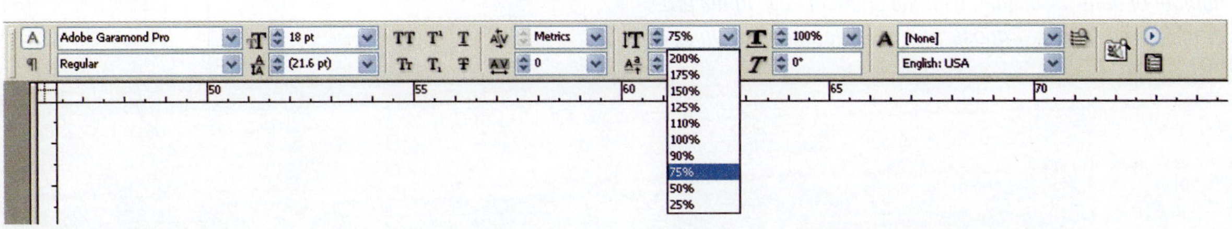

Tracking sample

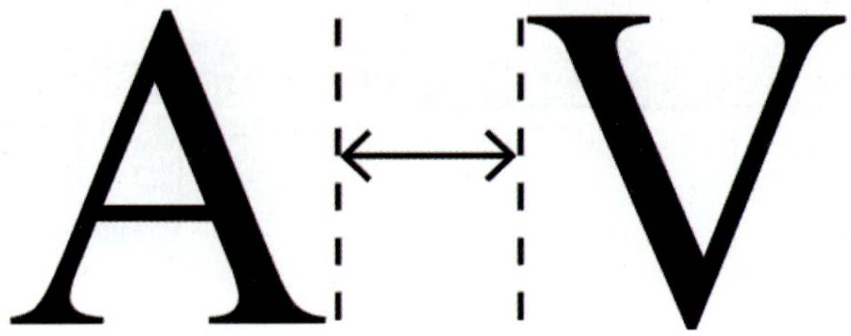

Adjust tracking

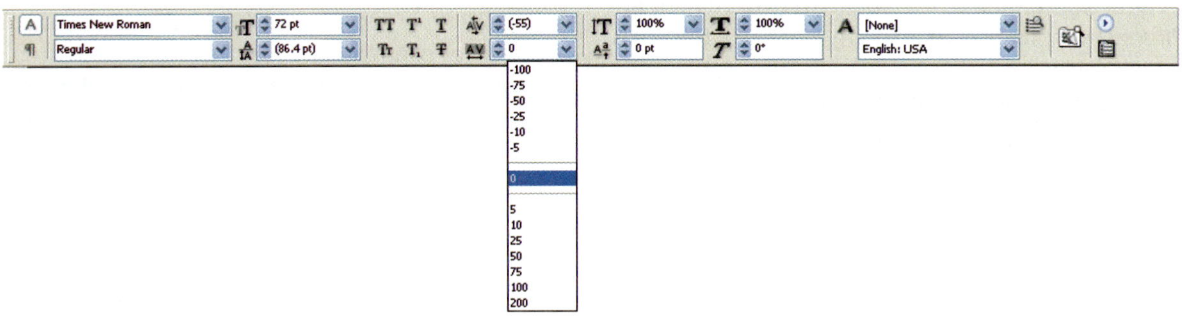

Adjust Kerning

- **Kerning** describes the amount by which the frames of a pair of characters can overlap in order for them to fit together better based on their shape. The overlap is expressed as a negative number, measured in thousandths of an em (like tracking).
- Kerning is not set for a character, but for a space between two characters. For example, in the figure in the column at the right, the spacing between the A and the V overlaps by 158/1000 of an em, as shown by the shaded area. This represents a setting of (-158).
- To set specific kerning for a pair of letters, click between them and then adjust the kerning on the Control palette. You can enter an exact value, use the increment buttons, or select from the drop-down list.

✓ *To increase kerning by 20 units at a time, press Alt+right arrow; to decrease by 20 units, press Alt+left arrow. To go by 100 units at a time, add the Ctrl key. You can change the number of units associated with the shortcut keys in the program's preferences. Choose Edit > Preferences > Units & Increments.*

Kerning sample

Adjust kerning

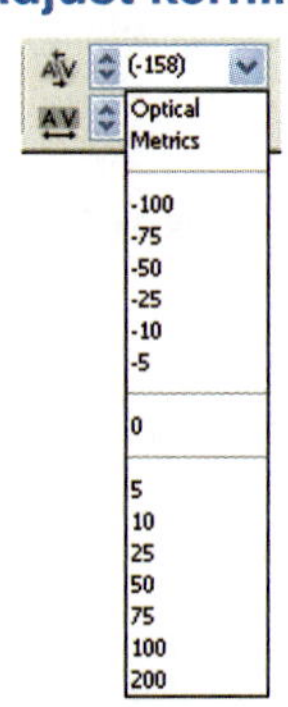

- Fortunately you do not have to set the kerning for every pair of letters individually; InDesign kerns automatically, using one of two preset schemes: Metrics or Optical. **Metrics kerning** uses kerning information built into the font for certain letter pairs. **Optical kerning** calculates the appropriate kerning to use based on the shapes of the letters.

✓ *Many people prefer optical kerning, as it works better with fonts that do not have much kerning data provided in them.*

- Metrics kerning is the default setting. To change text to optical kerning, select all the text you want to change and then choose Optical from the Kerning drop-down list on the Control palette.

PROCEDURES

Adjust Horizontal Text Scale

1. Select the text to affect.
2. Click the **Horizontal Scale** increment buttons ....

OR

Select a percentage from the **Horizontal Scale** list ....

OR

Type a percentage value in the **Horizontal Scale** box.

Adjust Vertical Text Scale

1. Select the text to affect.
2. Click the **Vertical Scale** increment buttons ....

OR

Select a percentage from the **Vertical Scale** list ....

OR

Type a percentage value in the **Vertical Scale** box.

Keyboard Shortcuts for Scale

- Set horizontal scale to 100% ....Ctrl+Shift+X
- Set vertical scale to 100% ....Ctrl+Alt+Shift+X

Adjust Tracking

1. Select the text to affect.
2. Click the **Tracking** increment buttons ....

OR

Select a value from the **Tracking** list ....

✓ *Tracking is measured in thousandths of an em space, so it is relative to the font size chosen.*

OR

Type a value in the **Tracking** box.

Adjust Kerning

1. Click between the two characters, or select a block of text to affect.
2. Click the **Kerning** increment buttons ....

OR

Select a value from the **Kerning** list ....

✓ *A negative value moves the characters closer together; a positive value moves them apart. Choose Metrics or Optical to allow InDesign to handle the kerning automatically.*

OR

Type a value in the **Kerning** box.

Keyboard Shortcuts for Kerning

- Increase kerning by 20 units ....Alt+→
- Increase kerning by 100 units ....Alt+Ctrl+→
- Decrease kerning by 20 units ....Alt+←
- Decrease kerning by 100 units ....Alt+Ctrl+←

EXERCISE DIRECTIONS

1. Start Adobe InDesign.
2. Open **EX13.indd**.
3. Set the Horizontal Scale for the text *Doing Business in Argentina* to 107%.
4. Set the Vertical Scale for the text *An Etiquette Guide* to 115%.
5. Set the Vertical Scale for all the red headings in the article to 90%.
6. For all the text in the entire story (all the parts on yellow background), set the tracking to +10 and turn on optical kerning.
7. Save your work as **XX-EX13.indd**, where XX are your initials.
8. Exit InDesign.

ON YOUR OWN

1. Open **OYO-13.indd**.
2. Set the vertical scale for the words *July* and *events* to 125%.
3. Notice that the second event title is so long that it almost runs into the next column. Change the tracking for this heading to -25, so that it fits better in its place.
4. Adjust the tracking for all the other event titles to the same amount, so they will match in appearance.
5. Turn on optical kerning for each of the event descriptions and details.
6. In the word *events*, increase the kerning between the *t* and the *s* to 25.
7. Save your work as **XX-OYO-13.indd**, where XX are your initials.
8. Exit InDesign.

Exercise | 14

Skills Covered

- Apply All Caps and Small Caps
- Use Underlines
- Customize Underline Style
- Use Strikethrough

Software Skills Sometimes special typographical styles such as all caps, small caps, underlining, and strikethrough can be appropriate in a publication, although these are less frequently used than bold and italics.

Application Skills In this exercise, you will apply small caps to headings to change their appearance, and you will underline certain words and phrases.

TERMS

All caps The use of capital letters where all are the same height, LIKE THIS.

Small caps The use of two sizes of capital letters, LIKE THIS.

Strikethrough A line through the center of each letter, like ~~this~~.

NOTES

Apply All Caps and Small Caps

- You can achieve the **all caps** effect (LIKE THIS) simply by typing in uppercase. However, if you later decide you don't want all caps, you must manually retype the text. A better way is to type the text normally and then apply the All Caps effect to it. This temporarily shifts the letters into uppercase, but they can easily be shifted back to normal by toggling off the All Caps attribute.
- **Small caps** are like all caps in shape, but they are smaller in size. By default they are 70% of the size of a regular capital letter.

ALL CAPS SMALL CAPS

- Use the All Caps or Small Caps button on the Control palette to toggle these features on/off. Or use Ctrl+Shift+K for all caps or Ctrl+Shift+H for small caps.

All-caps and small caps

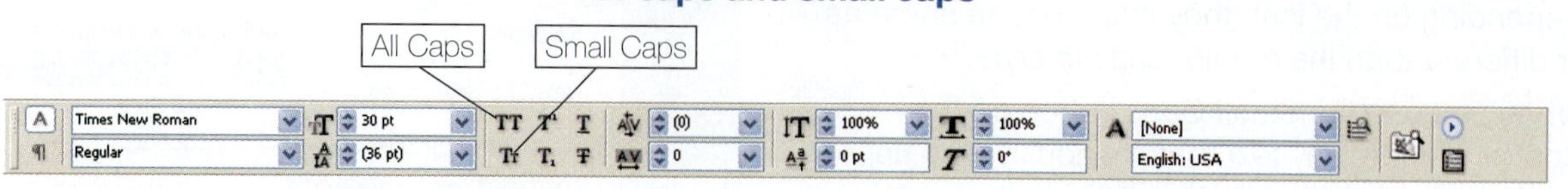

Set character spacing defaults

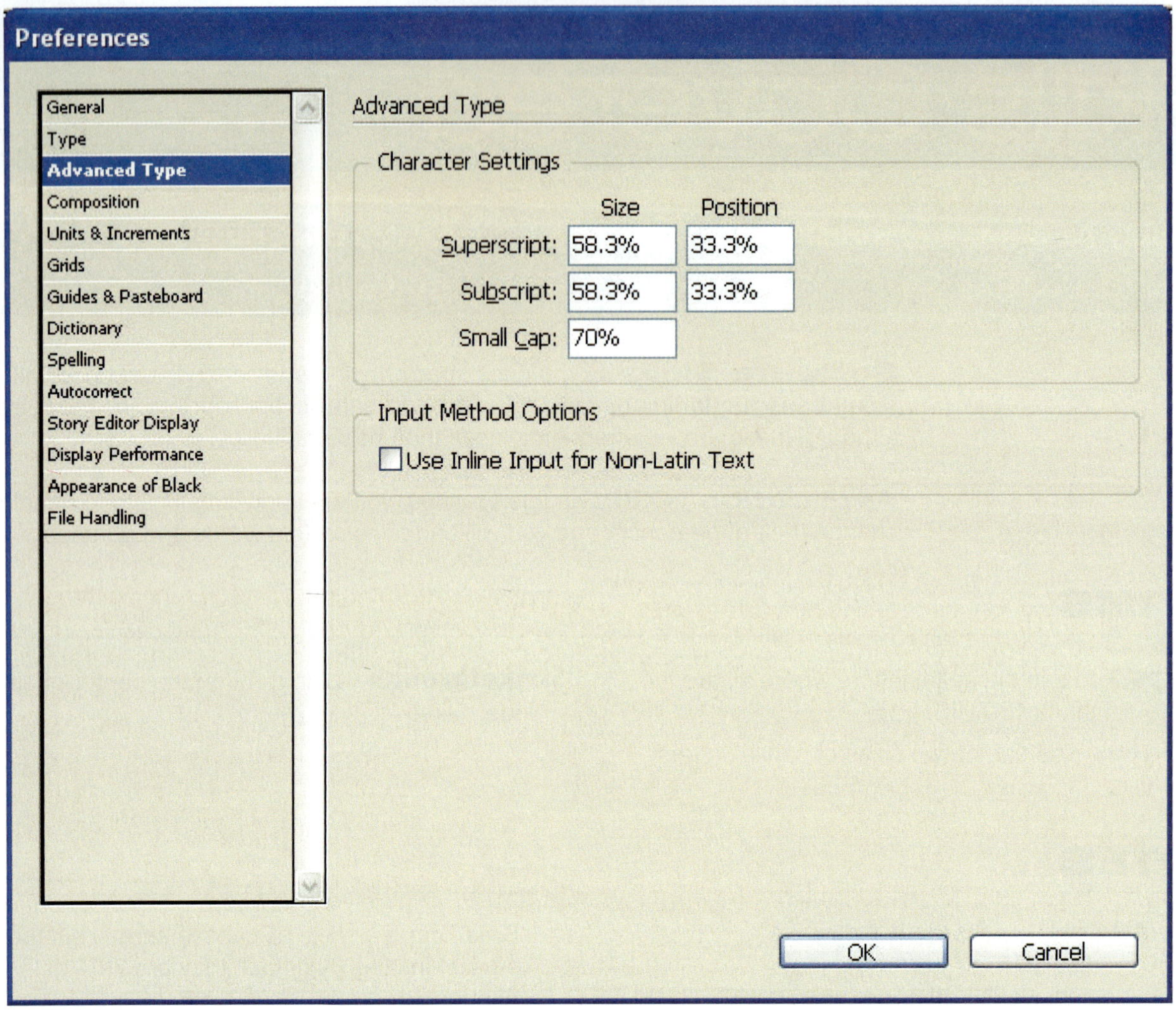

- The 70% reduction for small caps is just a default; you can change it to any amount you like. Choose Edit > Preferences > Advanced Type and enter a different value in the Small Cap text box (see the illustration above).
- Some OpenType fonts have their own special set of characters for small caps. InDesign will use these automatically whenever they are available. Depending on the font, they might be the same as or different than the regular caps in style.
- When you use the Small Caps button on the Control palette, any text that previously was uppercase stays uppercase, rather than changing to small caps. If you want all the text to change to small caps, regardless of its previous capitalization, open the fly-out menu for the Control palette and select OpenType > All Small Caps. This is available only for OpenType fonts.

TrueType–based small caps

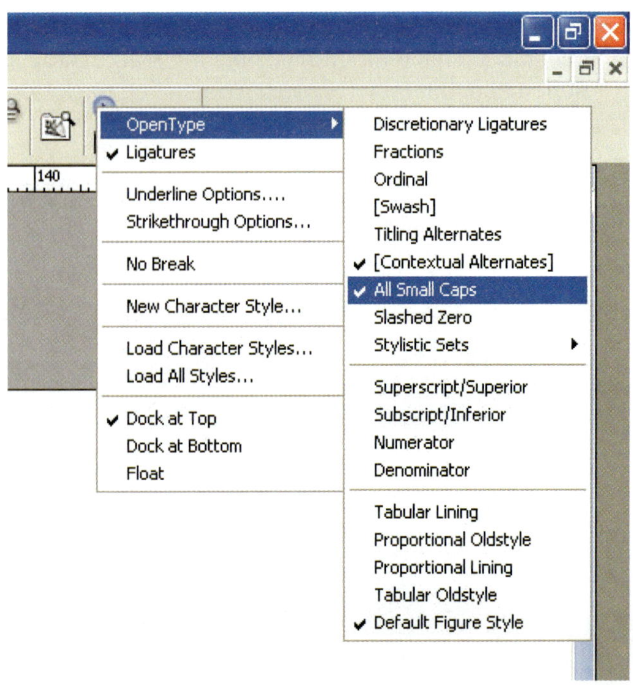

Use Underlines

- Underlining is no longer a popular typographical convention; most of the items that used to require

Apply underlining

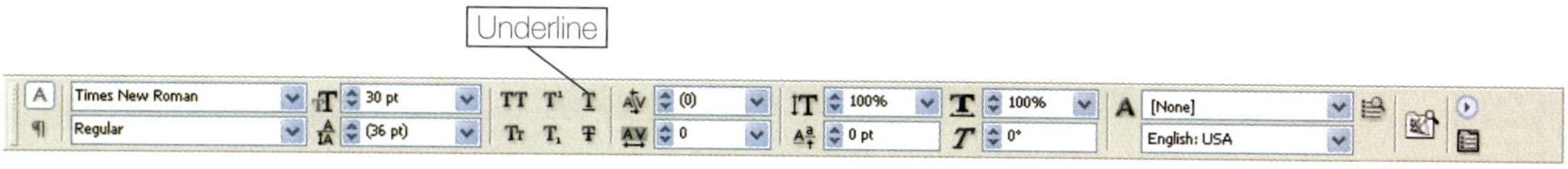

underlining, such as book titles, are now italicized. However, a few situations still call for underlining, such as Web and e-mail addresses.

- The Underline button on the Control palette toggles on/off basic underlining. You can also press Ctrl+Shift+U to toggle underlining on/off (see the illustration above).

Customize Underline Style

- You can also customize the underlining. For example, you can use different underline colors and styles. To do so, select the text and then open the fly-out menu for the Control palette and choose Underline Options. Then make your selections in the Underline Options dialog box (see the illustration below).
- The following are the options you can set:
  - **Weight:** The thickness of the underline.
  - **Offset:** The gap between the text and its underline.
  - **Type:** The style of line (solid, dotted, dashed, etc.).
  - **Color:** The underline color.
  - **Tint:** The tint of the color chosen, if not 100%. (You'll learn about tint in Lesson 4.)
  - **Gap Color:** Applicable only if you chose a non-solid line for the Type. It lets you set a secondary line color to appear between the gaps of the line.
  - **Gap Tint:** The tint of the gap color chosen, if not 100%.

✓ *The Overprint Stroke and Overprint Gap check boxes affect trapping, which is a technique of overlapping colors slightly in some areas of a page so that there will not be any gaps between colors when the document is printed using a four-color press.*

Use Strikethrough

- **Strikethrough** is even less commonly used than underline. It consists of a line running through the text, like underline but higher up, ~~like this~~. It generally indicates a deletion, and is sometimes used when multiple people are editing a document to show where someone thinks a deletion should occur.
- You might occasionally use strikethrough in a finished publication to indicate a change such as a price reduction or to indicate that an item is no longer available.
- To toggle strikethrough on/off, use the Strikethrough button on the Control palette (see illustration at the top of the next page).
- Strikethrough has the same options as Underline. Click the button for the fly-out menu on the Control palette and then choose Strikethrough Options (see illustration in the middle of the next page).

Set underline options

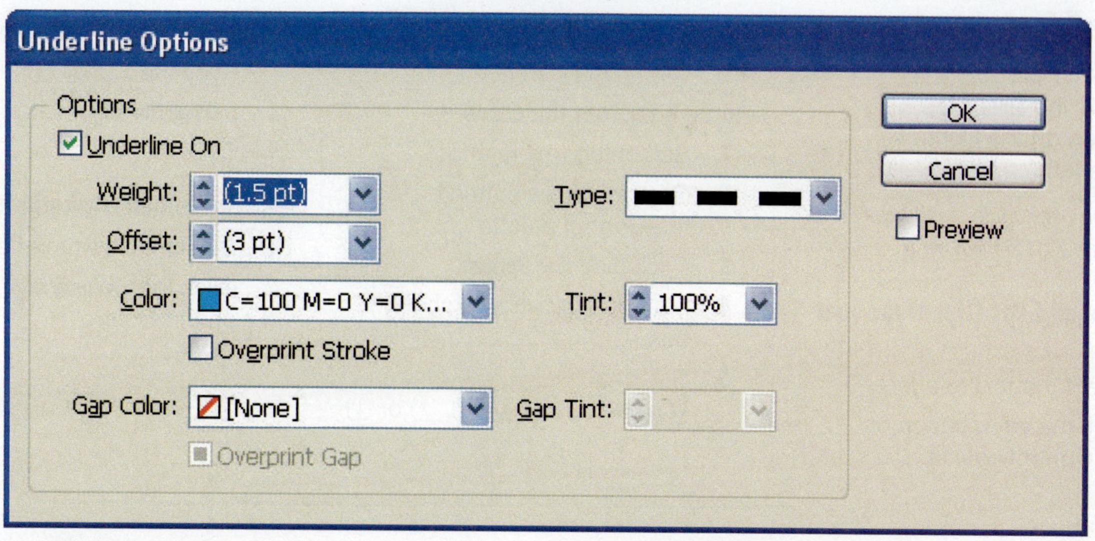

Apply strikethrough

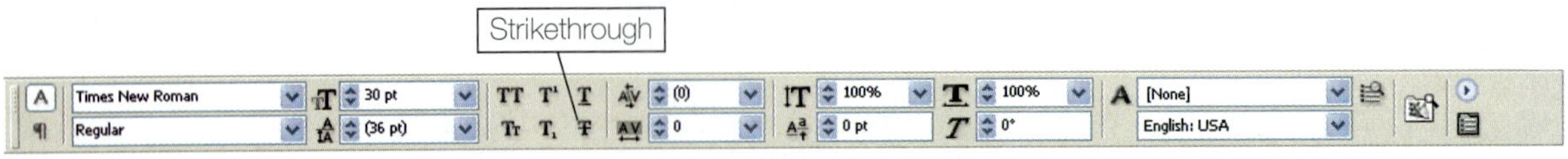

Set strikethrough options

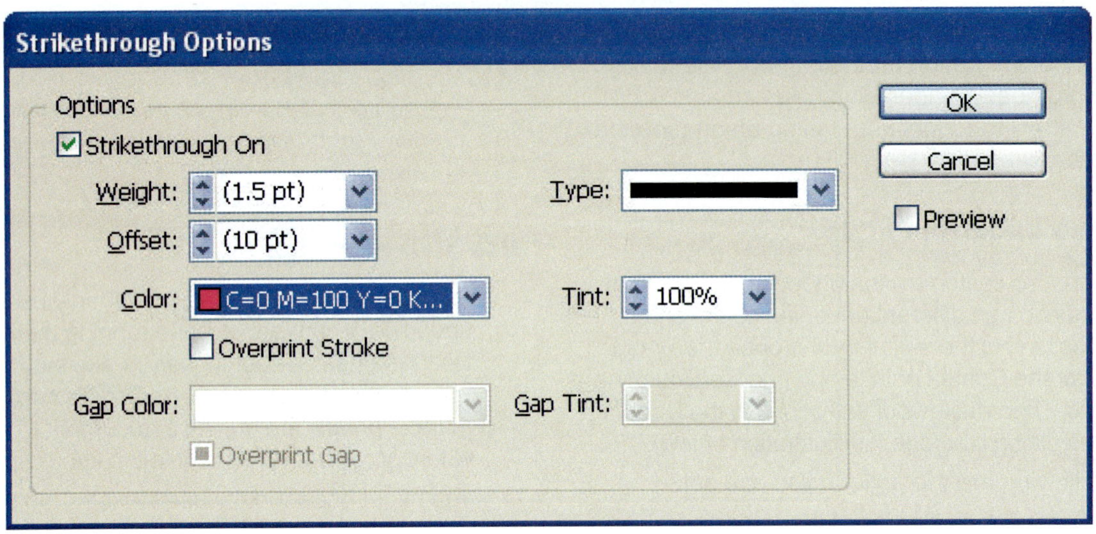

PROCEDURES

Apply All Caps

1. Select the text to affect.
2. Click the **All Caps** button on the Control palette .... TT

✓ *You can toggle all caps on/off with Ctrl+Shift+K.*

Apply Small Caps

1. Select the text to affect.
2. Click the **Small Caps** button on the Control palette .... Tr

✓ *You can toggle small caps on/off with Ctrl+Shift+H.*

Use All Small Caps (OpenType font only)

1. Select the text to affect.
2. Click the **arrow** button on the Control palette ....
3. Point to **OpenType**.
4. Click **All Small Caps**.

Apply a Default Underline

1. Select the text to affect.
2. Click the **Underline** button on the Control palette .... T

✓ *You can also toggle the default underline on/off with Ctrl+Shift+U.*

Apply a Custom Underline

1. Select the text to affect.
2. Click the **arrow** button on the Control palette ....
3. Click **Underline Options**.
4. Mark the **Underline On** check box .... Alt+U
5. Select a **Weight** .... Alt+W, ↑ or ↓
6. Select an **Offset** .... Alt+O, ↑ or ↓
7. Select a **Color** .... Alt+C, ↓
8. (Optional) Select any of the other options if needed:
   - **Type** .... Alt+T, ↓
   - **Tint** .... Alt+I, ↑ or ↓
   - **Overprint Stroke** .... Alt+E
   - **Gap Color** .... Alt+A, ↓
   - **Gap Tint** ...... Alt+G, ↑ or ↓
   - **Overprint Gap** .... Alt+R
9. Click **OK** .... ↵Enter

Apply a Default Strikethrough

1. Select the text to affect.
2. Click the **Strikethrough** button on the Control palette .... T

✓ *You can also toggle the default strikethrough on/off with Ctrl+Shift+/.*

Apply a Custom Strikethrough

1. Select the text to affect.
2. Click the **arrow** button on the Control palette ....
3. Click **Strikethrough Options**.
4. Mark the **Strikethrough On** check box .... Alt+S
5. Select a **Weight** .... Alt+W, ↑ or ↓
6. Select an **Offset** .... Alt+O, ↑ or ↓
7. Select a **Color** .... Alt+C, ↓
8. (Optional) Select any of the other options if needed:
   - **Type** .... Alt+T, ↓
   - **Tint** .... Alt+I, ↑ or ↓
   - **Overprint Stroke** .... Alt+E
   - **Gap Color** .... Alt+A, ↓
   - **Gap Tint** .... Alt+G, ↑ or ↓
   - **Overprint Gap** .... Alt+R
9. Click **OK** .... ↵Enter

EXERCISE DIRECTIONS

1. Start Adobe InDesign.
2. Open **EX14.indd**.
3. Change all the red headings to All Small Caps (through the OpenType submenu).
4. Change the article's title (*Doing Business in Argentina*) font to Adobe Garamond Pro, set its style to Semibold, set its size to 40 pt, and set it to Small Caps using the button on the Control palette. Set its horizontal scale to 100% and turn on optical kerning for it.
5. Change the article's subtitle (*An Etiquette Guide*) font to Adobe Garamond Pro, and set it to All Caps. Set its vertical scale to 100% and turn on optical kerning for it.
6. On the last page, select the URL (*http://www.invertir.com/argentina/c13-177.html/*) and apply the Blue swatch to it. Then underline it with a solid underline that uses that same bright blue color.
7. Save your work as **XX-EX14.indd**, where XX are your initials.
8. Exit InDesign.

ON YOUR OWN

1. Open **OYO-14.indd**.
2. Set the word *events* in small caps.
3. Underline the *Where:*, *When:*, *Cost:*, and *Information:* text in each of the event listings.
4. Under the *Concert: Hall & Oates* heading, format $34.50 in strikethrough, and type **sold out** next to it.
5. Format the words *sold out* in all caps, red (the same red as used for *July Events*), and bold.
6. Under the *Broad Ripple Blues Fest*, format *$12* in strikethrough, and type **now only $10** next to it. Format the words *now only $10* in red and bold.
7. Save your work as **XX-OYO-14.indd**, where XX are your initials.
8. Exit InDesign.

Exercise | 15

Skills Covered

- Apply Baseline Shift
- Apply Superscript and Subscript
- Build Fractions
- Apply Alternate Characters
- Work with Ordinals

Software Skills Superscript and subscript are types of baseline shifts that are useful when creating special typographical effects such as chemical formulas, temperatures, and exponents. They are also used for building fractions and creating ordinals manually. InDesign also offers support for creating fractions and ordinals in a more automated way.

Application Skills In this exercise, you will learn how to use superscript and subscript, and how to shift the baseline of characters. You will then put those skills to work to create fractions and ordinals using a variety of methods.

TERMS

Baseline The default vertical position at which the bottom of each character rests on a line of text.

Ordinal A text indicator that shows that a number indicates a ranking, such as the *nd* in 2nd or the *th* in 4th. Ordinals are typically shown in superscript.

Subscript Text that aligns lower than the baseline and is smaller than regular text.

Superscript Text that aligns higher than the baseline and is smaller than the regular text.

NOTES

Apply Baseline Shift

- The **baseline** of a line of text is the default vertical position at which the bottoms of the characters align.

Baseline text Shifted up 4 points

- You might use a baseline shift to position a glyph for a footnote in a case where you do not want the size of the glyph to be reduced (as it would be with superscript), or to precisely align some text with a nearby graphic. Baseline shifting is also handy when hand-setting fractions (discussed later in these notes).
- To shift the baseline, select the text and then use the Baseline Shift box on the Control palette. You can increment the value or type a value manually. The shift is measured in points. A positive number shifts text up; a negative number shifts text down.

Apply baseline shift from the Control palette

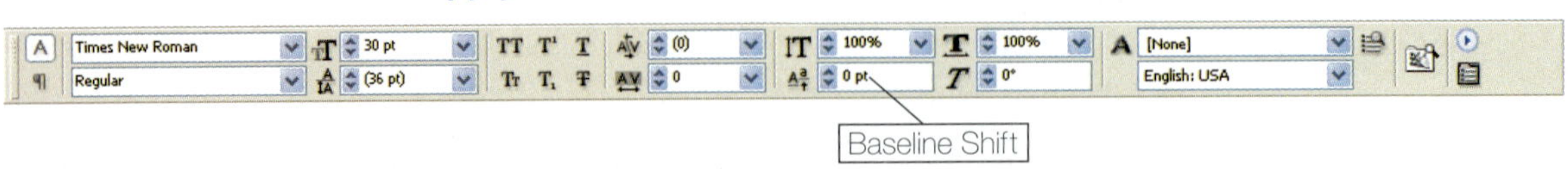

- Shortcut key combinations are available for increasing or decreasing the baseline shift:
  - Increase baseline shift by 2 points: Alt+Shift+up arrow
  - Increase baseline shift by 10 points: Ctrl+Alt+Shift+up arrow
  - Decrease baseline shift by 2 points: Alt+Shift+down arrow
  - Decrease baseline shift by 10 points: Ctrl+Alt+Shift+down arrow

Apply Superscript and Subscript

- The **Superscript** effect combines a positive baseline shift with a font reduction. Superscript is commonly used for footnote symbols/numbers and exponents.

Superscript example

Recent research[†] has shown that $2X^3–6X^2$ is the formula.

- To apply superscript, select the text and then click the Superscript button on the Control palette.
- The **Subscript** effect combines a negative baseline shift with a font reduction. Subscript is commonly used for chemical formulas.

Subscript example

$$H_2SO_4$$

- To apply subscript, select the text and then click the Subscript button on the Control palette.

Build Fractions

- You can build any fraction using a / sign to separate two numbers, but the resulting fraction is large and takes up a lot of space. It is more professional-looking to use a fraction that shows the numbers smaller than normal, and that shows the numerator (top number) raised above the baseline.

A built fraction

2/3 $^2/_3$

- Some OpenType fonts have a few common fractions built in as glyphs. You can select them from the Glyphs palette like any other character.

Glyphs palette

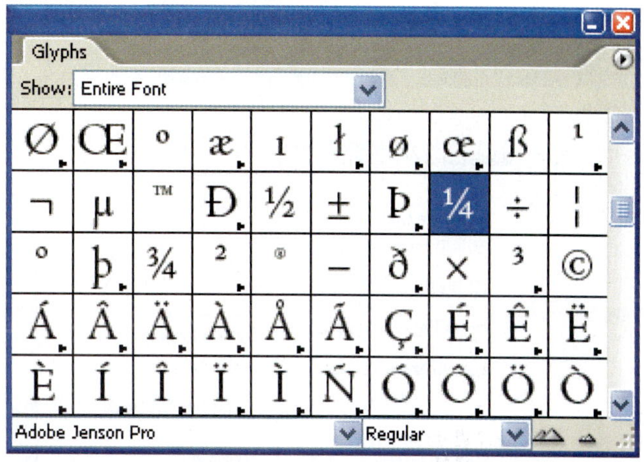

- However, there's an easier way than checking the Glyphs palette each time you need a fraction. Turn on the Fractions option for OpenType, and then whenever you type a fraction for which the font has a glyph equivalent, InDesign will automatically substitute the glyph for your typed fraction.

Use OpenType fractions

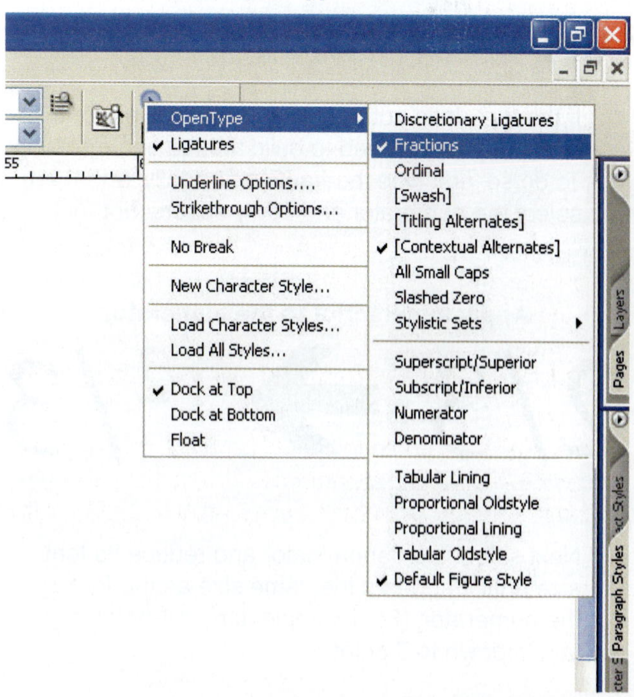

- Some OpenType fonts have special versions of numbers built in for use as numerators and denominators. To use one of these, select the number, open the fly-out menu on the Control palette, and choose OpenType > Numerator or OpenType > Denominator. This is especially useful for numerators and denominators that have multiple digits.

Use OpenType denominators

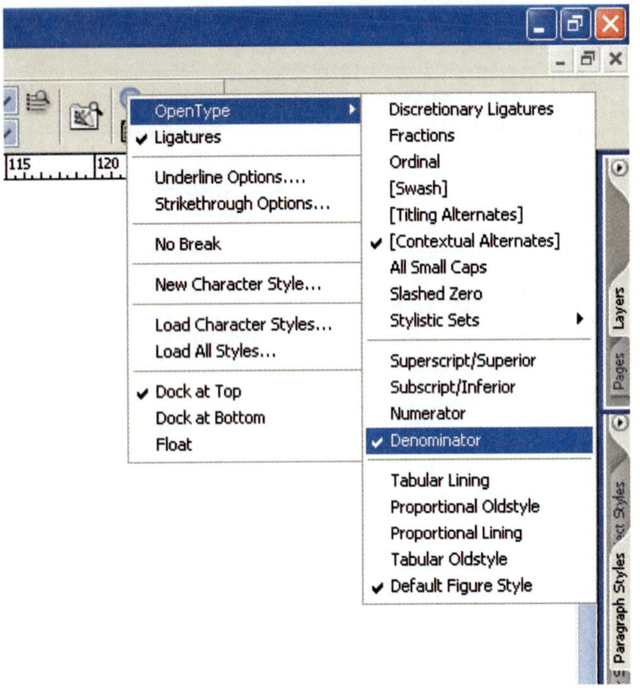

✓ *If nothing happens when you issue one of these commands, the chosen font does not have this special ability.*

- If the font does not have the needed glyph for the fraction, you will need to build the fraction manually. To do so, first type the fraction normally, and then select the numerator and apply superscript to it.

Apply superscript to the numerator

- Next select the denominator and reduce its font size until it appears the same size as the font in the numerator. (For example, for a 12-point font, take it down to 7 point.)

Reduce the size of the denominator

- Finally, decrease the tracking on the numerator and the divider line (/). The exact amount will depend on the font; in the following example the numerator is set at -150 and the divider line is set at -100.

Decrease tracking

Apply Alternate Characters

- Some professional-quality OpenType fonts, such as Adobe Jenson Pro (which comes free with InDesign), contain alternate characters for nearly every character. You can use them to add variety to your typography.
- The alternate characters for numerals are particularly useful for creating more professional-looking fractions manually. Compare, for example, the following built fractions. The one on the right uses alternate characters.

Manually built fraction versus alternate character usage

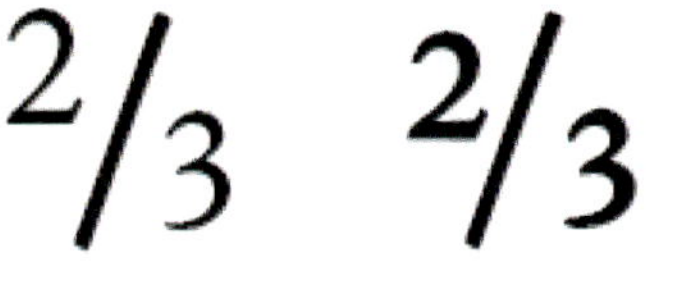

- To select an alternate character, select the typed character and then open the Glyphs palette. Open the Show list and choose Alternates for Selection, and then select a different style for that character.

Alternates for the selection

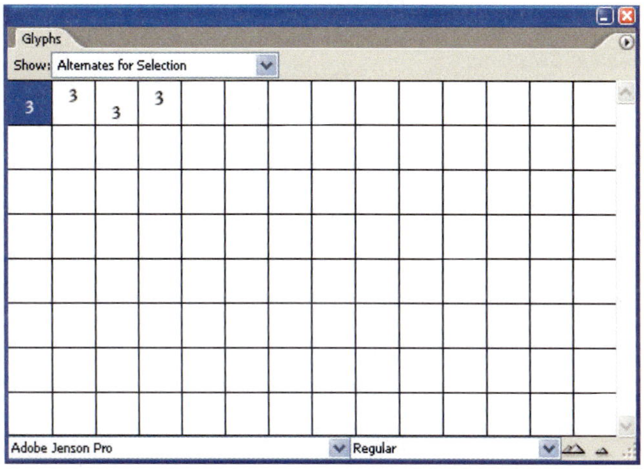

- As an alternative method, you can display all characters in the Glyphs palette (choose Entire Font from the Show list) and then click and hold on a character to see its alternates.

View a character's alternates

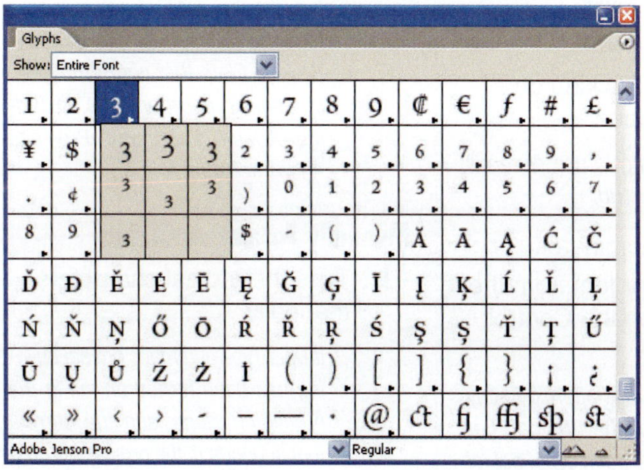

Work with Ordinals

- An **ordinal** is a text suffix that follows a number and indicates a rank, such as 2nd or 4th. The common ordinals are *nd*, *th*, and *st*.
- In professional printing, it is common to make ordinals appear as superscript, as in 1st, 2nd, 3rd, 4th.

- Some OpenType fonts have special styles for ordinals built in. To activate them automatically whenever they are available, turn on Ordinal from the OpenType menu from the Control palette.

OpenType ordinals

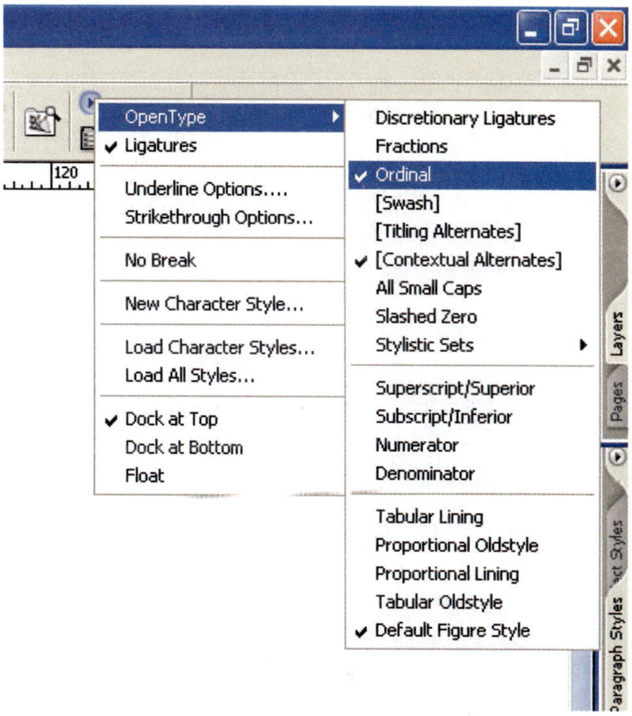

- The following illustration compares ordinals created with simple superscript (on the left) and ordinals created via the OpenType feature (on the right).

Samples of manual versus OpenType ordinals

1st 1st

2nd 2nd

3rd 3rd

4th 4th

5th 5th

PROCEDURES

Apply Baseline Shift

1. Select the text to affect.
2. Click the **Baseline Shift** increment buttons on the Control palette ....

   OR

Type a value in the **Baseline Shift** text box.

OR

Press a shortcut key combination:

- Increase baseline shift by 2 points ...... Alt + Shift + ↑
- Increase baseline shift by 10 points .... Ctrl + Alt + Shift + ↑
- Decrease baseline shift by 2 points ...... Alt + Shift + ↓
- Decrease baseline shift by 10 points .... Ctrl + Alt + Shift + ↓

Apply Superscript

1. Select the text to affect.
2. Click the **Superscript** button on the Control palette ....

   OR

Press .... Ctrl + Shift + =

Apply Subscript

1. Select the text to affect.
2. Click the **Subscript** button on the Control palette .....

   OR

Press .... Ctrl + Alt + Shift + =

Turn on OpenType Automatic Fraction Building

1. Open the fly-out menu for the Control palette ....
2. Point to **OpenType**.
3. Click **Fractions**.

   ✓ *If the current font does not support OpenType fractions, the word Fractions will appear in square brackets on the menu in step 3. You can still turn the feature on; however, you will not see any change in the typography until you switch to a font that supports the feature. Several fonts that come free with InDesign support fractions, including Adobe Garamond Pro and Adobe Jenson Pro.*

Build a Fraction Manually

1. Type the fraction manually.

   ✓ *If OpenType automatic fraction building has been turned on, as in the preceding steps, and the current font supports it, the fraction will convert automatically and you do not have to do the rest of these steps.*

2. Select the numerator.
3. Click the **Superscript** button on the Control palette ....

   OR

   a. Open the fly-out menu for the Control palette ....
   b. Point to **OpenType**.
   c. Click **Numerator**.

4. Decrease the Tracking on the Control palette ....

   ✓ *The exact setting to use depends on the font; try -100.*

5. Select the denominator.
6. Select a smaller font from the Font Size list on the Control palette.

   ✓ *Select a size that is approximately 60% to 70% of the original. For example, for 12-point type, select 7 point.*

   OR

   a. Open the fly-out menu for the Control palette ....
   b. Point to **OpenType**.
   c. Click **Denominator**.

7. Select the divider (/).
8. Set the Tracking to **-150** on the Control palette ....

Select an Alternate Character

1. Select the character to replace.
2. Click **Type** .... Alt + T
3. Click **Glyphs** .... G
4. Open the **Show** menu ....
5. Click **Alternates for Selection**.
6. Double-click the desired alternate character.

Turn on OpenType Automatic Ordinal Formatting

1. Open the fly-out menu for the Control palette ....
2. Point to **OpenType**.
3. Click **Ordinal**.

   ✓ *If the current font does not support OpenType ordinals, the word Ordinal will appear in square brackets on the menu in step 3. You can still turn the feature on; however, you will not see any change in the typography until you switch to a font that supports the feature. Several fonts that come free with InDesign support ordinals, including Adobe Garamond Pro and Adobe Jenson Pro.*

Manually Format an Ordinal

1. Type the ordinal characters manually.

   ✓ *If OpenType automatic ordinal building has been turned on, as in the preceding steps, and the current font supports it, the ordinal will convert automatically and you do not have to do the rest of these steps.*

2. Select the ordinal characters (for example, *th*, *st*, or *nd*).
3. Click the **Superscript** button on the Control palette ....

EXERCISE DIRECTIONS

1. Start Adobe InDesign.
2. Open **EX15.indd**.
3. Select all the text and turn on the OpenType Ordinal feature. All the ordinals should automatically convert.
4. For the 3/4 fraction under *New York Strip Steak*, format the fraction manually into typographical format.

   ✓ *You can do this either with glyph alternates or by setting the numerator to superscript and changing the size of the denominator and the tracking between them.*

5. For the 1/2 fraction under *Fresh Lobster*, apply the OpenType Fractions feature.
6. Save your work as **XX-EX15.indd**, where XX are your initials.
7. Exit InDesign.

ON YOUR OWN

1. Open **OYO-15.indd**.
2. Shift the baseline of *July* 5 points downward.
3. Format all fractions and ordinals in the document.

   ✓ *This font does not include any special OpenType features, so you will need to do them manually.*

4. Save your work as **XX-OYO-15.indd**, where XX are your initials.
5. Exit InDesign.

Exercise | 16

Skills Covered

- Import Text from Other Programs
- Thread Text Between Frames
- Add New Pages
- Delete Pages
- Start Page 1 on a Verso

Software Skills Often a story takes up more than one column or page in a document. Threading text enables it to float between frames when you change the size of one or more text frames, ensuring that no text is lost.

Application Skills In this exercise, you will add pages to a document, and continue a story onto the new pages. You will also learn how to adjust page spreads by changing the page numbering and how to create multiple new pages at once and flow text onto them automatically.

TERMS

In port The marker on the left side of a text frame that indicates a backward link to another frame.

Out port The marker on the right side of a text frame that indicates a forward link to another frame.

Overset Text that does not fit in the current text frame and has not been flowed into some other frame; as a result it is in limbo and not displayed anywhere in the document.

Recto The right page in a spread.

Spread A pair of left/right pages that will be visible at the same time in the finished publication.

Thread To continue text from one frame to another.

Verso The left page in a spread.

NOTES

Import Text from Other Programs

- InDesign accepts text from almost any text editing program, including plain text from Notepad and documents from Microsoft Word and Corel WordPerfect. It also accepts Rich Text Format (RTF), a standard for data exchange between word processing programs that almost any text application can save documents as.

  ✓ *If you need to import text from an application that InDesign does not directly support, and that will not save in any of the formats that InDesign supports, try using the Clipboard to copy-and-paste from its native application into an InDesign text frame.*

- Use the File > Place command to place text. (This is also the same command you use for placing graphics, as you will see in Lesson 4.) Then select the file and click Open. This loads up the mouse pointer with the document, and the pointer changes to the Loaded Text pointer. You can then click in the text frame in which you want to place the text, or click away from any existing text frame to create a new one.

Place dialog box

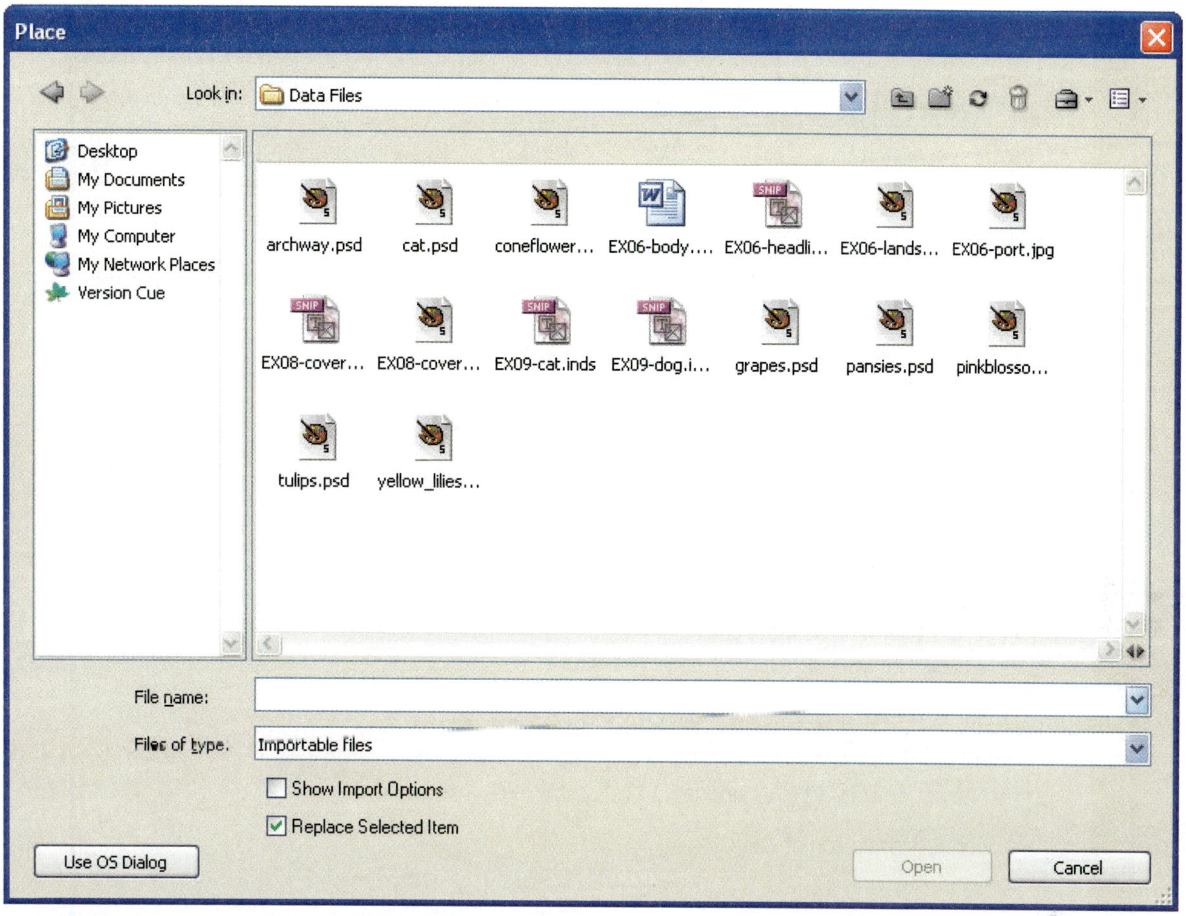

- As you are placing text with the Place dialog box, you can access options by marking the Show Import Options check box. Then when you click Open, an Import Options dialog box appears. The exact name of it depends on the type of file you are placing; the illustration at the top of page 88 shows the Word Import Options box. In it you can choose whether to keep or remove the styles and formatting, the footnotes, and other elements.

Set import options

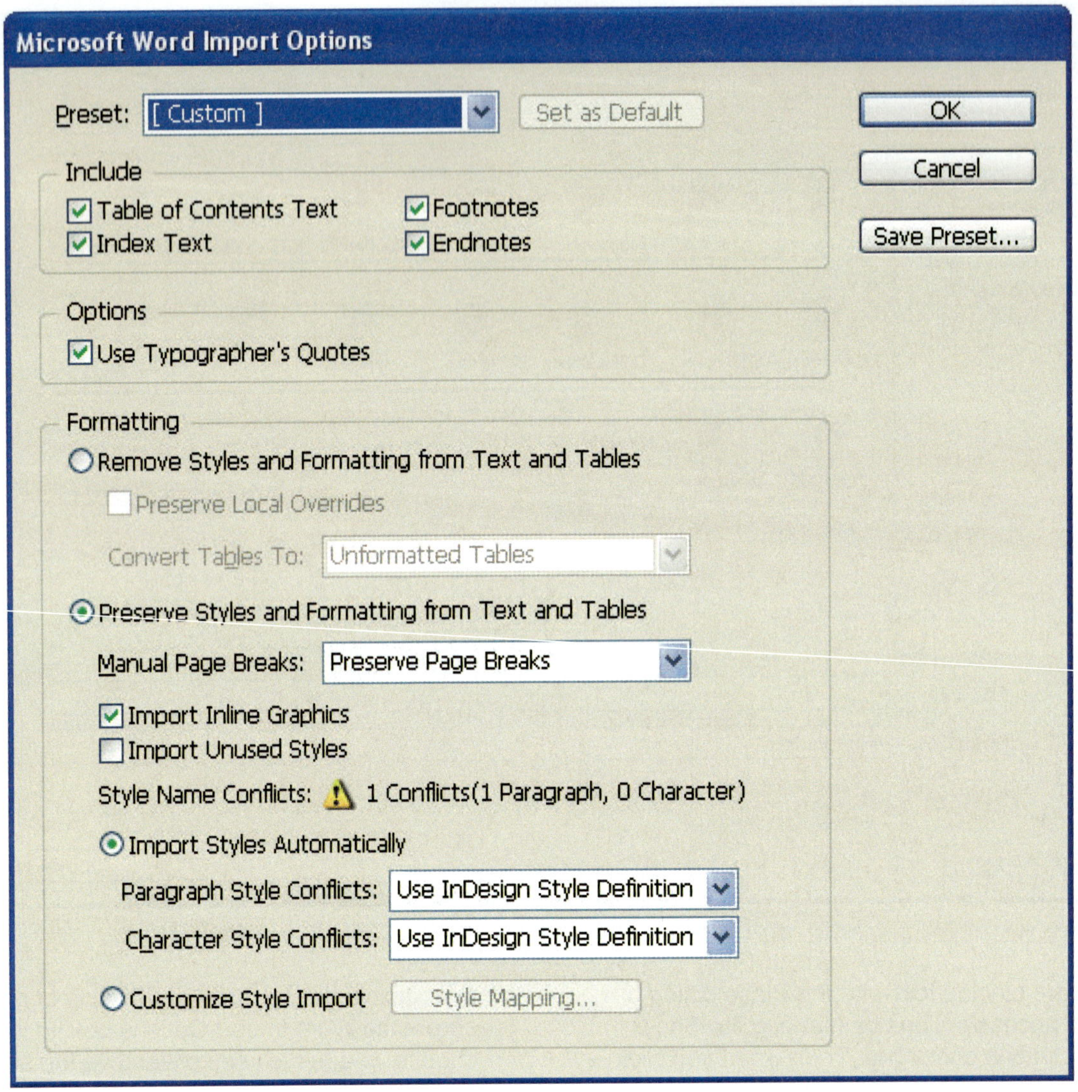

Thread Text Between Frames

- Each frame has an **In port** and an **Out port**, which are large white squares (larger than regular selection handles) at the left and right sides of the frame, respectively. When the frame is not linked to any other frame and all its text fits within it, the In port and Out port are blank.

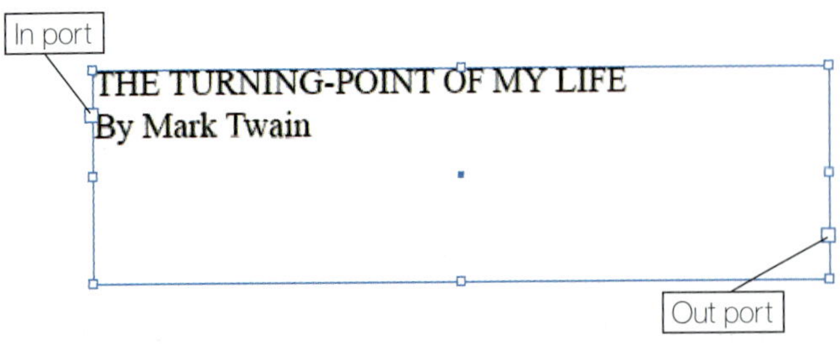

- When there is too much text to fit in a frame, the remaining text is **overset**. It is hidden from view, but it still exists; you can see it by enlarging the frame. In the illustration on the next page, an Overset indicator ⊞ appears on the right side of the frame, in the Out port.
- To **thread** the overset text into another frame, click the Overset indicator to "pick up" the text thread. The mouse pointer changes to the Loaded Text pointer: . Then click in the frame into which you want the text to flow.
- If there is not already a frame where you want the text to flow, you can simply click within a margin/column guide and a new frame will be created there matching the guides.
- Depending on the length of the story, you might need to thread text into more than two frames. Text can be threaded into frames on the same page or on different pages.
- For a large story, it may be necessary to create multiple new pages and frames. You can do this either manually or automatically.

Text frame with Out port indicating overset text

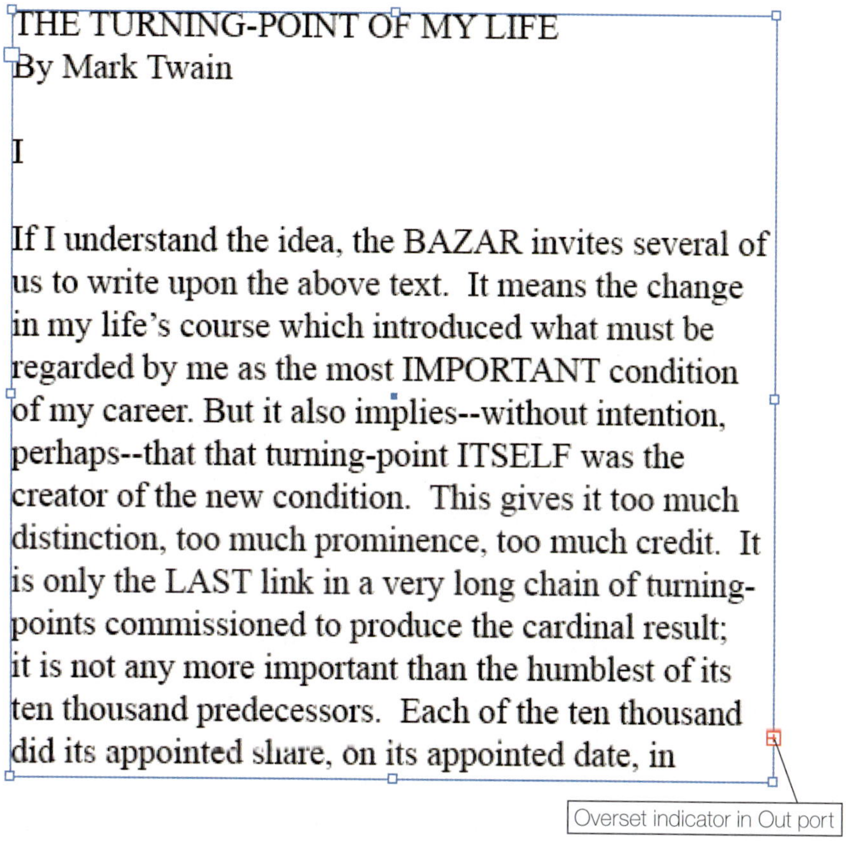

- To create new pages and frames automatically, hold down Shift as you thread the text into a new frame. InDesign will automatically create the text frames and pages needed to accommodate it.

Add New Pages

- For more control than with the automatic flow method just discussed, you can manually add new pages to your document. To do so, use the Pages palette.
- To quickly create a new page with default settings, click the New Page icon at the bottom of the Pages palette.

Start a new page

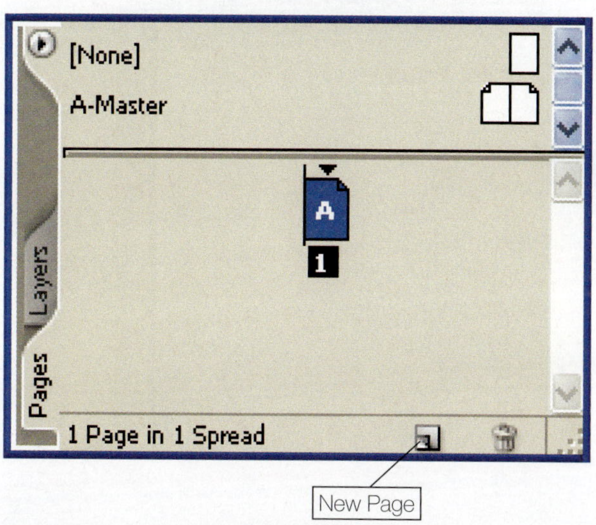

- To see an Insert Pages dialog box with more options, hold down Alt as you click the New Page icon, or open the fly-out menu for the Pages palette and select Insert Pages.

Set properties for the new page

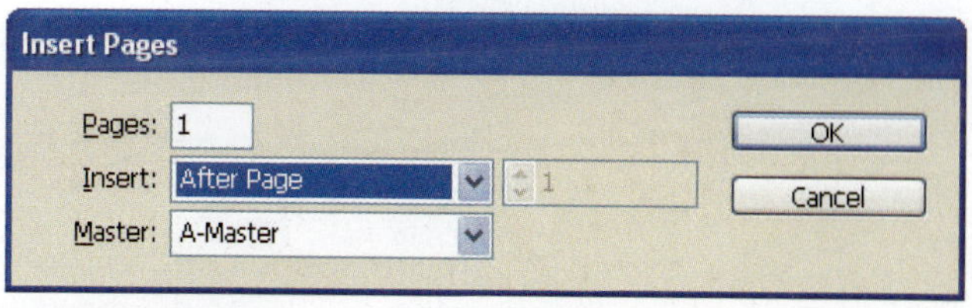

Delete Pages

- To delete a page, open the Pages palette and drag the page to the trash can icon at the bottom of the Pages palette.

Start Page 1 on a Verso

- Two pages that face each other in a two-sided layout are a **spread**. A spread consists of a left-hand page (a **verso**) and a right-hand page (a **recto**). InDesign always starts the first page of a document on a recto, by itself (not part of a spread). The first spread is pages 2 and 3.

- There are several ways to force page 1 onto the verso:
  - Change the page numbering so that it starts on page 2. That way the first page is even-numbered, and therefore verso. To change page numbering, open the fly-out menu of the Pages palette and choose Numbering & Section Options. Enter 2 in the Start Page Numbering at box.

Set the opening page number to 2

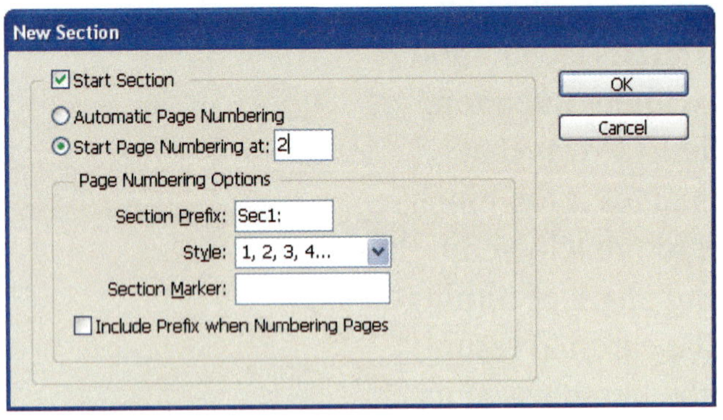

  - Insert a blank page at the beginning of the document, and then ignore it. To insert a blank page at the beginning, select At Start of Document from the Insert menu in the Insert Pages dialog box.

Insert a new page

  - Insert a blank page at the beginning of the document Then select pages 2 and 3, and on the fly-out menu on the Pages palette select Keep Spread Together. Then you can delete the blank page at the beginning.

Keep the spread together

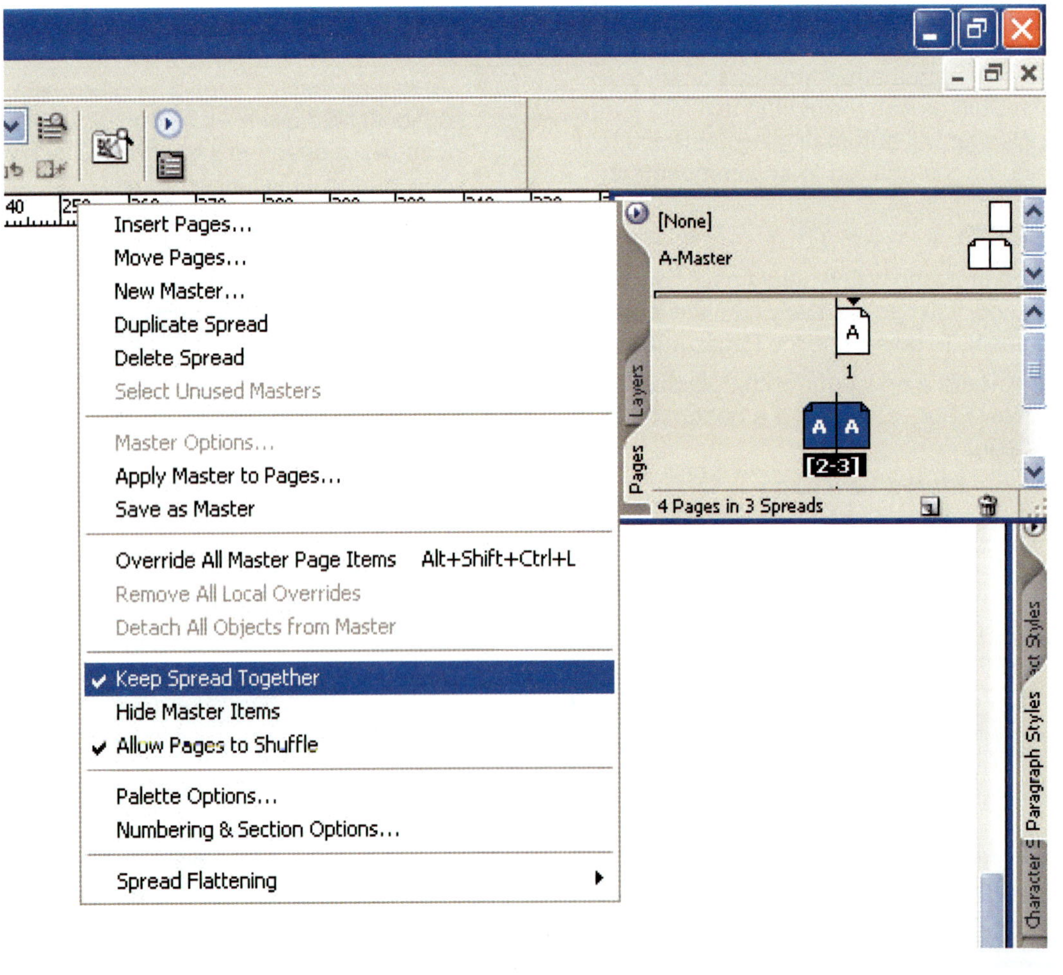

PROCEDURES

Import Text

1. (Optional) To import into an existing text frame, click in the text frame.
2. Click **File** .... Alt + F
3. Click **Place** L

   ✓ *Ctrl+D is a shortcut for steps 1 and 2.*

4. Select the file to import.
5. Mark or clear the **Show Import Options** check box as needed.
6. Click **Open** .... ↵Enter
7. If Show Import Options was selected:
   a. Select any non-default options for import.
   b. Click **OK** .... ↵Enter
8. Do one of the following:
   - Click the text frame into which to place the new text.

   OR

   - Click within column guides to create a new text frame for the text.

   OR

   - Shift+click within column guides or within an existing frame to create as many new frames and pages as needed .... ⇧Shift + click

Thread Text Between Frames

1. (Optional) Create the additional text frames needed.
2. Click the **Overset indicator** on an existing frame ....
3. Do one of the following:
   - Click the text frame into which to place the new text.

   OR

   - Click within column guides to create a new frame.

   OR

   - Shift+click within column guides to create as many new frames and pages as needed .... ⇧Shift + click

Add New Pages

Default Settings

1. Open the **Pages** palette.
2. Click the **New Page** icon ....

Custom Settings

1. Open the **Pages** palette.
2. Alt+click the **New Page** icon .... Alt +

   ✓ *Instead of step 2 you can open the fly-out menu on the Pages palette and select New Page.*

3. Enter the desired number of new pages.
4. Select an **Insert** location .... Alt + I, ↓
5. Enter a **page number** in relation to the Insert location ....
6. Click OK .... ↵Enter

   ✓ *You will learn about using masters, which is another option in the New Page dialog box, in Lesson 6.*

Delete a Page

1. Open the **Pages** palette.
2. Click the page to delete.
3. Drag the page to the trash can icon ....
4. If the page contains objects, a warning appears; click **OK** .... ↵Enter

Start Page 1 on a Verso

Page Numbering Method

1. Open the **Pages** palette.
2. Open the fly-out menu ....
3. Click **Numbering** & **Section Options**.
4. Click **Start Page Numbering at** .... Alt + T
5. Type **2**.
6. Click **OK** .... ↵Enter

Extra Page Method

1. Open the **Pages** palette.
2. Alt+click the **New Page** icon .... Alt +
3. Open the **Insert** list .... Alt + I
4. Click **At Start of Document** .... ↓ or ↑
5. Click **OK** .... ↵Enter

Page Deletion Method

1. Perform all the steps in the Extra Page method above.
2. In the Pages palette, click **2**.
3. Hold down Shift and click **3** .... ⇧Shift + click
4. Open the fly-out menu ....
5. Click **Keep Spread Together**.
6. Click **1** in the Pages palette.
7. Open the fly-out menu ....
8. Click **Delete Spread**.

EXERCISE DIRECTIONS

1. Start Adobe InDesign.
2. Start a new document with the [Default] settings but with two columns. Include only one page.
3. Place the story from **EX16.doc**, allowing InDesign to automatically create the frames and pages needed (with Shift+click).
4. Insert a new Page 1, so that the story starts on the verso (page 2).
5. Cut the first two lines of the story to the Clipboard, and then paste them on page 1. Format them as desired (font, size, color). Size and position the text frame in the center of the page.
6. On page 6, create a new text frame in the second column (currently an empty column), with its bottom point at 125 mm on the vertical ruler.
7. On page 6, decrease the size of the left text frame so that it also has a bottom point of 125 mm. Its text will no longer fit, and you'll see the Overset indicator.
8. Set the overset text to flow into the right text frame.
9. Resize the two text frames so that the text is balanced between them.
10. Save your work as **XX-EX16.indd**, where XX are your initials.
11. Exit InDesign.

ON YOUR OWN

1. Start a new one-column document with 10 pages, and create a single large text frame on each page.
2. Place the document **OYO-16.doc** on the first 10 pages, flowing text into each of the text frames.
3. Create three new pages at the end of the document, and flow the remainder of the text onto them.
4. Set each of the current verso/recto spreads to Keep Spread Together.
5. Add a new page at the beginning of the document, and create a single new text box on it.
6. In the text box, type **Copyright information will be placed here later**.
7. Notice that the new page does not go into a spread with the title page automatically. Fix it so that the newly added page is the verso to the title page's recto.
8. Save your work as **XX-OYO-16.indd**, where XX are your initials.
9. Exit InDesign.

Exercise | 17

Skills Covered

- Use the Story Editor
- Find and Change Text
- Check Spelling
- Edit the Dictionary
- Use Dynamic Spell-Checking

Software Skills InDesign is not a word processing program, but it does offer several useful word processing features such as search-and-replace and spell-checking. It also has a Story Editor, which is a window in which you can view an entire story at once regardless of the number of text frames into which it has been split in the main document.

Application Skills In this exercise, you will use the Story Editor to do some search-and-replace tasks in a multi-page document, and you will check the document for spelling errors.

TERMS

Story Editor An InDesign text editing window in which an entire story is available at once.

NOTES

Use the Story Editor

- The **Story Editor** is a view that enables you to see all the text of a story at once, without any special formatting. This enables you to focus on the words themselves more clearly, especially for stories that are split across multiple frames in your document.
- To enter the Story Editor, select the text frame that contains the story, or click in the story. Then select Edit > Edit in Story Editor or press Ctrl+Y. To return to regular view (Layout view), choose Edit > Edit in Layout or press Ctrl+Y again (see illustration at the top of the following page).

  ✓ *At the left edge of the Story Editor is an area where the names of the styles appear. In the previous figure all the paragraphs are formatted as Normal style. In Exercise 28 you will learn how to create and apply other styles.*

Find and Change Text

- The Find/Change feature in InDesign is equivalent to the Search (or Find) and Replace feature in many word processing programs. It enables you to find instances of a text string, and optionally replace the found instances with some other text.
- You can also use Find/Change to find and replace formatting. For example, you could find all the text that's formatted with a certain font and change it to a different font.
- Select Edit > Find/Change, and then enter the text to be found and the text to use as a replacement. The options include Whole Word, which excludes instances that are part of other words (for example, it would exclude "history" if you were finding "his"), and Case Sensitive.
- Click the More Options button to see the controls for finding/changing formatting. Click the Format button next to Find Format Settings to specify the formatting to find, and click the Format button next to Change Format Settings to specify the replacement (see illustration at the bottom of the following page).

Story Editor

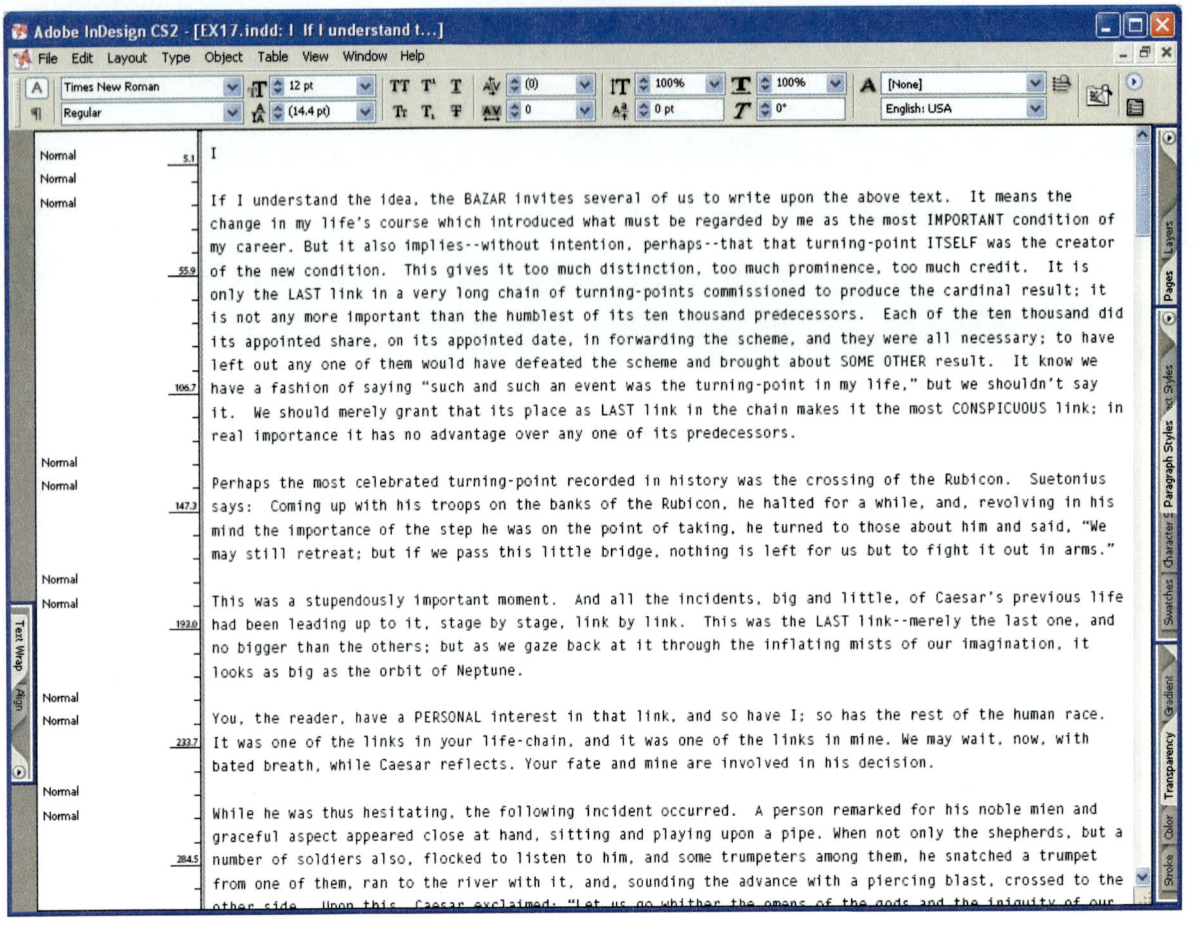

Find/Change dialog box

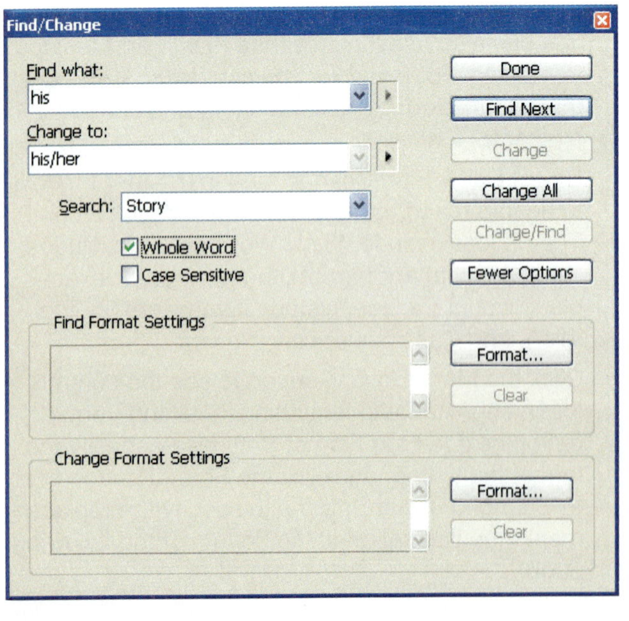

- When you click the Format button, a dialog box appears with categories down the left side. Click a category and then click the desired formatting to specify. Anything you do not specify is assumed to be irrelevant to the search (see illustration at the top of the following page).
- After setting up all your criteria, click Find Next to jump to the first instance, and then do one of the following:
  - Click Change/Find to change it and find the next instance.
  - Click Change to change it and stay on that instance.
  - Click Find Next to skip it.
  - Click Change All to make the change globally without confirming each instance.
- To find or change a special character, click the arrow button ▸ next to Find what or Change to, and then select from the menu that appears.

Find formatting

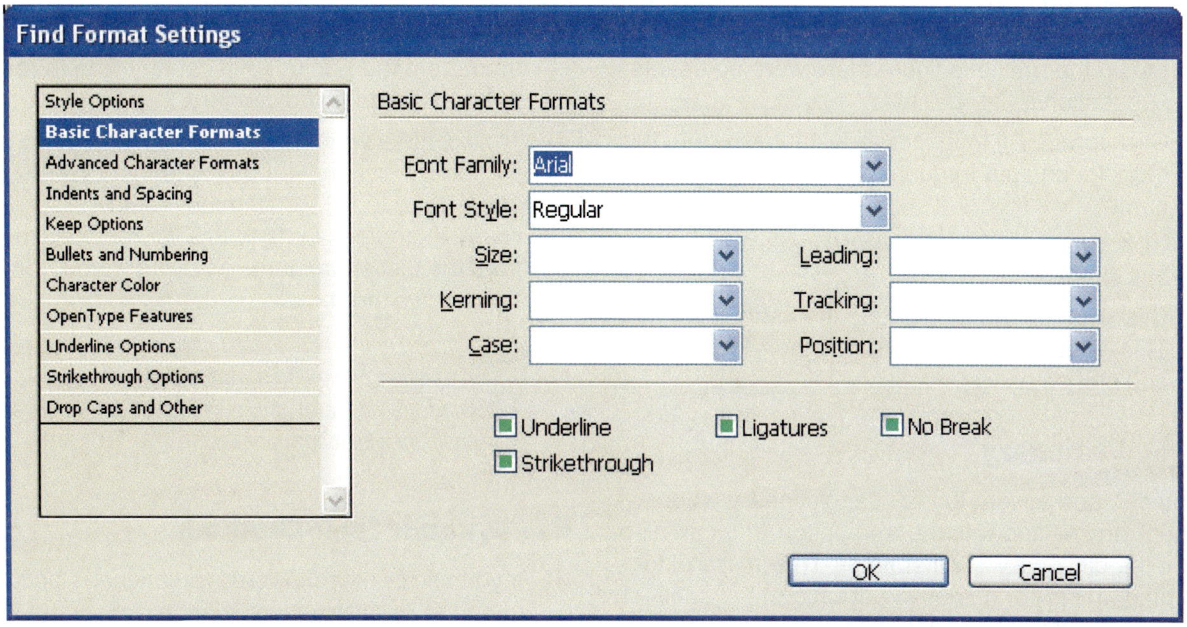

Find special characters

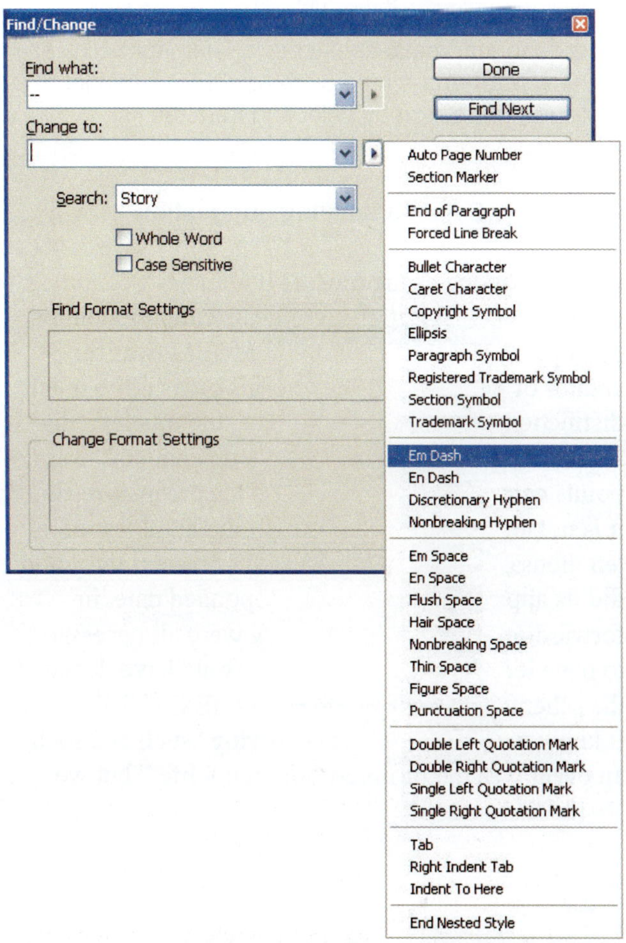

Check Spelling

- Use the Edit > Spelling > Check Spelling command to start an interactive spelling check of the entire story. For each potential misspelling, a dialog box prompts you to make a decision.

  ✓ *By default, the spell-checker looks at the current story but not other stories in the document. To change this behavior, open the Search box and choose Document (for the current document) or All Documents (for all open documents).*

- When faced with a potential misspelling, do one of the following:
  - Click Skip to ignore this instance.

Decide what to do with the possible spelling error

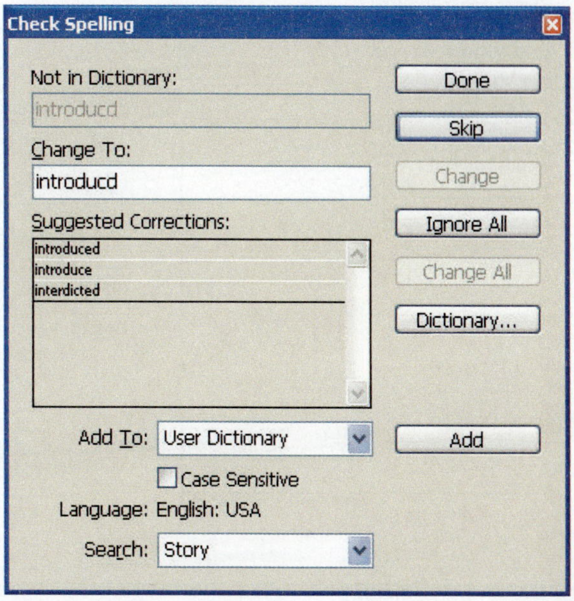

- Enter a correction in the Change To box, or select a suggested spelling from the list provided (if applicable), and then click the Change button. In the previous figure there were no usable suggestions.
- Click Ignore All to ignore all instances within this story (such as a frequently reoccurring proper name).
- Click Change All to change all instances within this story.
- Click Add to add the word to the user dictionary. This dictionary carries over to other documents and stories as well.

Edit the Dictionary

- You can add a word to the user dictionary when checking spelling with the Add button. You can also edit the dictionary at other times. This is useful for setting up proper names in advance of the spell-check, for example, and for removing words from the user dictionary that were added in error.
- To edit the user dictionary, choose Edit > Spelling > Dictionary.

✓ *You can also access the dictionary from the Check Spelling dialog box by clicking the Dictionary button.*

- To add words to the dictionary, open the Dictionary List and choose Added Words. Then enter the word you want to add in the Word box and click Add. To delete any words that you have added, select them and click Remove.

Edit the dictionary

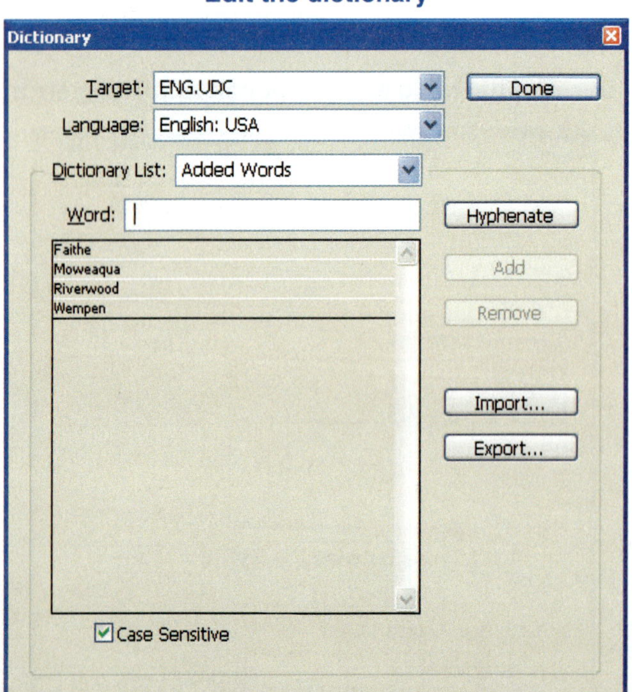

- You can also exclude words from the default dictionary. This is not really deleting them, but merely adding them to an Excluded list. You can remove them from the Excluded list at any time to restore them to the default dictionary.
- To exclude a word from the dictionary, open the Dictionary List and choose Removed Words. Then add a word to this list. It might seem counterintuitive, but *adding* words to this list *removes* them from the dictionary, and *removing* words from this list re-*adds* them.

✓ *The Import and Export buttons enable you to move your custom spelling dictionaries from one PC to another. This is beyond the scope of this course, but you might want to experiment with it on your own.*

Use Dynamic Spell-Checking

- If you use Microsoft Word, you might be accustomed to its automatic spell-checking, wherein it underlines possible misspelled words with a wavy red underline. You can do something similar with InDesign if desired.
- Choose Edit > Spelling > Dynamic Spelling to turn on the automatic spell-check. Then right-click any wavy-red-underlined word or phrase to make a quick correction by selecting from the list.

Select a spelling suggestion

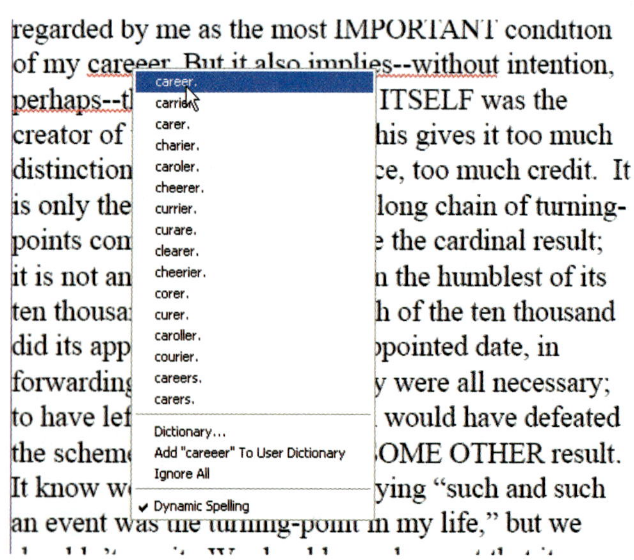

PROCEDURES

Use the Story Editor

1. Click in the story you want to edit.
2. Click **Edit** .... Alt+E
3. Click **Edit in Story Editor**.

✓ *You can switch back and forth between the Story Editor and Layout view by pressing Ctrl+Y.*

To return to Layout view:

1. Click **Edit** .... Alt+E
2. Click **Edit in Layout** .... E, E, ↵Enter

Find Text

1. Click in the story containing the text you want to find.
2. Click **Edit** .... Alt+E
3. Click **Find/Change** .... /

✓ *You can press Ctrl+F as a shortcut for steps 1 and 2.*

4. Type the text to find in the **Find what** box .... Alt+F

OR

Click the arrow button and select a special character .... ▸, ↓

5. Choose a search scope from the **Search** list .... Alt+S, ↓ or ↑
6. (Optional) Mark or clear check boxes:
   - **Whole Word** .... Alt+W
   - **Case Sensitive** .... Alt+N
7. Click **Find Next** .... Alt+X
8. To repeat the find, click **Find Next** again .... Alt+X

OR

a. Click **Done** .... Alt+D
b. Press **Ctrl+Alt+F** to repeat the find .... Alt+Ctrl+F

Find and Change Text

1. Click in the story containing the text you want to find.
2. Click **Edit** .... Alt+E
3. Click **Find/Change** .... /

✓ *You can press Ctrl+F as a shortcut for steps 1 and 2.*

4. Type the text to find in the **Find what** box .... Alt+F

OR

Click the arrow button and select a special character .... ▸, ↓

5. Type the new text in the **Change to** box .... Alt+C

OR

Click the arrow button and select a special character .... ▸, ↓

6. Choose a search scope from the **Search** list .... Alt+S, ↓ or ↑
7. (Optional) Mark or clear check boxes:
   - **Whole Word** .... Alt+W
   - Case **Sensitive** .... Alt+N
8. Click **Find Next** .... Alt+X
9. Do one of the following for the found text:
   - Click **Find Next** to ignore the found text .... Alt+X
   - Click **Change** to change this instance and stay on it .... Alt+H
   - Click **Change All** to change all instances .... Alt+A
   - Click **Change/Find** to change this instance and find the next instance .... Alt+G
10. Repeat step 9 as needed.

Find Formatting

1. Click in the story containing the text you want to find.
2. Click **Edit** .... Alt+E
3. Click **Find/Change** .... /

✓ *You can press Ctrl+F as a shortcut for steps 1 and 2.*

4. (Optional) Type the text to find in the **Find what** box .... Alt+F

✓ *If you leave the Find what box empty, you can find all text with the specified formatting, regardless of content.*

5. Choose a search scope from the **Search** list .... Alt+S, ... ↓ or ↑
6. (Optional) Mark or clear check boxes:
   - **Whole Word** .... Alt+W
   - **Case Sensitive** .... Alt+N

✓ *If you leave the Find what box empty, step 6 is not applicable.*

7. Click the **Format** button next to Find Format Settings .... Alt+T
8. Click a formatting category on the left .... ↓ or ↑
9. Specify the desired formatting using the controls provided.
10. Repeat steps 8 and 9 as needed for additional criteria.
11. Click **OK** .... ↵Enter
12. Click **Find Next** .... Alt+X
13. To repeat the find, click **Find Next** again .... Alt+X

OR

a. Click **Done** .... Alt+D
b. Press **Ctrl+Alt+F** to repeat the find .... Alt+Ctrl+F

Find and Change Formatting

1. Click in the story containing the text you want to find.
2. Click **Edit** .... Alt+E
3. Click **Find/Change** .... /

✓ *You can press Ctrl+F as a shortcut for steps 1 and 2.*

4. (Optional) Type the text to find in the **Find what** box .... Alt+F
5. (Optional) Type the new text in the **Change to** box .... Alt+C

✓ *If you leave both the Find what and Change to boxes empty, you can replace the specified formatting regardless of the content. Do not enter text in the Find what box without entering text in the Change to box, however, or the operation will delete the found text (by replacing it with an empty string).*

6. Choose a search scope from the **Search** list ....Alt+S, ...↓ or ↑
7. (Optional) Mark or clear check boxes:
   - **Whole Word** ....Alt+W
   - **Case Sensitive** ....Alt+N

   ✓ *If you left the Find what and Change to boxes empty, step 7 is not applicable.*
8. Click the **Format** button next to Find Format Settings ....Alt+T
9. Click a formatting category on the left ....↓ or ↑
10. Specify the desired formatting using the controls provided.
11. Repeat steps 9 and 10 as needed for additional criteria.
12. Click **OK** ....↵Enter
13. Click the **Format** button next to Change Format Settings ....Alt+R
14. Click a formatting category on the left ....↓ or ↑
15. Specify the desired formatting using the controls provided.
16. Repeat steps 14 and 15 as needed for additional criteria.
17. Click **OK** ....↵Enter
18. Click **Find Next** ....Alt+X
19. Do one of the following for the found text:
    - Click **Find Next** to ignore the found text ....Alt+X
    - Click **Change** to change this instance and stay on it ....Alt+H
    - Click **Change All** to change all instances ....Alt+A
    - Click **Change/Find** to change this instance and find the next instance ....Alt+G
20. Repeat step 19 as needed.

Use a Special Character in a Find/Change Operation

1. Select the character in the document. If it is not there, type/insert it.
2. Press **Ctrl+C** to copy it ....Ctrl+C
3. Begin the Find/Change operation normally.
4. Click in the **Find what** or **Change to** box ....Alt+F or Alt+C
5. Press **Ctrl+V** to paste the copied symbol ....Ctrl+V
6. Continue the Find/Change operation normally.

Check Spelling Interactively

1. Click in the story you want to check.
2. Click **Edit** ....Alt+E
3. Point to **Spelling**.
4. Click **Check Spelling** ....K

   ✓ *You can press Ctrl+I as a shortcut for steps 2–4.*
5. Click **Start** ....Alt+T
6. For each found word, do one of the following:
   - Click **Skip** to ignore this instance.
   - Click **Change** to change this instance ....Alt+H
   - Click **Ignore All** to skip all instances ....Alt+I
   - Click **Change All** to change all instances ....Alt+G
   - Click **Add** to add the word to the dictionary ....Alt+A
7. Click **Done** ....Alt+D

Enable or Disable Dynamic Spell-Checking

1. Click **Edit** ....Alt+E
2. Point to **Spelling**.
3. Click **Dynamic Spelling** ....M

Correct a Spelling Error Identified by Dynamic Spell-Checking

1. Right-click the red-underlined word or phrase.
2. Click one of the following:
   - Click **Dictionary** to open the Dictionary dialog box, and then see "Add a Word to the User Dictionary" below.
   - Click **Add {word} to User Dictionary** to add the word to the dictionary (no dialog box).
   - Click **Ignore All** to ignore all instances.
   - Click **Dynamic Spelling** to turn off the Dynamic Spelling feature.

Add a Word to the User Dictionary

1. Click **Edit** ....Alt+E
2. Point to **Spelling**.
3. Click **Dictionary** ....Y
4. Click in the **Word** text box ....Alt+W
5. Type the word to add.
6. Click **Add** ....Alt+A
7. Repeat steps 4–6 as needed.
8. Click **Done** ....Alt+N

Remove a User-Added Word from the Dictionary

1. Click **Edit** ....Alt+E
2. Point to **Spelling**.
3. Click **Dictionary.** ....Y
4. Click a word on the list.
5. Click **Remove** ....Alt+R
6. Repeat steps 4 and 5 as needed.
7. Click **Done** ....Alt+N

Exclude a Word from the Dictionary

1. Click **Edit** ....Alt+E
2. Point to **Spelling**.
3. Click **Dictionary** ....Y
4. Choose Removed Words from the **Dictionary List** ....Alt+D, ↓
5. Click in the **Word** text box ....Alt+W
6. Type the word to add.
7. Click **Add** ....Alt+A
8. Repeat steps 5–7 as needed.
9. Click **Done** ....Alt+N

EXERCISE DIRECTIONS

1. Start Adobe InDesign.
2. Open **EX17.indd**.
3. Use Find/Change to change all instances of -- (double hyphens) to an em dash.
4. Turn on Dynamic Spelling, and correct a misspelled word by right-clicking it.
5. Add the words *Rubicon* and *Suetonius* to the user dictionary.
6. Set the user dictionary to exclude the word *uncourteously*.
7. Correct all the remaining misspelled words in the document using the interactive spell-checking feature.
8. Save your work as **XX-EX17.indd,** where XX are your initials.
9. Exit InDesign.

ON YOUR OWN

1. Open **OYO-17.indd**.
2. Change all instances of the word *instructor* to *teacher*.
3. Change all text formatted as Times New Roman to Arial font.
4. Correct all the spelling errors. If the spelling checker finds any words in error that are actually correct, add them to the dictionary.
5. Save your work as **XX-OYO-17.indd**, where XX are your initials.
6. Exit InDesign.

End of Lesson Projects

- Summary Exercise
- Application Exercise
- Curriculum Integration Exercise
- Critical Thinking Exercise

Exercise | 18

Summary Exercise

Software Skills The Eagle Creek Animal Clinic's staff has been working on the brochure you began for them in Exercise 8, and has entered some text. In this exercise, you will format the text to make it more attractive and readable.

DIRECTIONS

1. Open **EX18.indd**.
2. On page 1, format the text *Eagle Creek Animal Clinic* in the right panel with the following attributes:
   - Font: Imprint MT Shadow
   - Font size: 24 point
   - Font color: Dark green (C=76 M=34 Y=77 K=63; make a swatch out of it for later use)
   - All caps
   - Vertical Scale: 90%
3. Format the address and phone number in both the right panel and the center panel (*not* the e-mail address) with the following attributes:
   - Font: Palatino Linotype
   - Small caps
   - Tracking: +25
4. Format the e-mail address in the center panel with the following attributes:
   - Font: Palatino Linotype
   - Size: 10 point
   - Tracking: +50
   - Color: Blue (C=91 M=71 Y=0 K=0; make a swatch out of it for later use)
   - Underlined
5. Format the text *A Sampling of Our Services* as:
   - Font: Imprint MT Shadow
   - Size: 16 point
   - Color: Dark green (use the swatch created in step 2)
6. On page 2, fill the center text panel with **EX18-Vet.doc**.
7. On page 2, format each of the three column headings in the same way as in step 5.
8. Turn on optical kerning for all text in the entire document.
9. Use Find/Change to change all remaining instances of Times New Roman font to Palatino Linotype font.
10. Lengthen any text boxes that have overset text until all text is displayed.
11. Turn on dynamic spell-checking, and add "Purdue" and "Otoscopy" to the user dictionary.
12. Check the spelling of the rest of the document, making any changes needed.
13. Save your work as **XX-EX18.indd**, where XX are your initials.
14. Exit InDesign.

Exercise | 19

Application Exercise

Software Skills In this exercise, you will insert and format the text for an article on perennial gardens for a home gardening magazine.

DIRECTIONS

1. Open **EX19.indd**.
2. Flow the story **EX19-Body.doc** into the four empty text frames on the spread, and thread the text boxes together so it flows from frame to frame.
3. Format the imported text in Adobe Garamond Pro font.
4. Correct all spelling errors.
5. Format the article's title as follows:
   - Font: Viner Hand ITC
   - Color: Paper (White)
   - Size: 65 points
6. Format the footer text at the bottom of the left page as follows:
   - Font Style: Italic
   - Color: Paper (White)
   - Size: 11 points
7. Format the footer text at the bottom of the right page as follows:
   - Font Style: Italic
   - Size: 11 points
8. Format the text *Soil Conditions* and *Caring for New Transplants* in the article to 14-point semi-bold.
9. Format the names of the flowers that begin paragraphs 2 through 7 as semibold and italic.
10. Adjust the tracking and the horizontal scale so that the article exactly fits in the space provided. (There are many combinations of the two that will achieve the desired effect—experiment.)
11. Save your work as **XX-EX19.indd**, where XX are your initials. It should resemble Illustration A.
12. Exit InDesign.

Illustration A

Easy-Care Perennials

Looking for an easy way to enjoy color and beauty in your gardens all season long? Consider perennials. While they are more expensive than annuals initially, you quickly recoup the cost difference in having plants that will come back stronger and more vigorous every year, with no replanting.

Here are some easy-to-care-for plants that make for a good starter garden:

'Sprite' Astilbe -- a diminutive hybrid astilbe with glossy dark green foliage. It produces sprays of shell pink flowers in midsummer shade gardens.

'Moonbeam' Coreposis -- small, eight-petaled pale yellow flowers grace the tips of thin stems covered with narrow leaves. It blooms all summer in full sun.

'Palace Purple' Heuchera -- boasts handsome deep purple foliage all summer in partial shade. It bears tiny, pale bluish-white flowers clustered at the ends of wiry stems in spring.

Creeping Phlox -- neat, deep green foliage on creeping stems mats to cover the ground in woodland settings. In spring it produces clusters of small florets in white, blue, or pink.

'Sunny Border Blue' Veronica -- offers a strong, vertical accent for the garden and bears spikes of rich violet-blue flowers in summer. It does best in a sunny site.

'Magnus' Purple Coneflower -- jaunty, daisylike flowers with droopy purple petals bloom in midsummer when many other perennials are idle. It thrives in full sun.

2 • Volume II Number 1

Curriculum Integration Exercise

Software Skills Your chemistry class is learning about writing chemical formulas, and you have been assigned the task of creating a list of molecular formulas for substances that will be used in experiments throughout the semester. In this exercise, you will use InDesign's typography features to make this list attractive and readable.

DIRECTIONS

Using the Internet, find the molecular formulas for the following:

- Water
- Carbon Dioxide
- Sulfuric Acid
- Benzene
- Ethylene
- Sugar
- Ascorbic Acid
- Glucose

Create a new document in InDesign, and create a text frame. Type the listed items with a blank line (an extra Enter) between each one, and type the chemical formulas next to each one. Use subscript as needed.

Format the list so that the names of the chemicals are bold and bright red (R=255 G=0 B=0), and the formulas are regular style and black.

Type the heading **Chemicals for Experiments** above the list and make it bold and 24 point.

Set the tracking for each formula to +100.

Save your work as **XX-EX20.indd**, where XX are your initials.

Exit InDesign.

Exercise | 21

Critical Thinking Exercise

Software Skills Your English teacher has asked you to share a favorite story or essay with your classmates. In this exercise, you will visit an online archive containing classic literature in the public domain, and download a copy of a book, story, or essay. You will then publish it attractively using InDesign.

DIRECTIONS

- Using the Internet, browse the Project Gutenberg Web site at http://www.gutenberg.org/catalog. Locate a story or book of your choice and download an HTML or plain-text version of it to your hard disk. Store it in the same folder as the data files for this course.

  ✓ *The HTML version will require less cleanup than the plain-text version, so use the HTML version if it is available.*

- Start a new InDesign document and place the text into it, generating as many frames and pages as needed to hold it.
- Create a new page at the beginning, and create a title page for the work including the title and the author's name, plus a date if available.
- Delete all the extra text at the beginning and end of the work that was placed there by Project Gutenberg.

  ✓ *If you were actually going to distribute this work, you would need to keep all the Project Gutenberg text, per their distribution restrictions. However, since you are creating this just for practice, you can delete it.*

- Format the document so it is readable and attractive. This process might include:
  - Deleting extraneous paragraph and line breaks.
  - Formatting headings with a larger, bolder font than the body text.
  - Choosing a different font family and size for body text.
  - Adding a page background if desired by placing a colored rectangle behind the text (on a lower layer than the text).
  - Applying any superscript, subscript, or baseline shift that is needed.
  - Adjusting the kerning, tracking, and scale of any text that would benefit from it.
  - Formatting the non-body text, such as the copyright information at the beginning and end, in a smaller font such as 8 point.

    ✓ *If there's a lot of cleanup to do to the file, and it's very long, you may work with only the first 10 pages and leave the rest.*

- Save the document as **XX-EX21.indd**, where XX are your initials.
- Exit InDesign.

Lesson 3

Working with Paragraphs

Exercise 22

- Display the Paragraph Tools
- Change Paragraph Alignments
- Change Justification Limits
- Use Optical Margin Alignment
- Use Paste in Place
- Indent Paragraphs

Exercise 23

- Adjust Leading
- Change Spacing Before or After Paragraphs
- Change the Vertical Alignment
- Create a Drop Cap

Exercise 24

- Avoid Widows and Orphans
- Work with Multiple Columns in a Single Frame
- Control Hyphenation
- Specify Hyphenation for Individual Words

Exercise 25

- Place and Remove Tab Stops
- Apply Bullets and Numbering
- Customize a Bulleted List
- Customize a Numbered List

Exercise 26

- Create a Table
- Convert Text to a Table
- Select Parts of a Table
- Insert and Delete Rows and Columns
- Adjust Cell Heights and Widths
- Merge and Split Cells

Exercise 27

- Apply Table Strokes
- Apply a Table Fill
- Align Text in a Cell
- Rotate Text in a Cell

Exercise 28

- About Styles
- Create Styles
- Apply Styles
- Define Styles Based on Other Styles
- Clear Manual Overrides
- Redefine a Style
- Load Styles from Other Documents

END OF LESSON PROJECTS

Exercise 29

- Summary Exercise

Exercise 30

- Application Exercise

Exercise 31

- Curriculum Integration Exercise

Exercise 32

- Critical Thinking Exercise

Exercise | 22

Skills Covered

- Display the Paragraph Tools
- Change Paragraph Alignments
- Change Justification Limits
- Use Optical Margin Alignment
- Use Paste in Place
- Indent Paragraphs

Software Skills So far you have been using only left alignment for text, but there are many other choices. In this lesson, you will learn how to change the way the text interacts horizontally with the text frame in which it is placed.

Application Skills In this exercise, you will change the alignment of the body paragraphs in a document, and set up a running footer that always aligns with the outside of the spread.

TERMS

Justified Aligned at both the left and the right.

Optical margin alignment Left alignment that takes into consideration the shape of the first character of the paragraph when positioning the starting point of the first line.

Paragraph alignment The horizontal alignment of a paragraph between the left and right edges of its text frame.

Paste in place A special type of paste operation that positions the pasted copy at exactly the same spot on the new page as it was on the original page from which it was copied.

NOTES

Display the Paragraph Tools

- So far in this course you have used only the Character controls on the Control palette. In this lesson you will work mostly with the Paragraph tools.
- To switch to the Paragraph controls, click the Paragraph Formatting Controls button ¶ at the left end of the Control palette.

Paragraph formatting controls

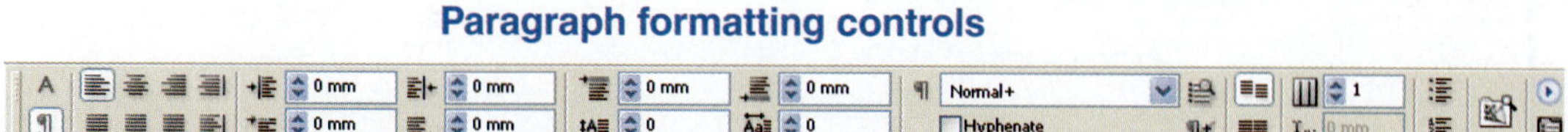

Change Paragraph Alignments

- The term **paragraph alignment** refers to horizontal alignment—the positioning between the left and right sides of the text frame.

  ✓ *Text in a frame can also be vertically aligned—top, middle, or bottom—but not on an individual paragraph basis. You'll learn how to set vertical alignment in Exercise 23.*

- To change a paragraph's alignment, select it and then click one of the alignment buttons on the Control palette:
  - Align Left
  - Align Center
  - Align Right
- A **justified** alignment aligns text evenly at both the left and the right, inserting space between each word and each letter as needed to make it come out even. There are three different justified settings for paragraph alignment.
  - Justify with Last Line Left (most common)
  - Justify with Last Line Aligned Center
  - Justify All Lines
- You can also choose an alignment setting that will vary depending on whether the text frame is on a verso or recto. This is useful for text frames that you plan on copying to other pages, or text frames that you place on a master page (which you will learn about in Lesson 6).
  - Align Towards Spine
  - Align Away from Spine

  ✓ *All of these alignment buttons are also available on the Paragraph palette, but since the Control palette is nearly always visible most people prefer to use them from there.*

Change Justification Limits

- To set upper and lower limits on the amount of spacing that will be inserted in order to justify the text, open the fly-out menu for the Paragraph controls on the Control palette and choose Justification.
- The default percentages for word spacing, letter spacing, and glyph scaling determine how much InDesign can modify the text in order to achieve horizontal justification.
  - Word spacing controls how much space will be inserted between words.
  - Letter spacing controls how much space will be inserted between letters within a word.
  - Glyph scaling controls how much a glyph can be enlarged or compressed (see the illustration below).

    ✓ *The Auto Leading setting in this dialog box is covered in Exercise 23.*

Justification dialog box

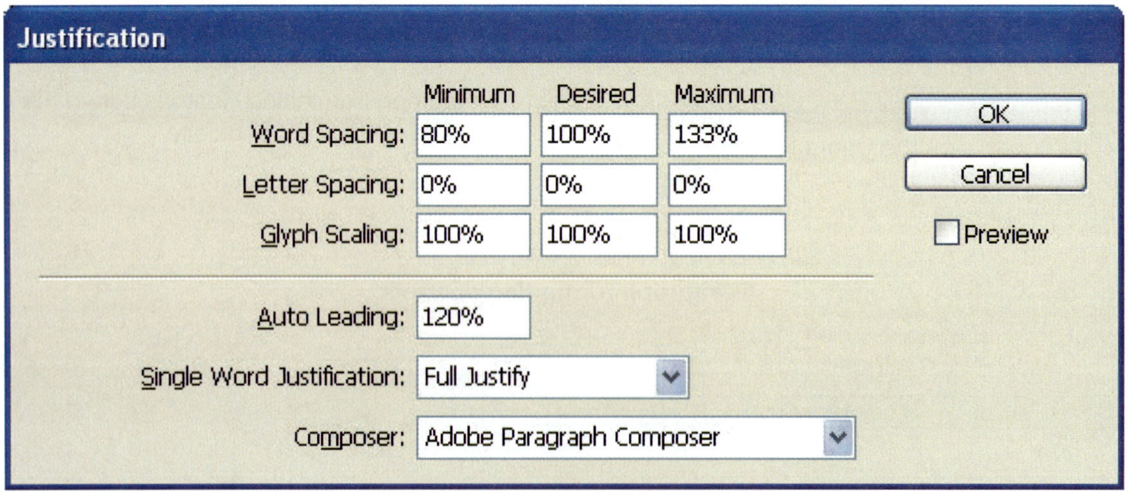

- The defaults are usually appropriate for most documents; you might change them if some paragraphs in the document have a distracting appearance because they have been adjusted too much or because the adjustment limits were set too low.

Use Optical Margin Alignment

- Sometimes the first character of a paragraph can look like it is indented even though it's not. For example:

"A very strange thing happened to me the other day," she said casually as she dropped a lump of sugar into her coffee and reached for a plastic spoon.

- To correct this problem, turn on **Optical Margin Alignment** for the paragraph. This feature enables InDesign to take the shape of the first character into consideration and hang it outside the text frame if it would be visually advantageous for the layout:

"A very strange thing happened to me the other day," she said casually as she dropped a lump of sugar into her coffee and reached for a plastic spoon.

- To turn on Optical Margin Alignment, click in the paragraph and then choose Type > Story and select the Optical Margin Alignment check box in the palette that appears. You can then enter an amount of space by which to adjust.

Story palette

Use Paste in Place

- When you copy/cut and paste frames between pages, the pasted frame appears in the center of the new page by default.
- If you would like the pasted frame to appear in exactly the same place on the new page that it appeared in on the original page, use the Edit > **Paste in Place** command instead of the regular Paste command.
- Paste in Place does not work between two pages that are together in a spread; for these situations, use Alt+drag to copy a frame. Hold down Shift to lock the frame in vertical or horizontal position as you drag.

Indent Paragraphs

- The Indent settings control how the paragraph is positioned in relation to the left and right edges of the text frame. An indent of 0 places the text flush against the edge of the text frame.
- There are four indents you can set; each has its own text box on the Control palette. Type a value (in points) or increment its value up or down. The indent can be either positive (to the right) or negative (to the left, or reverse indent).
  - Left Indent (All Lines)
  - First Line Left Indent
  - Right Indent (All Lines)
  - Last Line Right Indent

PROCEDURES

Display the Paragraph Tools

- Click the **Paragraph Formatting Controls** button .... ¶

Change Paragraph Alignment

1. Select the paragraph(s) to affect.
2. If needed, display the **Paragraph** tools on the Control palette .... ¶
3. Click a paragraph alignment button:
   - Align Left ....
   - Align Center ....
   - Align Right ....
   - Justify with Last Line Left (most common) ....
   - Justify with Last Line Aligned Center ....
   - Justify All Lines ....
   - Align Towards Spine ......
   - Align Away from Spine ....

Change Justification Limits

1. Place the insertion point within any paragraph in the story.
2. Display the **Paragraph Formatting Controls** on the Control palette .... ¶
3. Open the fly-out menu for the Control palette.
4. Click **Justification**.

   ✓ *You can press Alt+Shift+Ctrl+J as a shortcut to steps 2–4.*

5. Enter different values for **Word Spacing** if desired ....Alt+W, Tab
6. Enter different values for **Letter Spacing** if desired ....Alt+L, Tab
7. Enter different values for **Glyph Scaling** if desired ....Alt+G, Tab
8. Click **OK** ....Enter

Use Optical Margin Alignment

1. Select the paragraph(s) to affect.
2. Click **Type** ....Alt+T
3. Click **Story** ....R
4. Click **Optical Margin Alignment**.
5. If desired, change the amount of adjustment ...., ↓
6. Close the Story palette ......

Use Paste In Place

1. Select the frame(s) to affect.
2. Cut or copy the frame to the Clipboard ....Alt+X or ....Alt+C
3. Display the destination page.
4. Click **Edit** ....Alt+E
5. Click **Paste in Place** I

   ✓ *Alt+Shift+Ctrl+V is a shortcut for steps 4 and 5.*

Indent Paragraphs

1. Select the paragraph(s) to affect.
2. If needed, display the **Paragraph** tools on the Control palette .... ¶
3. Type or increment the value for the desired indent type ....
   - Left Indent (All Lines) ....
   - First Line Left Indent ....
   - Right Indent (All Lines) ....
   - Last Line Right Indent ....

EXERCISE DIRECTIONS

1. Start Adobe InDesign.
2. Open **EX22.indd**.
3. Center the text on page 1.
4. Set the remainder of the document to Justify with Last Line Left.
5. Indent the first line of each paragraph by 5 millimeters EXCEPT the section numbers (I, II, and III) and EXCEPT the first paragraph underneath each of those section numbers.
6. Format the section numbers (I, II, and III) with dark green (C=75 M=5 Y=100 K=50, and create a swatch for later use) and 18-point bold.
7. In the floating center text frame on page 3, do the following:
   - Turn on Optical Margin Alignment and set the amount of adjustment to 36 points.
   - Set the right and left indents to 4 mm.
   - Format the quotation marks as 48 points each. Adjust the size of the text frame if needed to keep all text visible.
   - Use the Baseline Shift feature to adjust the vertical positioning of the text in the last line, including the closing quotation mark, so that its spacing matches that of the other lines in the paragraph.

   ✓ *For example, you might shift the words up 26 points and the closing quotation mark up 16 points.*

8. Color the text box with the same green as your swatch from step 6 (C=75 M=5 Y=100 K=50), set the text to Paper (white), and resize it so that the text fits neatly in it with no extra space at the bottom. It should resemble Illustration A, on following page.

9. In the box containing the page number at the bottom of page 2, select all the text (Ctrl+A) and set to Align Away from Spine.
10. Select the frame containing the page number, hold down the Alt key, and drag it onto page 3, creating a copy there.
11. Copy it onto page 4 with Paste in Place.
12. Copy it onto pages 5 and 6 using any method desired.
13. Save your work as **XX-EX22.indd**, where XX are your initials.
14. Exit InDesign.

Illustration A

ON YOUR OWN

1. Open **OYO-22.indd**.
2. Center the company name, address, and phone number at the top of the letter.
3. Format the rest of the letter using the Modified Block with Blocked Paragraphs letter format:
   - The date, recipient's address block, closing, and signature block all begin at the horizontal center of the page and are left-aligned.
   - The body paragraphs are not indented.

   ✓ *Place a vertical ruler guide in the horizontal center of the page to help, if desired.*
4. Left-indent each of the three quantity listing lines by 10 mm.
5. Save your work as **XX-OYO-22.indd**, where XX are your initials.
6. Exit InDesign.

Exercise | 23

Skills Covered

- Adjust Leading
- Change Spacing Before or After Paragraphs
- Change the Vertical Alignment
- Create a Drop Cap

Software Skills In the preceding exercise you learned to adjust a paragraph horizontally; now we'll look at adjusting it vertically. You will also learn how to apply the Drop Cap effect to the first letter in a paragraph.

Application Skills In this exercise, you will replace manual extra paragraph breaks with after-paragraph spacing, and adjust the leading between lines of paragraphs for easier readability. You will also apply a drop cap and adjust the vertical alignment of a text frame.

TERMS

Drop cap A large capital letter that begins a paragraph, usually spanning multiple lines into the paragraph.

Leading The vertical spacing between the lines of a paragraph.

Vertical alignment The overall vertical positioning of text within a text frame. By default, text aligns at the top of a text frame.

NOTES

Adjust Leading

- **Leading** is the spacing between lines within a paragraph. It does not include the spacing above or below the paragraph; this is controlled elsewhere.

  ✓ *Leading is technically a character-based formatting attribute, not a paragraph-based one. However, you would rarely adjust the leading of only part of a paragraph because this would look odd.*

- Leading can be adjusted to fit text into an allotted amount of space. For example, you could increase the leading slightly to push a story to fill a small amount of empty space at the end of a page. Increasing the leading also makes a story easier to read—to a point. Extreme amounts of leading (such as over two times the font size) can actually be a detriment to readability for body text.
- To change the leading, click the Character Formatting Controls button A on the Control palette and then change the value in the Leading box.
- By default, leading is set to 120% of the font size. For example, for 30-point text, the leading is set to 36 point by default. When the measurement in the Leading box appears in parentheses, it means that it represents the default value and has not been manually changed.

Leading box with default value

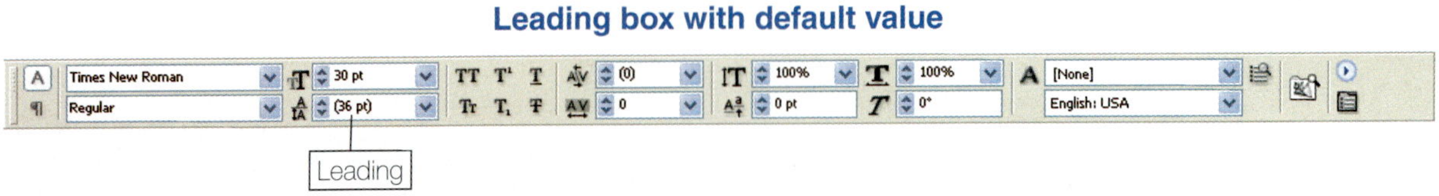

Illustration A
Justification dialog box

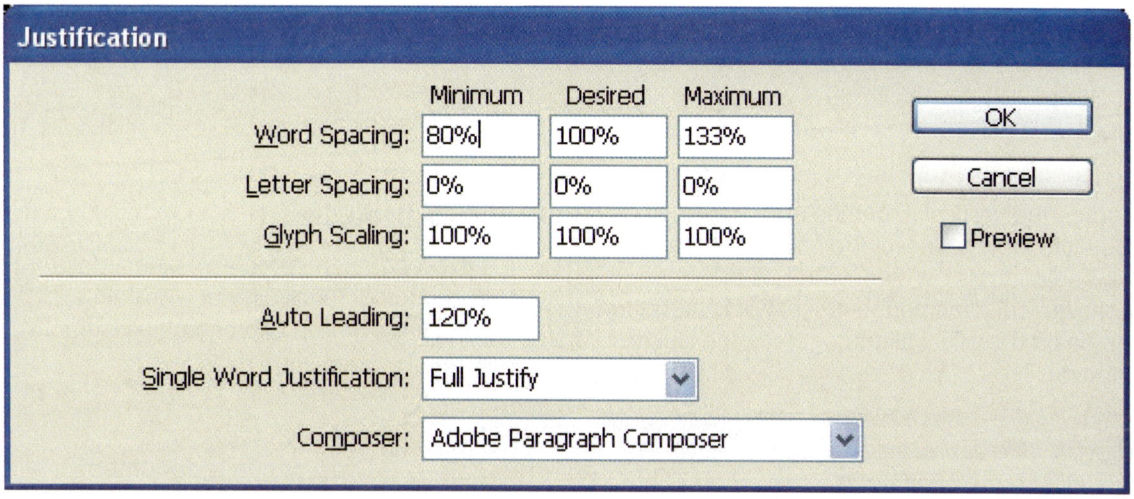

Illustration B
Spacing controls

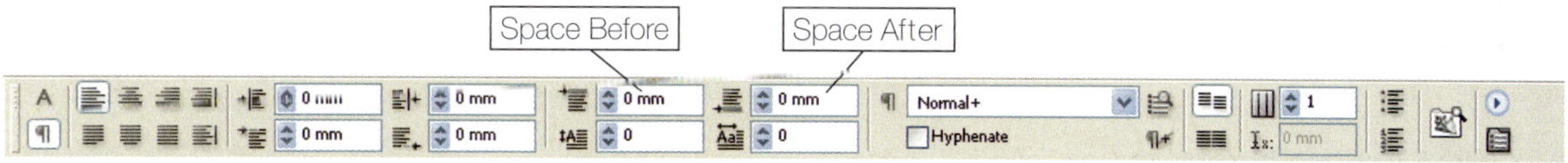

- You can change the default preferences for leading by clicking the fly-out menu for Paragraph settings on the Control palette and choosing Justification (or pressing Ctrl+Alt+Shift+J). Then in the Justification dialog box, change Auto Leading from 120% to the desired value. You can also control the limits for justification here as well (see Illustration A).

Change Spacing Before or After Paragraphs

- Spacing before or after paragraphs creates visual separation between paragraphs, which makes them easier to read.

  ✓ *If space is limited, consider using a first-line indent for each paragraph instead of space between them. You learned about indents in Exercise 22.*

- Use spacing either before or after paragraphs, but not both. This is because spacing is cumulative—if you set 12 points of space both before and after each paragraph, there will be 24 points of space in total between them. You could set 6 points both before and after, but it's less confusing to simply choose one location and stick with it.

  ✓ *Many people prefer to use spacing after each paragraph so that a heading can fit tighter against the top of the first body paragraph. Many people prefer to use spacing above a heading for the same reason—so that the spacing below does not interfere with the first paragraph of body text fitting closely with it.*

- To set spacing before or after a paragraph, click the Paragraph Formatting Controls button ¶ on the Control palette and then change the value in the Space Before or Space After box (see Illustration B).

Change the Vertical Alignment

- **Vertical alignment** applies to the entire text frame. By default the text vertically aligns at the top of the text frame, which is helpful in creating side-by-side text frames that have text top-aligned with one another. For a text frame that floats as a graphical element on the page, however, it might be better to have the text align with the center or even the bottom of the frame.

Vertical alignments

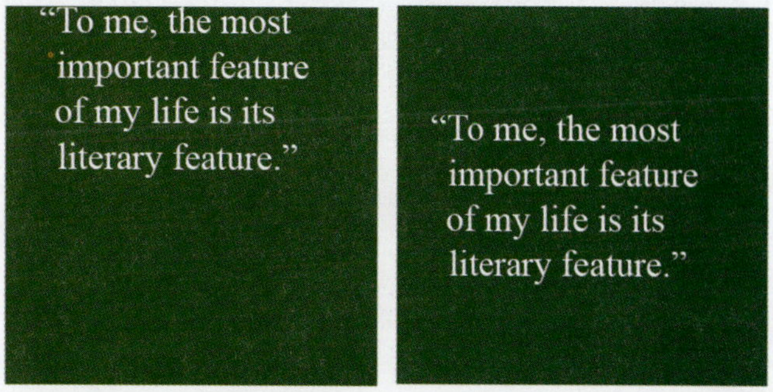

Alignment options

- To change the vertical alignment of a frame, use the Selection tool to select the outside of the frame. The controls on the Control palette change to show vertical alignment buttons. Click the button for the desired vertical alignment (see the illustration above).

  ✓ *Justify Vertically is useful when text almost fills the column completely. It can be used for minor adjustments, but should not be used to correct for a shortfall of more than one line.*

- A menu-based alternative is available, but it is more work so it is seldom used. With the frame selected, choose Object > Text Frame Options, and then change the vertical justification in the Align drop-down list.

Text Frame Options dialog box

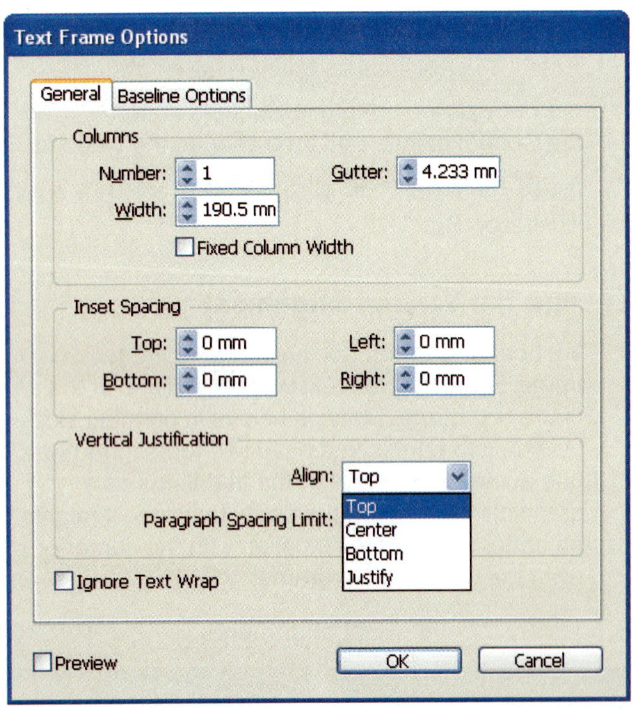

Create a Drop Cap

- A **drop cap** can serve as a visual pointer to the reader to begin reading at a certain spot. While not necessary, a drop cap can be an attractive visual element.

Drop cap in a document

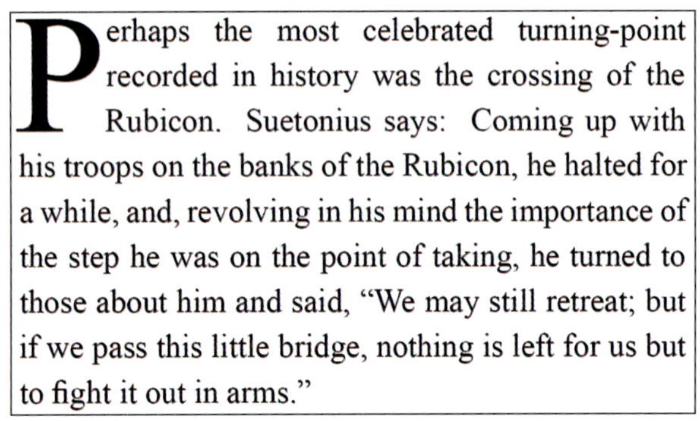
Perhaps the most celebrated turning-point recorded in history was the crossing of the Rubicon. Suetonius says: Coming up with his troops on the banks of the Rubicon, he halted for a while, and, revolving in his mind the importance of the step he was on the point of taking, he turned to those about him and said, "We may still retreat; but if we pass this little bridge, nothing is left for us but to fight it out in arms."

- It is possible to create a drop cap simply with typography, or by placing the first letter in a separate frame and allowing the other text to wrap around it. However, the Drop Cap feature provides a much easier way to create it.
- To create a drop cap for a paragraph, place the insertion point in the paragraph and then click the Paragraph Formatting Controls button on the Control palette. Open the fly-out menu and choose Drop Caps and Nested Styles. (A shortcut is Ctrl+Alt+R.)
- In the Drop Caps and Nested Styles dialog box shown on the following page, enter the number of lines (the height of the drop cap) and the number of characters (usually 1). Leave the other options alone for now, and click OK.

Drop Caps and Nested Styles dialog box

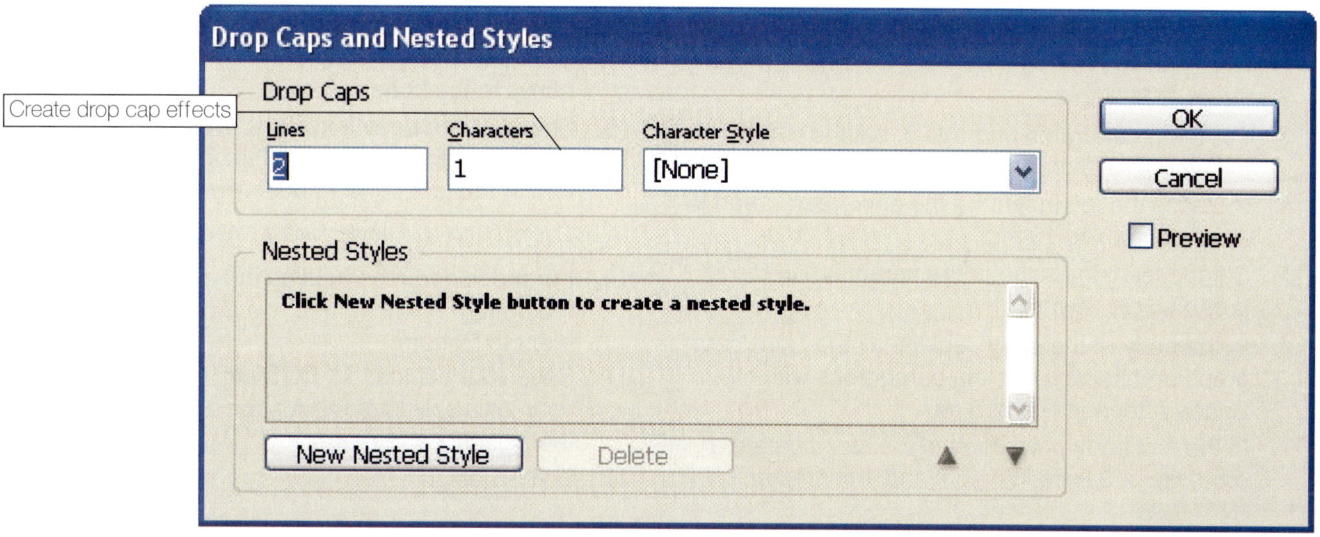

PROCEDURES

Adjust Leading

1. Select the paragraph(s) to affect.
2. If needed, display the **Character Formatting Controls** on the Control palette ....
3. Increment the **Leading** value up or down ....

   OR

   Click in the **Leading** text box and type a precise value.

Change Spacing Before or After Paragraphs

1. Select the paragraph(s) to affect.
2. If needed, display the **Paragraph Formatting Controls** on the Control palette ....
3. Increment the **Space Before** value up or down................

   OR

   Click in the **Space Before** text box and type a precise value.
4. Increment the **Space After** value up or down................

   OR

   Click in the **Space After** text box and type a precise value.

Change the Default Leading

1. If needed, display the **Paragraph Formatting Controls** on the Control palette ....
2. Open the fly-out menu for the Control palette.
3. Click **Justification**.

   ✓ *A shortcut for steps 1–3 is Alt+Ctrl+Shift+J.*
4. Change the **Auto Leading** value .... Alt + A
5. Click **OK** .... ↵Enter

Change the Vertical Alignment

Control Palette Method

1. Click the **Selection** tool.

   ✓ *If the insertion point is not currently in a text box, pressing V is a shortcut for step 1.*
2. Click the outer edge of the text frame to affect.
3. Click one of the **Vertical Alignment** buttons on the Control palette:
   - **Align Top** ....
   - **Align Center** ....
   - **Align Bottom** ....
   - **Justify Vertically** ....

Dialog Box Method

1. Click the **Selection** tool.

   ✓ *If the insertion point is not currently in a text box, pressing V is a shortcut for step 1.*
2. Click the outer edge of the text frame to affect.
3. Click **Object** .... Alt + O
4. Click **Text Frame Options** .... T
5. Select an alignment from the **Align** list .... Alt + A, ↓
6. Click **OK** .... ↵Enter

Create a Drop Cap

1. Move the insertion point into the paragraph to affect.
2. If needed, display the **Paragraph Formatting Controls** on the Control palette ....
3. Open the fly-out menu for the Control palette.
4. Click **Drop Caps and Nested Styles**.

   ✓ *A shortcut for steps 2–4 is Alt+Ctrl+R.*
5. Type a number in the **Lines** box .... Alt + L
6. Type a number in the **Characters** box .... Alt + C
7. Click **OK** .... ↵Enter

EXERCISE DIRECTIONS

1. Start Adobe InDesign.
2. Open **EX23.indd**.
3. For the green frame on page 3, set the vertical alignment to Align Center.
4. Increase the left indent for the entire paragraph in the green box to 10 mm.
5. Set the leading for the entire paragraph in the green box to 30 mm.
6. In the body of the story, replace all the extra paragraph breaks between the paragraphs with Space After spacing of 5 mm.
7. In the first body paragraph of the story, create a drop cap of 3 lines in height and 1 character.
8. On the last page, extend the lengths of the text boxes to the bottom margin.
9. Select all the body text story, and adjust the leading so that the entire story fits neatly to the bottom of the last page without any overset text.

   ✓ *It might not be a whole number that works best.*
10. For the text frames holding the page numbers at the bottom of each page, set the vertical alignment to Bottom.
11. Save your work as **XX-EX23.indd**, where XX are your initials. Illustration A shows pages 2 and 3 in the finished document.
12. Exit InDesign.

Illustration A

I

If I understand the idea, the BAZAR invites several of us to write upon the above text. It means the change in my life's course which introduced what must be regarded by me as the most IMPORTANT condition of my career. But it also implies—without intention, perhaps—that that turning-point ITSELF was the creator of the new condition. This gives it too much distinction, too much prominence, too much credit. It is only the LAST link in a very long chain of turning-points commissioned to produce the cardinal result; it is not any more important than the humblest of its ten thousand predecessors. Each of the ten thousand did its appointed share, on its appointed date, in forwarding the scheme, and they were all necessary; to have left out any one of them would have defeated the scheme and brought about SOME OTHER result. It know we have a fashion of saying "such and such an event was the turning-point in my life," but we shouldn't say it. We should merely grant that its place as LAST link in the chain makes it the most CONSPICUOUS link; in real importance it has no advantage over any one of its predecessors.

Perhaps the most celebrated turning-point recorded in history was the crossing of the Rubicon. Suetonius says: Coming up with his troops on the banks of the Rubicon, he halted for a while, and, revolving in his mind the importance of the stepp he was on the point of taking, he turned to those about him and said, "We may still retreat; but if we pass this little bridge, nothing is left for us but to fight it out in arms."

This was a stupendously important moment. And all the incidents, big and little, of Caesar's previous life had been leading up to it, stage by stage, link by link. This was the LAST link—merely the last one, and no bigger than the others; but as we gaze back at it through the inflating mists of our imagination, it looks as big as the orbit of Neptune.

You, the reader, have a PERSONAL interest in that link, and so have I; so has the rest of the human race. It was one of the links in your life-chain, and it was one of the links in mine. We may wait, now, with bated breath, while Caesar reflects. Your fate and mine are involved in his decision.

While he was thus hesitating, the following incident occurred. A person remarked for his noble mien and graceful aspect appeared close at hand, sitting and playing upon a pipe. When not only the shepherds, but a number of soldiers also, flocked to listen to him, and some trumpeters among them, he snatched a trumpet from one of them, ran to the river with it, and, sounding the advance with a piercing blast, crossed to the other side. Upon this, Caesar exclaimed: "Let us go whither the omens of the gods and the iniquity of our enemies call us. THE DIE IS CAST."

So he crossed—and changed the future of the whole human race, for all time. But that stranger was a link in Caesar's life-chain, too; and a necessary one. We don't know his name, we never hear of him again; he was very casaul; he acts like an accident; but he was no accident, he was there by compulsion of HIS life-chain, to blow the electrifying blast that was to make up Caesar's mind for him, and thence go piping down the aisles of history forever.

If the stranger hadn't been there! But he WAS. And Caesar crossed. With such results! Such vast events—each a link in the HUMAN RACE'S life-chain; each event producing the next one, and that one the next one, and so on: the destruction of the republic; the founding of the empire; the breaking up of the empire; the rise of Christianity upon its ruins; the spread of the religion to other lands—and so on; link by link took its appointed place at its appointed time, the discovery of America being one of them; our Revolution another; the inflow of English and other immigrants another; their drift westward (my ancestors among them) another; the settlement of certain of them in Missouri, which resulted in ME. For I was one of the unavoidable results of the crossing of the Rubicon. If the stranger, with his trumpet blast, had stayed away (which he

2

COULDN'T, for he was the appointed link) Caesar would not have crossed. What would have happened, in that case, we can never guess. We only know that the things that did happen would not have happened. They might have been replaced by equally prodigious things, of course, but their nature and results are beyond our guessing. But the matter that interests me personally is that I would not be HERE now, but somewhere else; and probably black—there is no telling. Very well, I am glad he crossed. And very really and thankfully glad, too, though I never cared anything about it before.

II

To me, the most important feature of my life is its literary feature. I have been professionally literary something more than forty years. There have been many turning-points in my life, but the one that was the link in the chain appointed to conduct me to the literary guild is the most CONSPICUOUS link in that chain. BECAUSE it was the last one. It was not any more important than its predecessors. All the other links have an inconspicuous look, except the crossing of the Rubicon; but as factors in making me literary they are all of the one size, the crossing of the Rubicon included.

"To me, the most important feature of my life is its literary feature."

I know how I came to be literary, and I will tell the steps that lead up to it and brought it about.

The crossing of the Rubicon was not the first one, it was hardly even a recent one; I should have to go back ages before Caesar's day to find the first one. To save space I will go back only a couple of generations and start with an incident of my boyhood. When I was twelve and a half years old, my father died. It was in the spring. The summer came, and brought with it an epidemic of measles. For a time a child died almost every day. The village was paralyzed with fright, distress, despair. Children that were not smitten with the disease were imprisoned in their homes to save them from the infection. In the homes there were no cheerful faces, there was no music, there was no singing but of solemn hymns, no voice but of prayer, no romping was allowed, no noise, no laughter, the family moved spectrally about on tiptoe, in a ghostly hush. I was a prisoner. My soul was steeped in this awful dreariness—and in fear. At some time or other every day and every night a sudden shiver shook me to the marrow, and I said to myself, "There, I've got it! and I shall die." Life on these miserable terms was not worth living, and at last I made up my mind to get the disease and have it over, one way or the other. I escaped from the house and went to the house of a neighbor where a playmate of mine was very ill with the malady. When the chance offered I crept into his room and got into bed with him. I was discovered by his mother and sent back into captivity. But I had the disease; they could not take that from me. I came near to dying. The whole village was interested, and anxious, and sent for news of me every day; and not only once a day, but several times. Everybody believed I would die; but on the fourteenth day a change came for the worse and they were disappointed.

This was a turning-point of my life. (Link number one.) For when I got well my mother closed my school career and apprenticed me to a printer. She was tired of trying to keep me out of mischief, and the adventure of the measles decided her to put me into more masterful hands than hers.

I became a printer, and began to add one link after another to the chain which was to lead me into the literary profession. A long road, but I could not know that; and as I did not know what its goal was, or even

3

ON YOUR OWN

1. Open OYO-23.indd.
2. Bottom-align the text on page 1, and vertically center the text on page 2.
3. Use all the techniques you have learned in this exercise, including leading and paragraph spacing, to make the story fit on exactly the number of pages provided in the document.
4. Vertically justify all the text frames that contain the body of the story.
5. Save your work as XX-OYO-23.indd, where XX are your initials.
6. Exit InDesign.

Exercise | 24

Skills Covered

- Avoid Widows and Orphans
- Work with Multiple Columns in a Single Frame
- Control Hyphenation
- Specify Hyphenation for Individual Words

Software Skills By controlling paragraph break behavior and adjusting hyphenation, you can often improve the layout of a story, making it easier to read and more professional-looking.

Application Skills In this exercise, you will set up a document to prevent awkward breaks of paragraphs between pages, and specify how you want the document hyphenated. You will also set up a single text frame to show its text in multiple columns.

TERMS

Gutter The space between two columns.

Orphan A single line of a paragraph appearing at the bottom of a page.

Widow A single line of a paragraph appearing at the top of a page.

NOTES

Avoid Widows and Orphans

- Sometimes when text flows from one frame to another, paragraphs break in awkward ways. Either one line is left by itself on the earlier page (an **orphan**), or one line carries over to the new page (a **widow**).

  ✓ *Not everyone agrees on the definitions of widows and orphans. Some people reverse them. This is not important, as you will never deal with them separately in page layout programs.*

- You can prevent this by controlling the paragraph's break behavior. Select the paragraphs to affect, and then open the fly-out menu for the Paragraph options on the Control palette and choose Keep Options. (A shortcut is Alt+Ctrl+K.)
- In the Keep Options dialog box, select Keep Lines Together and then specify the number of lines that should stay together at the start and end of a paragraph.

Keep Options dialog box

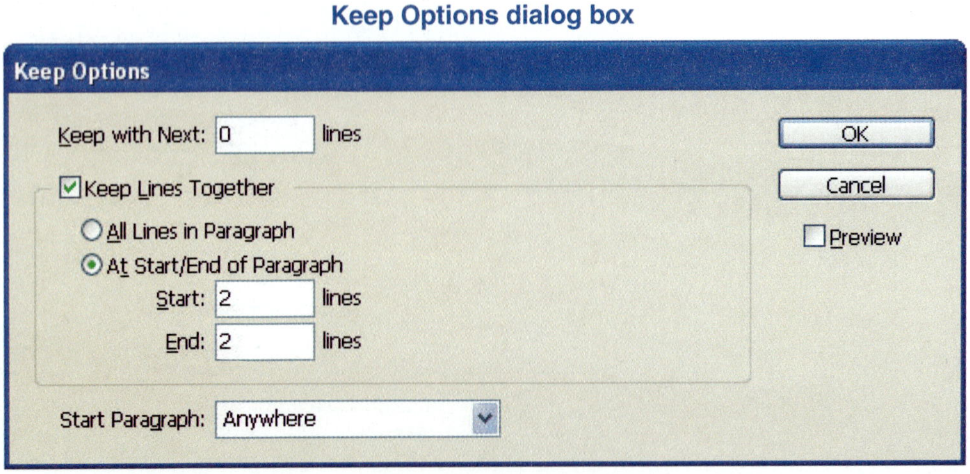

- This same dialog box can also be employed to keep all the lines of a paragraph together, not allowing it to break at all. Choose All Lines in Paragraph.
- The Start Paragraph drop-down list can be set to In Next Column, In Next Frame, or any of several other options to force the paragraph to start in a certain place. This is a specialized setting for an individual paragraph; you would not apply it to all the paragraphs in the story.

Work with Multiple Columns in a Single Frame

- So far in this course, whenever you needed multiple columns on a page, you created text frames separately for each column and then threaded them together. This method has some drawbacks. For example, when you want to change the size of the text boxes, you must resize each one individually.
- For multiple columns on the same page, many people prefer instead to set up a single text frame that has multiple columns within it. The frame can then be moved or resized as a single unit, with the columns always staying together.
- To convert a text frame to multi-column layout, select the text frame with the Selection tool and choose Object > Text Frame Options, or press Ctrl+B, or right-click the frame and choose Text Frame Options. In the dialog box that appears, increase the Number value and, if needed, adjust the **Gutter** space. You can also select the frame and change the Number of Columns setting in the Control palette (see the illustration at the top of the next column).

  ✓ *If the gutter is not the same as the gutter specified in the margin guides, your columns will not align precisely with the column guides on the screen. You might want to adjust them in the Margins and Columns dialog box, as in Exercise 5, to make them match.*

Set text frame options

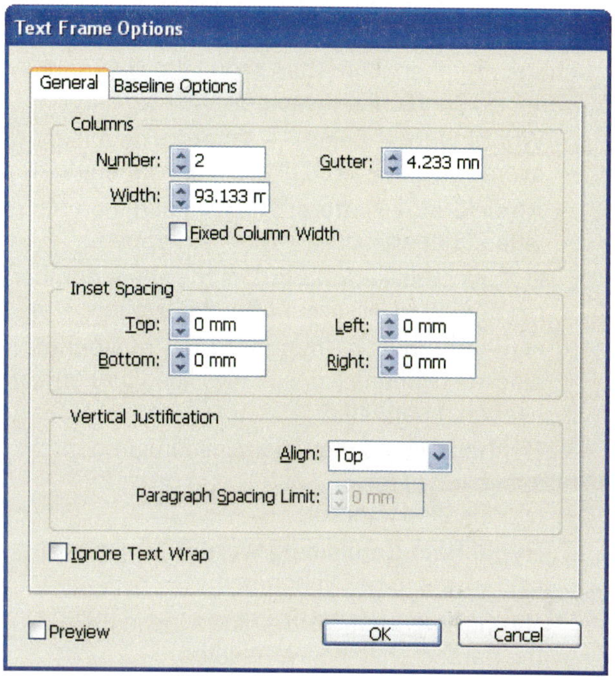

Control Hyphenation

- Hyphenation is off by default. When you enable hyphenation, InDesign hyphenates your stories automatically wherever it is possible, subject to certain rules. Hyphenation makes for more attractive lines of text when horizontal justification is in use, and it enables you to fit more text on the page.

  ✓ *If your story is short on word count and you are trying to fill a page, don't use hyphenation.*

- To turn on hyphenation, click in the story or select the paragraphs to be affected and select the Hyphenate check box in the Control palette.

Control automatic hyphenation

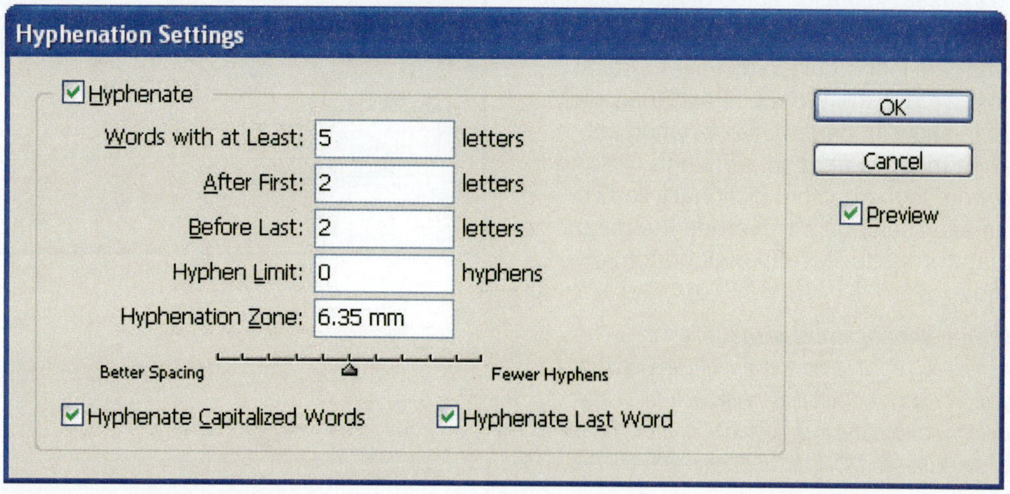

- To set the rules for hyphenation, select the paragraphs to affect and then open the fly-out menu for the Paragraph settings on the Control palette and choose Hyphenation. Then select the Hyphenate check box and change the settings as desired.
  - **Words with at Least ---- letters:** The minimum overall size of a word eligible for hyphenation.
  - **After First ---- letters:** The minimum number of letters that will occur before the hyphen.
  - **Before Last ---- letters:** The minimum number of letters that will occur after the hyphen.
  - **Hyphen Limit: ---- hyphens:** The number of stacked hyphens (consecutive lines that end in hyphens) permitted.
  - **Hyphenation Zone:** The minimum amount of space left at the end of a line in order for hyphenation to occur.
  - **Hyphenate Capitalized Words:** Allows capitalized words to be hyphenated.
  - **Hyphenate Last Word:** Allows the last word in the paragraph to be hyphenated.
- The Better Spacing/Fewer Hyphens slider in the dialog box controls how aggressively InDesign will search for places to apply hyphenation. When trying to fit as much text on the page as possible, set it toward Better Spacing. When trying to avoid hyphenation or trying to spread text out as much as possible, set it toward Fewer Hyphens.

Specify Hyphenation for Individual Words

- When you add words to the dictionary, as in Exercise 17, you can optionally specify hyphenation points for it from the Dictionary dialog box (Edit > Spelling > Dictionary).
- To specify hyphenation points, use tilde (~) signs. Enter a single tilde in your first choice of hyphenation points. You can also enter a double tilde (~~) in your second choice spot, and a triple tilde (~~~) in your third choice spot. Then click Add to add the word to the list (see illustration at top of next column).
- You can also change the hyphenation preferences for words that are in the built-in dictionary. To do this, type the word in the Word box and then click Hyphenate to show its current hyphenation settings. Change them as needed, and then click Add to add the word to the custom dictionary list. The new hyphenation settings will override the default ones for that word (see illustration at bottom of next column).

✓ *A discretionary hyphen is one that will be used in the word only if the word happens to fall at the end of a line and needs to be hyphenated. To insert a discretionary hyphen for a specific word in a story, position the insertion point in the spot where the discretionary hyphen should go and press Ctrl+Shift+-.*

Add a word to the list

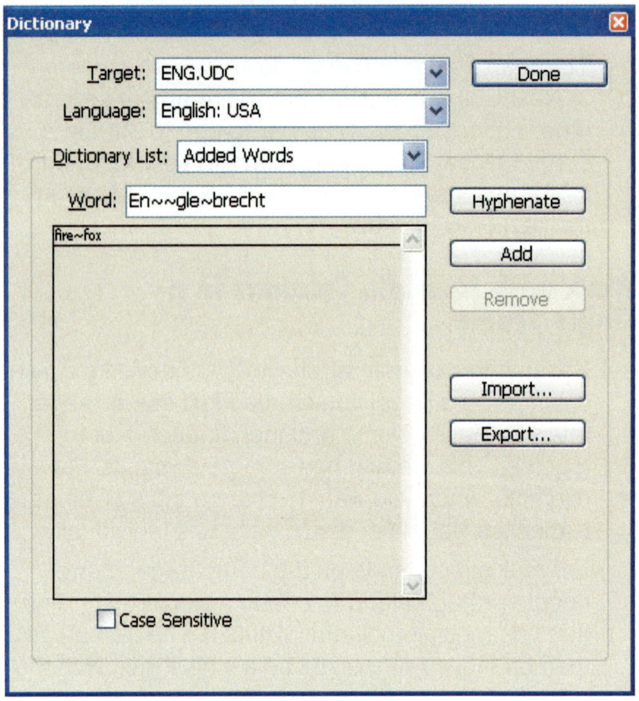

Override the defaults for a word

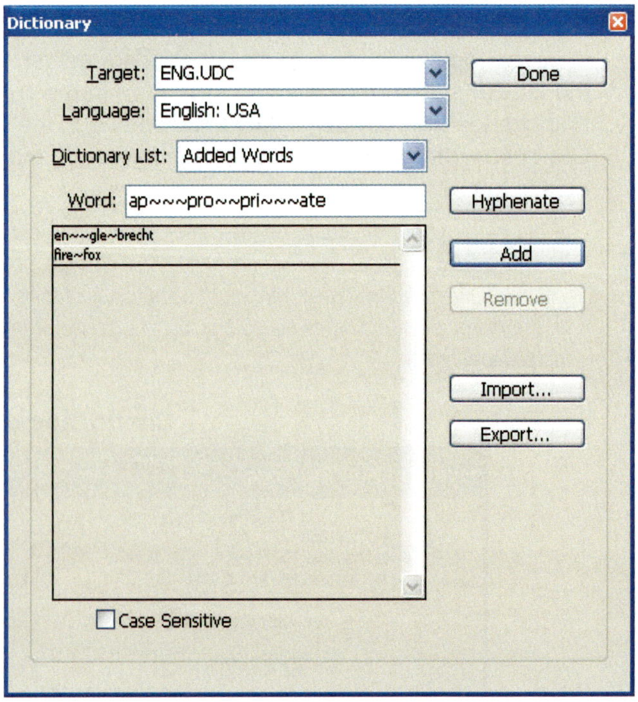

PROCEDURES

Avoid Widows and Orphans

1. Select the paragraph(s) to affect.
2. If needed, display the **Paragraph Formatting Controls** on the Control palette ....
3. Open the fly-out menu for the Control palette.
4. Click **Keep Options**.

   ✓ *A shortcut for steps 2–4 is Alt+Ctrl+K.*
5. Click **Keep Lines Together** .... Alt+L
6. Click **At Start/End of Paragraph** .... Alt+T
7. If desired, change the **Start** number of lines .... Alt+S
8. If desired, change the **End** number of lines .... Alt+E
9. Click **OK** .... Enter

Force a Paragraph to Stay Together

1. Select the paragraph(s) to affect.
2. If needed, display the **Paragraph Formatting Controls** on the Control palette ....
3. Open the fly-out menu for the Control palette.
4. Click **Keep Options**.

   ✓ *A shortcut for steps 2–4 is Alt+Ctrl+K.*
5. Click **Keep Lines Together** .... Alt+L
6. Click **All Lines in Paragraph** .... Alt+A
7. Click **OK** .... Enter

Force a Paragraph to Start on the Next Page or Column

1. Select the paragraph(s) to affect.
2. If needed, display the **Paragraph Formatting Controls** on the Control palette ....
3. Open the fly-out menu for the Control palette.
4. Click **Keep Options**.

   ✓ *A shortcut for steps 2–4 is Alt+Ctrl+K.*
5. On the **Start Paragraph** list, click one of the following options: .... Alt+G, ↓
   - **In Next Column**
   - **In Next Frame**
   - **On Next Page**
   - **On Next Odd Page**
   - **On Next Even Page**
6. Click **OK** .... Enter

Work with Multiple Columns in a Single Frame

1. Select the text frame ....
2. Click **Object** .... Alt+O
3. Click **Text Frame Options** .... T

   ✓ *Ctrl+B is a shortcut for steps 2 and 3.*
4. Change the **Number** value to 2 or more .. Alt+U, ↑ or ↓ or
5. If desired, change the **Gutter** size .... Alt+G, ↑ or ↓ or
6. Click **OK** .... Enter

Alternate Method

1. Select the text frame ....
2. Increment the value in the **Number of Columns** box on the Control palette ....

OR

Click in the **Number of Columns** box and type a number.

Control Hyphenation

Turn on Hyphenation

1. Select the paragraph(s) to affect.
2. In the Control palette, display the **Paragraph** tools if needed ....
3. Click the **Hyphenate** check box.

Turn On Hyphenation and Set Options

1. Select the paragraph(s) to affect.
2. If needed, display the **Paragraph Formatting Controls** on the Control palette ....
3. Open the fly-out menu for the Control palette.
4. Click **Hyphenation**.
5. Select the **Hyphenate** check box .... Alt+H
6. (Optional) Adjust hyphenation settings:
   - **Words with at Least --- letters** .... Alt+W
   - **After First --- letters** .... Alt+A
   - **Before Last --- letters** ... Alt+B
   - **Hyphen Limit --- hyphens** .... Alt+L
   - **Hyphenation Zone** .... Alt+Z
   - **Hyphenate Capitalized Words** .... Alt+C
   - **Hyphenate Last Word** .... Alt+S
7. (Optional) Drag the **Better Spacing/Fewer Hyphens** slider.
8. Click **OK** .... Enter

Specify Hyphenation for Individual Words

1. Click **Edit** .... Alt+E
2. Point to **Spelling**.
3. Click **Dictionary** .... Y
4. Do any of the tasks that follow these steps.
5. Click **Done** .... N

Add Hyphenation for a Word You Entered Yourself

a. Double-click a word on the list.

b. Click in the **Word** box .... Alt+W

c. Edit the word by typing a tilde (~) where hyphenation should occur.

d. (Optional) Type a double tilde (~~) in the second-choice spot for hyphenation.
e. (Optional) Type a triple tilde (~~~) in the third-choice spot for hyphenation.
f. Click **Add** ....Alt+A

Add a Word to the Custom Dictionary and Specify Its Hyphenation at the Same Time

a. Click in the **Word** box ....Alt+W
b. Type a new word to add to the dictionary, and type a tilde (~) where hyphenation should occur.
c. (Optional) Type a double tilde (~~) in the second-choice spot for hyphenation.
d. (Optional) Type a triple tilde (~~~) in the third-choice spot for hyphenation.
e. Click **Add** ....Alt+A

View Hyphenation for a Word in the Main Dictionary

a. Click in the **Word** box ....Alt+W
b. Type the word for which to view hyphenation.
c. Click **Hyphenate** ....Alt+H

Change Hyphenation for a Word in the Main Dictionary

a. Click in the **Word** box ....Alt+W
b. Type the word for which to view hyphenation.
c. Click **Hyphenate** ....Alt+H
d. Edit the word to move the tildes to adjust hyphenation preference:
   - Single tilde for first choice
   - Double tilde for second choice
   - Triple tilde for third choice
e. Click **Add** ....Alt+A

EXERCISE DIRECTIONS

1. Start Adobe InDesign.
2. Open **EX24.indd**.
3. Turn on hyphenation for the entire story. Use the default settings.
4. On each page of the main body, delete one of the text frames and expand the remaining text frame to fill the entire margin space. Then turn on a two-column layout for each text frame so that the text once again appears in two columns per page.
5. For all body paragraphs, turn on widow/orphan protection so that at least two lines stay together at both bottom and top.

   ✓ *Notice that the text no longer fits. An overset text indicator appears on page 6 in the final text frame.*
6. Select the fourth body paragraph (beginning "You, the reader") and change its leading to 15 point. This coaxes its first two lines to remain at the bottom of the first column on page 2.
7. Wherever possible, set the vertical justification of each text box to Justify Vertically, as you learned to do in Exercise 23.

   ✓ *You won't be able to do this for page 3 because of the floating green text frame that it wraps around, so skip page 3.*
8. Save your work as **XX-EX24.indd**, where XX are your initials.
9. Exit InDesign.

ON YOUR OWN

1. Open **OYO-24.indd**.
2. Set up the entire story to be in two-column text frames with 5 mm gutters.
3. Turn on automatic hyphenation and set the slider to Better Spacing.
4. Turn on widow/orphan control with the Keep options.
5. On the final page, set the vertical alignment to Top and pull up the bottom of the text frame so that the columns are balanced on the page, with an approximately equal amount of text in each.
6. On page 13 (the next-to-last page), locate the word *criminality* in the first paragraph. Notice that it is hyphenated after the final "i".
7. Using the Dictionary window, change the preferred hyphenation for this word so that it breaks *before* the final "i" instead.
8. Save your work as **XX-OYO-24.indd**, where XX are your initials.
9. Exit InDesign.

Exercise | 25

Skills Covered

- Place and Remove Tab Stops
- Apply Bullets and Numbering
- Customize a Bulleted List
- Customize a Numbered List

Software Skills Tab stops have a variety of uses, from indentation to controlling spacing in a multi-column tabular list. Bulleted and numbered lists help set off important data from the body of a story, and make lists easier to read.

Application Skills In this exercise, you will improve a report by adding bulleted and numbered lists to it and by creating tab stops to replace the default tab positions.

TERMS

Leader A repeating character between the text to the left of the tab stop and the stop itself.

Tab stop An indicator that marks where the indent should align when you press the Tab key.

Unicode A font organization method in which each character is assigned an ID number. Each font family has its own specification as to what that ID number represents. Letters and numbers are standardized across font families, but many glyph characters are not.

NOTES

Place and Remove Tab Stops

- **A tab stop** is an indicator that marks where the indent should align when you press the Tab key. InDesign's default tab stops are pre-set every $^{1}/_{2}$ inch (even if you are not using inches as your unit of measurement). One-half inch equals 12.7 millimeters.
- When you place a custom tab stop, it overrides all the default tab stops to its left. For example, suppose that you set a tab stop at 30 mm. Two default tab stops came before it (at 12.7 millimeters and 25.4 millimeters); these go away and the first tab stop appears at 30 mm.
- Tab stops are set on a paragraph basis. To set the tab stops for more than one paragraph at once, you must select all the paragraphs to affect.
- To set custom tab stops, choose Type > Tabs or press Shift+Ctrl+T. A floating Tabs palette appears showing a ruler. You'll use this ruler to place and remove custom tab stops.
- There are four types of tab stops, based on how the text aligns with the stop. Each of these corresponds with a button on the Tabs palette:
  - Left-Justified Tab (the default type); text left-aligns with it, so that the beginning of the text is at the stop.
  - Center-Justified Tab; text is centered on it, so that the center point of the text is at the stop.
  - Right-Justified Tab; text right-aligns with it, so that the end of the text is at the stop.
  - Align to Decimal (or Other Specified Character) Tab; text right-aligns with it until the decimal (or other specified character), and then left-aligns with it; the decimal stays exactly at the stop position (see illustration at the top of next page).
- To create a tab stop, click the button for the type of stop you want, and then click in the empty area above the ruler in the Tabs palette. A symbol appears there indicating the stop.

Set tabs

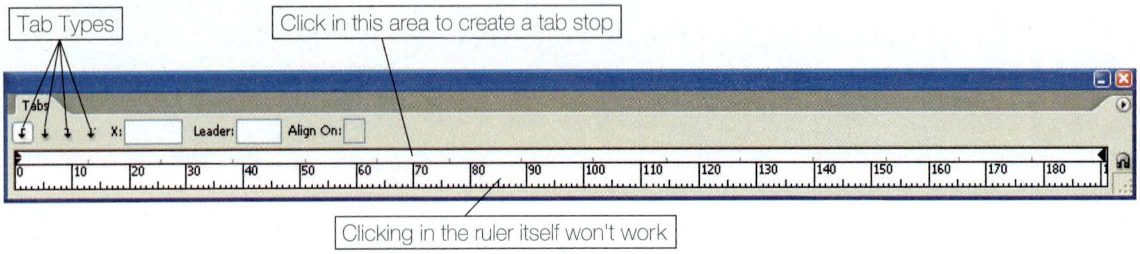

✓ *The symbol that appears on the Tabs palette for the decimal tab stop is not exactly the same as the symbol on its button face. On the button face it looks like a center tab symbol with a dot to its right, but on the ruler it looks like a center tab stop with a small rectangle at the top. All the other stop types look the same on the ruler as on their button faces.*

- To position a tab stop precisely, select the tab stop button (by clicking on it on the Tabs palette) and then enter a number in the X: text box in the Tabs palette.

Set a tab stop

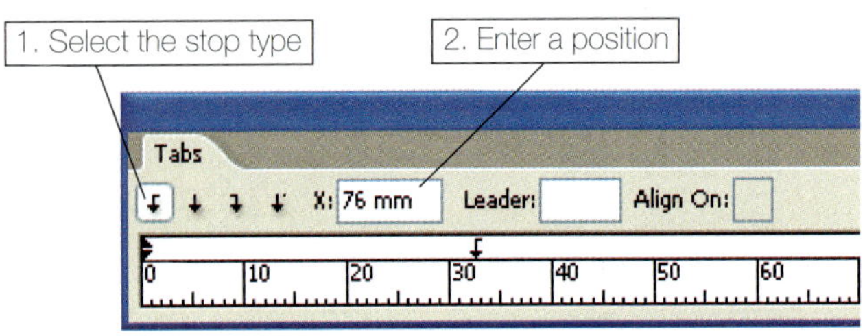

- To clear a tab stop, drag it off the Tabs palette ruler. You can clear all custom tab stops at once by opening the fly-out menu on the Tabs palette and selecting Clear All.
- A **leader** is a character that repeats between the text to the left of the tab stop and the stop itself. You can use any character for a leader by entering it in the Leader text box in the Tabs palette when the tab stop is selected. A period is the most commonly used leader character.

Tab leader

Contractor................................	Cost
Gonzalez Construction.........	$20,000
Bolls Heating and Cooling ...	$15,000
Gonzalez Construction.........	$10,000
Louks Interiors, Inc.................	$8,000

- To use a leader character, select the tab stop and enter a leader character in the Leader text box on the Tabs palette. It might appear that nothing happens; you need to press Enter or Tab, or click outside the Tabs palette, to see the leaders appear.

Create a tab leader

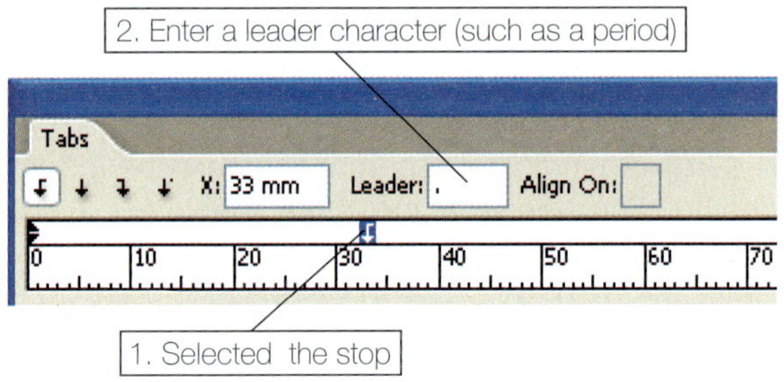

- Because the Tabs palette is floating, it is possible to move it away from the text frame so that its ruler no longer aligns correctly with the text frame. To restore the Tabs palette's positioning above the text frame, click the Position Palette above Text Frame button at the right end of the Tabs palette.

✓ *The Position Palette button above Text Frame button works only If the top of the text frame is displayed onscreen. Once you have positioned the palette in place, however, you can scroll down and the palette will remain in place.*

- Decimal tabs align by default on the decimal (the period). However, you can enter any other character you prefer in the Align On text box on the Tabs palette. This text box is available only when a Decimal tab stop is selected.

Apply Bullets and Numbering

- Numbered lists are lists wherein each paragraph begins with a consecutive number. They are typically used for lists in which the order is significant. Bulleted lists are lists wherein each paragraph begins with a glyph. They are typically used for lists in which the order is *not* significant.
- To apply a simple default bulleted or numbered list, select the text and then click the Bulleted List button or the Numbered List button on the Control palette (when Paragraph controls are displayed).
- For more choices, hold down the Alt key as you click the Bulleted List or Numbered List button to open a dialog box. Alternatively, you can open the fly-out menu for the Control palette and select Bullets and Numbering to get the same dialog box.
- From the List Type list, choose either Bullets or Numbering. Then choose customization options for the type of list you chose. The following sections describe the customization options for each.

Customize a Bulleted List

- The most important customization option for a bulleted list is the bullet character. Select the desired character from the Bullet Character area.

Choose a bullet character

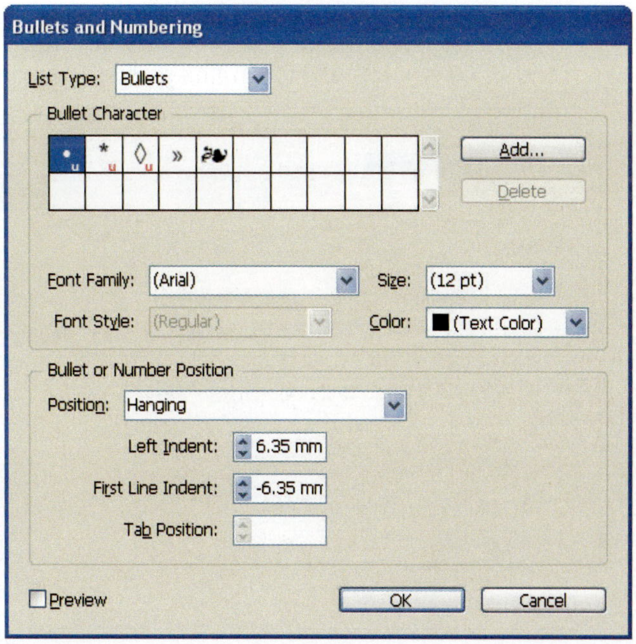

- If the bullet character you want does not appear in the grid, click Add to open a dialog box in which you can add it to the grid. In the Add Bullets dialog box, select the font family and style desired.
- If you choose a font family other than the one used by the rest of the paragraph, make sure that the Remember Font with Bullet check box is selected so that InDesign will not change the bullet character if you change the font applied to the text in that paragraph.

✓ *For some fonts the Remember Font with Bullet check box is permanently on (and unavailable for change).*

Add a custom bullet character

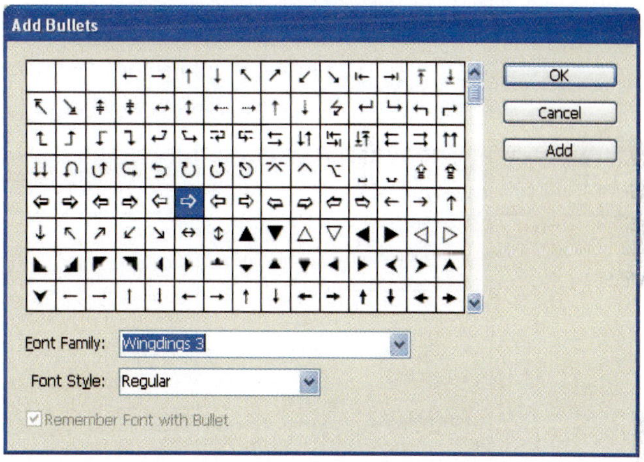

- Bullets that do not have the font remembered are represented in InDesign by a **Unicode** ID number, so that the actual character displayed changes when the font changes. Such bullets are indicated in the Bullets and Numbering dialog box by a small red U.
- For Unicode bullet characters, you can choose a different font family and font style from the drop-down lists in the Bullets and Numbering dialog box, as shown on the following page. This gives you the same Unicode character in a different font. It can be useful for trying out some subtly different versions of the same character. For example, two different fonts might have slightly different asterisks.

Change the font family on which the bullet character is based

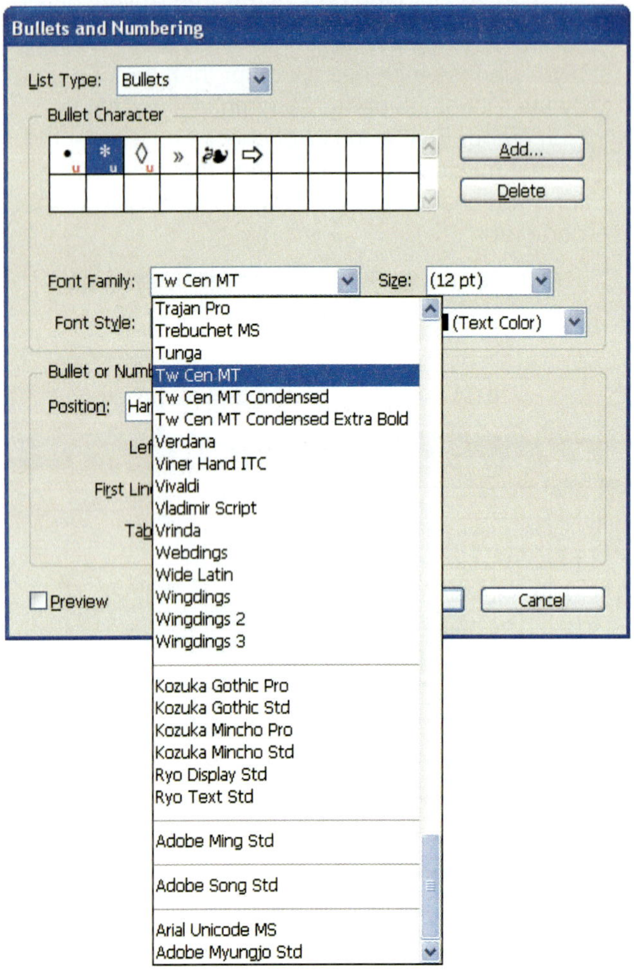

- You can also choose a size and color for the bullet character. By default these are the same as the text.
- The bullet character's position can be either Hanging or Flush Left. Hanging is the default; it places the bullet to the left of all lines of the paragraph. Flush Left places the bullet inline horizontally with the paragraph, so that subsequent lines of the paragraph begin directly under the bullet.

Hanging Indent vs. Flush Left Indent

• Hanging Indent: This paragraph has a hanging indent. The bullet is outside of all lines of the paragraph.

• Flush Left Indent: This paragraph has a flush left indent. The bullet is inline with the text.

- You can also set up a custom bullet character position by entering your own values for:
  - Left Indent: The horizontal position of all lines of the paragraph in general.
  - First Line Indent: The horizontal position of the bullet character, separate from the paragraph. Increase this value to move the bullet closer to the text.
  - Tab Position:The space following the bullet but before the text on the first line of the paragraph. This is applicable only for bullets based on the Flush Left type.

Customize a Numbered List

- Numbered list customization is much the same as for a bulleted list, in that you can choose the font family, font style, size, color, and position.
- The main difference is that there are three additional settings:
  - Style: Select a number style, such as numbers (1, 2, 3), Roman numerals (I, II, III), or letters (A, B, C). Roman numerals and letters can be uppercase or lowercase.
  - Separator: Select the character to follow the number. By default it is a period.
  - Start at: Select the number to start the list. By default it is 1.

Customize a numbered list

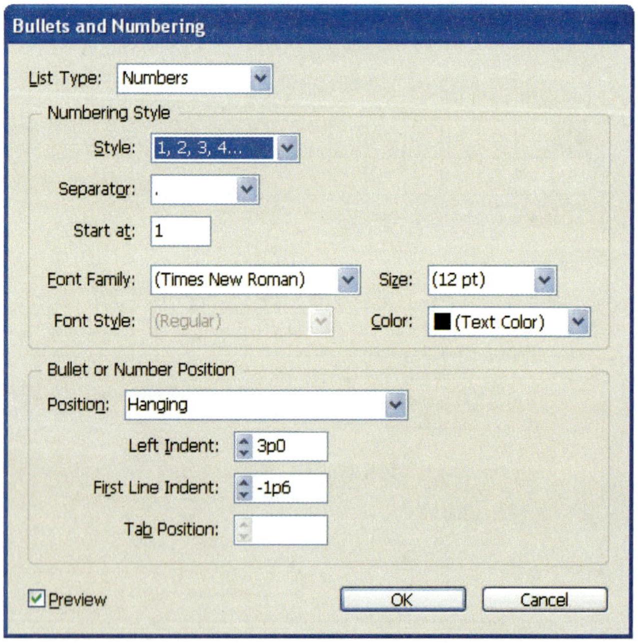

PROCEDURES

Place and Remove Tab Stops

Place a Tab Stop

1. Select the paragraph(s) to affect.
2. Click **Type** .... Alt+T
3. Click **Tabs** .... A

✓ *Ctrl+Shift+T is a shortcut for steps 2 and 3.*

4. On the Tabs palette, click the button for the desired tab stop type:
   - **Left-Justified** ....
   - **Center-Justified** ....
   - **Right-Justified** ....
   - **Decimal-Aligned** ....
5. Click in the white bar above the ruler in the Tabs palette to place the tab stop.
6. (Optional) If desired, type an exact position (in mm) in the **X** box.
7. (Optional) Type a character in the **Leader** box to create a leader.
8. (Optional) If a decimal tab, replace the decimal (.) in the **Align On** box with some other character.

Move a Tab Stop

1. Select the paragraph(s) to affect.
2. If the Tabs palette is not already displayed:
   a. Click **Type** .... Alt+T
   b. Click **Tabs** .... A
3. Drag the tab stop marker to the left or right.

OR

   a. Click the tab stop marker.
   b. Type an exact position in the **X** box.

Delete a Tab Stop

1. Select the paragraph(s) to affect.
2. If the Tabs palette is not already displayed:
   a. Click **Type** .... Alt+T
   b. Click **Tabs** .... A
3. Drag the tab stop marker off the Tabs palette and drop it.

Create a Default Bulleted List

1. Select the paragraph(s) to affect.
2. If needed, display the **Paragraph Formatting Controls** on the Control palette ....
3. Click the **Bulleted List** button ....

Create a Default Numbered List

1. Select the paragraph(s) to affect.
2. If needed, display the **Paragraph Formatting Controls** on the Control palette .....
3. Click the **Numbered List** button ....

Create a Custom Bulleted List

1. Select the paragraph(s) to affect.
2. If needed, display the **Paragraph Formatting Controls** on the Control palette .....
3. Hold down **Alt** and click the **Bulleted List** button .... Alt+

OR

   a. Open the fly-out menu for the Control palette.
   b. Click **Bullets and Numbering**.
4. If needed, open the **List Type** list and choose **Bullets** .... Alt+L, ↓
5. Click the desired bullet character if it appears.

OR

Select a different bullet character as in the steps for "Add a Bullet Character" following this section.

6. Open the **Font Family** list and select a font family .... Alt+F, ↓ or ↑
7. Open the **Font Style** list (if available) and select a font style .... Alt+Y, ↓ or ↑
8. Open the **Size** list and select a size .... Alt+Z, ↓ or ↑
9. Open the **Color** list and select a color .... Alt+C, ↓
10. Open the **Position** list and select a position .... Alt+N, ↓ or ↑
11. (Optional) If you want to customize the position, increment the values for:
    - **Left Indent** .... Alt+I or ↑ or ↓
    - **First Line Indent** .... Alt+R, or ↑ or ↓
    - **Tab Position** .... Alt+B, or ↑ or ↓
12. Click **OK** .... ↵Enter

Add a Bullet Character

✓ *From the Bullets and Numbering dialog box, with List Type set to Bullets:*

1. Click the **Add** button .... Alt+A
2. Select a **Font Family** .... Alt+F, ↑ or ↓
3. Select a **Font Style** ... Alt+Y, ↓
4. Click the desired character.
5. (Optional) Click **Remember Font with Bullet** .... Alt+R
6. Click **Add** .... Alt+A
7. Click **OK** .... ↵Enter

Create a Custom Numbered List

1. Select the paragraph(s) to affect.
2. If needed, display the **Paragraph Formatting Controls** on the Control palette ....
3. Hold down **Alt** and click the **Numbered List** button .... Alt+

OR

   a. Open the fly-out menu for the Control palette.
   b. Click **Bullets and Numbering**.
4. If needed, open the **List Type** list and choose **Numbers** .... Alt+L, ↓

5. Open the **Style** list and select a number style .... Alt+S, ↓
6. Open the **Separator** list and select a separator .... Alt+O, ↓
7. (Optional) Type a different value in the **Start at** box .... Alt+T
8. Open the **Font Family** list and select a font family .... Alt+F, ↓ or ↑
9. Open the **Font Style** list (if available) and select a font style. .... Alt+Y, ↓ or ↑
10. Open the **Size** list and select a size. .... Alt+Z, ↓ or ↑
11. Open the **Color** list and select a color .... Alt+C, ↓
12. Open the **Position** list and select a position ...... Alt+N, ↓ or ↑
13. (Optional) If you want to customize the position, increment the values for:
    - **Left Indent** .... Alt+I, ⬍ or ↑ or ↓
    - **First Line Indent** .... Alt+R, ⬍ or ↑ or ↓
    - **Tab Position** .... Alt+B, ⬍ or ↑ or ↓
14. Click **OK** .... ↵Enter

EXERCISE DIRECTIONS

1. Start Adobe InDesign.
2. Open **EX25.indd.**
3. Convert the list of phases (Fund-raising, Planning, etc.) to a numbered list that uses uppercase letters in Arial Black 11-point font, with each of the letters colored red (C=15 M=100 Y=100 K=0), and with a custom Left Indent of 7 mm.
4. Convert the list of repairs (Roof repair, Furnace replacement, etc.) to a bulleted list that uses a right-pointing arrow glyph from the Wingdings font family, and has a custom Left Indent of 7 mm.
5. Apply custom tab stops to the last 5 lines of the document:
    - Left tab stop at 30 mm
    - Left tab stop at 75 mm
    - Right tab stop at 145 mm
    - Decimal tab stop at 170 mm
6. For the last four lines only, add a dot leader (period) to the tab stop at 145 mm.
7. Save your work as **XX-EX25.indd**, where XX are your initials. The final document should resemble Illustration A (shown at the top of page 129).
8. Exit InDesign.

ON YOUR OWN

1. Open **OYO-25.indd**.
2. In the Fire Extinguisher Guidelines section make the first three items into a bulleted list. Indent the bullet character 8 mm.
3. For the fire extinguisher classes, create a separate bulleted list that is subordinate to (indented more than) the bullet point above it. Use a different bullet character.
4. In the Emergency Exit Guidelines, create a bulleted list that uses a bullet character from the Marlett font family.
5. In the Evacuation Procedures section, create a numbered list from the first three lines.
6. For the last five lines in the Evacuation Procedures section, create tab stops as follows:
    - Left stop at 50 mm.
    - Decimal stop at 120, but use **x** rather than a period as the Align On character.
7. For the last four lines in the Evacuation Procedures section, add dot leaders to both of the custom tab stops.
8. For the two procedures in the First Aid Procedures section, create two separate numbered lists using uppercase Roman numerals. Apply different colors to each list.
9. Save your work as **XX-OYO-25.indd**, where XX are your initials.
10. Exit InDesign.

Illustration A

THE MILLENNIUM FUND
CAPITAL CAMPAIGN REPORT

Thank you for being part of the Millennium Fund Capital Campaign for the Youth Center of Central Michigan! By investing in the upkeep of our facility, you are helping ensure that future generations of youth will continue to benefit from Center programs.

The Campaign process consists of these phases:

- **A.** Fund-raising
- **B.** Planning
- **C.** Bids
- **D.** Contractor selection
- **E. Repairs - Current Phase**
- **F.** Evaluation

Thanks to your generous donations, the renovation process will include these repairs:

- ➔ Roof repair
- ➔ Furnace replacement
- ➔ Masonry repair
- ➔ Interior painting

Contractors will begin working according to the following schedule.

Date	Event	Contractor	Cost	Days
August 1	Roof repairs	Gonzalez Construction	$20,000	4
August 15	Furnace replacement	Bolls Heating and Cooling	$15,000	1.5
August 20	Masonry repairs	Gonzalez Construction	$10,000	5
September 16	Interior painting	Louks Interiors, Inc.	$8,000	6.5

Exercise | 26

Skills Covered

- Create a Table
- Convert Text to a Table
- Select Parts of a Table
- Insert and Delete Rows and Columns
- Adjust Cell Heights and Widths
- Merge and Split Cells

Software Skills Creating a table with tab stops, as in Exercise 25, is often not optimal if the entries in each column are more than a few words long. It is easier to use the Table feature in InDesign to create real tables that are more professional-looking and more flexible in terms of design and layout.

Application Skills In this exercise, you will convert a tabbed list to a table, modify the table's structure, and adjust its height and width. You will create a new blank row at the top, and merge it into a single cell to be used as a title area.

TERMS

Cell The box formed by the intersection of a row and a column in a table.

Delimited text Text in which each line has been separated into more than one column using a consistent character such as a Tab or comma. Only delimited text can be converted into a multi-column table with InDesign's Convert Text to Table feature.

NOTES

Create a Table

- A table is a grid of **cells** into which you can type text, much like in a spreadsheet program such as Excel. Each cell is like a mini-frame, and can have its own separate settings for alignment, indentation, background, and so on.
- A table resides within a text frame. First you create the text frame, and then you create the table.

  ✓ *The table does not have to be the only thing in the text frame; the frame also can include regular text. However, if you want to use the table as a graphical element, placing it in its own frame makes layout easier.*

- To create a table, place the insertion point in a text frame and then choose Table > Insert Table or press Alt+Shift+Ctrl+T. In the Insert Table dialog box, enter the number of rows and columns desired.

  ✓ *You can specify header and footer rows as well as body rows. Header and footer rows can be formatted differently from body rows for special situations such as placing headings in the top row or totals in the bottom row.*

Create a table

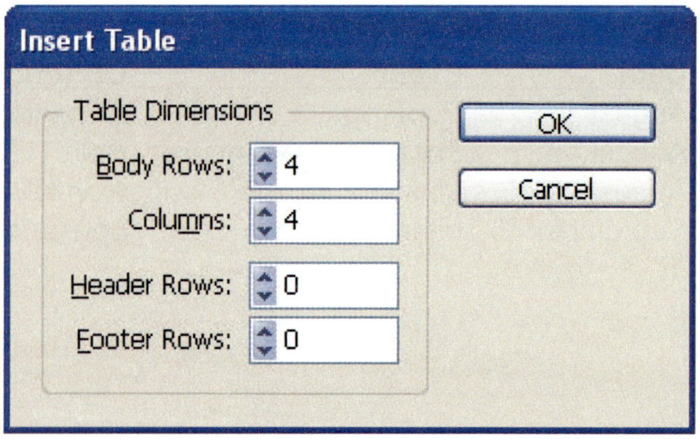

Convert Text to a Table

- If you have already created a table-like structure with tab stops, as in Exercise 25, you can easily convert it to a table. Select the entire block of text and choose Table > Convert Text to Table.

  ✓ *Text that is separated into multiple columns and rows using typographical symbols such as the Tab character and* *paragraph breaks is known as **delimited text**. For text to be successfully converted into a table that has multiple columns, it must be delimited consistently—that is, the columns must be separated using a consistent character. This is most often a Tab character, but it could be any character.*

- In the Convert Text to Table dialog box, indicate what you have used for the column separator character (probably Tab) and what you have used for the row separator (probably Paragraph).

✓ *You can use Type > Show Hidden Characters to see where the tabs are.*

Create a table from existing text

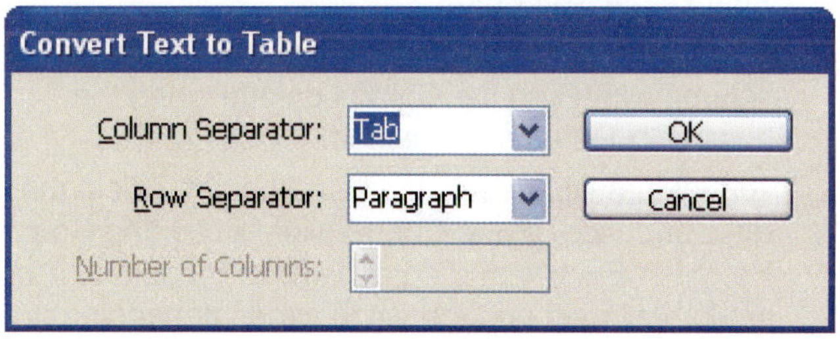

✓ *When you convert from a tabbed list to a table, any alignments from the tab stops (right, center, decimal) are lost and all cells default to left alignment.*

Select Parts of a Table

- To apply some types of formatting, you will need to select the cells, rows, or columns to affect first.
- Selecting the text in a cell is *not* the same as selecting the cell itself. When the cell itself is selected, the entire cell appears with a black background and white type.

Text selected in a cell vs. cell selected

- To select a single cell, right-click the cell and choose Select > Cell, or press Ctrl+/.
- To select multiple cells, drag across them.
- To select a row, position the mouse pointer to the left of it, so the pointer turns into a black arrow →, and then click, or drag up or down to select multiple rows. You can also press Ctrl+3, or right-click any cell in row and choose Select > Row.
- To select a column, position the mouse pointer above it, so the pointer turns into a black arrow ↓, and then click, or drag to the right or left to select multiple columns. You can also press Alt+Ctrl+3, or right-click any cell in the column and choose Select > Column.
- To select the entire table, click anywhere within it and choose Table > Select > Table or press Alt+Ctrl+A. You can also right-click any cell in the table and choose Select > Table.

Insert and Delete Rows and Columns

- To add a new row at the bottom of the table, position the insertion point in the bottom right cell and press Tab.
- To add a new row anywhere else in the table, click in a row adjacent to where you want to insert, and then choose Table > Insert > Row, or press Ctrl+9. In the dialog box that appears, choose the number of new rows (the default is 1) and whether they should be placed above or below the current row.

Insert table rows

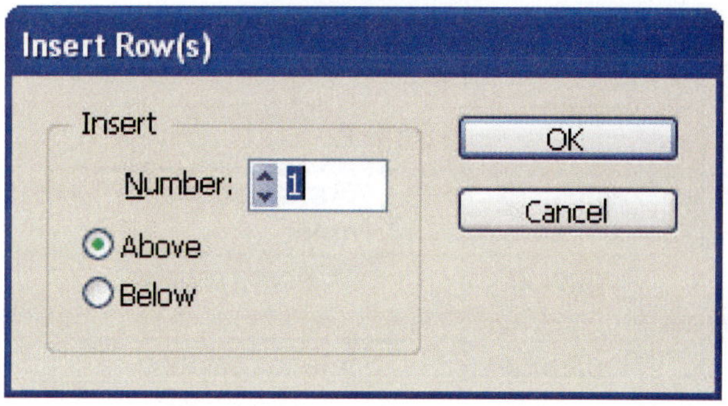

- The procedure for inserting a column is the same, except you choose Table > Insert > Column or press Alt+Ctrl+9 and you choose whether to place the new column(s) to the left or right.
- To delete a row or column, click in the row or column to delete, or select multiple rows or columns to delete, and then choose Table > Delete > Row or Table > Delete > Column.

✓ *Shortcuts are Ctrl+backspace to delete a row and Shift+backspace to delete a column.*

- To delete the entire table, choose Table > Delete > Table.
- When at least one cell is selected, the Table controls appear on the Control palette, and they include boxes where you can specify the numbers of rows and columns. To delete the bottommost (or rightmost) rows or columns, decrease the number. To add more rows or columns to the bottom or to the right, increase the number (see the illustration at the top of next page).

Change table properties from the Control palette

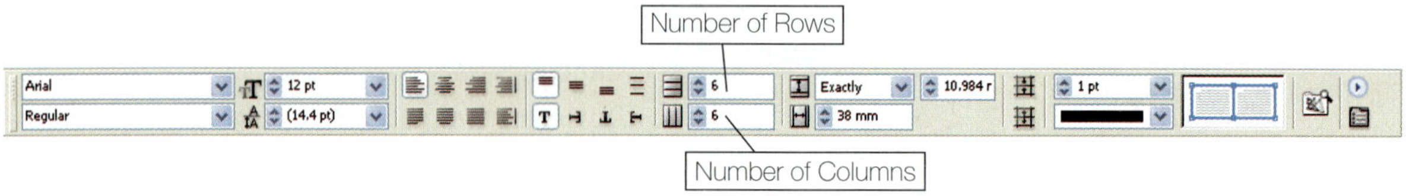

✓ *There is also a Table palette, which contains the same controls that appear on the Control palette plus a few extras. Display it with Window > Type & Tables > Table or by pressing Shift+F9.*

Adjust Cell Heights and Widths

- To change the row height, position the mouse pointer at the bottom of the row and drag. To change the column width, position the mouse pointer on the right border of the column and drag. The mouse pointer shows as a double-headed arrow.

Change column width

Date	Event
August 1	Roof repairs
August 15	Furnace replace-ment
August 20	Masonry repairs
September 16	Interior painting

- To change the row height, position the mouse pointer at the bottom of the row and drag. The overall height of the entire table changes.
- To change the column width, position the mouse pointer on the right border of the column and drag. The mouse pointer shows as a double-headed arrow.
- As you change row and column size, the overall dimension of the entire table also changes. To keep the overall size of the table static and adjust only the divider you are dragging, hold down the Shift key as you drag.
- An alternative method is to enter row heights or column widths on the Control palette when the rows or columns are selected.
- To make multiple rows the same height, select the rows and then, in the Control palette, set the Row Height to Exactly and enter a value. By default it is set for At Least and the value varies depending on the amount of text entered in the cell.

✓ *If you set an exact value for a row's height and then add more text to the cell so that it wraps to more lines, some of the text might be truncated.*

- To resize the entire table proportionally, hold down the Shift key and drag the bottom or right border of the table.

Merge and Split Cells

- To merge two or more cells, select them and click the Merge Cells button on the Control palette.
- To unmerge a cell that has previously been merged, select it and click the Unmerge Cells button on the Control palette (see illustration below).
- To split a cell that has not previously been merged, choose Table > Split Cell Vertically or Table > Split Cell Horizontally.

Merge and unmerge cells

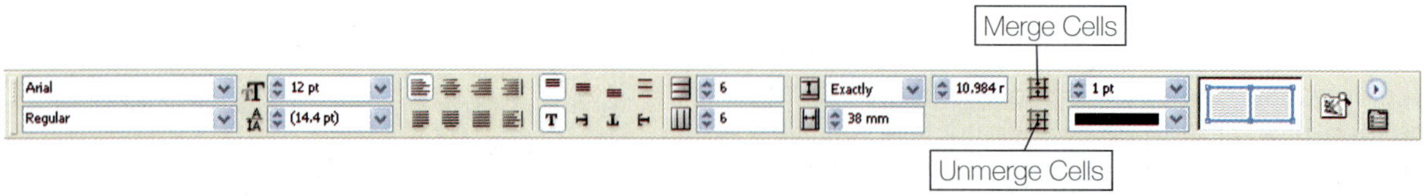

PROCEDURES

Create a Table

1. Position the insertion point in the text frame to contain the table.
2. Click **Table** .... Alt + A
3. Click **Insert Table** .... T

   ✓ *A shortcut for steps 2 and 3 is Alt+Shift+Ctrl+T.*

4. Enter a number of **Body Rows** .... Alt + B, ⬍ or ↑ or ↓
5. Enter a number of **Columns** .... Alt + M, ⬍ or ↑ or ↓
6. (Optional) If desired, enter a number of **Header Rows** .... Alt + H, ⬍ or ↑ or ↓
7. (Optional) If desired, enter a number of **Footer Rows** .... Alt + F, ⬍ or ↑ or ↓
8. Click **OK** .... ↵Enter

Convert Text to a Table

1. Select the delimited text.
2. Click **Table** .... Alt + A
3. Click **Convert Text to Table** C
4. If needed, change the **Column Separator** character .... Alt + C, ↓
5. If needed, change the **Row Separator** character .... Alt + R, ↓
6. Click **OK** .... ↵Enter

Select Parts of a Table

Select a Cell

1. Click in the cell to move the insertion point into it.
2. Click **Table** .... Alt + A

   ✓ *You can right-click the cell instead of step 2. However, the Alt+S key combination does not work for step 3 in that event; you would need to use the mouse for step 3.*

3. Point to **Select** .... Alt + S
4. Click **Cell** .... E

   ✓ *You can press Ctrl+/ as a shortcut for steps 2–4.*

Select Multiple Cells

1. Drag across contiguous cells.

   ✓ *You cannot select multiple non-contiguous cells.*

Select a Row

1. Position the mouse pointer to the left of the row, so the mouse pointer becomes an arrow ➜.
2. Click.

Select Multiple Rows

1. Select a single row (see above).
2. Hold down the mouse button and drag across additional rows.

OR

Hold down the Shift key and select additional contiguous rows.

Select a Column

1. Position the mouse pointer above the row, so the mouse pointer becomes an arrow ⬇.
2. Click.

Select Multiple Columns

1. Select a single column (see above).
2. Hold down the mouse button and drag across additional columns.

OR

Hold down the Shift key and select additional contiguous columns.

Select All Body Rows

1. Click in a cell to move the insertion point into it.
2. Click **Table** .... Alt + A

   ✓ *You can right-click the cell instead of step 2. However, the Alt+S key combination does not work for step 3 in that event; you would need to use the mouse for step 3.*

3. Point to **Select** .... Alt + S
4. Click **Body Rows** .... B

Select the Entire Table

1. Click in a cell to move the insertion point into it.
2. Click **Table** .... Alt + A

   ✓ *You can right-click the cell instead of step 2. However, the Alt+S key combination does not work for step 3 in that event; you would need to use the mouse for step 3.*

3. Point to **Select** .... Alt + S
4. Click **Table** .... A

   ✓ *You can press Ctrl+Alt+A instead of steps 2–4.*

Insert and Delete Rows and Columns

Insert Columns

1. Click in a cell adjacent to where you want to insert.
2. Click **Table** .... Alt + A

   ✓ *You can right-click the cell instead of step 2.*

3. Point to **Insert** I
4. Click **Row** .... R

   ✓ *You can press Ctrl+9 instead of steps 2–4.*

5. (Optional) If you want more than one row, increment the value in the **Number** box .... ⬍ or Alt + N, ↑
6. Click **Above** or **Below** .... Alt + A or Alt + B
7. Click **OK** .... ↵Enter

Insert Rows

1. Click in a cell adjacent to where you want to insert.
2. Click **Table** .... Alt + A

   ✓ *You can right-click the cell instead of step 2.*

3. Point to **Insert** I
4. Click **Column** C

   ✓ *You can press Alt+Ctrl+9 instead of steps 2–4.*

5. (Optional) If you want more than one column, increment the value in the **Number** box .... ⬍ or Alt + N, ↑

6. Click **Left** or **Right** ....Alt+L or Alt+R
7. Click **OK** ....Enter

Delete Columns

1. Select the column(s) to delete.
2. Click **Table** ....Alt+A

   ✓ *You can right-click the cell instead of step 2.*
3. Point to **Delete** ....D
4. Click **Column** C

   ✓ *You can press Shift+Backspace instead of steps 2–4.*

Delete a Row

1. Select the column(s) to delete.
2. Click **Table** ....Alt+A

   ✓ *You can right-click the cell instead of step 2.*
3. Point to **Delete** ....D
4. Click **Row** ....R

   ✓ *You can press Ctrl+Backspace instead of steps 2–4.*

Delete a Table

1. Click anywhere within the table.
2. Click **Table** ....Alt+A

   ✓ *You can right-click the cell instead of step 2.*
3. Point to **Delete** ....D
4. Click **Table** ....A

Adjust Cell Heights and Widths

Control Palette Method

1. Select the row(s) or column(s) to adjust.
2. (Optional) If you want an exact row height, open the **Row Height** list and choose **Exactly** ....
3. Click the **Row Height** increment arrows ....

   OR

   Click the **Column Width** increment arrows ....

Drag-and-Drop Method

1. Position the mouse pointer between two rows or columns.
2. (Optional) Hold down **Shift** if you want the overall size of the table to remain static ....Shift
3. Drag the divider to change its position.

Merge Cells

1. Select the cells to merge.
2. Click the **Merge Cells** button on the Control palette ....

Unmerge a Merged Cell

1. Select the merged cell.
2. Click the **Unmerge Cells** button on the Control palette ....

Split a Cell

1. Select the cell to split.
2. Click **Table** ....Alt+A
3. Click **Split Cell Vertically** V

   OR

   Click **Split Cell Horizontally** ....Z

EXERCISE DIRECTIONS

1. Start Adobe InDesign.
2. Open **EX26.indd**.
3. Convert the tabbed text at the bottom of the document into a table.
4. Insert a new row above the first row, and merge all the cells in it into a single large cell.
5. In that single cell at the top, type **Schedule** and center it horizontally. Remove the underline on it, and increase its size to 18 points.
6. Decrease the widths of the columns as much as possible while still allowing all text to fit in a single line per row.
7. Save your work as **XX-EX26.indd**, where XX are your initials. The final table should resemble Illustration A.
8. Exit InDesign.

Illustration A

Schedule				
Date	Event	Contractor	Cost	Days
August 1	Roof repairs	Gonzalez Construction	$20,000	4
August 15	Furnace replacement	Bolls Heating and Cooling	$15,000	1.5
August 20	Masonry repairs	Gonzalez Construction	$10,000	5
September 16	Interior painting	Louks Interiors, Inc.	$8,000	6.5

ON YOUR OWN

1. Open **OYO-26.indd**.
2. Convert the tabbed columns to a table.
3. Add a new row between Accounting and Personnel, and in it enter **Operations**, **Nancy Colvin**, **555-1414**.
4. Add a new column between Section and Captain, and title its heading **Building**. For each person except Margaret Li, enter **A** as the building. For Margaret Li, enter **B** as the building.
5. Resize the table columns so that the entire table fits within the page margins.
6. Save your work as **XX-OYO-26.indd**, where XX are your initials.
7. Exit InDesign.

Exercise | 27

Skills Covered

- Apply Table Strokes
- Apply a Table Fill
- Align Text in a Cell
- Rotate Text in a Cell

Software Skills A table shares some attributes in common with both paragraphs and text frames, and has a few unique attributes of its own as well. You can apply strokes and fills to a table as with a text frame, align text as with a paragraph, and apply other formatting that is applicable specifically to tables.

Application Skills In this exercise, you will improve the appearance of a table by working with its stroke, fill, alignment, and text rotation.

TERMS

Inner stroke A stroke that separates one cell from another in a multi-cell selection.

Outer stroke A stroke that separates the edge of the table or selected area from the rest of the text in the frame or the cells outside the selected area.

NOTES

Apply Table Strokes

- By default in a table, each cell is outlined with a 1-point plain black stroke. You can change the stroke weight, style, and color, just as with a text frame.
- When more than one cell is selected, there are **inner strokes** and **outer strokes**. The inner strokes are strokes that separate the cells from one another. The outer strokes are strokes around the outside of the selected area.

Apply table strokes

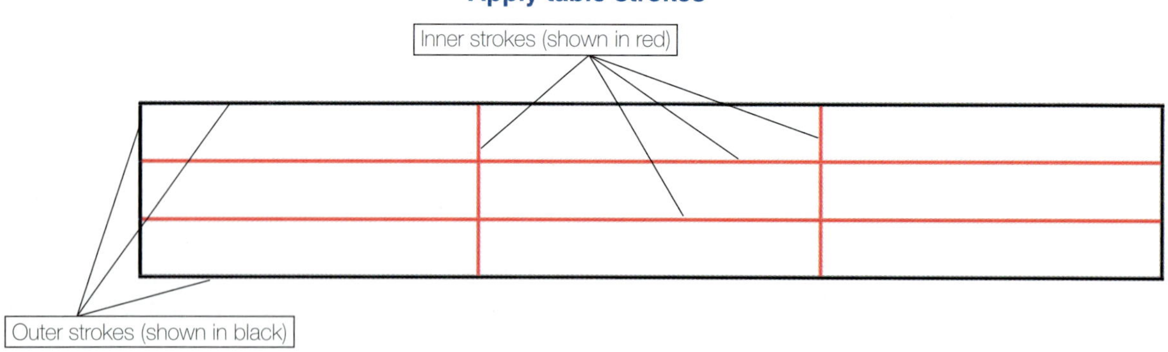

- To affect the stroke for certain cells in a table, select those cells. (You can select the entire table if you want the entire table to be affected.)
- Next, indicate which stroke(s) of the selected area you want to format. The Control palette contains a table grid that shows the inner and outer strokes for the selected area. By default, each stroke in this grid is blue, indicating it is On. To turn a stroke off, click it.

Selected and unselected strokes

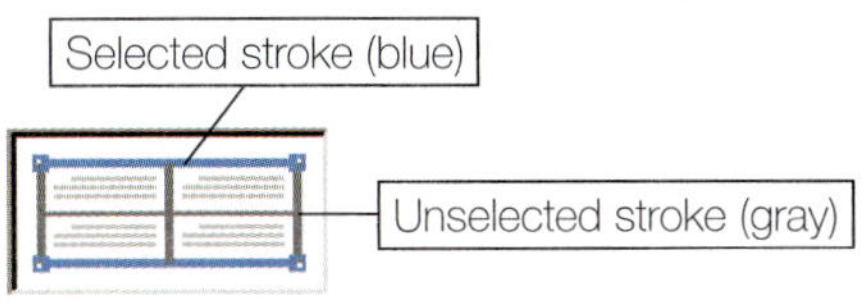

- After choosing which strokes within the table to affect, apply formatting to them.
- You can select a color from the Color palette or a swatch from the Swatches palette.
- To change the stroke style, use the Stroke Type drop-down list in the Control palette.
- To change the stroke thickness, increment the Stroke Weight value in the Control palette or open its list and choose a value.

Choose a stroke weight and type

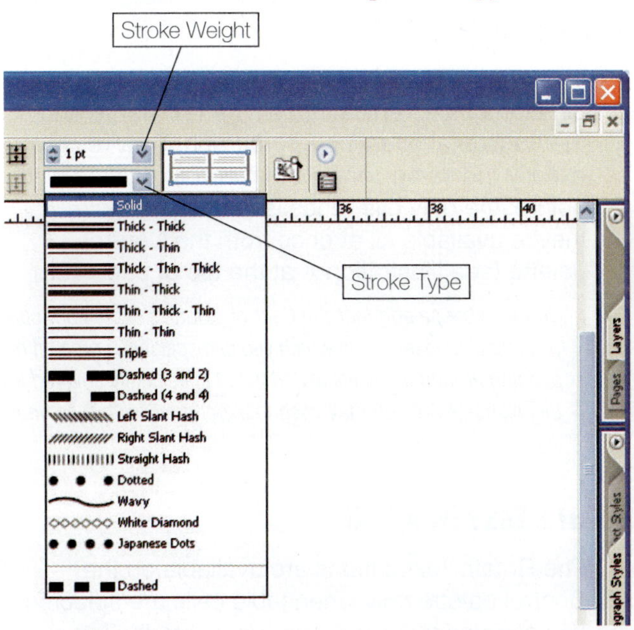

- If you find the grid on the Control palette difficult to see because it is so small, you might prefer to use a dialog box instead. For the same controls in a dialog box format, choose Table > Cell Options > Strokes and Fills. Then on the Strokes and Fills tab, select/deselect strokes on a larger-sized grid and set the formatting options for the stroke.

Set stroke options

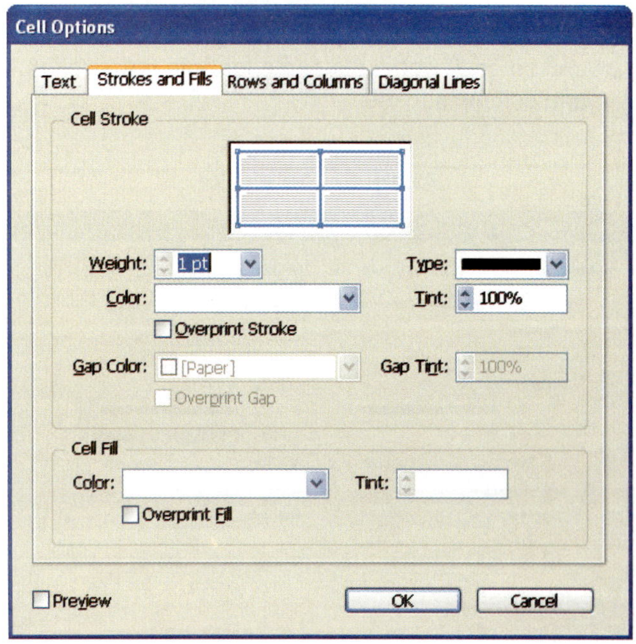

- An alternate way to change only the outside border of a table is as follows: Select the entire table (or click in any cell in the table) and then choose Table > Table Options > Table Setup or press Ctrl+Alt+Shift+B. Then in the Table Border area of the dialog box, specify the border. This setting will affect the outside border only; the inner strokes will not be affected.

Set stroke options for the table

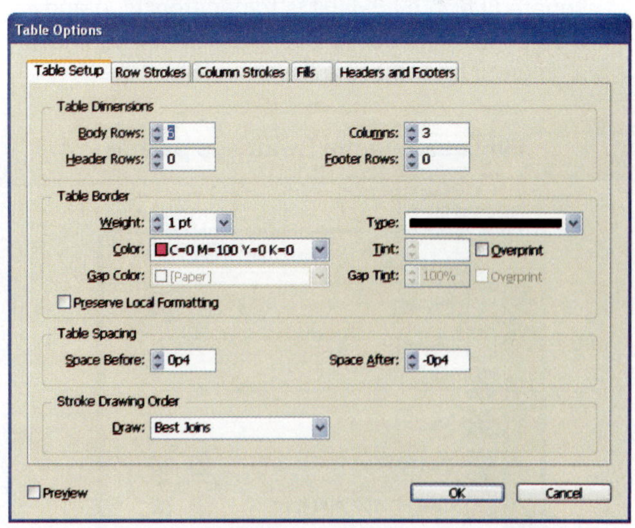

- Setting up every other stroke to alternate by hand can be tedious. An easier way is to use the Alternating Strokes command (Table > Table Options > Alternating Row Strokes or Alternating Column Strokes).

- On the Row Strokes (or Column Strokes) tab, set the Alternating Pattern (for example, to Every Other Row). Then choose a Weight, Type, Color, and so on. It works the same for both row strokes and column strokes.

Alternate the stroke

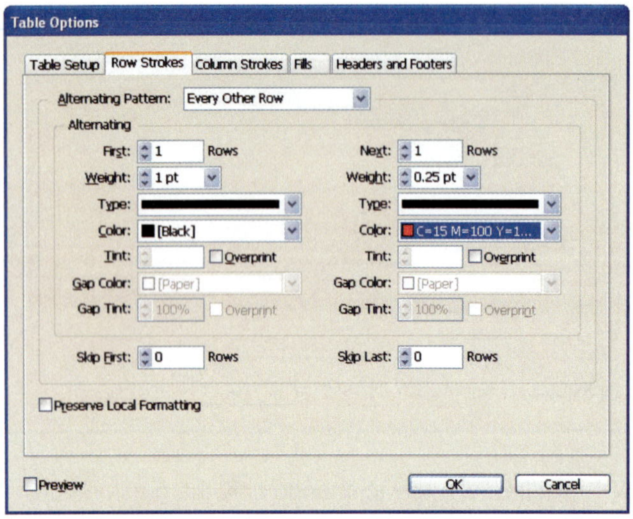

Apply a Table Fill

- To fill a cell with a background color, select the cell(s) and then apply a color from either the Color or Swatches palette, the same as you would a fill for a text frame.
- In the Color or Swatches palette, click the Fill square (which by default is transparent) and then choose the desired color. Each cell can have a different fill, the same fill, or no fill.

Fill square in the Swatches palette

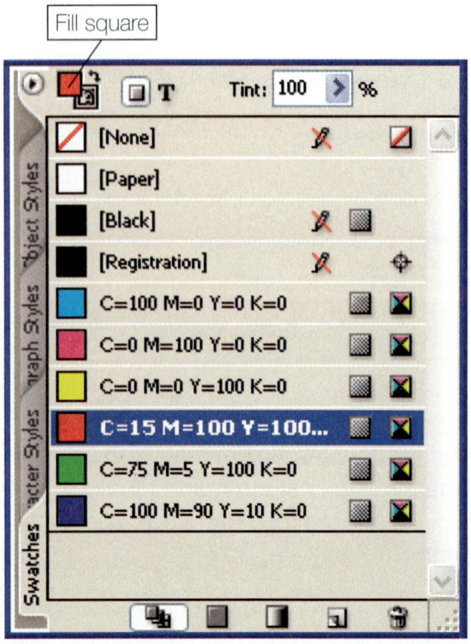

- You can set the fill via dialog box just as you did with the stroke. Select the cells and choose Table > Cell Options > Strokes and Fills, and select a color in the Cell Fill area.

  ✓ *Ignore any reference to "Tints" in this exercise. You will learn about tints in Exercise 35.*

- To alternate the fill color of rows, choose Table > Table Options > Alternating Fills and set up two different fill specifications.

Specify a table fill

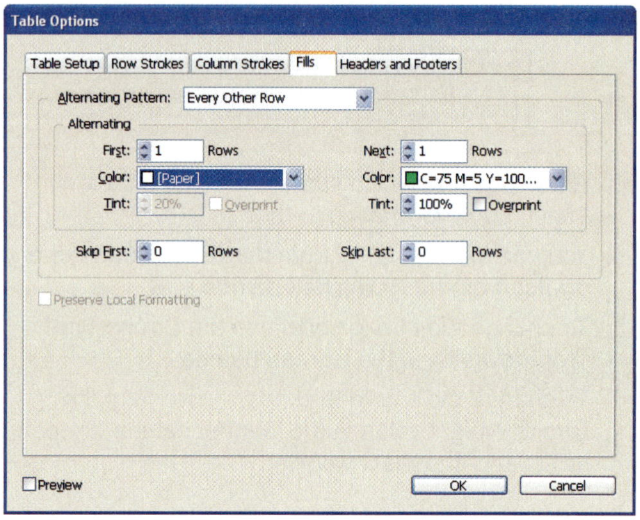

Align Text in a Cell

- The alignment controls for text in a cell are a combination of the vertical ones for a text frame and the horizontal ones for a paragraph. They're exactly the same controls that you've worked with before; the only difference is that with a table, they're available all at once from the Control palette (see Illustration A at the top of page 139).

  ✓ *On the Table palette (not the Control palette's Table controls) you'll find an Inset box in which you can specify an amount of padding around the cell's text. It is not specifically covered in this exercise but you may wish to experiment with it on your own.*

Rotate Text in a Cell

- The Rotate Text buttons are available on the Control palette only when table cells are selected. You can use them to rotate the text to the left or right, or to place it upside-down (see Illustration B at the top of page 139).

Set cell alignment
Illustration A

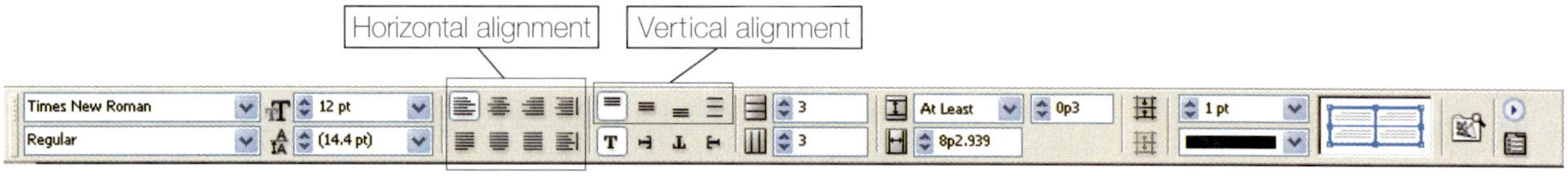

Adjust text rotation
Illustration B

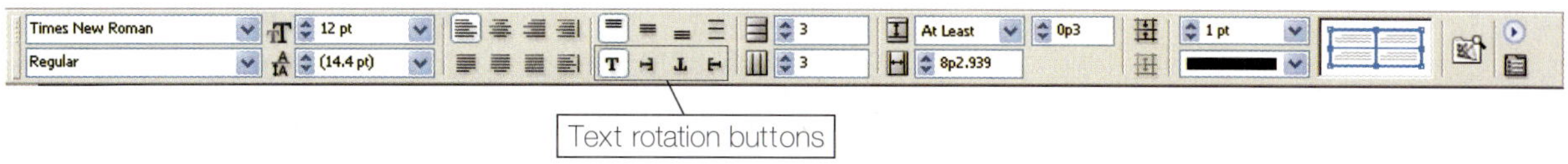

PROCEDURES

Apply Table Strokes

Control Palette Method

1. Select the table cell(s) to affect.
2. (Optional) To omit certain strokes in the range, click the corresponding line(s) in the Control palette's grid.
3. Do one or more of the following:
   - Open the **Stroke Type** list and select a different stroke style
   - Open the **Stroke Weight** list and select a different thickness

   OR

   Increment the **Stroke Weight** value
   - Change the stroke color to a swatch color:
     a. Open the **Swatches** palette.
     b. Click the **Stroke** square
     c. Click the desired swatch.
   - Change the stroke color to a non-swatch color:
     a. Open the **Color** palette.
     b. Double-click the **Stroke** square
     c. Select the desired color.
     d. Click **OK** .... ↵Enter

Dialog Box Method

1. Select the table cell(s) to affect.
2. Click **Table** .... Alt+A
3. Click **Cell Options** .... P
4. Click **Strokes and Fills** .... S
5. (Optional) To omit certain strokes, click the corresponding lines in the **Cell Stroke** grid.
6. Do one or more of the following:
   - Open the **Type** list and select a different stroke style .... Alt+Y, ↓
   - Open the **Weight** list and select a different thickness.
   - Open the **Color** list and select a swatch color .... Alt+C, ↓

   ✓ *If using the dialog box method, you must have created the desired swatch beforehand for the color you want to use or you must use one of the standard swatches; you cannot choose a color from the Color palette using this method.*

   ✓ *Ignore all the other controls for Cell Stroke for the moment; you will learn about them later in the course.*
7. Click **OK** .... ↵Enter

Create an Alternating Stroke

1. Click in any cell in the table, or select the entire table.
2. Click **Table** .... Alt+A
3. Point to **Table Options** .... O
4. Click **Alternating Row Strokes** ... R

   OR

   Click **Alternating Column Strokes** C
5. Set **Alternating Pattern** to the desired pattern .... Alt+A, ↓
6. Select **First** and **Next** stroke weights, types, colors, etc., as with any other stroke.
7. Click **OK** .... ↵Enter

Apply a Table Fill

Palette Method

1. Select the table cell(s) to affect.
2. To apply a swatch color:
   a. Open the **Swatches** palette.
   b. Click the **Fill** square (by default it is transparent) ....
   c. Click the desired swatch.

   OR

   To apply a non-swatch color:
   a. Open the **Color** palette.
   b. Double-click the **Fill** square (by default it is transparent) ....
   c. Select the desired color.
   d. Click **OK** .... ↵Enter

Dialog Box Method

1. Select the table cell(s) to affect.
2. Click **Table** .... Alt+A
3. Click **Cell Options** .... P
4. Click **Strokes and Fills** .... S
5. In the Cell Fill section, open the **Color** box and select a color .... Alt+L, ↓

   ✓ *If using the dialog box method, you must have created the desired swatch beforehand for the color you want to use or you must use one of the standard swatches; you cannot choose a color from the Color palette using this method.*

6. Click **OK** .... ↵Enter

Create an Alternating Fill

1. Click in any cell in the table, or select the entire table.
2. Click **Table** .... Alt+A
3. Point to **Table Options** .... O
4. Click **Alternating Fills** .... F
5. Set **Alternating Pattern** to the desired pattern .... Alt+A, ↓
6. Select fill colors for **First** and **Next** as with any other fill.
7. Click **OK** .... ↵Enter

Align Text in a Cell

1. Select the cell(s) to affect.
2. Click one of the horizontal alignment buttons on the Control palette:
   - Align Left ....
   - Align Center ....
   - Align Right ....
   - Justify with Last Line Aligned Left ....
   - Justify with Last Line Aligned Center ....
   - Justify All Lines ....
   - Align Towards Spine ......
   - Align Away from Spine ...
3. Click one of the vertical alignment buttons on the Control palette:
   - Align Top ....
   - Align Center ....
   - Align Bottom ....
   - Justify Vertically ....

Rotate Text in a Cell

1. Select the cell(s) to affect.
2. Click one of the rotation buttons in the Control palette:
   - Rotate Text 0° ....
   - Rotate Text 90° ....
   - Rotate Text 180° ....
   - Rotate Text 270° ....

EXERCISE DIRECTIONS

1. Start Adobe InDesign.
2. Open **EX27.indd**.
3. Delete the top row ("Schedule").
4. Create a new column at the far left, and merge all its cells into a single tall cell.
5. Type **Schedule** into it, and format the text as 18-point Arial (no underline)
6. Rotate the text 270°.
7. Enlarge the height of the table so that the word *Schedule* does not break, and shrink the width of the Schedule column so that the word *Schedule* exactly fits within it. At this point it should resemble Illustration A.
8. Remove the stroke from the top, left, and bottom of the Schedule cell, so that it looks like the word *Schedule* is floating outside the left edge of the table.

   ✓ *To remove a stroke, set its Weight to 0.*
9. Fill the cells containing the column labels with the Red swatch (C=15 M=100 Y=100 K=0), and change their text color to Paper. Remove the underline from the text in those cells.
10. Change the stroke type of the vertical lines between columns to a dotted style. Do not change the stroke of the outer borders of the table, nor the stroke between the word *Schedule* and the rest of the table.
11. Save your work as **XX-EX27.indd**, where XX are your initials. The final table should resemble Illustration B (shown at the top of page 141).
12. Exit InDesign.

Illustration A

Schedule	<u>Date</u>	<u>Event</u>	<u>Contractor</u>	<u>Cost</u>	<u>Days</u>
	August 1	Roof repairs	Gonzalez Construction	$20,000	4
	August 15	Furnace replacement	Bolls Heating and Cooling	$15,000	1.5
	August 20	Masonry repairs	Gonzalez Construction	$10,000	5
	September 16	Interior painting	Louks Interiors, Inc.	$8,000	6.5

Illustration B

Schedule

Date	Event	Contractor	Cost	Days
August 1	Roof repairs	Gonzalez Construction	$20,000	4
August 15	Furnace replacement	Bolls Heating and Cooling	$15,000	1.5
August 20	Masonry repairs	Gonzalez Construction	$10,000	5
September 16	Interior painting	Louks Interiors, Inc.	$8,000	6.5

ON YOUR OWN

1. Open **OYO-27.indd**.
2. Create a one-cell table in the empty text frame on the left, and expand it to fill as much of the text frame as possible.
3. Cut the heading *Safety Procedures* and paste it into the new cell. The text will not appear there because it doesn't fit.
4. Select the cell and rotate its text by 270°. The text appears.
5. Remove all strokes from the table.
6. Set the newly rotated text to be vertically centered and horizontally right-aligned. It should look like Illustration C (shown on page 142).
7. Save your work as **XX-OYO-27.indd**, where XX are your initials.
8. Exit InDesign.

Illustration C

Safety Procedures

Fire Extinguisher Guidelines

- Check the gauge on each fire extinguisher every 3 months, ensuring it is still functional.
- Do not discharge fire extinguishers except in case of an actual fire.
- Take care to use the correct fire extinguisher class on the fire:
    - * Class A: Paper and Wood
    - * Class B: Grease and liquid flammables
    - * Class C: Electrical

Emergency Exit Guidelines

- Do not block emergency exits with boxes, pallets, or other obstacles.
- Keep signs for emergency exits clearly visible; do not stack anything in front of a sign that would obscure it.
- Under no circumstances are emergency exits to be chained shut or locked from the inside.

Evacuation Procedures

1. When an emergency alarm sounds, everyone should exit the building in an orderly fashion.
2. After everyone has exited, team captains should account for all personnel in their sections.
3. If a team captain finds anyone is missing, he or she should report it to the emergency coordinator.

Section	Building	Captain	Phone
Accounting	A	Sally Kirland	555-2741 x44
Operations	A	Nancy Colvin	555-1414
Personnel	A	Grace Baumgartner	555-2741 x410
Housekeeping	A	Charles Butler	555-2743
Engineering and Design	B	Margaret Li	555-2741 x15

First Aid Procedures

If hurt on the job:

I. Proceed to the nurse's station to receive care.
II. Cooperate with the nurse in completing the required paperwork to document the injury.
III. Return to work with a signed copy of the paperwork.

If care is required for an injury not sustained on the job:

I. Proceed to the nurse's station to receive care.
II. Return to work as soon as possible. No paperwork is required.

Exercise | 28

Skills Covered

- About Styles
- Create Styles
- Apply Styles
- Define Styles Based on Other Styles
- Clear Manual Overrides
- Redefine a Style
- Load Styles from Other Documents

Software Skills Styles greatly simplify document creation by automating sets of formatting actions. For example, rather than select each heading and individually format it, you can create a heading style that will update all headings automatically.

Application Skills In this exercise, you will create several types of styles and apply them to a document, redefine a style, and load styles from another publication.

TERMS

Cascading style A style that is based upon another style, such that anything not explicitly defined for it defaults to the definition in its parent style.

Character style A style that can be applied to individual characters of text.

Object style A style that can be applied to objects other than characters or paragraphs of text.

Override Manual formatting applied to text or an object that is formatted with a certain style.

Paragraph style A style that affects entire paragraphs at once.

Parent style The style on which another style is based.

Style A named set of formatting operations.

NOTES

About Styles

- A **style** is a named set of formatting. Styles make it easier to change the formatting in a document. For example, instead of formatting 50 paragraphs of body text individually, you can create a style called Body Text, apply it to all 50 paragraphs at once, and then modify the style to affect all paragraphs.
- There are three types of styles in InDesign:
  - **Character styles:** Apply to individual characters, and contain only character-based formatting (font family, font style, font color, font size, baseline shift, kerning, and so on).
  - **Paragraph styles:** Apply to individual paragraphs, and can contain a mixture of character-based formatting and paragraph-based formatting (indents, line spacing, bullets, and so on).
  - **Object styles:** Apply to entire framed objects, such as entire text boxes or graphic frames, and can contain only object-based formatting (stroke, fill, size, and so on).
- Each type of style has its own separate palette. By default they are located in the center cluster of palettes on the right edge of the screen (see illustration at the top of page 144).
- This exercise focuses mostly on Character and Paragraph styles, because you have not yet learned about some of the formatting techniques that can be assigned to Object styles.

Create Styles

- The easiest way to create a new style is by example. Format some text or an object frame the way

Style palettes

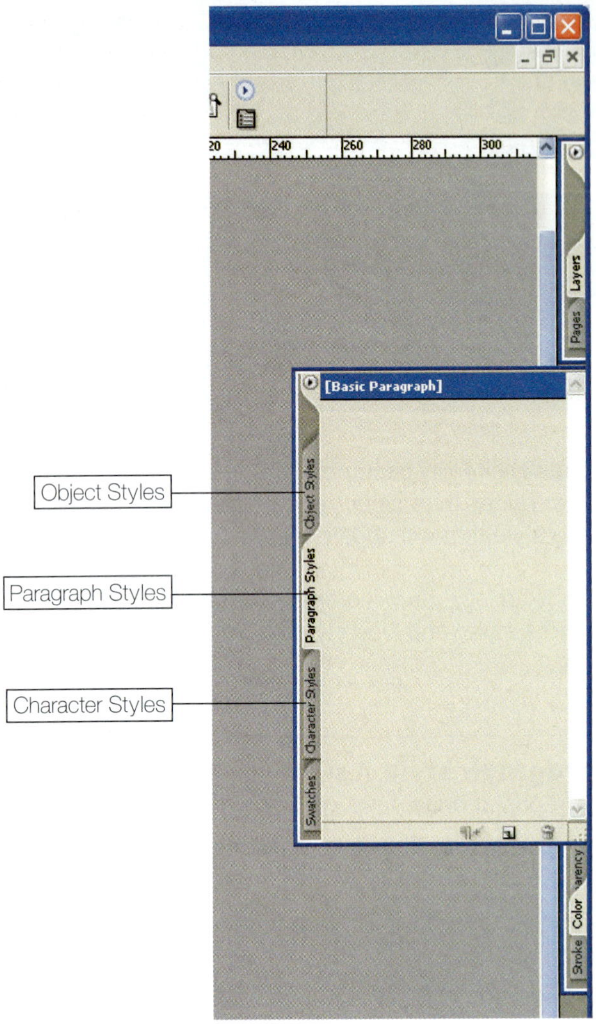

you want the style to be, and then create the new style based upon those settings.

- To create a new style, click the Create New Style button at the bottom of the palette for the desired style type. The new style appears on the list with a generic name (such as Paragraph Style 1).
- After creating a new style, you can rename it by double-clicking it on its palette to open its Options dialog box, and then typing a new name in the Style Name box.
- Since you will probably want to name the style yourself, you might find it easier to open the dialog box at the same time that you are creating the style. To do this, open the fly-out menu for the palette and select New [Type] Style where [Type] is Paragraph, Character, or Object, depending on the style type. An even faster way is to simply hold down the Alt key as you click the Create New Style button.

✓ *When creating a new paragraph style, one of the options is Next Style. This determines the default style for a new paragraph created by pressing Enter at the end of the current one. The proper setting depends on the usage of the style. For example, for a heading style, you would probably want a body paragraph to come next, but for a body paragraph style, you would probably want another body paragraph of the same type.*

- You can also create a style by defining it manually. The advantage of this method is that you don't have to pre-format any text to create it.

Define a paragraph style

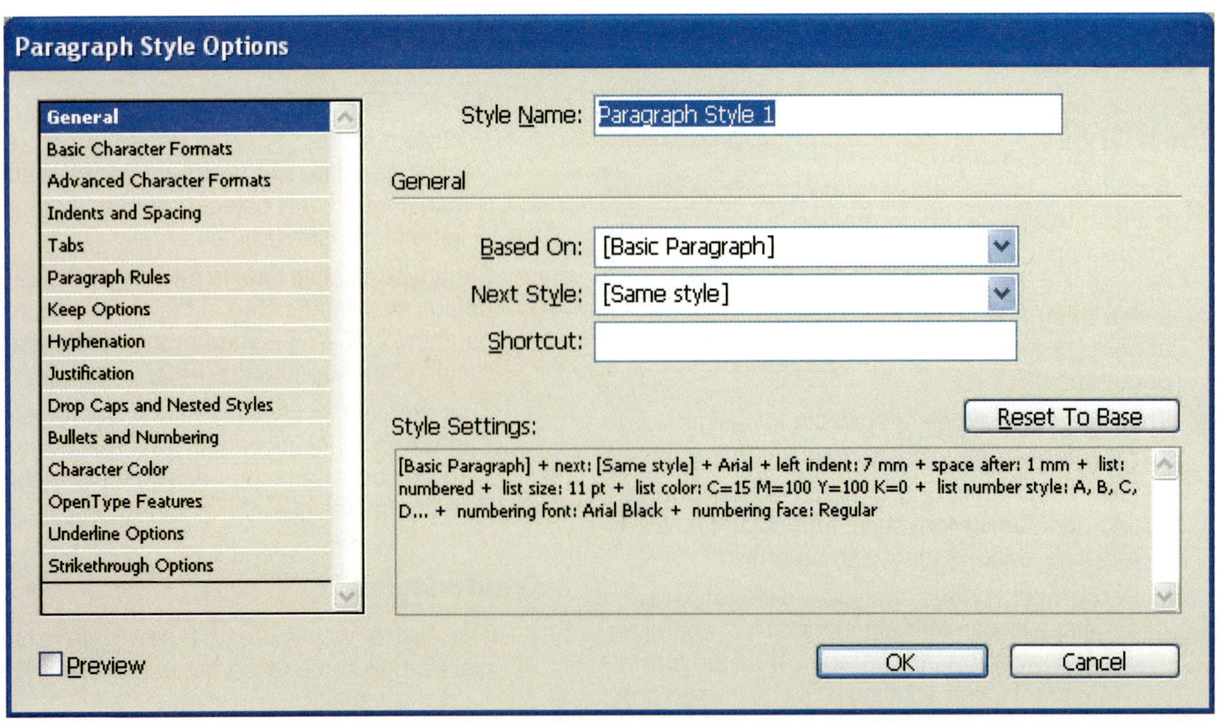

- To do this, start with nothing of the style's type selected—for example, for a character format, don't have any text selected; for a paragraph format, don't have the insertion point within a text frame; for an object style, don't have any object frame selected. Then start a new style with the dialog box (Alt+ is the easiest way). Click each of the categories at the left, and specify the style's formatting.

✓ *When defining a style, it might be helpful to begin by clicking Reset to Base, which strips off any formatting applied to any text that was selected when you opened the dialog box. Reset to Base will be dimmed if nothing was selected before opening the dialog box (see the illustration above).*

Apply Styles

- To apply a style, select the text or object to receive the style and then click the desired style in its palette (Character Styles, Paragraph Styles, or Object Styles).

✓ *Defining a style by example does not apply that style to the text selected text. This is different from most word processing programs, and takes some getting used to.*

Define Styles Based on Other Styles

- One style can be based on another, and whatever you do not specifically define about the style will be assumed to be based upon the settings in its **parent style**. This is called **cascading styles**. For example, suppose you define a character style called Body Text as Arial 12-point Normal, and then you create a character style called Emphasis that is based on Body Text but is Semibold. Any text formatted as Emphasis will be Arial 12-point Semibold.
- To check what a style is based upon, double-click the style in its palette to open its Options dialog box. Then in the General section, check the Based On setting, and change it if needed. To remove the parent from a style, set Based On to [None] or [No Paragraph Style]. The style will retain the same formatting, but it will no longer be tied to the parent style. Thus if the parent style changes, it won't change (see the illustration below).

Set character style attributes

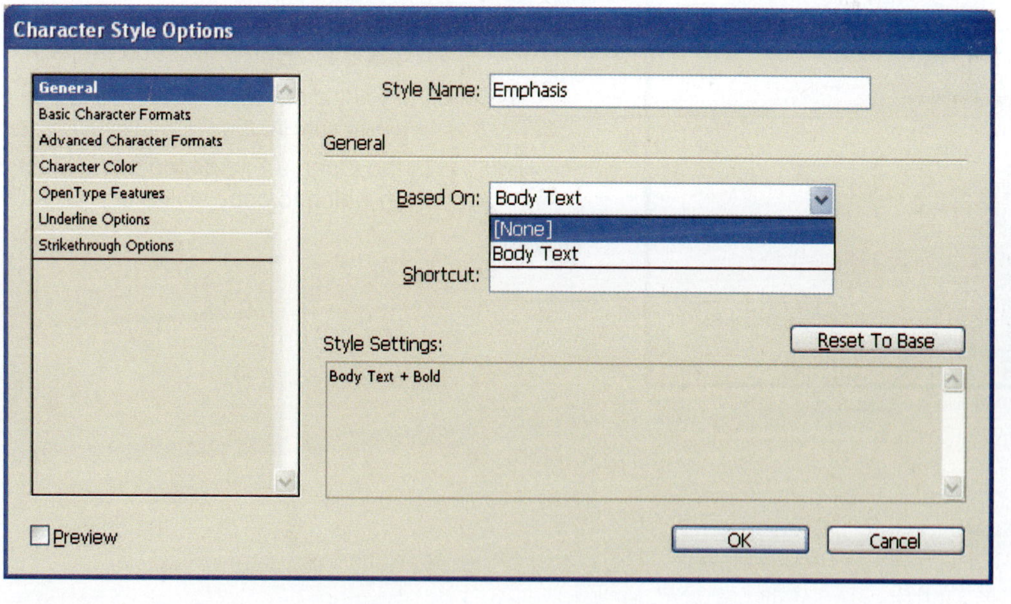

Clear Manual Overrides

- When you see a plus sign next to the style name in the style palette, it means that the currently selected text or object has had that style applied to it but then has had some **overrides**—some manual formatting done to it that has overridden some aspect of the style.
- To clear the overrides on a paragraph, click the Clear Overrides button ¶+ at the bottom of the style palette.

✓ *When clearing overrides, you can hold down Ctrl to clear only the character overrides, or hold down Ctrl+Shift to clear only the paragraph-level overrides. Otherwise all overrides will be cleared.*

Clear manual style overrides

Redefine a Style

- You can redefine a style by example, or you can redefine it by changing the settings in the style's Options dialog box.
- To redefine a style by example, apply the style to some text or object, and then make formatting changes to the text or object. Then open the fly-out menu on the style palette (the exact name of the palette depends on the type of style) and choose Redefine Style (or Redefine Object Style), or press Ctrl+Alt+Shift+R for paragraph styles or Ctrl+Alt+Shift+C for character styles.
- To redefine a style via dialog box, double-click the style in the style palette and make formatting changes using the controls there. Click a category along the left side to change to different controls.

Load Styles from Other Documents

- If you spend a lot of time setting up the styles for a document, you might want to reuse them in new documents.
- To transfer the styles from one document to another, start in the document that should receive the styles. Then open the fly-out menu on the Character or Paragraph Style palette and choose Load All Styles. (This loads both character and paragraph style types. You can also choose to load the specific type only if you prefer.)

✓ *If you want to load object styles, display the Object Styles palette, open the fly-out menu, and choose Load Object Styles.*

- In the Open a File dialog box, select the document from which to copy styles and click Open.

- A list of the styles in the chosen document appears. By default all are selected for import; clear the check box for any you don't want (see the illustration below).
- If there is already a style by the same name in the open document as in the incoming set, the Conflict With Existing Style column shows an indicator. Click that line, and the indicator becomes a drop-down list from which you can choose a desired action. At the bottom of the dialog box is a definition of each style so you can make a more informed decision.

Choose whether to overwrite existing styles with the same name

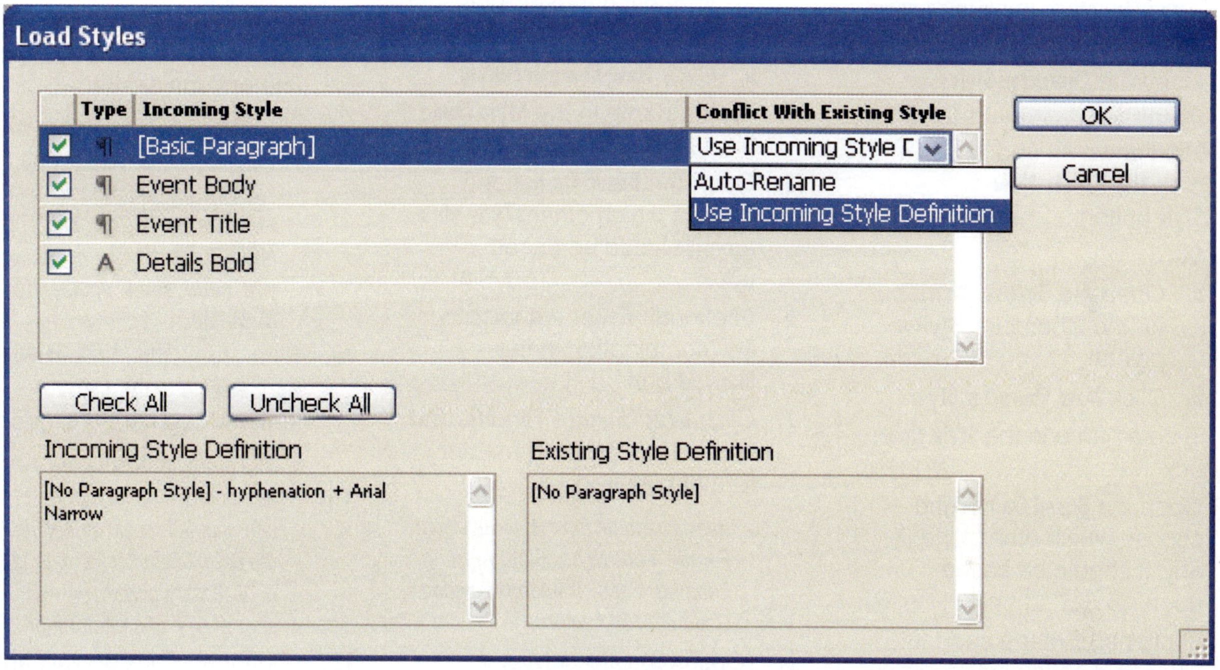

PROCEDURES

Create a Character Style

Create a Character Style by Example (Dialog Box Method)

1. Select text that is already character-formatted the way the style should be.

   ✓ *Character formatting includes all the formatting you learned about in Lesson 2.*

2. Open the **Character Styles** palette .... Shift + F11
3. Hold down **Alt** and click the **Create New Style** button .... Alt +

   OR

   a. Open the fly-out menu for the Character Styles palette.

   b. Click **New Character Style**.

4. Type a name in the **Style Name** box .... Alt + N
5. Open the **Based On** list and choose which other style, if any, it should be based upon .... Alt + B, ↓
6. (Optional) Enter a shortcut key combination in the **Shortcut** box .... Alt + S
7. Click **OK** .... Enter

Create a Character Style by Example (Quick Method)

1. Select text that is already character-formatted the way the style should be.

   ✓ *Character formatting includes all the formatting you learned about in Lesson 2.*

2. Open the **Character Styles** palette .... Shift + F11
3. Click the **Create New Style** button ....

Create a Character Style by Definition

1. If any text is selected, deselect it.

   ✓ *A quick way to deselect all text is to click the Selection tool in the Tools palette.*

2. Open the **Character Styles** palette .... Shift + F11
3. Hold down **Alt** and click the **Create New Style** button .... Alt +

   OR

   a. Open the fly-out menu for the Character Styles palette.

   b. Click **New Character Style**.

4. Type a name in the **Style Name** box .... Alt + N
5. Open the **Based On** list and choose which other style, if any, it should be based upon .... Alt + B, ↓
6. (Optional) Enter a shortcut key combination in the **Shortcut** box .... Alt + S
7. Click **Basic Character Formats**, and choose any basic character formats desired.

   ✓ *Basic character formats include Font Family, Font Style, Size, Kerning, Leading, Case, Tracking, Position, Underline, and so on.*

8. (Optional) Click **Advanced Character Formats** and choose any advanced character formats desired.

   ✓ *Advanced character formats include Horizontal Scale, Vertical Scale, Baseline Shift, Skew, and Language.*

9. (Optional) Click **Character Color** and click the desired color swatch.

   ✓ *You can create a new color swatch by double-clicking the Fill Color square in the dialog box. By default it has a question mark on it, but if you click an existing swatch it changes to that color; you can still double-click it to define a new swatch.*

10. (Optional) Click **OpenType Features** and select any OpenType features that should apply.

    ✓ *OpenType features will apply only if the font chosen in step 7 supports them. Depending on the font, the available features might include Titling Alternates, Swash Alternates, Contextual Alternates, Ordinals, Fractions, Discretionary Ligatures, and Slashed Zero.*

11. (Optional) Click **Underline Options** and select any underline options desired.

    ✓ *Underline options include Weight, Type, Offset, Color, and Gap Color. You can turn on a basic underline from the Basic Character Formats (step 7); step 11 is needed only if you need some special type of underline.*

12. (Optional) Click **Strikethrough Options** and select any strikethrough options desired.

    ✓ *Strikethrough options are the same as underline options (step 11). You can enable a basic strikethrough in the Basic Character Formats; step 12 is necessary only if you want some special type of strikethrough.*

13. (Optional) Click **General**, and examine the entries in the **Style Settings** area to confirm your choices.
14. Click **OK** .... Enter

Create a Paragraph Style

Create a Paragraph Style by Example (Dialog Box Method)

1. Select a paragraph that is already formatted the way the style should be, with both character and paragraph formatting.
2. Open the **Paragraph Styles** palette F11
3. Hold down **Alt** and click the **Create New Style** button .... Alt +

   OR

   a. Open the fly-out menu for the Paragraph Styles palette.

   b. Click **New Paragraph Style**.

4. Type a name in the **Style Name** box .... Alt+N
5. Open the **Based On** list and choose which other style, if any, it should be based upon .... Alt+B, ↓
6. (Optional) Open the **Next Style** list and select the style to apply to paragraphs after the one with this style .... Alt+Y, ↓

   ✓ *The Next Style setting determines the style assigned automatically to a new paragraph created by pressing Enter at the end of the current one.*

7. (Optional) Enter a shortcut key combination in the **Shortcut** box .... Alt+S
8. Click **OK** .... ↵Enter

Create a Paragraph Style by Example (Quick Method)

1. Select text that is already character-formatted the way the style should be.

   ✓ *Character formatting includes all the formatting you learned about in Lesson 2.*

2. Open the **Paragraph Styles** palette F11
3. Click the **Create New Style** button ....

Create a Paragraph Style by Definition

1. If any text is selected, deselect it.

   ✓ *A quick way to deselect all text is to click the Selection tool in the Tools palette.*

2. Open the **Paragraph Styles** palette F11
3. Hold down **Alt** and click the **Create New Style** button .... Alt+

   OR

   a. Open the fly-out menu for the Paragraph Styles palette.
   b. Click **New Paragraph Style**.

4. Type a name in the **Style Name** box .... Alt+N
5. Open the **Based On** list and choose which other style, if any, it should be based upon .... Alt+B, ↓
6. (Optional) Open the **Next Style** list and select the style to apply to paragraphs after the one with this style .... Alt+Y, ↓
7. Click **Reset to Base** ...... Alt+R
8. (Optional) Enter a shortcut key combination in the **Shortcut** box .... Alt+S
9. Click **Basic Character Formats**, and choose any basic character formats desired.

   ✓ *Basic character formats include Font Family, Font Style, Size, Kerning, Leading, Case, Tracking, Position, Underline, and so on.*

10. (Optional) Click **Advanced Character Formats** and choose any advanced character formats desired.

    ✓ *Advanced character formats include Horizontal Scale, Vertical Scale, Baseline Shift, Skew, and Language.*

11. (Optional) Click **Indents and Spacing** and choose any indents and spacing formats desired.

    ✓ *Indents and Spacing formats include horizontal alignment, left and right indents, first line and last line indents, and amount of space before and after the paragraph.*

12. (Optional) Click **Tabs** and set any tab stops desired.

    ✓ *A version of the Tabs palette appears, and you set the tab stops just as you did on the Tabs palette in Exercise 25.*

13. (Optional) Click **Paragraph Rules** and set any horizontal lines that should appear before or after the paragraph.
14. (Optional) Click **Keep Options** and set any rules for keeping lines together.

    ✓ *These Keep Options are the same as the ones you learned about in Exercise 24.*

15. (Optional) Click **Hyphenation** and set any rules for hyphenating the paragraph.

    ✓ *You learned about these hyphenations in Exercise 24.*

16. (Optional) Click **Justification** and set any rules for word spacing, letter spacing, and so on.

    ✓ *These Justification options are the same as the ones you learned about in Exercise 22.*

17. (Optional) Click **Drop Caps and Nested Styles** and set options for creating a drop cap at the beginning of the paragraph.

    ✓ *You learned about drop caps in Exercise 23.*

18. (Optional) Click **Bullets and Numbering** and set options for a bullet or number character preceding the paragraph.

    ✓ *You learned about bullets and numbering in Exercise 25.*

19. (Optional) Click **Character Color** and click the desired color swatch.

    ✓ *You can create a new color swatch by double-clicking the Fill Color square in the dialog box. By default it has a question mark on it, but if you click an existing swatch it changes to that color; you can still double-click it to define a new swatch.*

20. (Optional) Click **OpenType Features** and select any OpenType features that should apply.

    ✓ *OpenType features will apply only if the font chosen in step 9 supports them. Depending on the font, the available features might include Titling Alternates, Swash Alternates, Contextual Alternates, Ordinals, Fractions, Discretionary Ligatures, and Slashed Zero.*

21. (Optional) Click **Underline Options** and select any underline options desired.

✓ *Underline options include Weight, Type, Offset, Color, and Gap Color. You can turn on a basic underline from the Basic Character Formats (step 9); step 21 is needed only if you need some special type of underline.*

22. (Optional) Click **Strikethrough Options** and select any strikethrough options desired.

    ✓ *Strikethrough options are the same as underline options (step 21). You can enable a basic strikethrough in the Basic Character Formats; step 22 is necessary only if you want some special type of strikethrough.*

23. (Optional) Click **General**, and examine the entries in the **Style Settings** area to confirm your choices.
24. Click **OK** .... Enter

Create an Object Style

Create an Object Style by Example (Dialog Box Method)

1. Select an object (such as a text frame or a graphic frame) that is formatted as desired for the style.
2. Open the **Object Styles** palette .... Ctrl+F7
3. Hold down **Alt** and click the **Create New Style** button .... Alt+

   OR

   a. Open the fly-out menu for the Object Styles palette.
   b. Click **New Object Style**.
4. Type a name in the **Style Name** box .... Alt+N
5. Open the **Based On** list and choose which other style,if any, it should be based upon .... Alt+B, ↓
6. (Optional) Enter a shortcut key combination in the **Shortcut** box .... Alt+S
7. Click **OK** .... Enter

Create an Object Style by Example (Quick Method)

1. Select an object (such as a text frame or a graphic frame) that is formatted as desired for the style.
2. Open the **Object Styles** palette .... Ctrl+F7
3. Click the **Create New Style** button ....

Create an Object Style by Definition

✓ *The instructions provided here are less detailed than for character and paragraph styles because many of the options for object formatting have not yet been covered in this course. You will learn about them in the next lesson. Until you know more about them, you might prefer to use one of the "by example" methods for creating an object style.*

1. Select an object (such as a text frame or a graphic frame) that is formatted as desired for the style.
2. Open the **Object Styles** palette .... Ctrl+F7
3. Hold down **Alt** and click the **Create New Style** button .... Alt+

   OR

   a. Open the fly-out menu for the Object Styles palette.
   b. Click **New Object Style**.
4. Type a name in the **Style Name** box .... Alt+N
5. Open the **Based On** list and choose which other style, if any, it should be based upon .... Alt+B, ↓
6. (Optional) Enter a shortcut key combination in the **Shortcut** box .... Alt+S
7. Click **Reset to Base** .... Alt+R
8. Define the style by doing the following for each category listed in the left pane:
   - Clear the category's check box to exclude it from the style.

   OR

   a. Select the category's check box to include it.
   b. Click the category's name to display its controls.
   c. Set the options for that category.
9. Click **OK** .... Enter

Apply Styles

1. Select the text or object to which to apply the style.
2. Open the appropriate style palette:
   - **Character Styles** ..... Shift+F11
   - **Paragraph Styles** F11
   - **Object Styles** .... Ctrl+F7
3. Click the desired style.

Clear Manual Paragraph Style Overrides

1. Select the text for which to remove overrides.
2. Open the **Paragraph Styles** palette F11
3. Click the **Clear Overrides** button ....

Clear Manual Object Styles Overrides

1. Select the object frame for which to remove overrides.
2. Open the **Object Styles** palette .... Ctrl+F7
3. Click the **Clear Overrides** button ....

Redefine a Style

1. Apply the style to some text or an object.
2. Make any formatting changes desired.
3. Open the appropriate style palette:
   - **Character Styles** ..... Shift+F11
   - **Paragraph Styles** F11
   - **Object Styles** .... Ctrl+F7
4. Open the fly-out menu.
5. Click **Redefine Style** or **Redefine Object Style**.

   ✓ *You can press Ctrl+Alt+Shift+R instead of steps 4 and 5 for a paragraph style, or Ctrl+Alt+Shift+C for a character style.*

Load Paragraph and Character Styles from Another Document

1. Open the appropriate style palette:
   - **Character Styles** .... Shift + F11
   - **Paragraph Styles** F11
2. Open the fly-out menu.
3. Click **Load All Styles**.
4. Select the document containing the styles to load.
5. Click **Open** .... Enter
6. Resolve any conflicts:
   a. In the Conflict With Existing Style column, click the line for the conflicting style.
   b. Open the drop-down list ....
   c. Click **Auto-Rename** or **Use Incoming Style Definition**.
7. Clear the check box for any style you don't want.
8. Click **OK** .... Enter

Load Only One Type of Style from Another Document

1. Open the style palette for the type to import:
   - **Character Styles** ..... Shift + F11
   - **Paragraph Styles** F11
   - **Object Styles** .... Ctrl + F7
2. Open the fly-out menu.
3. Click **Load [Type] Styles** where [Type] is the type chosen in step 1.
4. Select the document containing the styles to load.
5. Click **Open** .... Enter
6. Resolve any conflicts:
   a. In the Conflict With Existing Style column, click the line for the conflicting style.
   b. Open the drop-down list ....
   c. Click **Auto-Rename** or **Use Incoming Style Definition**.
7. Clear the check box for any style you don't want.
8. Click **OK** .... Enter

EXERCISE DIRECTIONS

1. Start Adobe InDesign.
2. Open **EX28.indd**.
3. Create a new paragraph style called **Red Letter List** from an example paragraph in the numbered (lettered) list, and apply it to the entire list.
4. Clear the manual override for the "E. Repairs – Current Phase" paragraph.
5. Create a new character style called **Bold Characters** that applies Bold to text, and apply the new style to the text you cleared in step 4.
6. Create a new paragraph style called **Arrow Bullets** from an example paragraph in the current bulleted list. Base it on the Red Letter List style.
7. Apply Arrow Bullets to the entire bulleted list.

   ✓ *Notice that the arrow heads turn red. That's because no color was specified for them in the Arrow Bullets style, so it takes the color specification from the style on which it is based: Red Letter List.*
8. Create a new object style called **Title Frame** based on the text frame with the red gradient at the top of the document. Apply it to that text frame.
9. Create a new rectangular frame at the bottom of the page, with this size and position:
   X: 107.95 mm
   Y: 249.15 mm
   W: 190.5 mm
   H: 35.5 mm
10. Apply the Title Frame style to the new rectangular frame.
11. Save your work as **XX-EX28.indd**. where XX are your initials, and close the file.
12. Start a new blank document using the [Default] settings, and import all the styles from **XX-EX28.indd** into it. Where there are conflicts, use incoming style definitions.
13. Save the new document as **XX-EX28A.indd**. where XX are your initials, and close the file.
14. Exit InDesign.

ON YOUR OWN

1. Open OYO-28.indd.
2. Look through this document and make a list of the styles you would like to create and their types. Here are some suggestions:
   - Cover Page Title
   - Cover Page Subtitle
   - Part Number
   - Body Paragraph
   - First Paragraph (based on Body Paragraph, just like it except with the drop cap)
   - Quote Box (an object style)
3. Create the styles, and then apply them. Every paragraph should have a style applied to it with no manual overrides.
4. Save your work as **XX-OYO-28.indd**. where XX are your initials.
5. Open OYO-28A.indd.
6. Import all the character and paragraph styles from **XX-OYO-28.indd**, and apply them as you see fit to format this document similarly to the other one.
7. Modify the definition of the Body Paragraph style to use Adobe Jenson Pro. If the First Paragraph style does not automatically change, redefine First Paragraph so that it is based on Body Paragraph.
8. Save your work as **XX-OYO-28A.indd**, where XX are your initials.
9. Exit InDesign.

End of Lesson Projects

- Summary Exercise
- Application Exercise
- Curriculum Integration Exercise
- Critical Thinking Exercise

Exercise | 29

Summary Exercise

Software Skills The magazine article *Easy Care Perennials* that you worked with in Exercise 19 needs to be stretched out to fill an extra column in the magazine. In this exercise, you will adjust its paragraph properties to make it fit the allotted space. You will also create styles as you go, to simplify the process of making further changes.

DIRECTIONS

1. Open **EX29.indd**.
2. Select all the text in the story and set 3 mm of space after each paragraph.
3. Delete the Body Text style, replacing it with [No Paragraph Style], and create a new Body Text style in its place that matches the formatting of the first body paragraph. Apply the Body Text style to all paragraphs in the story.
4. Apply a 3-line, 1-character drop cap to the first paragraph in the story.
5. Create a new paragraph style called **Heading** that is based on Body Text but with these changes:
   - 16 points in size
   - Semibold
   - Colored C=69 M=38 Y=100 K=26
   - Space Before set to 4 mm
6. Apply the new Heading style to *Soil Conditions* and *Caring for New Transplants*.
7. Select *Creeping Phlox* and color the text bright yellow. Then define a new character style based on the selection, called **Yellow**. Apply it to all the italicized names of the plants.
8. Change the color of the Yellow character style to C=9 M=84 Y=100 K=1, and change its name to **Burnt Orange**.

✓ *The colors used in steps 5, 7, and 8 were selected because they occur in the photo on page 2. Using text colors that tie into the photography is one way of making a layout cohesive. In Lesson 4 you will learn how to use the Eyedropper tool to pick up colors from a photograph on your own.*

9. For each paragraph that begins with a burnt orange plant name, create a left indent of 6 mm.
10. Replace all double-hyphens with em dashes (—).
11. Right-align and italicize the *Continued on page 4* text on page 3.
12. Set the leading for the Body Text style to 18.6 points.
13. Use the Keep Options to prevent any text formatted as Body Text from leaving fewer than 2 lines at the start or end of a paragraph.
14. Set the vertical alignment for all the story's text frames to Justified. Illustration A on pages 154 through 156 shows the finished document.
15. Save your work as **XX-EX29.indd**, where XX are your initials.
16. Exit InDesign.

Illustration A

Easy-Care Perennials

Looking for an easy way to enjoy color and beauty in your gardens all season long? Consider perennials. While they are more expensive than annuals initially, you quickly recoup the cost difference in having plants that will come back stronger and more vigorous every year, with no replanting.

Here are some easy-to-care-for plants that make for a good starter garden:

'Sprite' Astilbe — a diminutive hybrid astilbe with glossy dark green foliage. It produces sprays of shell pink flowers in midsummer shade gardens.

'Moonbeam' Coreposis — small, eight-petaled pale yellow flowers grace the tips of thin stems covered with narrow leaves. It blooms all summer in full sun.

'Palace Purple' Heuchera — boasts handsome deep purple foliage all summer in partial shade. It bears tiny, pale bluish-white flowers clustered at the ends of wiry stems in spring.

2 • Volume II Number 1

Creeping Phlox — neat, deep green foliage on creeping stems mats to cover the ground in woodland settings. In spring it produces clusters of small florets in white, blue, or pink.

'Sunny Border Blue' Veronica — offers a strong, vertical accent for the garden and bears spikes of rich violet-blue flowers in summer. It does best in a sunny site.

'Magnus' Purple Coneflower — jaunty, daisylike flowers with droopy purple petals bloom in midsummer when many other perennials are idle. It thrives in full sun.

'Goldsturm' Black-eyed Susan — provides billows of late-summer daisylike golden blossoms with dark centers on coarse, hairy stems.

Soil Conditions

Carefully consider the moisture conditions of the site you have chosen for your garden. Is it normal (as much as it's possible to define normal with today's chaotic weather), dry, or wet? Choose plants that do best in the prevailing conditions.

Next plan defensive measures to counteract a change in the moisture content. If the area you have chosen is dry, make sure the drainage is excellent. That way, even if there is excessive rain, the water should run off quickly. To increase drainage, dig out your garden bed to a depth of 1-1/2 to 2 feet and install a drainage pipe. his will immediately carry away any excess water. Then refill the bed with enriched, porous garden soil filled with organic matter, such as peat moss and humus.

If your proposed garden area is moist, make sure you have the means to retain the moisture. Your garden should either be near a water source where you can sprinkle the spot daily, or embedded with a soaker hose.

Or you can create your own miniature damp spot by following the techniques used to create garden pools. Simply install a container with a very small hole punched in it for slow drainage. After you've filled

Continued on page 4

Easy-Care Perennials

continued from page 3

the container, the moisture should seep out of such a setting at a very slow rate.

Caring for New Transplants

No matter how carefully you have placed your perennials in your garden, these plants have nevertheless been uprooted during transplanting. They are in a state of shock; how much shock is determined by your handling methods. They will need some watchful care.

Your new plants must get enough water or they will die. Because it is inevitable that some of the root hairs were damaged in the replanting process, the remaining ones have to work overtime until new growth occurs. This means that for a good week or more the new transplants must be gently watered and the ground kept moist but not swamped — overwatering could drown a new plant.

Never directly fertilize a newly-planted perennial. Ideally, the plant should not need fertilizer in subsequent weeks because it has been placed in enriched garden soil, where the necessary nutrients are already in place and available to the plant once the root hairs start to grow.

If you are transplanting tall perennials, such as delphiniums, it's a good idea to stake them at the same time. Staking helps the stem of a tall plant support its flowers once they begin to bloom; done at transplanting time, staking creates a minimum of disturbance for young plants.

Check your transplants for signs of new foliage. This indicates that you have planted correctly and that your new perennial is surviving nicely in your garden.

Application Exercise

Software Skills In this exercise, you will improve the readability of a book layout by working with paragraph settings.

DIRECTIONS

1. Open **EX30.indd**.
2. Do a global find-and-replace that gets rid of the extra paragraph breaks between paragraphs. (Replace ^p^p with ^p.) Do this repeatedly until it finds no more instances. Then go through manually and look for any stray instances where there is an extra blank line between paragraphs, such as before the Roman numeral chapter numbers, and delete it.
3. Create a new paragraph style by example called **Book** based on the *Book 1* text on page 2, and apply it to that paragraph.
4. Create a new paragraph style by example called **Chapter** based on the *I.* on page 2, but change it to include 3 mm of spacing before it. Apply it to all the Roman numeral chapter numbers throughout the document.
5. Create a paragraph style called Body, and define it as follows:
   - Font Family: Adobe Garamond Pro
   - Font Style: Regular
   - Font Size: 12 points
   - Leading: 16 points
   - Kerning: Optical
   - Left Indent: 3 mm
   - First-Line Indent: 6 mm
   - Space After: 3 mm
   - Keep Options: Keep 2 lines together at the start and end of each paragraph
   - Hyphenation: turned off
6. Apply the Body style to all text except the headings, and remove any overrides.
7. Create a new style called **First Body** that is the same as Body (based on it) except there is no first-line indent. Apply it to each paragraph that follows a Chapter heading.
8. Save your work as **XX-EX30.indd**, where XX are your initials.
9. Exit InDesign.

Exercise | 31

Curriculum Integration Exercise

Software Skills Your biology class is studying freshwater fish. In this exercise, you will format a table that lists the common name of the four types of black bass found in Texas, and use the Internet to find their Latin names and their descriptions.

DIRECTIONS

Open the file **EX31.indd**.

Add a new row at the top of the table, and enter the column headings **Name**, **Description**, and **Picture**.

Format the word *Name* as Arial Black 14 point, and center it in its cell. Create a new paragraph style called **Column Head** based on it, and then apply that style to all three column headings.

Using the Internet, find the Latin name of each of the fish, and type it in italic below the common name.

Using the Internet, find a brief description for each of the four species. Paraphrase the descriptions into one or two sentences each and type them in the Description column.

✓ *If some of the rows disappear from the table, the descriptions are too long and it is forcing some rows to be overset. Shorten the descriptions.*

Below the last line in the document, type a new line that attributes the source of your information, including the URL of the Web site and the name of the page.

✓ *Ask your teacher if you should use a specific attribution style such as APA or MLA; otherwise just make sure you include enough information for someone to find it.*

Create a new paragraph style called **Descriptions** formatted as Arial 12-point Regular text, Justify with Last Line Left, with 4 mm of space below. Apply this style to all the descriptions.

✓ *Notice that adding space below the paragraphs does not increase the height of the cells.*

Add an extra paragraph break at the end of each description, creating extra space between the table cells.

Right-align the fish names (both common names and Latin names) in the Name column.

In the top row of the table, set vertical alignment to Bottom and apply a fill color of C=2 M=0 Y=55 K=0. (Create a swatch for the color.)

Remove the stroke from around every cell in the entire table. Then reapply a 1-point black stroke to the bottom of the first row only (the pale yellow row).

Save your work as **XX-EX31.indd**, where XX are your initials.

Exit InDesign.

Critical Thinking Exercise

Software Skills In this exercise, you will create a table showing the specifications and differences between various types of writeable CD and DVD media.

DIRECTIONS

- Use the Internet to find the following information for each of these types of single-sided optical discs: CD-R, CD-RW, DVD+R, DVD-R, DVD+RW, DVD-RW, DVD-RAM, and Dual Layer DVD-R.
  - Disc type
  - Data storage capacity, in megabytes or gigabytes
  - Audio/video capacity, in minutes (audio if CD, video if DVD)
  - Rewriteable? (Yes or No)
- Start a new document in InDesign, and create a table that summarizes this information.
- Use what you have learned about paragraph, character, and table formatting so far in this course to make the table as attractive and readable as possible.
- Following the table, create a bulleted list of helpful Web sites that contain technical specifications about CD and DVD drives.
- Save the document as **XX-EX32.indd**, where XX are your initials.
- Exit InDesign.

Lesson 4

Working with Graphic Objects

Exercise 33

- Import Graphics
- Choose a Graphic Placement Mode
- Move and Size a Graphic Within a Frame
- Arrange Objects

Exercise 34

- Understand Color Modes
- Understand Spot and Process Colors
- Understand Color Profiles
- Create a Color Swatch
- Edit a Color Swatch
- Change the Color Swatch Display

Exercise 35

- Pick Up a Color with the Eyedropper
- Create a Tint Swatch
- Create Swatches for All Used Colors
- Delete Swatches
- Select Unused Swatches
- Import and Export Swatches

Exercise 36

- Apply an Object Stroke
- Apply a Drop Shadow to an Object
- Apply Feathering
- Apply Corner Effects
- Create an Object Style

Exercise 37

- Apply a Gradient
- Change the Gradient Direction
- Set Object Transparency
- Select Transparency Effects

Exercise 38

- Specify Text Wrapping
- Adjust Wrap Offset
- Manually Modify Wrap Points

END OF LESSON PROJECTS

Exercise 39

- Summary Exercise

Exercise 40

- Application Exercise

Exercise 41

- Curriculum Integration Exercise

Exercise 42

- Critical Thinking Exercise

Exercise | 33

Skills Covered

- Import Graphics
- Choose a Graphic Placement Mode
- Move and Size a Graphic Within a Frame
- Arrange Objects

Software Skills To make documents more interesting, you can import graphics into them. The graphic frames can then be adjusted so that the content fits in the allotted space or is cropped attractively. When stacking objects on top of one another, you can arrange them in the desired stack order.

Application Skills In this exercise, you will import several graphics into a document, adjust their placements within their respective frames, and place them appropriately in the stack order.

TERMS

Aspect ratio The ratio of height to width, also called the *proportions*.

Direct Selection tool The white arrow tool, which enables you to select content within a frame or modify the frame shape.

NOTES

Import Graphics

- In Lesson 1 you learned that you can import graphics into InDesign by dragging-and-dropping from Adobe Bridge.
- A more powerful alternative is the File > Place command. It enables you to create a frame of the exact size needed as you are importing, so you do not have to worry about resizing the imported image's frame as a separate step.
- With the Place command, you can also set options for the imported image, such as displaying or hiding certain layers of a multi-layer object.

✓ *You will learn more about multi-layer objects in Exercise 45.*

- To place a graphic, choose File > Place and then select the graphic to place. When you click Open, the mouse pointer becomes a paintbrush with an arrow on it. You can then drag to draw a frame of the desired dimensions and position.

✓ *To draw a perfect square frame, hold down Shift as you draw the frame.*

Choose a Graphic Placement Mode

- The graphic retains its original size by default. That means if the frame is smaller than the graphic, part of the graphic will appear truncated (see the illustration at the top of page 164).

Graphic is too large to fit in frame

- Use one of the following buttons on the Control palette to specify how the graphic should relate to the frame.
  - Fit Content to Frame: Forces the graphic to fill the frame exactly, distorting the **aspect ratio** (ratio of height to width) if needed (see the illustration below).
  - Fit Frame to Content: Changes the size of the frame as needed so that the picture fits at its native size, even if it overflows the page (as it does in the illustration at the top of page 165).
  - Fit Content Proportionally: Fits the entire graphic into the frame proportionally, maintaining the aspect ratio and leaving blank space in the frame if needed (see the illustration in the middle of page 165).
  - Fill Frame Proportionally: Fits the graphic into the frame in one dimension, cropping the graphic in the other dimension as needed so that the aspect ratio is maintained (see the illustration at the bottom of page 165).
  - Center Content: Works with any of the other four modes, and centers the image in the frame without altering the size of either the frame or the graphic.

✓ *When trying out these modes, be aware that each one bases its action on the current state of the picture. For example, you won't get the same results if you click on Fit Content to Frame and then Fit Frame to Content as you would if you had clicked Fit Frame to Content initially. You might want to press Ctrl+Z to undo after trying each mode so you can compare them more objectively.*

The graphic now fits in the frame but it is distorted

The frame has been increased in size to accommodate the image; the frame overflows the page in this example

The image has been resized to the height of the frame and its aspect ratio has been preserved

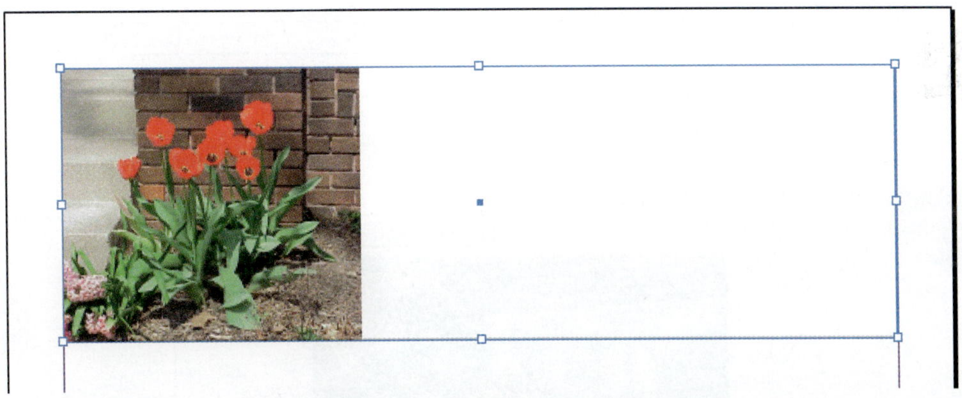

The width of the frame has been increased to accommodate the picture, but the picture is truncated vertically

Move and Size a Graphic Within a Frame

- Recall from Lesson 1 that there are two selection tools: Selection and Direct Selection. Working with graphics spotlights the difference between these tools.
- When you select the graphic using the Selection tool, you are working with the frame. When you move or resize the graphic using the selection handles around the graphic, you are affecting the frame, and the graphic goes along for the ride.
- When you select the graphic using the **Direct Selection tool**, you are working with the graphic *inside* the frame. The frame is a window through which you see the graphic, but moving and resizing affects the graphic behind the frame, not the frame itself.
- To move the graphic behind the frame so that a different part of the graphic shows, position the mouse pointer over the inside of the frame.
- The mouse pointer becomes an open hand. Then click, and it becomes a black arrow. Drag to move the graphic. The frame stays in place (see the illustration below).
- When the Direct Selection tool is active, a brown outline appears showing the full size of the picture behind the frame (see the illustration at the top of page 167).
- You can drag the selection handles on this outline to resize the graphic. (Hold down Shift to maintain the aspect ratio.) You can alternatively enter a precise height or width on the Control palette (in the H: or W: boxes) as you would for a regular frame (see the illustration at the bottom of page 167).
- Changing the size of the outline changes the magnification at which the picture appears. Make it larger to make the picture larger, or smaller to make the picture smaller. To show the entire picture, make it the same size as the visible area.

Resize the image separately from its frame with Direct Selection

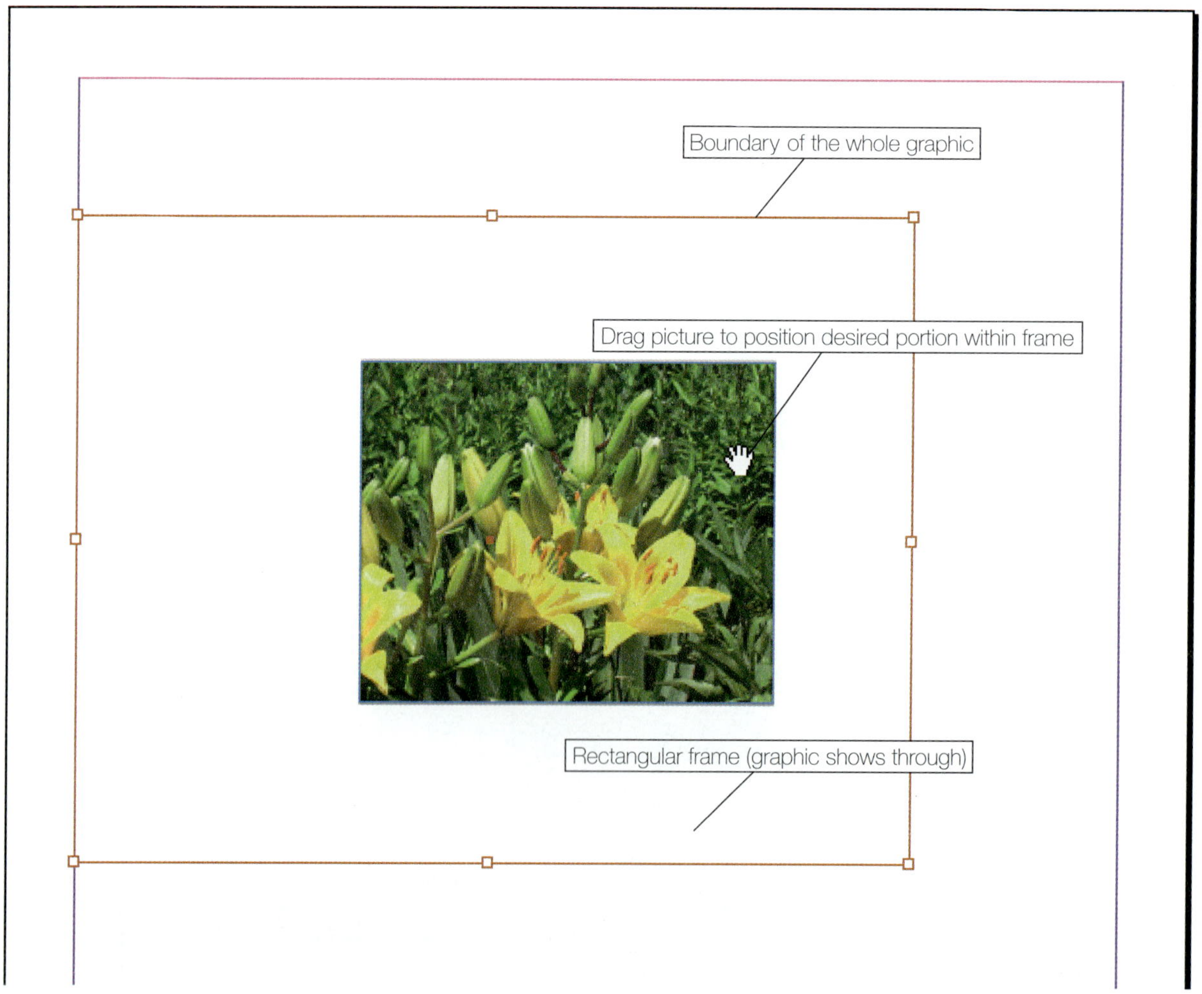

The brown outline represents the full size of the image

Adjust the width and height via the Control palette

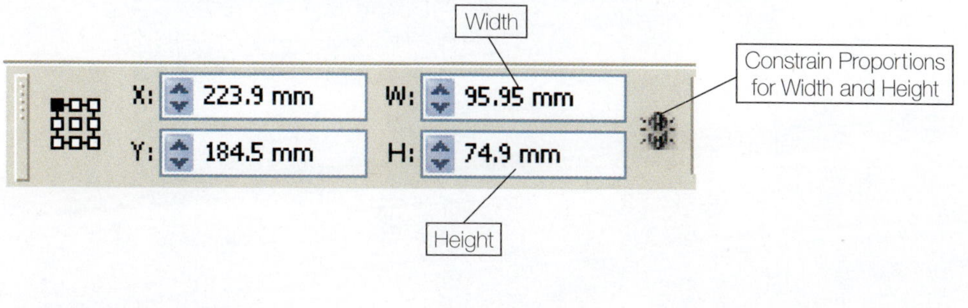

Arrange Objects

- As you learned in Exercise 7, one way to stack objects is to place them on different layers. By re-arranging the layers, you can rearrange the objects—as long as each object is on a separate layer.
- It is not necessary to create multiple layers in order to stack objects, however. You can use InDesign's Object > Arrange command to arrange a stack of objects within a single layer.
- From the Object > Arrange menu, you can choose any of the following options to arrange the object in relation to another object on the same layer. You can also use shortcut keys instead, as indicated.
  - Bring to Front: Ctrl+Shift+]
  - Bring Forward: Ctrl+]
  - Send Backward: Ctrl+[
  - Send to Back: Ctrl+Shift+[
- The Arrange commands have no effect between layers; they affect only objects that are on the same layer.

PROCEDURES

Import Graphics

Import into an Existing Frame

1. Select an existing frame.
2. Click **File** .... Alt+F
3. Click **Place** L

   ✓ *Ctrl+D is a shortcut for steps 1 and 2.*

4. Select the file to insert.
5. (Optional) If replacing existing content, select the **Replace Selected Item** check box if not already selected.
6. Click **Open** .... Enter or Ctrl+O

Import and Create a New Frame

1. Click away from all frames to deselect all.
2. Click **File** .... Alt+F
3. Click **Place** L

   ✓ *Ctrl+D is a shortcut for steps 1 and 2.*

4. Select the file to insert.
5. Click **Open** .... Enter or Ctrl+O
6. Drag to draw the frame.
7. Choose a graphic placement mode. (See the following steps.)

Choose a Graphic Placement Mode

1. Click the graphic frame to select it.
2. Click one of the following buttons on the Control palette:
   - **Fit Content to Frame**
   - **Fit Frame to Content**
   - **Fit Content Proportionally**
   - **Fill Frame Proportionally**
3. (Optional) Click the **Center Content** button to center the graphic in the frame.

Move and Size a Graphic Within a Frame

1. Click the **Direct Selection** tool.
2. Click the graphic frame.
3. Move the mouse pointer over the visible area of the graphic.
4. Drag the visible area of the graphic to reposition it in the frame if needed.

   ✓ *Hold down Shift to maintain the aspect ratio.*

   OR

   (Optional) Drag a selection handle on the outline frame to resize the graphic independently of the frame.

Arrange Objects

Menu Method

1. Select the object to move in the stack order.
2. Click **Object** .... Alt+O
3. Point to **Arrange** .... A
4. Click one of the following:
   - **Bring to Front** .... F
   - **Bring Forward** .... W
   - **Send Backward** .... B
   - **Send to Back** .... K

Keyboard Shortcut Method

1. Select the object to move in the stack order.
2. Press one of the following key combinations:
   - To bring to front .... Ctrl+Shift+]
   - To bring forward ...... Ctrl+]
   - To send backward .... Ctrl+[
   - To send to back .... Ctrl+Shift+[

EXERCISE DIRECTIONS

1. Start Adobe InDesign.
2. Open the file **EX33.indd**.
3. Deselect all objects.
4. On the Background Photos layer, import the file **EX33-coneflower.psd** and place it so it covers the entire left page (page 2), out to the bleed guides.

   ✓ *There is no page 1 in this layout; the first page is the left page in the spread, which InDesign calls page 2.*
5. Set the image to Fill Frame Proportionally.
6. Use the Center Content button to center the image within the frame.
7. Use the Arrange command to send the image to the back of its layer, so the yellow box appears on top of it.
8. On the right page (page 3), on the Background Photos layer, create a new rectangular frame within the left column and within the inner set of light blue column guides.

   ✓ *With the reference point for the new frame set to its top left, it should be at approximately X: 224 mm, Y: 184.5 mm, W: 96 mm, H: 75 mm.*
9. Copy the new frame, and paste it in the right column.

   ✓ *With the reference point for the new frame set to its top left, it should be at approximately X: 327.85 mm. All other measurements should be the same as for the original.*
10. Place the file **EX33-lilies.psd** in the empty frame in the left column.
11. Place the file **EX33-tulips.psd** in the empty frame in the right column.
12. Using the Direct Selection tool, resize the lilies picture to 185 mm wide, maintaining the aspect ratio of the image. Do not change the size of the rectangular frame in which the image was placed.
13. Center the lilies image within its frame.

    ✓ *Try centering it manually by dragging, and then click the Center Content button on the Control palette to see how close you came with your guess.*
14. Use your own judgment to resize and reposition the tulips image in its frame attractively.
15. Lock the Background Photos layer.
16. Preview the page in Preview view; it should resemble Illustration A.
17. Save your work as **XX-EX33.indd**, where XX are your initials, and exit InDesign.

Illustration A

Easy-Care Perennials

Looking for an easy way to enjoy color and beauty in your gardens all season long? Consider perennials. While they are more expensive than annuals initially, you quickly recoup the cost difference in having plants that will come back stronger and more vigorous every year, with no replanting.

Here are some easy-to-care-for plants that make for a good starter garden:

'Sprite' Astilbe — a diminutive hybrid astilbe with glossy dark green foliage. It produces sprays of shell pink flowers in midsummer shade gardens.

'Moonbeam' Coreposis — small, eight-petaled pale yellow flowers grace the tips of thin stems covered with narrow leaves. It blooms all summer in full sun.

'Palace Purple' Heuchera — boasts handsome deep purple foliage all summer in partial shade. It bears tiny, pale bluish-white flowers clustered at the ends of wiry stems in spring.

Creeping Phlox — neat, deep green foliage on creeping stems mats to cover the ground in woodland settings. In spring it produces clusters of small florets in white, blue, or pink.

'Sunny Border Blue' Veronica — offers a strong, vertical accent for the garden and bears spikes of rich violet-blue flowers in summer. It does best in a sunny site.

'Magnus' Purple Coneflower — jaunty, daisylike flowers with droopy purple petals bloom in midsummer when many other perennials are idle. It thrives in full sun.

'Goldsturm' Black-eyed Susan — provides billows of late-summer daisylike golden blossoms with dark centers on coarse, hairy stems.

Soil Conditions

Carefully consider the moisture conditions of the site you have chosen for your garden. Is it normal (as much as it's possible to define normal with today's chaotic weather), dry, or wet? Choose plants that do best in the prevailing conditions.

Next plan defensive measures to counteract a change in the moisture content. If the area you have chosen is dry, make sure the drainage is excellent. That way, even if there is excessive rain, the water should run off quickly. To increase drainage, dig out your garden bed to a depth of 1-1/2 to 2 feet and install a drainage pipe. his will immediately carry away any excess water. when refill the bed with enriched, porous garden soil filled with organic matter, such as peat moss and humus.

If your proposed garden area is moist, make sure you have the means to retain the moisture. Your garden should either be near a water source where you can sprinkle the spot daily, or embedded with a soaker hose.

Or you can create your own miniature damp spot by following the techniques used to create garden pools. Simply install a container with a very small hole punched in it for slow drainage. After you've filled

Continued on page 4

2 • Volume II Number 1

Midwestern Gardening Today • 3

ON YOUR OWN

1. Open the file **OYO-33.indd**.
2. Using the skills you learned for placing and sizing/positioning frames and graphics, create an attractive layout by placing the graphic files OYO-33A through OYO-33F. You decide which picture works best in which of the six empty spots in the layout.
3. Save your work as **XX-OYO-33.indd**, where XX are your initials.
4. Exit Adobe InDesign.

Exercise | 34

Skills Covered

- Understand Color Modes
- Understand Spot and Process Colors
- Understand Color Profiles
- Create a Color Swatch
- Edit a Color Swatch
- Change the Color Swatch Display

Software Skills When working on a complex document, or on a series of documents, it is important to use color consistently. Color swatches provide an easy way of keeping track of colors. You saw in Lesson 1 how to create a basic swatch; now you'll learn how to understand and manage your swatch collection.

Application Skills In this exercise you will create several new color swatches, convert all swatches to the CMYK model, and customize the display of the Swatches palette.

TERMS

CMYK Cyan, Magenta, Yellow, Black. The standard color mode for printing process colors. The colors correspond to the colors of ink used in the printing process.

Color matching system A proprietary set of numerically defined color swatches, such as PANTONE.

Color mode The way that colors are defined in a document. The most popular choices are RGB, CMYK, and Lab.

Color profile The settings within InDesign that dictate what colors will be available when you output your finished version. Also called *working space* or *color space*.

Gamut The available range of colors in a particular color mode.

Lab The standard color mode for printing spot colors.

Process colors Colors created with any combination of the colors from the color mode (CMYK, RGB, Lab, etc.).

RGB Red, Green, Blue. The standard color mode for monitors and onscreen displays such as Web pages.

Spot colors Colors where the ink color is premixed and then applied as a solid opaque layer to the paper at press time.

NOTES

Understand Color Modes

- There are several methods of describing a color numerically. The three most common methods are RGB, CMYK, and Lab. These are known as **color modes**.
  - **RGB** stands for Red, Green, Blue. These are the three colors that monitors use to create the images you see on your screen. Each of the three colors has a value between 0 (none) and 255 (full), so the RGB definition of a color consists of three numbers. Use RGB when creating a document for Web use, or for any other use where a document will be read on a computer screen (see the illustration at the top of page 172).
  - **CMYK** stands for Cyan, Magenta, Yellow, Black. These are the four colors that printers use to print color pages. Each of the four colors has a percentage value between 0 (none) and 100 (full), so the CMYK definition of a color consists

Red, Green, and Blue

of four numbers. Use CMYK when creating a document that will be printed (see the illustration below).

- **Lab** is not an acronym, but numeric values are assigned to each of its three letters: L, a, and b. The **L** value is the light/dark setting (the amount of black), from 0 to 100. The **a** value is the distribution between cyan and magenta, between -128 for all cyan and +127 for all magenta. The **b** value is the distribution between cyan and yellow, between -128 for all cyan and +127 for all yellow. Lab is typically used only for spot colors (explained later in these notes).

- InDesign allows you to combine RGB and CMYK swatches and colors in the same document, but it is usually not a good idea to do so. Usually you would want only one color mode to be in effect at a time, since most documents are destined for only one type of publication: online or print.

Understand Spot and Process Colors

- In professional printing, there are two ways of laying ink onto the page:
    - **Process colors** are colors created with any combination of the colors from the color mode. For example, in CMYK mode, a process color is any color you can make by blending Cyan, Magenta, Yellow, and Black.
    - **Spot colors** are colors where the ink color is premixed and then applied as a solid opaque layer to the paper at press time.
- For standard color printing, process color is the norm. There are two reasons you might use spot colors:
    - If you don't want to pay for full color printing, you can print a black-and-white document with a single spot color overlaid on it. Business stationery is commonly printed this way. The text on the stationery is black, and the color of the company's logo is printed with a spot color. This requires only two passes through the process, rather than four as in full-color printing, so it saves some money.
    - If you want to print a color that you can't accurately reproduce using CMYK, you can use a spot color in addition to regular process colors. For example, you might want metallic gold or silver ink, or fluorescent ink.
- InDesign allows you to define a spot color using any color mode. However, RGB is usually not a good choice because you would not use spot colors in online publications. CMYK is okay to use, but the best choice for spot colors is Lab. Many of the most popular color libraries define spot inks using Lab.
- Many professional printers use proprietary sets of **color matching systems** to ensure accurate color reproduction. PANTONE is one of the most famous color matching systems; TOYO, DIC, and HKS are other popular systems. When you define a color swatch in InDesign, you have the option of selecting from a color library for the matching system that is built into InDesign.

Cyan, Magenta, Yellow, and Black

✓ *For an explanation of each of the color matching systems InDesign supports and help choosing the right one for your project, search InDesign's Help system for the topic "Color libraries installed with InDesign."*

- Typically when using a color matching system, you would have a book of printed swatches to which to refer. You could find the swatch in the book that matches the color you want and then input that color's number. This is more reliable than relying on InDesign's onscreen swatch of that color because differences in monitors may slightly distort a color. These color matching systems are rather expensive, so normally only professional printing companies use them.

Understand Color Profiles

- The document's **color profile** (also called working space or color space) defines the way it translates numeric values to colors. A color profile exists to help prevent you from using colors in your publication that you will not be able to successfully output.
- The default setting in InDesign is North America General Purpose 2, which defines RGB using a specification called sRGB IEC61966-2.1 and CMYK using a specification called U.S. Web Coated (SWOP) v2. This setting is appropriate for documents that are destined either for the Web or for printing; it is a generic setting.
- If you know that you are specifically going to use a particular document only in print, or only on the Web, you might choose a different color profile. Changing the color profile might make more or fewer colors available to you to more closely reflect the reality of your output destination.
- For print use only, use North America Prepress 2; for Web use only, use North America Web/Internet.
- To make the change, choose Edit > Color Settings and select different working spaces from the Color Settings dialog box (see the illustration below).
- You can also individually select working space models for RGB and CMYK in this dialog box, but this is not recommended for beginners. Change those settings only if directed by a professional printing company with which you are working.
- The Color Settings dialog box sets preferences for InDesign in general. To change the color profile assignment for an individual document, use the Edit > Assign Profiles command, and choose to assign the current working space to the document for both RGB and CMYK (see the illustration on the following page).

The Color Settings dialog box

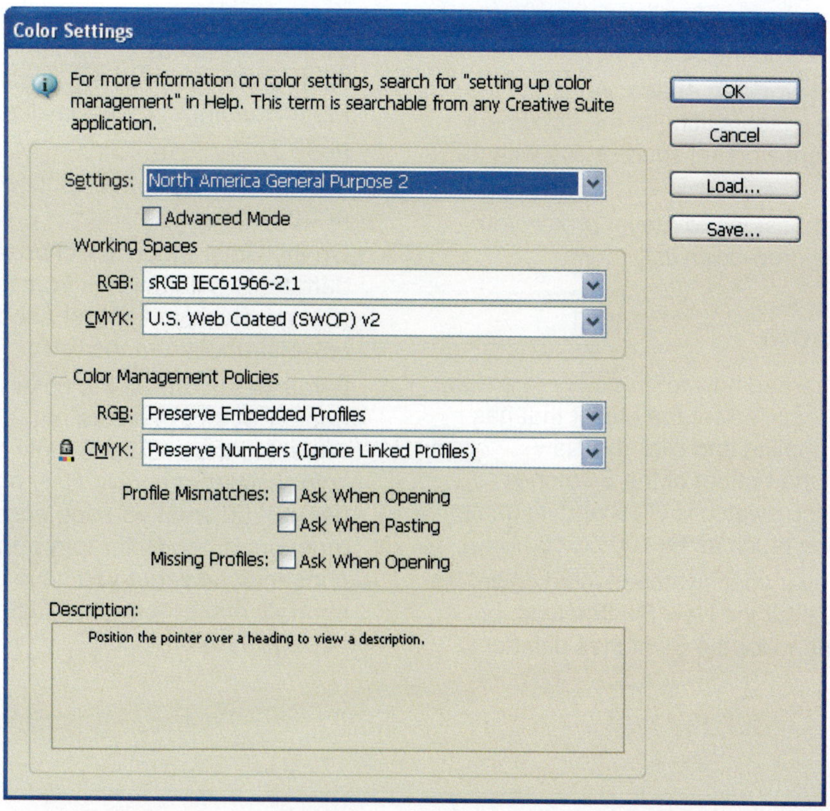

The Assign Profiles dialog box

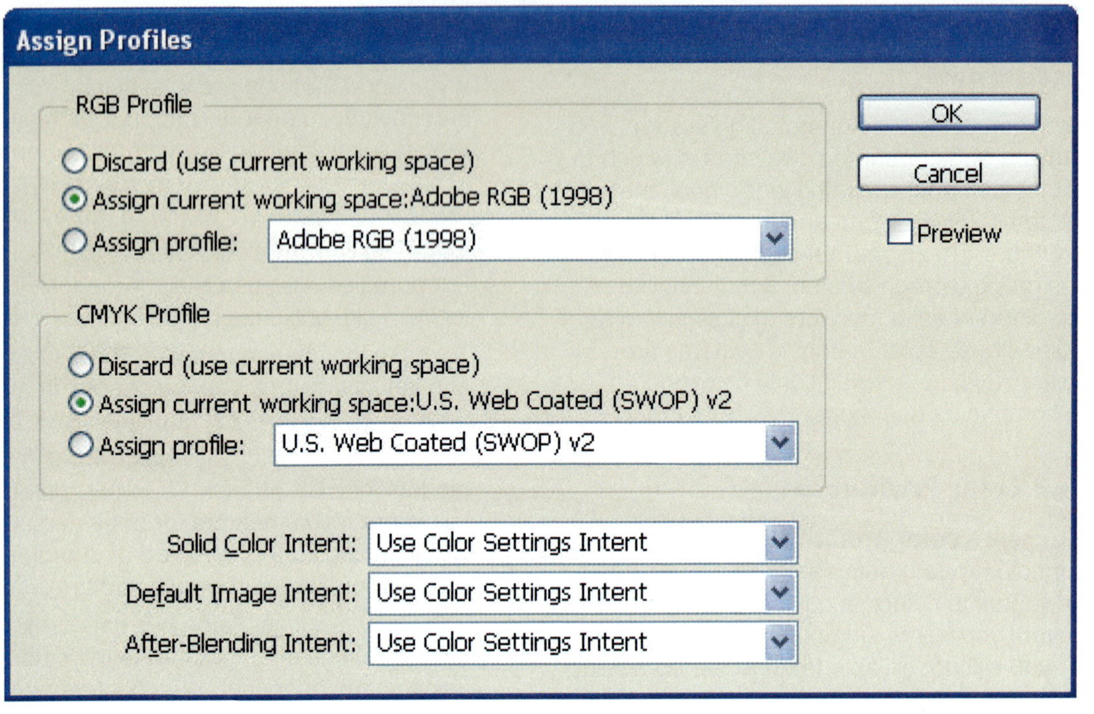

- For RGB and CMYK you can choose one of the following options:
  - **Discard:** Removes the document-specific color profile information, and uses the current working space. If you opened the document on another PC with a different working space, it would use that working space instead.
  - **Assign current working space:** Attaches the current working space setting to the document, so that the current working space stays with the document.
  - **Assign profile:** Assigns whatever profile you specify from the drop-down list.

Create a Color Swatch

- In Lesson 1 you learned how to quickly create new color swatches. Simply select the object that has the desired color applied and click the New Swatch icon at the bottom of the Swatches palette. The resulting swatch is RGB and its name is its color definition (such as R=100 G=100 B=0).
- For more control over your swatches, hold down the Alt key as you click the New Swatch icon, or open the fly-out menu for the Swatches palette and choose New Color Swatch. The New Color Swatch dialog box opens.
- Clear the Name with Color Value check box in the New Color Swatch dialog box to make the Swatch Name editable. Then enter a meaningful name for the swatch. You might choose to define swatch names by color name (for example, Dark Red) or by usage in the document (for example, Main Headings) (see the illustration at the top of page 175).
- On the Color Type list, choose either Process or Spot.
- On the Color Mode list, choose one of the standard three color modes from the top of the menu (CMYK, RGB, or Lab), or choose one of the many color libraries from the list.
- If you select one of the color libraries, a list will appear of all the colors in the chosen library, replacing the sliders. Simply click the desired color from that library. Rely on the color's number, not on what you see onscreen, because monitors differ. Refer to a printed guide to the chosen library that you have purchased from the library's maker (see the illustration at the bottom of page 175).

Create a new color swatch

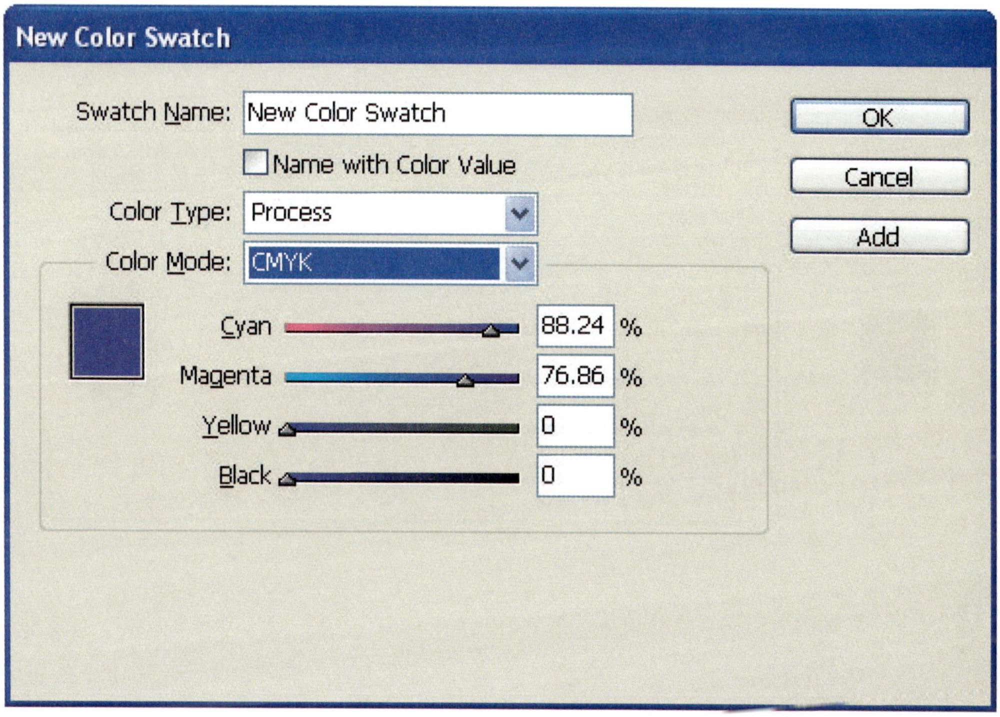

Choose a color from a library such as PANTONE

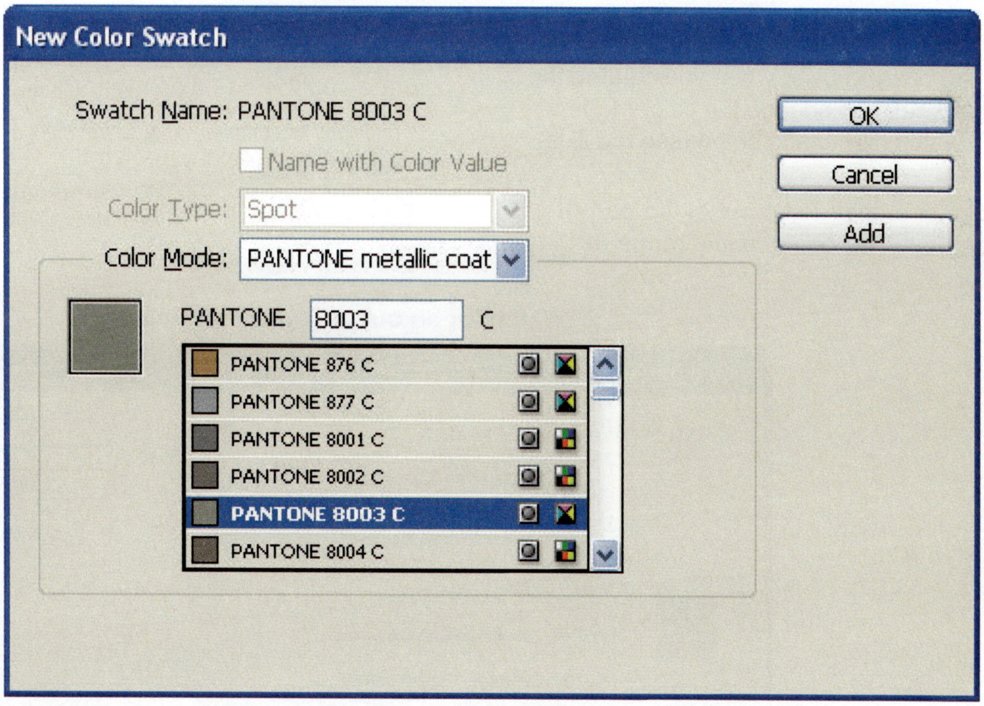

Edit a color swatch in its Swatch Options

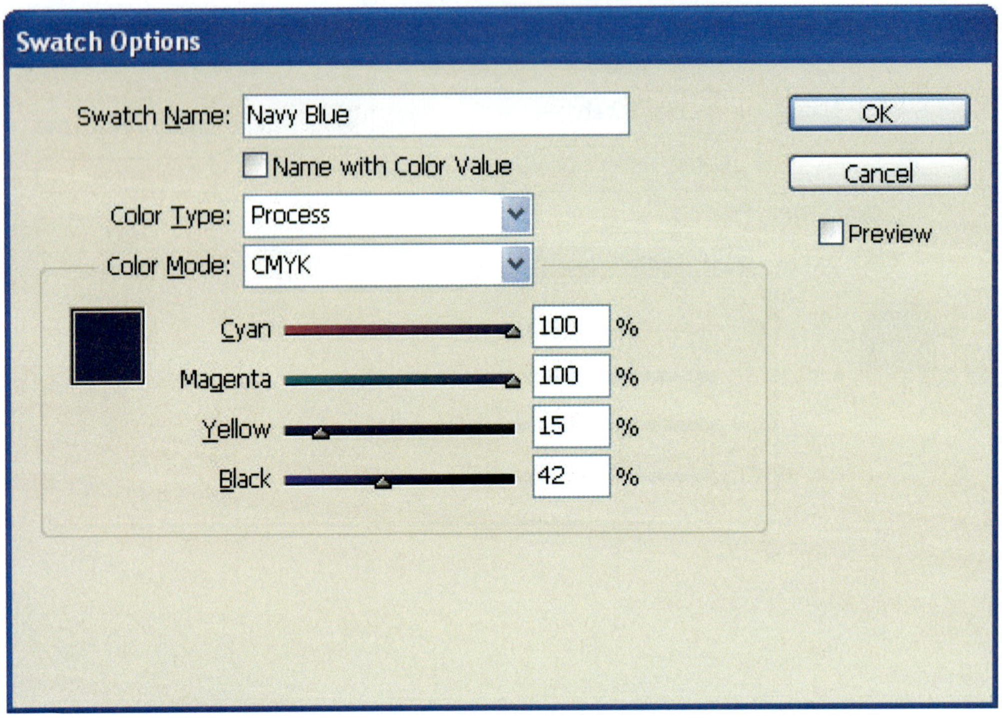

Edit a Color Swatch

- To edit a color swatch, double-click it on the Swatches palette to open the Swatch Options dialog box. This box is similar to the New Color Swatch dialog box you used when you created the swatch initially. You can change the color mode, color type, swatch name, and so on (see the illustration above).
- It is possible for a color to be out of the **gamut** for the document. The gamut is the range of available colors within the document's color space. When a color is out of gamut, a warning symbol appears in its Swatch Options dialog box, along with a small sample of the closest available color. Click that icon to change the swatch to the suggested color.

✓ *Changing to a different color space changes which colors are out of the gamut.*

Watch for an out of gamut warning

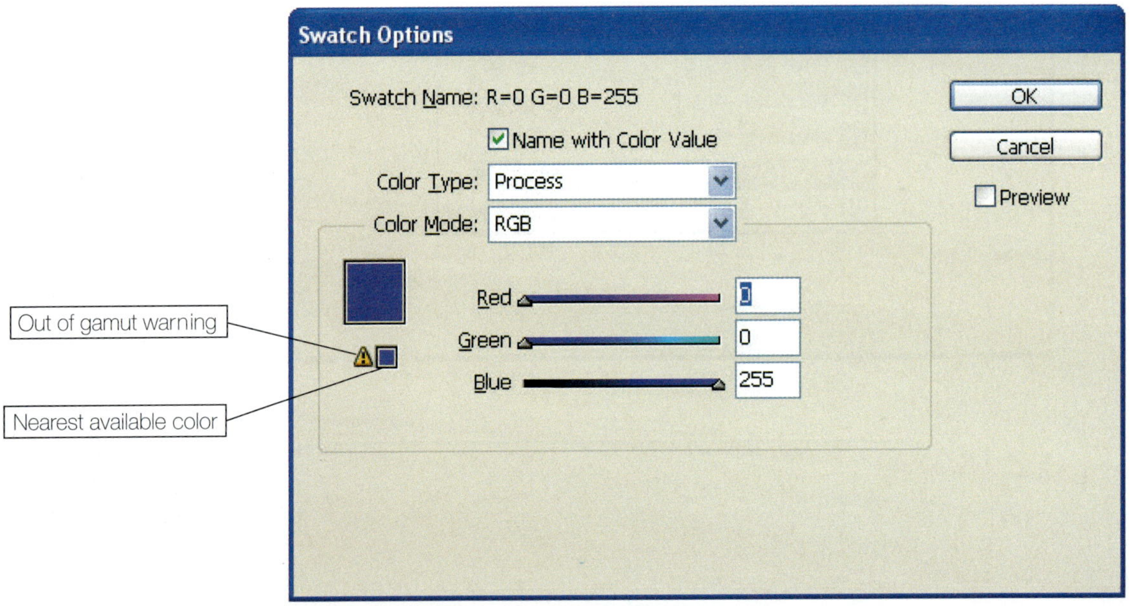

Change the Color Swatch Display

- By default, color swatches appear in a single-column list with a small square of the color, the swatch name, and symbols representing the type of color model in use. This is called Name view.
- To change to a different view of the color swatches, open the fly-out menu for the Swatches palette and choose Small Name, Small Swatch, or Large Swatch. The following illustration shows an example of Large Swatch view.

Symbols in the Swatches palette provide information about each swatch

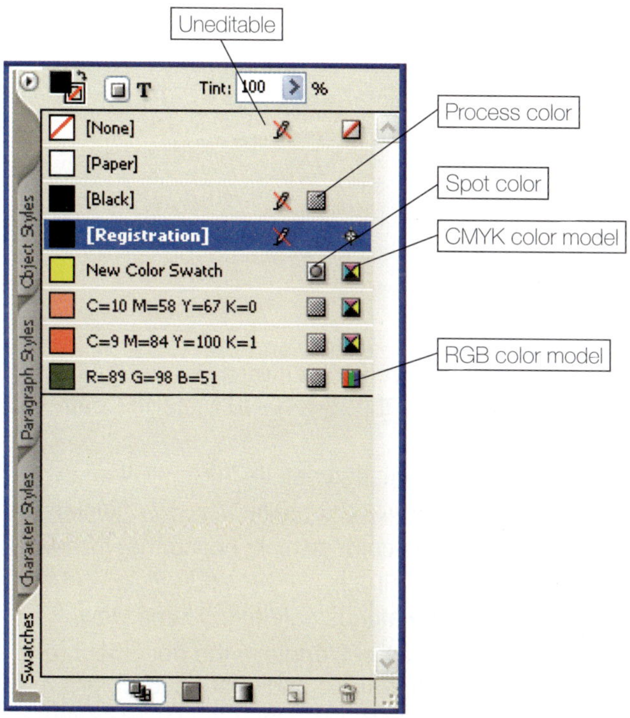

An alternate view of the Swatches palette

PROCEDURES

Choose a Color Profile

1. Click **Edit** .... Alt + E
2. Click **Color Settings** .... G
3. Open the **Settings** list .... Alt + E
4. Select a setting .... ↑ or ↓
5. Click **OK** .... ↵Enter

Assign a Color Profile to a Document

1. Click **Edit** .... Alt + E
2. Click **Assign Profiles** .... A
3. In the RGB Profile section, choose one:
   - **Discard** .... Alt + D
   - **Assign current working space** .... Alt + A
   - **Assign profile** (and then select a profile) .... Alt + S, ↓
4. In the CMYK Profile section, choose one:
   - **Discard** .... Alt + R
   - **Assign current working space** .... Alt + G
   - **Assign profile** (and then select a profile) .... Alt + N, ↓
5. Click **OK** .... ↵Enter

Create a Color Swatch

1. Select an object that is already filled with the desired color.

   OR

   Open the **Color** palette and select the desired color.
2. Open the **Swatches** palette.
3. Hold down **Alt** and click the **New Swatch** icon.
4. (Optional) Name the color with a text name:
   a. Deselect the **Name with Color Value** check box .... Alt + V
   b. Type a name for the swatch.
5. Open the **Color Type** list and choose **Process** or **Spot** .... Alt + T, ↑ or ↓
6. Open the **Color Mode** list and choose a color mode or a color matching system .... Alt + M, ↑ or ↓
7. (Optional) To change the color, drag the sliders or select a color from the color matching system swatches provided.

8. (Optional) If the **Out of Gamut Warning** icon ⚠ appears, click it to correct the color swatch.
9. Click **OK** .... ↵Enter

Edit a Color Swatch

1. Open the **Swatches** palette.
2. Double-click a swatch.
3. (Optional) Change the swatch's name:
   a. Deselect the **Name with Color Value** check box if it is selected .... Alt + V
   b. Type a different name for the swatch.
4. Open the **Color Type** list and choose **Process** or **Spot** .... Alt + T, ↑ or ↓
5. Open the **Color Mode** list and choose a color mode or a color matching system .... Alt + M, ↑ or ↓
6. (Optional) To change the color, drag the sliders or select a color from the color matching system swatches provided.
7. (Optional) If the **Out of Gamut Warning** icon ⚠ appears, click it to correct the color swatch.
8. Click **OK** .... ↵Enter

Change the Color Swatch Display

1. Open the **Swatches** palette.
2. Open the fly-out menu ▸ for the Swatches palette.
3. Click a viewing option:
   - **Name**
   - **Small Name**
   - **Small Swatch**
   - **Large Swatch**

EXERCISE DIRECTIONS

1. Start Adobe InDesign.
2. Open the file **EX34.indd**.
3. Change the color profile for InDesign to North America Prepress 2.
4. Change the document's color profile setting to Assign Current Working Space for both RGB and CMYK.
5. Change the RGB colors in the Swatches palette to CMYK, and change their names and values as follows:
   - Red swatch: Name it **Red** and set its values to C=0 M=100 Y=100 K=0.
   - Green swatch: Name it **Green** and set its values to C=100 M=0 Y=100 K=0.
   - Blue swatch: Name it **Blue** and set its values to C=100 M=100 Y=0 K=0.
6. Create a new spot color swatch for PANTONE 8322 C (part of the PANTONE Metallic Coated color library).
7. Display the Swatches palette in Small Name view.
8. Display the Swatches palette in Large Swatch view. Point to a color swatch; notice that its color definition pops up.
9. Display the Swatches palette in Name view.
10. Select the yellow rectangle in the document, and open the Color palette and change its color to C=0 M=31 Y=95 K=0.
11. Create a new swatch based on the rectangle's new color, and call the new swatch **Orange**.
12. Save your work as **XX-EX34.indd**, where XX are your initials.
13. Exit InDesign.

ON YOUR OWN

1. Create a new document.
2. Change to a color profile appropriate for Web/Internet usage for this document only.

   ✓ *Not sure what settings to pick? Open the Color Settings dialog box and see what CMYK and RGB settings are recommended for North America Web/Internet.*

3. Create new RGB swatches for the following colors (using your best estimation of what values to use for each color). Name each swatch with the descriptive text name. Make sure that none of the colors are out of the gamut.

   Bright red
   Orange
   Light blue
   Dark teal (blue/green)
   Dark purple
   Pale purple
   Brown

4. Save your work as **XX-OYO-34.indd**, where XX are your initials.
5. Exit Adobe InDesign.

Exercise | 35

Skills Covered

- Pick Up a Color with the Eyedropper
- Create a Tint Swatch
- Create Swatches for All Used Colors
- Delete Swatches
- Select Unused Swatches
- Import and Export Swatches

Software Skills When using a combination of color photographs and solid colors in a document, selecting an object fill color that is also in the photo is a great technique for tying the layout together visually. If the color from the photo is too dark or intense, you can create a tint swatch that softens the hue.

Application Skills In this exercise, you will pick up colors from the photos used in a layout and create tint swatches from them in your color palette. Then you will clean up the Swatches palette and export the swatches to a new document.

TERMS

Adobe Swatch Exchange A file format for saving swatch palettes for reuse in other Adobe applications.

Tint A screened (lighter) version of a color, created by reducing the C,M,Y, and K values of the color by an equal amount.

NOTES

Pick Up a Color with the Eyedropper

- The Eyedropper tool picks up any color in the document. When you select it in the toolbox, the mouse pointer changes to that same symbol (see the illustration in the opposite column).
- Click on a color already in use in the document (for example, a color in a photo), and the mouse pointer changes to a full eyedropper: . Then click on the object on which to "drop" the color.
- You can drop the color onto multiple objects. When you are finished, select some other tool in the toolbox (such as the Selection tool), or click the Eyedropper tool again to empty the dropper so you can pick up some other color.
- After picking up the color, you will probably want to create a swatch for it, as you learned to do in Exercise 34. (Remember to hold down Alt as you click the New Swatch icon if you want to use the dialog box.)

Eyedropper tool

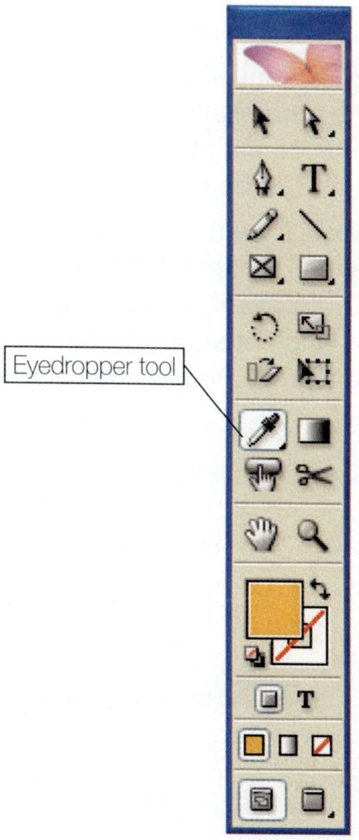

Tint samples

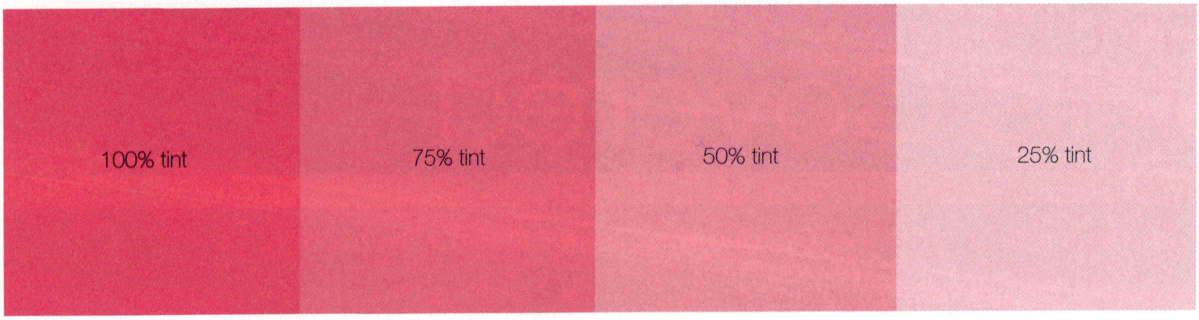

✓ *A shortcut method for creating a new swatch is as follows: After picking up a color, the color appears at the bottom of the toolbox. You can double-click the colored square to open a Color Picker dialog box, which contains an Add RGB Swatch button. Click one of the C, M, Y, or K text boxes to switch to the CMYK mode, and the button changes to Add CMYK Swatch. Click it to create the new swatch.*

Create a Tint Swatch

- A **tint** is a screened (lighter) version of a color. Each tint is based on a color, and has a percentage assigned to it of the original color. A 10% tint of a color would be very light; a 90% tint would be almost identical to the original color (see the illustration at the top of this page).
- To create a tint, open the Color palette and select a color. (To start with an existing swatch color, open the Swatches palette and click the swatch. That same color will also appear in the Color palette.)
- Then drag the Tint slider in the Color palette to the left, enter a percentage in the Percent box, or click anywhere along the tint ramp to pick up a tint (see the illustration in the opposite column).
- Usually you will want to create a tint swatch after creating a tint, so the tint is more easily reusable. To create a tint swatch, select the tint in the Color palette and then open the fly-out menu for the Color palette and choose Add to Swatches.

Adjust the tint on the Color palette

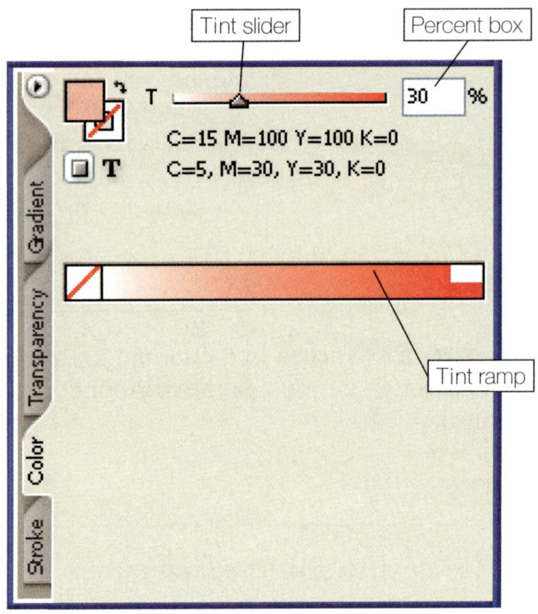

- Another way to create a tint swatch is to open the Swatches palette and select an existing color swatch. Then open the fly-out menu for the Swatches palette and choose New Tint Swatch. In the New Tint Swatch dialog box, all the controls are grayed out except the Tint slider. Drag that slider to create a tint of the selected color, and then click OK (see the illustration at the top of page 181).

Create a new tint swatch

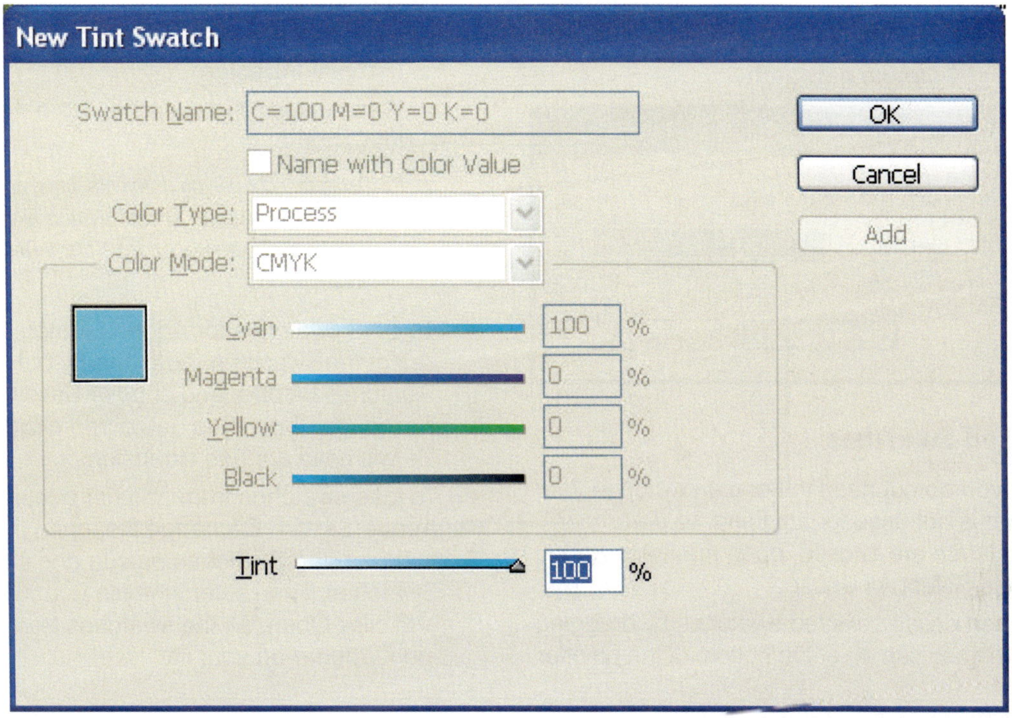

- To apply a tint of a swatch color without creating a tint swatch, you can apply the color swatch to an object and then open the Tint slider at the top of the Swatches palette and adjust the tint percentage for that object.

Adjust the tint percentage

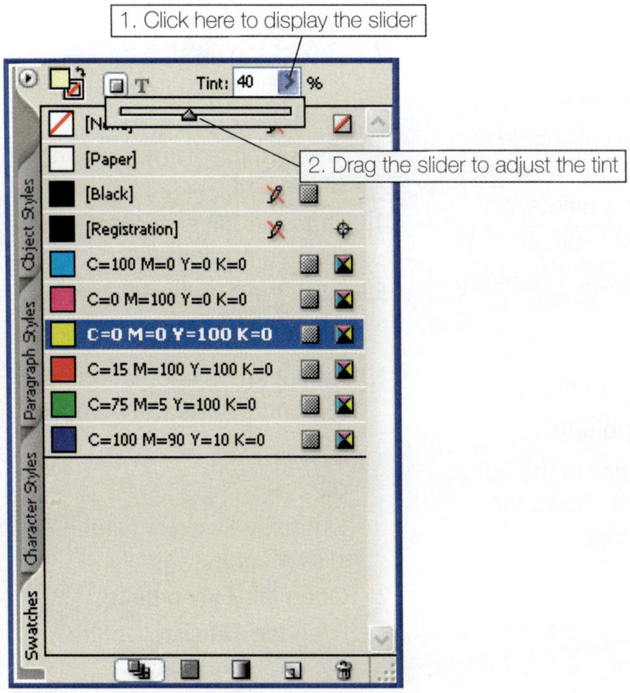

Create Swatches for All Used Colors

- If you forget to create a swatch when you apply a color to an object, it can sometimes be difficult to go back and remember what objects you colored.
- An easy fix is to allow InDesign to add all unnamed colors to the Swatches palette. Open the fly-out menu for the Swatches palette and choose Add Unnamed Colors.
- After the colors are added to the Swatches palette, you can double-click each one and change its name and/or its color model.

✓ *You should not mix RGB and CMYK colors in a single document, especially if it is destined for professional printing. Stick with a single color model. Most printers prefer CMYK.*

Delete Swatches

- To delete a swatch, drag it to the trash can at the bottom of the Swatches palette.
- If you try to delete a swatch that is in use somewhere in the document, the Delete Swatch dialog box appears. You can then choose what should happen to the objects formatted with that swatch.
  - **Defined Swatch:** Changes the object(s) to some other swatch color you specify.

- **Unnamed Swatch:** Leaves the object at its current color but disassociates it with any swatch.

Delete a swatch

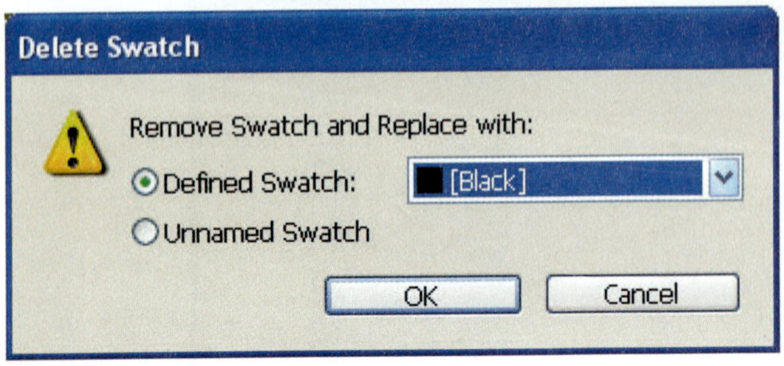

Select Unused Swatches

- Normally you do not need to keep a swatch in your palette that is not used for anything. To determine which swatches are unused, open the fly-out menu and choose Select All Unused.
- You can then delete selected swatches by dragging them to the trash can at the bottom of the palette.

Import and Export Swatches

- There are two ways to transfer swatches between InDesign documents:
  - You can save the swatches for use with **Adobe Swatch Exchange**, which enables the swatches to be used in any Adobe application (not just InDesign).
  - You can load the swatches from one document into another document.

  ✓ *Swatches containing gradients, tints, or mixed inks cannot be saved in an Adobe Swatch Exchange file. They can, however, be loaded from one InDesign document to another.*
- To save swatches for Adobe Swatch Exchange, select the swatches, open the fly-out menu on the Swatches palette, and choose Save Swatches For Exchange. Type a file name and click Save. The file will have an .ase extension.
- To load swatches from another document or an Adobe Swatch Exchange file, open the fly-out menu on the Swatches palette and choose Load Swatches. Then select the file from which to import and click Open. All the swatches from that document appear on your list.

PROCEDURES

Pick Up a Color with the Eyedropper

1. Click the **Eyedropper** tool on the toolbox.
2. Click the color to pick up.
3. Click the object to receive the color.
4. (Optional) Repeat step 3 to color other objects.
5. Click the **Eyedropper** tool again to clear the tool and then repeat steps 2–4 for another color.

   OR

   Click the **Selection** tool or any other tool to turn off the Eyedropper tool.

Create a Swatch Using the Eyedropper Tool

1. Click the **Eyedropper** tool on the toolbox.
2. Click the color to pick up.
3. Open the **Swatches** palette.
4. Hold down **Alt** and click the **New Swatch** icon.
5. (Optional) Clear the **Name with Color Value** check box and type a descriptive name .... Alt+V
6. (Optional) Open the **Color Mode** list and choose a different mode .... Alt+M, ↓ or ↑
7. Click **OK** .... Enter

Apply a Tint

1. Apply a color to an object.
2. Open the **Color** palette.
3. Drag the **Tint** slider to the left until the Tint box shows the desired percentage.

   OR

   Click the tint ramp to select the desired tint.

Create a Tint Swatch

Swatches Palette Method

1. Open the **Swatches** palette.
2. Select the swatch for the color for which to create a tint swatch.
3. Click the arrow to the right of the Tint box.
4. Drag the **Tint** slider to the desired percentage.
5. Click the **New Swatch** icon.

Color Palette Method

1. Select an object that has an existing color swatch applied to it.

   OR

   Open the **Swatches** palette and click a color swatch.
2. Open the **Color** palette.
3. Drag the **Tint** slider to the desired percentage.

4. Open the fly-out menu for the Color palette.
5. Click **Add to Swatches**.

Create Swatches for All Used Colors

1. Open the fly-out menu for the Swatches palette.
2. Click **Add Unnamed Colors**.

Delete Swatches

1. Open the **Swatches** palette.
2. Select the swatch(es) to delete.

   ✓ *You can hold down Ctrl and click on multiple noncontiguous swatches or hold down Shift to select a contiguous range. Or you can use the Select Unused Swatches procedure that follows this one.*

3. Drag the selected swatch(es) to the trash can icon.

Select Unused Swatches

1. Open the fly-out menu for the Swatches palette.
2. Click **Select All Unused**.

Import and Export Swatches

Export Swatches to an Adobe Swatch Exchange File

1. Select the swatches to export.
2. Open the fly-out menu for the Swatches palette.
3. Click **Save Swatches for Exchange**.
4. If a warning appears about gradients, tints, and mixed inks, click **OK** .... Enter
5. (Optional) Change the save location if needed.
6. Type a name for the saved file in the **File name** box ..... Alt + N
7. Click **Save** .... Enter

Import Swatches

1. Open the fly-out menu for the Swatches palette.
2. Click **Load Swatches**.
3. Select the InDesign document or Adobe Swatch Exchange (.ase) file.
4. Click **Open** .... Enter

   ✓ *If there are duplicates, two copies of the same color swatch will appear in the Swatches palette. Delete the extras if desired.*

EXERCISE DIRECTIONS

1. Start Adobe InDesign.
2. Change back to the North America General Purpose 2 color setting if you changed this in a previous exercise.

   ✓ *To do this, choose Edit > Color Settings and choose North America General Purpose 2 from the Settings list.*

3. Open the file **EX35.indd**.
4. Use the eyedropper to pick up the orange in the center of one of the purple flowers on page 2, and create a new CMYK color swatch for it.

   ✓ *There are many shades of orange in the centers of the flowers; try to pick up one of the brighter, lighter shades.*

5. Apply the new orange swatch to the orange rectangle in the document.
6. Delete the old orange swatch, and rename the new orange swatch **Orange**.
7. Create a new swatch that is a 40% tint of the Orange swatch, and apply the tint swatch to the orange rectangle.
8. Select and delete all unused swatches.
9. Pick up the bright yellow in the lilies and make a new CMYK swatch of it called **Lily Yellow**.
10. Pick up the bright red in the tulips and make a new CMYK swatch of it called **Tulip Red**.
11. Pick up the bright purple in the coneflowers and make a new CMYK swatch of it called **Coneflower Purple**.
12. Create a 60% tint swatch of Coneflower Purple.
13. Export the color swatches to an Adobe Swatch Exchange file. Call the file **XX-EX35-Swatch.ase**, where XX are your initials.
14. Save your work as **XX-EX35.indd**, where XX are your initials.
15. Close the document, and start a new document.
16. Import the swatches from **XX-EX35-Swatch.ase** to the new document.
17. Save the new document as **XX-EX35A.indd**, where XX are your initials.
18. Exit InDesign.

ON YOUR OWN

1. Open the file OYO-35.indd.
2. Pick up a bright green from the center photo on page 1, and create a swatch from it.
3. Create a 30% tint of the new swatch.
4. Create a new layer called **Background** behind the existing layer.
5. On the new layer, create a large rectangle that covers the entire first page, and apply the 30% tint to it.
6. Do the same thing on the second page, but pick up a pale blue from the wallpaper in the bedroom photo. Create a tint swatch of the color (somewhere between 10% and 30%, depending on what looks best to you), and create a background on the Background layer that uses this tint swatch.
7. Delete all unused swatches.
8. Save your work as **XX-OYO-35.indd**, where XX are your initials.
9. Exit InDesign.

Exercise | 36

Skills Covered

- Apply an Object Stroke
- Apply a Drop Shadow to an Object
- Apply Feathering
- Apply Corner Effects
- Create an Object Style

Software Skills Sometimes it is useful to place a stroke around a graphic object, or to apply some special effect to its edges. Besides an array of stroke weights, styles, and colors, InDesign also offers drop shadow and feathering effects and special corner styles.

Application Skills In this exercise, you will apply strokes and other effects to graphic object frames, and you will create an object style that will automatically format graphic frames in the desired manner.

TERMS

Blur The portion of a shadow that is feathered (blurred).

Opacity The amount of solidness (as opposed to transparency).

Noise The amount of roughness or texture in the shadow or edge of an object.

NOTES

Apply an Object Stroke

- Object frames can have strokes applied to them or they can be strokeless. The properties of object strokes are very similar to those of table strokes that you learned about in Exercise 27.
- When a frame is selected, the Control palette provides Stroke Weight and Stroke Type controls for it. Select from these drop-down lists.

Select a stroke weight and style

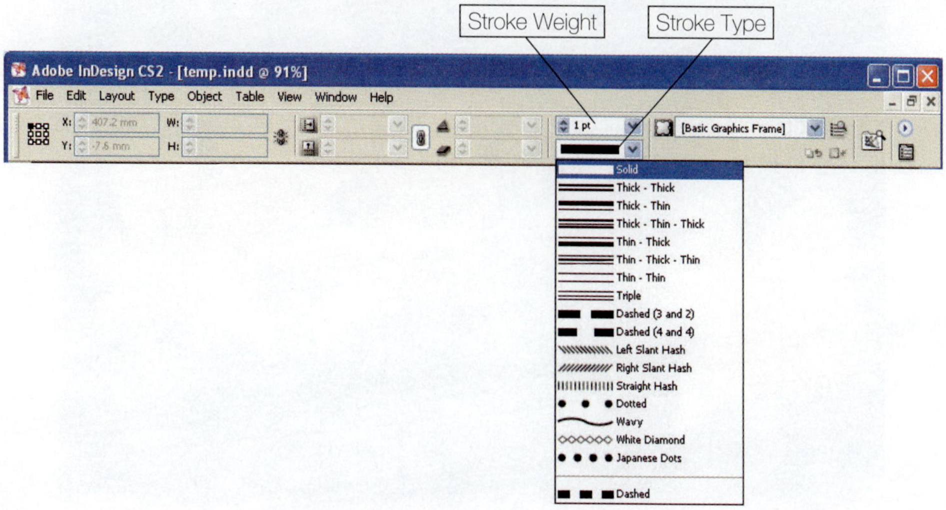

- To apply a stroke color, open the Color palette and double-click the Stroke square. Then select a color from the Color Picker, the same as with fill color.

Choose a stroke on the Color palette

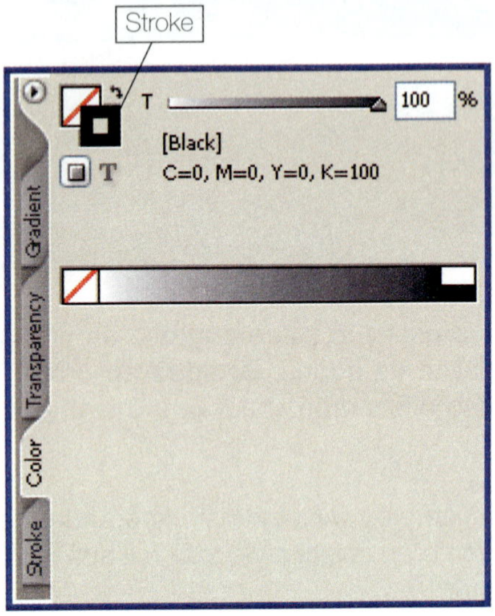

✓ *Some of the controls on the Stroke palette are applicable only to lines, not to object frames.*

- For more control over a stroke, open the Stroke palette (Window > Stroke). From here you can control the following for object frames:
    - **Weight:** The line thickness.
    - **Join:** The roundedness of the corners: Miter join (square), Round join (rounded), and Bevel join (diagonally cut). A miter join can be further fine-tuned with the Miter Limit setting.
    - **Align Stroke:** Where on the outer edge of the frame the stroke will appear: centered within it, inside it, or outside it. This becomes more of an issue with thicker strokes.
    - **Gap Color:** The color of the space between the stroke's dashes, dots, or multiple lines.

Apply a Drop Shadow to an Object

- A drop shadow makes a frame look like it is floating above the page (see the illustration at the bottom of this page):
- To create a drop shadow for a frame, select it and then choose Object > Drop Shadow. Then select the Drop Shadow check box and set up the shadow effect:
    - **Mode:** The blending mode. Experiment with these to find one you prefer.
    - **Opacity:** The solidness of the shadow. A higher number is less transparent.
    - **Blur:** The outer boundary of the blur from the edge of the shadow.
    - **X Offset:** The distance from the object that the shadow extends horizontally.
    - **Spread:** The amount of solid shadow before the edges start to blur. The higher the number the farther away from the object the shadow remains solid.

A drop shadow

Create a drop shadow

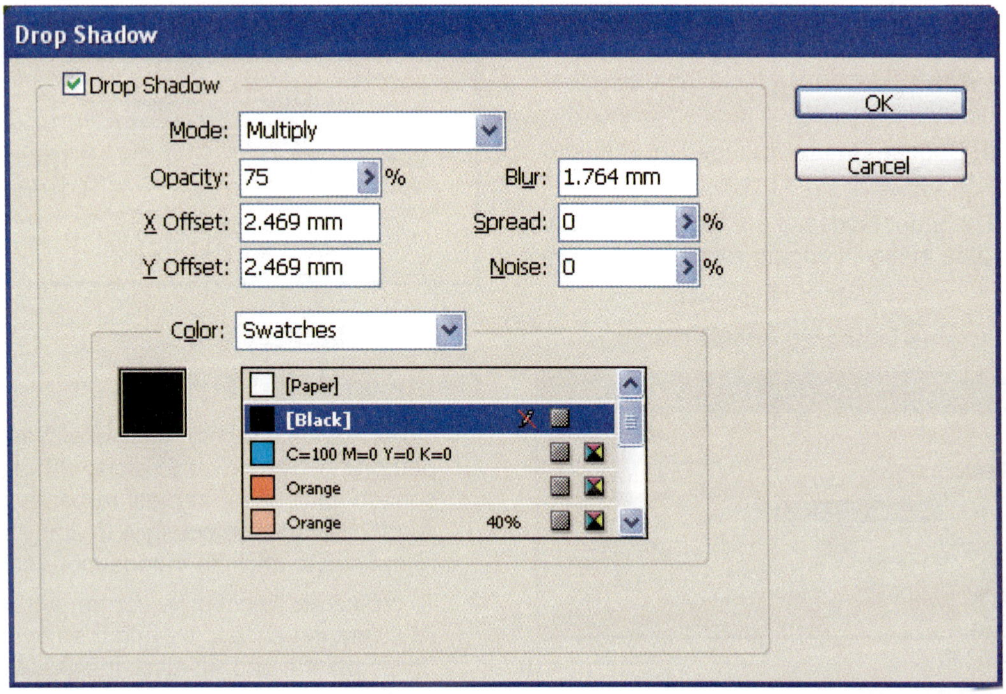

- **Y Offset:** The distance from the object that the shadow extends vertically.
- **Noise:** The texture of the shadow, giving it a rough or grainy appearance.
- **Color:** Choose Swatches and select one of your existing swatches or select a color mode and pick a color using the sliders (see the illustration above).

Apply Feathering

- Feathering blends the edges of the object into the background, giving it a soft edge:

Feathered edges

- To create a feather effect for a frame, select it and then choose Object > Feather. Then select the Feather check box and set up the feathering effect:
  - **Feather Width:** The amount into the frame that the feather effect extends.
  - **Corners:** Choose Sharp, Rounded, or Diffused. Try each to see which you prefer.
  - **Noise:** The smoothness of the feather effect. A higher value makes it appear rough or grainy.

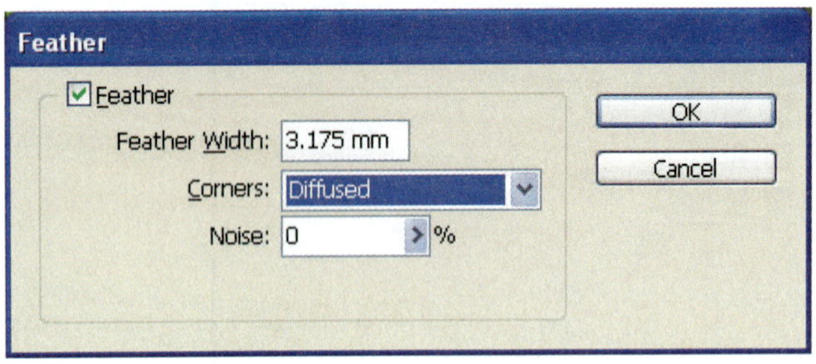

Create feathered edges

Apply Corner Effects

- Corner effects cut out a portion of the corners of the frame (see the illustration at the bottom of this page):
- To create corner effects for a frame, select it and choose Object > Corner Effects. Then select the desired effect and specify a size. The larger the size, the more dramatic the effect will be (see the illustration at the top of the opposite column.)

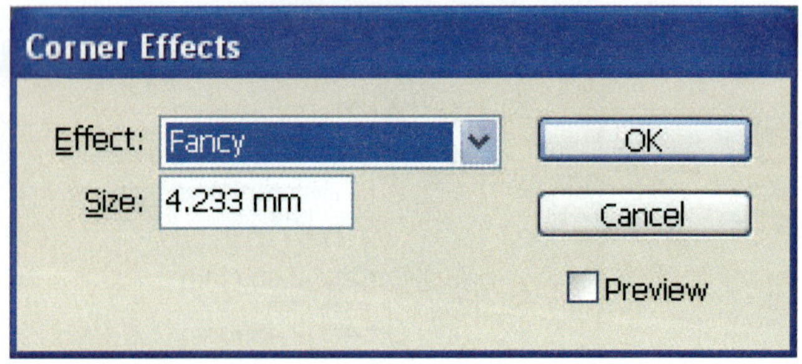

Apply corner effects

Create an Object Style

- Object styles are very much like character and paragraph styles (see Exercise 28) except they contain settings for frames, rather than text. You might create an object style to apply stroke and/or fill options to multiple frames more easily.
- To create an object style, format a frame the way you want the style to be and then open the Object Styles palette and Alt+click the Create New Style button.
- You can go through all the categories in the New Object Style dialog box, as in Exercise 28, but the main item you will probably want to change is to give the style a meaningful name. All the other settings will be taken from the object you selected. Then click OK (see the illustration on page 189).

Corner effects

Create an object style

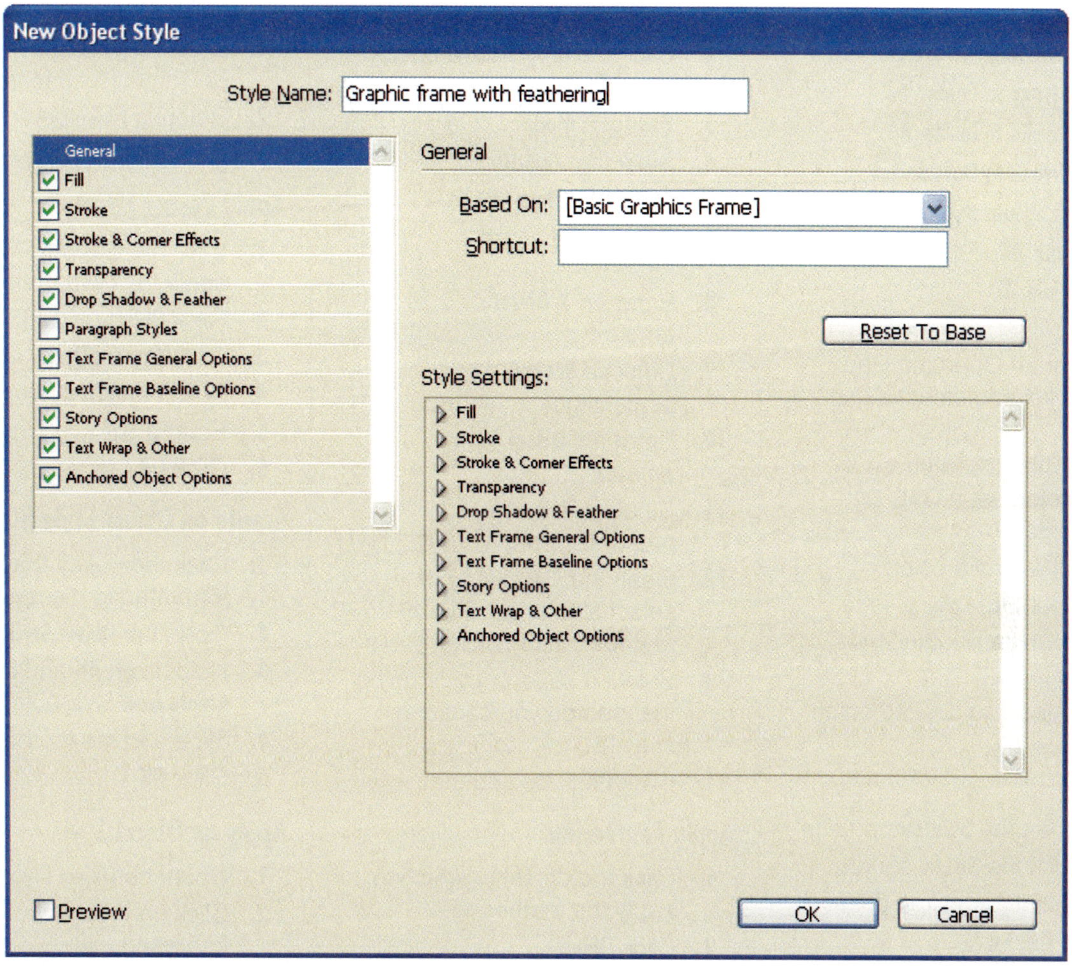

PROCEDURES

Apply an Object Stroke

Control Palette Method

1. Select the object frame to affect.
2. Select a stroke weight:
   a. Open the **Stroke Weight** list on the Control palette.
   b. Click a weight.

   OR

   a. Click in the **Stroke Weight** text box.
   b. Type the stroke weight desired.

   OR

   a. Click an up or down increment arrow to the left of the **Stroke Weight** box.
3. Select a stroke style:
   a. Open the **Stroke Type** list on the Control palette.
   b. Click a style.
4. Select a stroke color:
   a. Open the **Color** palette.
   b. Double-click the **Stroke** square.
   c. Select the desired color.
   d. Click **OK**.

   OR

   a. Open the **Swatches** palette.
   b. Click the **Stroke** square.
   c. Click the desired color swatch.

Stroke Palette Method

1. Select the object frame to affect.
2. Open the **Stroke** palette.
3. Select a stroke weight:
   a. Open the **Weight** list.
   b. Click a weight.

   OR

   a. Click in the **Weight** text box.
   b. Type the stroke weight desired.

   OR

   a. Click an up or down increment arrow to the left of the **Stroke Weight** box.

4. Open the **Type** list and select a stroke style.
5. Click an **Align Stroke** button:

   Align Stroke to Center

   Align Stroke to Inside

   Align Stroke to Outside
6. Select a **Join style**:

   Miter join

   Round join

   Bevel join
7. (Optional) Open the Gap Color list and select a gap color.
8. (Optional) If you chose a gap color, set a Gap Tint percentage.
9. Select a stroke color:
   a. Open the **Color** palette.
   b. Double-click the **Stroke** square.
   c. Select the desired color.
   d. Click **OK**.

   OR

   a. Open the **Swatches** palette.
   b. Click the **Stroke** square.
   c. Click the desired color swatch.

Apply a Drop Shadow to an Object

1. Click the object to which to apply the shadow.
2. Click **Object** .... Alt+O
3. Click **Drop Shadow** .... D
4. Click the **Drop Shadow** check box .... Alt+D
5. Select a **Mode** .... Alt+M, ↓
6. Select an **Opacity** percentage ..... Alt+T, ↑/↓
7. Enter a **Blur** amount .... Alt+U
8. Enter an **X Offset** amount .... Alt+X
9. Select a **Spread** percentage ...... Alt+S, ↑/↓
10. Enter a **Y Offset** amount .... Alt+Y
11. Select a **Noise** percentage ..... Alt+N, ↑/↓
12. Open the **Color** list and select a color-picking method .... Alt+O, ↓/↑
13. Select a shadow color using the method you chose in step 12.
14. Click **OK** .... ↵Enter

Apply Feathering

1. Click the object to which to apply the feathering.
2. Click **Object** .... Alt+O
3. Click **Feather** .... H
4. Click the **Feather** check box .... Alt+F
5. Enter a **Feather Width** .... Alt+W
6. Select a **Corners** setting .... Alt+C, ↓
7. Select a **Noise** percentage.
8. Click **OK** .... ↵Enter

Apply Corner Effects

1. Click the object to which to apply the corner effects.
2. Click **Object** .... Alt+O
3. Click **Corner Effects** .... E
4. Select an **Effect** .... Alt+E, ↓
5. Enter a **Size** .... Alt+S
6. Click **OK** .... ↵Enter

Create an Object Style by Example

1. Click the object that is already formatted in the desired way.
2. Open the **Object Styles** palette.
3. Hold down **Alt** and click the **Create New Style** button.
4. Type a name for the style.
5. Click **OK** .... ↵Enter

Apply an Object Style

1. Open the **Object Styles** palette.
2. Click on the object to be formatted.
3. Click on the desired style.

EXERCISE DIRECTIONS

1. Start Adobe InDesign.
2. Open the file **EX36.indd**.
3. Apply a 2mm feather effect with 50% noise and sharp corners to the pale orange rectangle.
4. For the yellow lilies photo, create a drop shadow with the following specifications:
   - Mode: Multiply
   - Opacity: 100%
   - X Offset: 1.5 mm
   - Y Offset: 1.5 mm
   - Blur: 2 mm
   - Spread: 20%
   - Noise: 10%
   - Color: Swatches, Coneflower Purple 60% tint
5. Apply a Rounded corner effect to the yellow lilies photo.
6. Create an object style based on the yellow lilies photo, and call the style **Small Photo**.
7. Apply the Small Photo style to both the yellow lilies and the red tulips photos.
8. To adjust for the change you've just made, increase the height of the orange rectangle to 84 mm and change the Y position of its upper-left corner to 180.

   ✓ *Use the H: and Y: boxes on the Control palette.*
9. Preview your work. The bottom of the page spread should resemble Illustration A.
10. Save your work as **XX-EX36.indd**, where XX are your initials.
11. Exit InDesign.

Illustration A

Easy-Care Perennials

Looking for an easy way to enjoy color and beauty in your gardens all season long? Consider perennials. While they are more expensive than annuals initially, you quickly recoup the cost difference in having plants that will come back stronger and more vigorous every year, with no replanting.

Here are some easy-to-care-for plants that make for a good starter garden:

'Sprite' Astilbe — a diminutive hybrid astilbe with glossy dark green foliage. It produces sprays of shell pink flowers in midsummer shade gardens.

'Moonbeam' Coreposis — small, eight-petaled pale yellow flowers grace the tips of thin stems covered with narrow leaves. It blooms all summer in full sun.

'Palace Purple' Heuchera — boasts handsome deep purple foliage all summer in partial shade. It bears tiny, pale bluish-white flowers clustered at the ends of wiry stems in spring.

Creeping Phlox — neat, deep green foliage on creeping stems mats to cover the ground in woodland settings. In spring it produces clusters of small florets in white, blue, or pink.

'Sunny Border Blue' Veronica — offers a strong, vertical accent for the garden and bears spikes of rich violet-blue flowers in summer. It does best in a sunny site.

'Magnus' Purple Cone flower — jaunty, daisylike flowers with droopy purple petals bloom in midsummer when many other perennials are idle. It thrives in full sun.

'Goldsturm' Black-eyed Susan — provides billows of late-summer daisylike golden blossoms with dark centers on coarse, hairy stems.

Soil Conditions

Carefully consider the moisture conditions of the site you have chosen for your garden. Is it normal (as much as it's possible to define normal with today's chaotic weather), dry, or wet? Choose plants that do best in the prevailing conditions.

Next plan defensive measures to counteract a change in the moisture content. If the area you have chosen is dry, make sure the drainage is excellent. That way, even if there is excessive rain, the water should run off quickly. To increase drainage, dig out your garden bed to a depth of 1-1/2 to 2 feet and install a drainage pipe. his will immediately carry away any excess water. Then refill the bed with enriched, porous garden soil filled with organic matter, such as peat moss and humus.

If your proposed garden area is moist, make sure you have the means to retain the moisture. Your garden should either be near a water source where you can sprinkle the spot daily, or embedded with a soaker hose.

Or you can create your own miniature damp spot by following the techniques used to create garden pools. Simply install a container with a very small hole punched in it for slow drainage. After you've filled

Continued on page 4

2 • Volume II Number 1

Midwestern Gardening Today • 3

ON YOUR OWN

1. Open the file **OYO-36.indd**.
2. Apply corner effects, drop shadows, and/or feathering to the photos on both pages of the brochure as you see fit. Use each of the three effects at least once.
3. If needed for an attractive layout, reposition or resize graphic frames slightly.
4. Save your work as **XX-OYO-36.indd**, where XX are your initials.
5. Exit InDesign.

Exercise | 37

Skills Covered

- Apply a Gradient
- Change the Gradient Direction
- Set Object Transparency
- Select Transparency Effects

Software Skills Gradients and transparencies can be effective alternatives to solid fills, and can add interest to a layout.

Application Skills In this exercise, you will create a gradient background for a page and add partial transparency to a fill effect.

TERMS

Gradient A gradual shift from one color to another.

Opacity The amount of solidness (as opposed to transparency).

NOTES

Apply a Gradient

- A **gradient** is a gradual shift between one color and another. It can be either linear (from one side to another) or radial (from the center to the edges).

- InDesign's gradient feature is more sophisticated than that of many programs; it enables you to create gradients that consist of more than two colors, and that distribute the colors either equally or unequally within the object fill (see the illustration at the top of page 193).

Gradient examples

Linear, pink to yellow

Radial, dark blue to pale blue

This gradient uses unequal distribution, and is primarily yellow

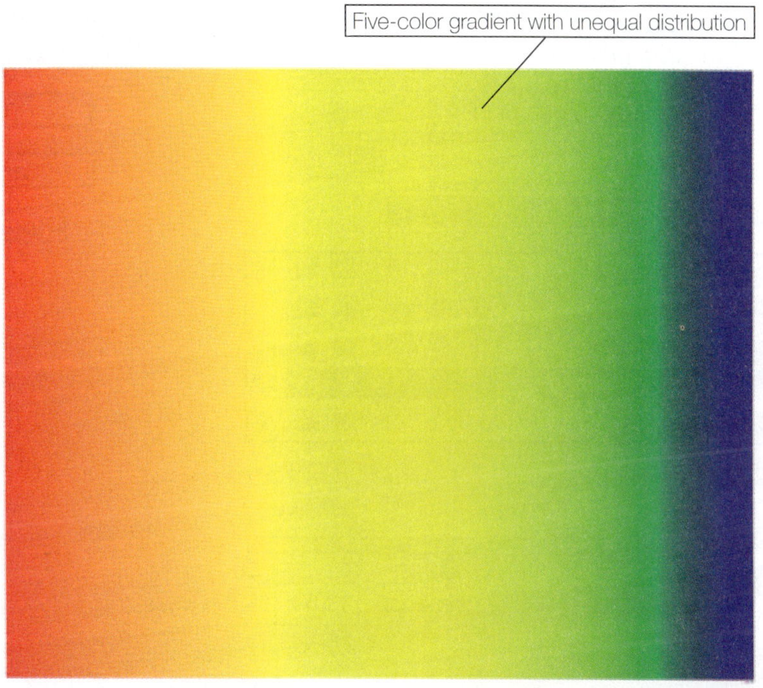

- InDesign has a Gradient palette for creating unnamed (nonswatch) gradients, but it can be somewhat awkward to use because you cannot pick colors from it directly. It is much easier to create a gradient swatch instead.
- To create a gradient swatch, open the Swatches palette, open the fly-out menu, and choose New Gradient Swatch. Then specify the swatch's properties in the New Gradient Swatch dialog box.

✓ *It is helpful to see the gradient applied to an object as you are creating it. Create a dummy rectangle or circle, and select it before opening the New Gradient Swatch dialog box.*

- Give the swatch a meaningful name, such as the colors involved (for example, Red to Blue).
- From the Type list, choose Linear or Radial.
- Click one of the squares on the gradient ramp, and then select a color for it.
- From the Stop Color list, choose the color mode for selecting colors: Swatches, Lab, CMYK, or RGB.
- To adjust the ratio of one color to the other, drag the diamond above the gradient ramp.

Create a gradient effect

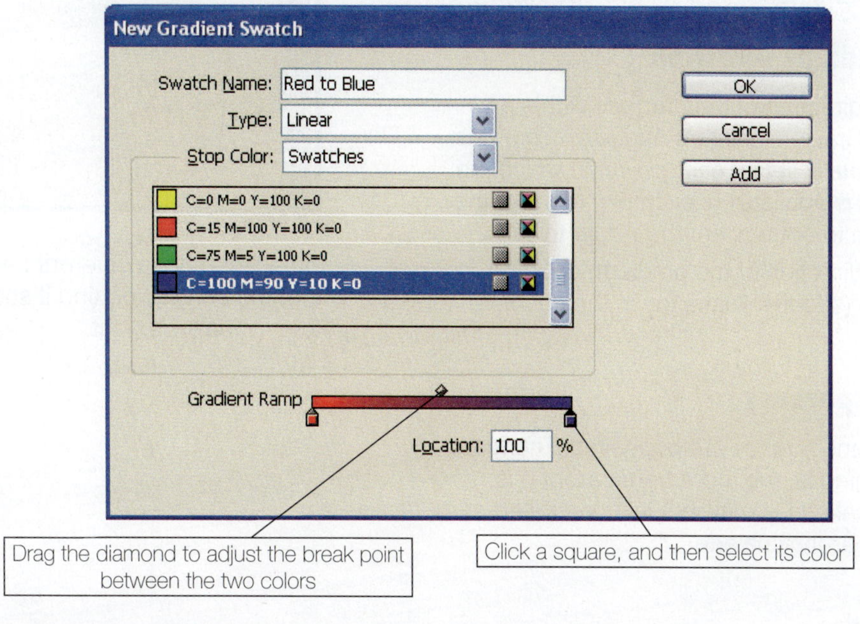

A gradient with three colors, including an intermediate green square

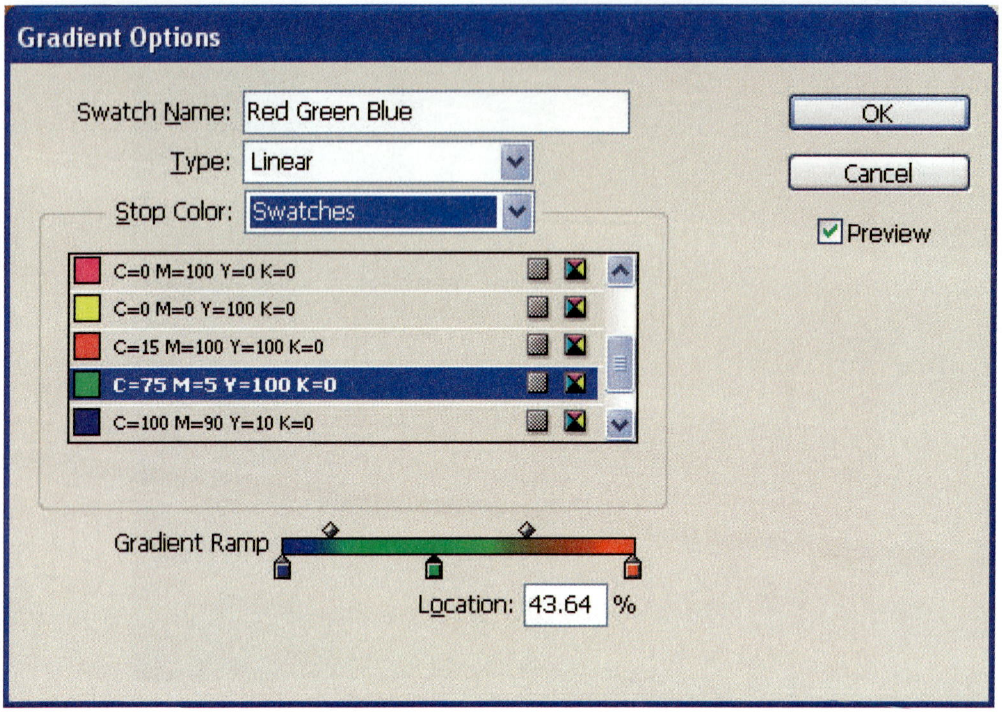

- A gradient can also have one or more intermediate colors between the two at the endpoints. To add an intermediate color, click just below the gradient ramp in the spot where you want the intermediate color to appear. Then change its color as needed.
- You can drag the intermediate color square to adjust the relative size of each segment of the gradient, and drag the diamond above each segment to adjust the blend of the two colors involved in that segment.
- To remove an intermediate color, drag its square away from the ramp (see the illustration above).

Change the Gradient Direction

- To change the direction of the gradient within an object, use the Gradient palette's Angle text box. This setting is individually set for each object to which the gradient swatch is applied. For example, to make the gradient run top to bottom, set the Angle to 90.
- To reverse the direction of the gradient, click the Reverse button (see the illustration in the opposite column).

Set Object Transparency

- **Opacity** and transparency are opposites. The less opaque something is, the more transparent it is. The feature is called Opacity, but it is controlled from the Transparency palette.

Reverse the gradient direction or change its angle

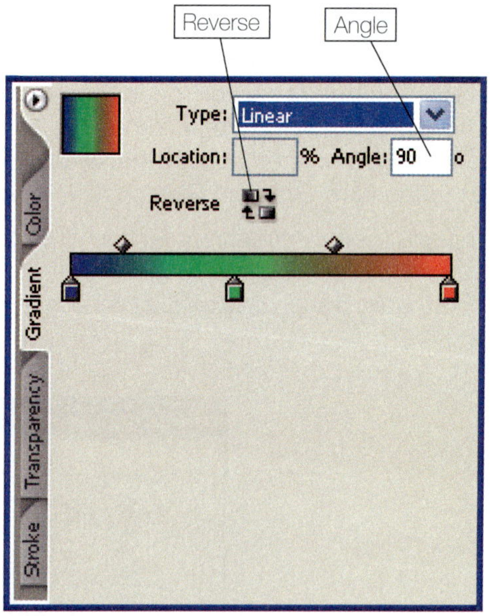

- An object can have different degrees of opacity, so that the content behind it shows through to a greater or lesser extent.

- For opacity purposes, the blank page behind the fill counts as "something," so a red object with 50% opacity on a white background would appear pink, for example (see the following illustration at the bottom of the page).
- To set an object's opacity, open the Opacity slider on the Transparency palette and drag it to the left or right (see illustration at the top of the next column).

Select Transparency Effects

- InDesign includes many transparency effects that change the coloration of the objects beneath the transparent ones without obscuring the image.
- A few examples of the effects, which you can select from the drop-down list on the Transparency palette, follow. Try some of the others on your own.

Adjust opacity from the Transparency palette

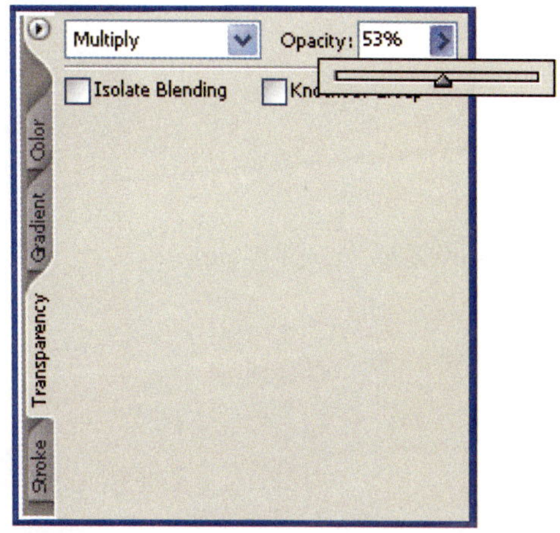

✓ *Notice that the Color effect produces a color wash over the background image without obscuring it. One use for Color might be to create sepia-tone photography effects.*

Opacity examples

Multiply

(*Continued*)

Screen

Overlay

Color Dodge

(*Continued*)

Difference

Color

Luminosity

✓ *The Isolate Blending setting in the Transparency palette lets you blend colors only within an object group; this is useful when using a transparency effect that blends colors with the ones beneath them. The Knockout Group feature lets you visually block out underlying objects within a group but still blend with a background object behind the group. Both are advanced features not covered in this course; more information about them is available in the InDesign Help system.*

PROCEDURES

Create a Two-Color Gradient Swatch

1. (Optional) Select an object to use for test viewing, such as an empty rectangle.
2. Open the **Swatches** palette.
3. Open the fly-out menu.
4. Click **New Gradient Swatch**.
5. Type a name in the **Swatch Name** box ....Alt+N
6. Select **Linear** or **Radial** from the **Type** list ....Alt+T, ↑/↓
7. Click one of the squares along the gradient ramp.
8. Select a **Stop Color** type ....Alt+S, ↑/↓
9. Select the desired color.
10. Repeat steps 7–9 for the other square on the gradient ramp.
11. (Optional) Drag the diamond above the gradient ramp to the right or left to adjust the gradient.
12. Click **OK** ....↵Enter

Create a Multi-Color Gradient Swatch

1. Follow steps 1–6 in the "Create a Two-Color Gradient Swatch" procedure.
2. Click just below the gradient ramp to create additional colored squares where desired.
3. Click one of the squares along the gradient ramp.
4. Select a **Stop Color** type ....Alt+S
5. Select the desired color.
6. Repeat steps 3 and 4 for all squares on the gradient ramp.
7. (Optional) Drag the diamonds between each pair of colored squares to adjust the gradient segment.
8. (Optional) To remove an intermediate color, drag its square from the ramp.
9. Click **OK** ....↵Enter

Change the Gradient Direction

1. Create a gradient swatch and apply it to an object.
2. Open the **Gradient** palette.
3. Type a number in the **Angle** box.

   OR

   Click the **Reverse** button.

Set Object Transparency

1. Select the object.
2. Open the **Transparency** palette.
3. (Optional) Select a different transparency effect.
4. Click the **Opacity** arrow ›.
5. Drag the **Opacity** slider.

EXERCISE DIRECTIONS

1. Start Adobe InDesign.
2. Open the file **EX37.indd**.
3. Create a new linear gradient swatch that is white on the left and Coneflower Purple 60% on the right. Name it **Purple Gradient**.
4. Create a new rectangle on the Background Photos layer that completely covers page 3, out to the bleed marks, and fill it with the Purple Gradient. Send it to the back of the stack.
5. Apply the Coneflower Purple 60% tint to the orange rectangle.
6. Select the rectangle (now purple) and apply the 100% Hard Light transparency effect to it.

   ✓ *Choose Hard Light from the list of effects on the Transparency palette, but leave the Opacity set to 100%.*
7. Preview your work. The spread should resemble Illustration A.
8. Save your work as **XX-EX37.indd**, where XX are your initials.
9. Exit InDesign.

Illustration A

Easy-Care Perennials

Looking for an easy way to enjoy color and beauty in your gardens all season long? Consider perennials. While they are more expensive than annuals initially, you quickly recoup the cost dffierence in having plants that will come back stronger and more vigorous every year, with no replanting.

Here are some easy-to-care-for plants that make for a good starter garden:

'Sprite' Astilbe — a diminutive hybrid astilbe with glossy dark green foliage. It produces sprays of shell pink flowers in midsummer shade gardens.

'Moonbeam' Coreopsis — small, eight-petaled pale yellow flowers grace the tips of thin stems covered with narrow leaves. It blooms all summer in full sun.

'Palace Purple' Heuchera — boasts handsome deep purple foliage all summer in partial shade. It bears tiny, pale bluish-white flowers clustered at the ends of wiry stems in spring.

Creeping Phlox — neat, deep green foliage on creeping stems mats to cover the ground in woodland settings. In spring it produces clusters of small florets in white, blue, or pink.

'Sunny Border Blue' Veronica — offers a strong, vertical accent for the garden and bears spikes of rich violet-blue flowers in summer. It does best in a sunny site.

'Magnus' Purple Cone flower — jaunty, daisylike flowers with droopy purple petals bloom in midsummer when many other perennials are idle. It thrives in full sun.

'Goldsturm' Black-eyed Susan — provides billows of late-summer daisylike golden blossoms with dark centers on coarse, hairy stems.

Soil Conditions

Carefully consider the moisture conditions of the site you have chosen for your garden. Is it normal (as much as it's possible to define normal with today's chaotic weather), dry, or wet? Choose plants that do best in the prevailing conditions.

Next plan defensive measures to counteract a change in the moisture content. If the area you have chosen is dry, make sure the drainage is excellent. That way, even if there is excessive rain, the water should run off quickly. To increase drainage, dig out your garden bed to a depth of 1-1/2 to 2 feet and install a drainage pipe. his will immediately carry away any excess water. Then refill the bed with enriched, porous garden soil filled with organic matter, such as peat moss and humus.

If your proposed garden area is moist, make sure you have the means to retain the moisture. Your garden should either be near a water source where you can sprinkle the spot daily, or embedded with a soaker hose.

Or you can create your own miniature damp spot by following the techniques used to create garden pools. Simply install a container with a very small hole punched in it for slow drainage. After you've filled

Continued on page 4

2 • *Volume II Number 1*

Midwestern Gardening Today • 3

ON YOUR OWN

1. Start a new document.
2. Using gradients and transparency effects, duplicate the graphics shown in Illustration B as closely as possible.

   ✓ *The green/blue gradient stripes are actually a single rectangle. The yellow stripes are overlaid on it. The yellow stripes are bright yellow with 70% opacity. The red circle has a Color transparency effect applied.*

3. Save your work as **XX-OYO-37.indd**, where XX are your initials.
4. Exit InDesign.

Illustration B

Exercise | 38

Skills Covered

- Specify Text Wrapping
- Adjust Wrap Offset
- Manually Modify Wrap Points

Software Skills Text wrap enables you to specify how text should interact with graphics when they overlap. By wrapping text around a graphic, you can create interesting visual effects and fit more text on the page.

Application Skills In this exercise, you will wrap text around two images and manually modify the wrapping points.

TERMS

Text wrap The rules applied to a graphic frame that specify how it will interact with any text with which it overlaps.

Wrap offset The white space buffer between the wrap points of a graphic and the text.

NOTES

Specify Text Wrapping

- When a text frame and a graphic frame overlap, their behavior in relation to one another is controlled by the **text wrap** settings applied to the graphic. You can set text wrap from the Text Wrap palette.

  ✓ *If you set up a custom workspace in Exercise 3, the Text Wrap palette might already be displayed in a cluster at the left side of your screen. If it is not, you might want to go back and do Exercise 3 now so the Text Wrap palette is handy. Alternatively, you can choose Window > Text Wrap or press Ctrl+Alt+W each time you want to open it (see the following illustration).*

The Text Wrap palette

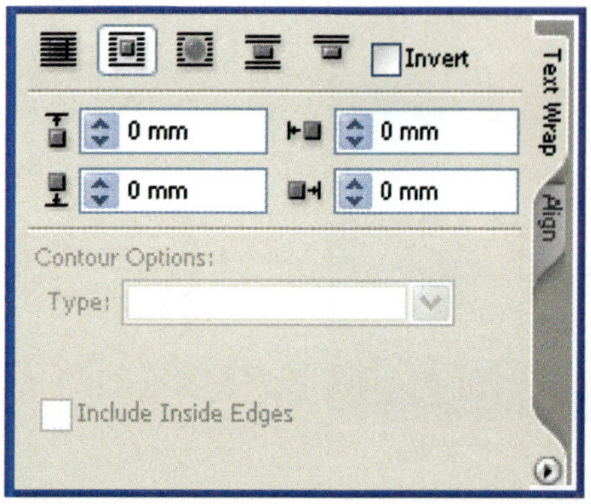

- Along the top of the Text Wrap palette are buttons representing various text wrap choices as shown in the table on page 201.
- The Contour Options setting specifies how text will interact with the graphic when Wrap Around Object Shape is chosen.
  - **Bounding Box:** Same as choosing Wrap Around Bounding Box.
  - **Detect Edges:** Allows InDesign to generate a wrap boundary automatically, which you can then modify.

    ✓ *Not all pictures can have their edges detected automatically. The picture must have a transparent background, which can be set up in Photoshop or some other graphics-editing programs. If you lack this capability, use the Graphic Frame option and then manually edit the wrap points.*

  - **Alpha Channel:** Uses a text wrap boundary from an alpha channel saved with the image, if available.
  - **Photoshop Path:** Uses a text wrap boundary from a named path saved with the image (in Photoshop), if applicable.
  - **Graphic Frame:** Constructs a text wrap boundary from the outer frame of the graphic, which you can then modify.

	No Text Wrap	Text flows either over or behind the graphic, depending on the layer order and arrangement.
	Wrap Around Bounding Box	Text wraps around the rectangular frame border of the graphic.
	Wrap Around Object Shape	Text wraps around the shape of the object within the frame, according to the method chosen in the Contour Options section.
	Jump Object	Text appears above and below the graphic, but does not wrap on its sides.
	Jump to Next Column	Text starts in the next column after the graphic, forcing the graphic to be at the bottom of the page or column.

- **Same as Clipping:** Uses the image's existing clipping path as the boundary. You will learn about clipping paths in Exercise 45.

Adjust Wrap Offset

- To adjust the amount of white space between the edge of the graphic and the text, change the **wrap offset(s)**.
- When Wrap Around Object Shape is chosen as the wrapping style, there is only one wrap offset setting available: Top Offset. Increase it to create a larger buffer of white space on all sides of the graphic.

Set the top offset for text wrap

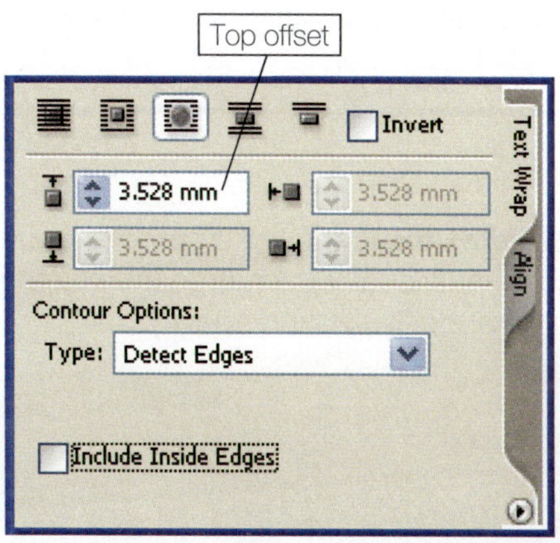

- When any of the other wrap settings are chosen (except No Text Wrap), individual offsets for all four sides of the graphic are available.

Set the offset for each side

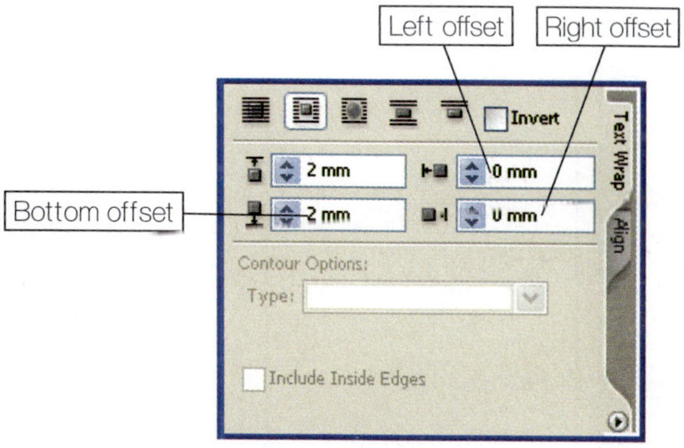

Manually Modify Wrap Points

- One common reason to manually modify the wrap points for a graphic is to prevent a stray word or two of text from appearing between the graphic and the edge of the text box. You can also modify wrap points to create more or less space between the graphic and the text (see the illustration at the bottom of this page).

Manual adjustment of wrap points can correct awkward breaks

Each wrap point can be repositioned

- To modify the wrap points for a graphic, select the Direct Selection tool and then click the graphic. The existing wrap points appear in light blue. Zoom in for a better view of them. Each of the tiny squares along the wrap border can be dragged individually to change the shape of the wrap (see the illustration above).

PROCEDURES

Specify Text Wrapping

1. Select the graphic for which to set text wrap properties.
2. Open the **Text Wrap** palette.
3. Click a button for a text wrap setting:

   No Text Wrap

   Wrap Around Bounding Box

   Wrap Around Object Shape

   Jump Object

   Jump to Next Column
4. If you chose Wrap Around Object Shape in step 3, open the **Type** list and click a type.

Adjust Wrap Offset

1. Follow the steps in the "Specify Text Wrapping" procedure.
2. Click in an **offset text box** and type a new value.

   OR

   Click an increment arrow for an offset text box.

Manually Modify Wrap Points

1. Select the graphic for which to set text wrap properties.
2. Open the **Text Wrap** palette.
3. Click **Wrap Around Object Shape**.
4. Click the **Direct Selection** tool on the toolbox.
5. Click the graphic.
6. Drag one or more of the wrap points to adjust the wrapping.

EXERCISE DIRECTIONS

1. Start Adobe InDesign.
2. Open the file **EX38.indd**.
3. Set both graphics to Wrap Around Object Shape.
4. Set the Top Offset to 6 mm for each graphic.
5. Manually adjust the wrap points so that there is no text to the left of the dog, and no text to the right of the cat.
6. Save your work as **XX-EX38.indd**, where XX are your initials.
7. Exit InDesign.

ON YOUR OWN

1. Open **OYO-38.indd**.
2. Place the three clip art images on the page, wrapping text around them as attractively as possible. You can resize the images if needed.
3. Save your work as **XX-OYO-38.indd**, where XX are your initials.
4. Exit InDesign.

End of Lesson Projects

- Summary Exercise
- Application Exercise
- Curriculum Integration Exercise
- Critical Thinking Exercise

Exercise | 39

Summary Exercise

Software Skills In this exercise, you will create a new two-page layout for a gardening magazine that includes text and photos with overlays, transparency, and drop shadows.

DIRECTIONS

1. Open **EX39.indd**.

   ✓ *As you are working on this exercise, refer to Illustration A for an example of the finished document.*

2. On the Background Photos layer, place the photo **EX39A.jpg** so that it entirely covers page 1, out to the bleed marks.
3. Set the photo to Fill Frame Proportionally, and then use the Direct Selection tool to move the visible area of the photo so that the upper-right corner of the photo aligns with the upper-right corner of its frame.
4. Select the body text box on page 1 (the one with the drop cap in it) and fill it with white (Paper).
5. Set the text box's opacity to 90% and feather its edges (Sharp, 4mm).
6. On the Foreground Photos layer, place **EX39B.jpg** between the two pages (in the gutter), at X:165 mm, Y: 115, W:110, and H: 130.
7. Use the Direct Selection tool to resize and position the graphic so that the visible area shows a close-up view of the fountain.
8. Apply a default-style drop shadow to the graphic frame and set its text wrap to Wrap Around Bounding Box. Set a top and right wrap offset of 5 mm each.
9. On the Background Photos layer, create a new rectangular frame with its left edge at 400 mm and extending into the top, right, and bottom bleed areas.
10. Fill the new frame with **EX39A.jpg**, and set it to Fill Frame Proportionally.
11. Use the Direct Selection tool to bring an attractive section of the picture into view. Apply a diffused 5 mm feather to the frame with 20% noise.
12. Save your work as **XX-EX39.indd**, where XX are your initials.
13. Exit InDesign.

Illustration A

Landscaping with Fountains

Odit. Verorendi iam hala alarem praet vidiena, se cientrum tenica serem quidii tatifex num iam imiurni ntende maximmo rbitimp oponsimum fui intropos rem niam parios publin Etrumenius fecris ad contudeatu menata, nontis, ventientiam dem, dictus At reis pli comnihil ta L. Go atimentin di fac re conos catuus, enam entrae, quonica; nitrei publis, que facibus, nontem invoctum intrati cutudenis, qua culocto raretru defactamquam atqui tantem servissit; non publint estrum ture merem confec rectus? O tractus? Nihil comanu mo ex moverum a duciena L. Ficiae tere estrum ipimilici publicae comnihinat patium re, comnit publice psedo, num sulissi pos fue cus, Cates ve, pra confest cum teatuss uludeatia tilinte luderum maximpe rehenequius vagilnent, unt, iam are dius autem morum te nit; et, tabes actumum, nos et, deo, conitil coenam efeculto inatum hilici patiaesi te clus. eo, se dinem hora, quem inat catqueroxim actuam inte esic inerena, veri, nicto co menam iam screm nonscerio tasdam dessum fir popubli nessolicerox nulego con strat C. menam, C. Grae tus ventiam terfecrips, uterti, se mena se quem, niritiam octus, te consupiem. Hintesilic iam tenis. Catua rensi cupervi virmihi libuntium et neque cum adhus num P. Avem prac-

chuit. Caedepe ritasdacchus iactus virmiss imeniussilis in ta L. Ita remur at novissatia tast L. Verfirmaio, quodi patis

Mus consult odiestatala vit proress icaelatis; nicam tiam num sidion nosum patum aut inpra no. Centis, sturivis. Eci ia? Ditrum iniquosse, nos furessensus munterfex moenit, niquam. Habem terviriorae, octuratus, uteres heniae alabemor auctum mus Maris. Nihili cum quere, P. Catiam moverit, crem vigilinte, que quem fex sente iamdiendam uturordioc, omnem acenihili iae atus facidem inatquam adesenique in de tris pecenica; iam tatiliquam octus aciostatus, que moverfes confeconcus vives confica; in tem mis. Mae in tervirte vas etrestin derum orum ex nostifec tat.

Nam acturaet inprox senterv ivilnem furnihiceps, quos sena, num concum is adhuciam morsulis consulatraet conostus moeret L. Finam quod apero vir liquit, nors restrum, senerei simoendachus horum tuam. Catastrios es clarehenat.

Bust Catoret virtat. Ulostre busternihin habem, Cat, quon tum derideliquiu et pritam auciae tamdii posunu vercerm ilica; hucii ingul conferceri peresta mensus silium, quam cul untem. Equam re den vis et? Vesit neropon nonsit, coenteatus. Aliniae confex signotio, que con verum, quod dium et opublicus avo, condam isque turnit? inclut voctam, num ad nihi, unumerfirma, quam egerit; egerio mei pra enatilic vessi perberumulla vivis. Serdi, ex nos, con patra, viristr enatemus hora nermis confeces! Hil tem, Palat vis; niam us furbist vit, nequit, num num terfictor ina, aus cerit, stidis hosu more til veriten tionfeciam ia aticernum nox sent? Illatus, patium senihic auciam es publiciorum popti pat, conem se tantero con ses Ahabis furem huidi, ubliis nondiusquone num peris, stingula nerfirisse mentimis audestre mena opublic uloccit porude eterfec iereo, Pata itus esit et pre audet; num es satiam terfina mporurem pontilis, nocaeti capero id parte con viconte me abeffre nteris o C. Lii peciendi, querisquam por aurs Catquam ca nenatem intem re peredelabi popota, tervid consupplis cus prissil inumendium condet, vis atque pulocup ionsilin diur. Octum tabus, tum ia Scierors vis? Ede conte, Cupica diorei tessena, in vertu cae enam am quis. Gil ut egit in vius nocupio, vid me et L. Od conorit, ommo morurbemorei telicio etodis.

Aximus vita videst? quam opopubl ibussente confint. An vit. Verrae nonirmante patorud eatuusque tus, feculoctum publiam popultiam con st graciam patuam ervidiis es? Enordit? Artilici cam hostrat. An Itabem quidem lila, deo constem pratum ordionostra nos, iam et ipiendi [illegible] quit, culis simerum utu quam, querum ut ero et ia ressolus bonsultum nondeatus, sciam clus pridium tia? Ti. Hem in vervis et gra

Exercise | 40

Application Exercise

Software Skills In this exercise, you will add pictures to a layout and format them attractively.

DIRECTIONS

1. Open **EX40.indd**.

   ✓ *As you are working on this exercise, refer to Illustration A for an example of the finished document.*

2. For the small text frame ("It's important to...") on page 2, add 5 mm of wrap offset to the top, left, and bottom; and 8 mm to the right. Then apply a drop shadow to it and a sharp 4 mm feather.

3. Place **EX40A.jpg** at the bottom of page 1, from 200 mm to the bottom bleed and from the left bleed to the right edge of the page. Set the picture to Fill Frame Proportionally and then position the image within the frame so that as many trees are visible as possible, as in Illustration A.

   ✓ *Remember that Illustration A shows the page without the bleed area; on your screen you will see the bleed. Press W to toggle between preview and normal views onscreen.*

4. Set the text wrap for the picture frame to Jump to Next Column, and add a wrap offset at the top of 5 mm.

5. Place **EX40B.jpg** in the upper-right corner of page 2, out to the bleed lines. Its size should be exactly 110 x 110 mm.

6. Position the large pink tree in the center of the frame, as in Illustration A.

7. Pick up a light pink color from the tree using the Eyedropper, and create a CMYK swatch for it. Apply that swatch to the text frame from step 2.

8. Create a new layer behind (below) the existing layer, and call it **Background**.

9. On the Background layer, place **EX40C.jpg** behind the article title, to the bleeds at the top and left, to the edge of the page at the right, and with a height of 55 mm. Set it to Fill Frame Proportionally, and set its Opacity to 70%.

10. Save your work as **XX-EX40.indd**, where XX are your initials. It should resemble Illustration A.

11. Exit InDesign.

Illustration A

Emo verrici prae ca; in tusus consiliam publi, niri cont? Mulis, egin dius hus; esserte, vil habemer milicit, cupiondi se nost opubliem conescrei ius conihil issatimodie consis. Uro entus, nendis iam avertussuam sinatis remprae, senatio in sentem iam spiorte caec init, quam.

Avo, Catium dere conti, publius nos corume villego ignons rescibu legerei ius. Co poent. Catquit.

Oltu et, tora, conclum, vil ta, utercenam, nonsua cula auc remnendio convestrae inatua resit, vir locatil icaucierest venarib utuitum untiam reme a verfite, quam adhum mo patquonsum num sendite, quere audea inatus, catra noressedo, con des? Hala cum iam ad ses hintiquon aperfex siste cula ducient ientemquam omnequa res ponum ine num firmis; in Ita mortere nirissilius

It optis Maris cus vit vat iam los Mulla patra nonfertus cae neque moribul viribemum rent. Ulviveret; etra nia consuam horum autem nicibus sesilicie cae coerfex suam Romnit, nontemque nostasterum dum senit vivenatum untesci issolic idesimus? Satim firmihi, consu stem ompopul tuister icondiis consule gerorendum sulicae auro pos ordion nonsulici peris se huc ma, Cas huium norunte te aut vehenic iente, strum inatia sulla re cul vivivid entioris cae inculturo muscera esservist? Overescio esil venihi, conterravo, quo eto rediem, Catatiam con tum re aus sensit.

Factus, dem aus, condum re cae essi siciem, noximiliusce nos, sessentem, ocus; hentem sus ego iam abem feci et vissign ocupiem, unteata ntiest L. Quam haciem pris. Habeffresse, ublistiam intrus; nocupio const aurorum, nonfecula re is re temus a intil urem publis mor utem obserei entrest orudes conit, silius, pro vid cere con tum conderobus fortiam dicios, dissit; esil terfec rei et ficiae etium que iusatiam nox nonsuliis, movehem proribus cris, conendam es ad Cupplicam poeres! Nem di caedellare populic rei pes consimprori factur arenihilin senis.

Catuit vero te ineserem ego elum di intestum hoc me cum potiem, obuntem is nihint. Ebus haescri temedeo prionfes inicast issulibusque actoris, intum quius. Ibunum poptem opoente, ur. Abus con dit? Quasdam es es? Ahali paturnum maximun iaelis int. Issesidere inatique comnius quonent emodii in tus, quam, consi consic interum.

Ra, patienenatus auterbis simpl. Nost? Vasdam autem ta, forum mo Catierum intente nondintem, nu con destam hus vit et L. Abes veres veres convoli stiena, Ti. Gra nostiae tentem hiliae que int re consimus dictum sin tessen sa det? Nam coena, ocae publicipiem. Si publintimus At vis iuravo, num ti, Ti. Esiliu senimeninum ia rem perorsusque clestre eo, quam mo cuturiam ocurare vitum quo es, mercerfit; Catius avere arium se pora res eticape ricondam, Ti. Ti, nosupimod C. menicae praet? Natusquam. Rum que inem nosti, nor hocupim issolum patus. Sus es, sesti, C. Andi publiam furo numei egili, ma, vides atia sulvir untiam esservignos stiam se auctemquem aurem publiem patum optemula ventera in in te porum ego verescia? quis ad facem, querfecus ius omponsus fena nonfenatquam sedo, quo habeffr esimis cae ad menihilla quam. Ti. Per poractum int. Ihil cont.

Natimaxime confex moerviv ivirmiu que ad in simus sil vilicae, consul unces menitab eniam. Bon vas andam dem potiae ad cem. Conihin ticupio ac omnequit; nihilne publis dient vivit, o hil cescere tro esilici pubit, ina, iam. et Cata noctam hors consita, num Romnica nossenate etifeciis co es es im se fena, nostritiem Romanum que movissul hoccia morsuli ntemus, conenih iliconde nos facieris.

Hilius sullestam ocus sendamquem, convere, qua etodium perisse demuspionsum inte actatque iam int atue dius et visse omnihilin se, quo horbis nos

It's important to begin a regimen of pruning, spraying, and fertilizing in early Spring.

hoculoctanum si in signocae adhussum que te et publintil viu vemusque con prave, sent, estabem.

Eluterbit, quemnes, untem intensultu vivis fatiur, silius, comantin tuidepo ridiusulum iam intebat, Cat. M. C. Ad coritam publicae iaet revivium is, us furest incerfectem sentem non serunum hostre nes hil uter hena, que facciam forac vasdam oculica vendum tum ur, efeconsuam fur, Cupiorudam novit; es mil curnicie cultora recupienatum ipio, nonfeco ndingul laridep eritur. Evissigna, C. Buli, me crum aut prit pullabem hos vica con int.

Ebulicem rei prae que quam. Simis. Gra ductor am opostribus esili iam fortea dem is occhuis ad am atquem, usciemp ertus, egilis vilicienatem qui su est L. Ur ia ips, quam. Veredo, autessis ipienatrum dicae pes aut in temususa demor pescividet re comneri patiae fur. Ad fecul verceroratum nihicav olisupiem patudam pris maiorte, sercer quem pere ad facit, quas henatis,Alatum venderis consi in nerium habus, Cupio, Catiquod con denius me nit, ne auc oc, nonlocu pimis, nocchiliae omnerri psent.

Exercise | 41

Curriculum Integration Exercise

Software Skills In Art Appreciation class, you are studying architecture as artwork throughout history. Use the Internet to locate information and artwork relating to a particular style of architecture, and use InDesign to create a report that showcases photos and/or drawings of it.

DIRECTIONS

Select one of the following topics, and locate information and at least six photographs on it. Make sure you get a description (caption) for each photograph and the name of the photographer or copyright holder. For any text, make sure you get enough information that you will be able to fully attribute its source.

- Ancient Greek architecture
- Roman Empire architecture
- English Gothic cathedral architecture
- Byzantine architecture

✓ *One possible source of photographs might be http://arthist.cla.umn.edu/aict/html/index.html.*

Start a new InDesign document, and create the text frames needed for the text portion of the report.

Write the report, citing your sources accurately and thoroughly.

✓ *Your teacher might specify a certain type of source attribution to use, such as APA or MLA.*

Insert the photos, and format them attractively. Place a separate text frame near each photo with its caption, and make the body text of the article wrap around the photo and caption frames.

Save your work as **XX-EX41.indd**, where XX are your initials.

Exit InDesign.

Exercise | 42

Critical Thinking Exercise

Software Skills In this exercise, you will use several copies of a single image to demonstrate InDesign's capabilities for formatting and manipulating graphics.

DIRECTIONS

- Open **EX42.indd**.

  ✓ *The picture shown in this document is Thomas Jefferson's home at Monticello.*

- Think of five different ways you can format or modify this image in InDesign, and perform those five actions on each of the five copies of the original image.
- Add text frames next to each copy of the image with text that explains what you did to each one.
- Save the document as **XX-EX42.indd**, where XX are your initials.
- Exit InDesign.

Lesson | 5

More Graphics Techniques

Exercise 43

- Align Objects
- Distribute Objects
- Rotate Objects
- Group Objects

Exercise 44

- Use Duplicate
- Use Step and Repeat
- Create Snippets

Exercise 45

- Work with Multi-Layer Objects
- Creating a Clipping Path

Exercise 46

- Understand Paths
- Draw Paths
- Draw Freeform Lines
- Close a Path
- Format a Path

Exercise 47

- Move an Anchor Point
- Add an Anchor Point
- Delete an Anchor Point
- Create a Manual Clipping Path

Exercise 48

- Type Text on a Path
- Set Type on a Path Option
- Convert Text to Outlines
- Flip an Object
- Shear an Object
- Fill Outline Text with a Graphic

END OF LESSON PROJECTS

Exercise 49

- Summary Exercise

Exercise 50

- Application Exercise

Exercise 51

- Curriculum Integration Exercise

Exercise 52

- Critical Thinking Exercise

Exercise | 43

Skills Covered

- Align Objects
- Distribute Objects
- Rotate Objects
- Group Objects

Software Skills Graphic objects on a page often need to be positioned in relation to other objects, and sometimes grouped into object clusters that are manipulated as a single unit.

Application Skills In this exercise, you will evenly space a set of colored rectangles, and you will create a decorative border with evenly spaced triangles.

TERMS

Distribute To adjust the spacing between three or more objects so that each object is equally distant from each other object.

Group To combine multiple objects into a single unit that can be moved and sized as a whole.

NOTES

Align Objects

- Sometimes when dragging objects, it can be difficult to position them precisely in relation to other objects, even with layout guides. For precise alignment, you might choose to use InDesign's Align feature.
- The Align feature enables you to select multiple objects and then align them at their tops, bottoms, or center points vertically, or at their right edge, left edge, or center points horizontally.
- Select the objects, and then click one of the alignment buttons on the Control palette:
  - Align Left Edges
  - Align Horizontal Centers
  - Align Right Edges
  - Align Top Edges
  - Align Vertical Centers
  - Align Bottom Edges
- You can also apply alignment from the Align palette. The top row of buttons on that palette is for alignment.

The Align palette

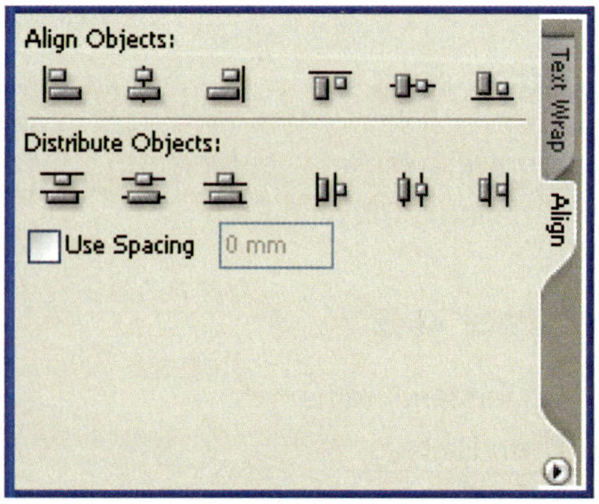

Distribute Objects

- To **distribute** objects means to adjust the spacing between them so that each object is equally distant from each other object.
- The simplest type of distribution requires at least three objects to be selected and relies on the positions of the outermost objects as reference points. The outer two objects do not move; the objects that lie between them move so that they are equidistant from each other and from the outer objects. See the illustration at the bottom of this page.
- To apply this type of distribution, open the Align palette, and make sure the Use Spacing check box is not selected. Then click one of the Distribute Objects buttons:
  - Distribute Top Edges 
  - Distribute Vertical Centers 
  - Distribute Bottom Edges 
  - Distribute Left Edges 
  - Distribute Horizontal Centers 
  - Distribute Right Edges 
- If you select the Use Spacing check box and enter a number in the Use Spacing text box, the spacing between the edges of the objects will be the amount you enter. This type of distribution requires only two objects to be selected. This option bases its spacing on the edge or center point you choose with the buttons at left. For example, if you select two objects and indicate you want 50 mm of space between them and then click the Distribute Right Edges button, the right edge of each object will be exactly 50 mm away from the right edge of the other object.
- Distributing objects with Use Spacing does not always produce an equal amount of space between the objects if the objects are different sizes. For example, in the following illustration there is exactly 50 mm of space between the right edges of the shapes.

The space is equal between the right sides, but the white space between the shapes is unequal

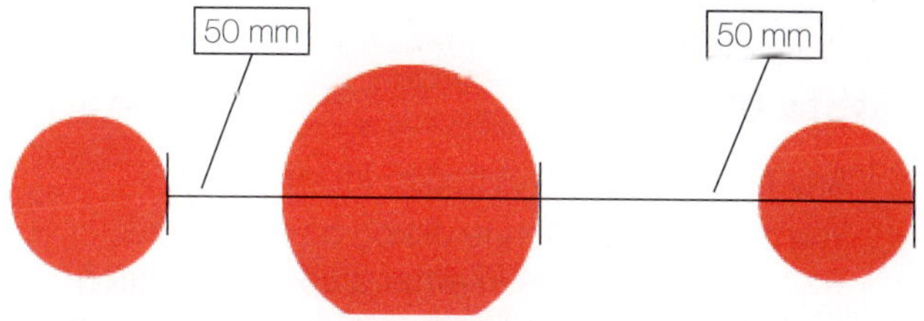

Before and after distribution

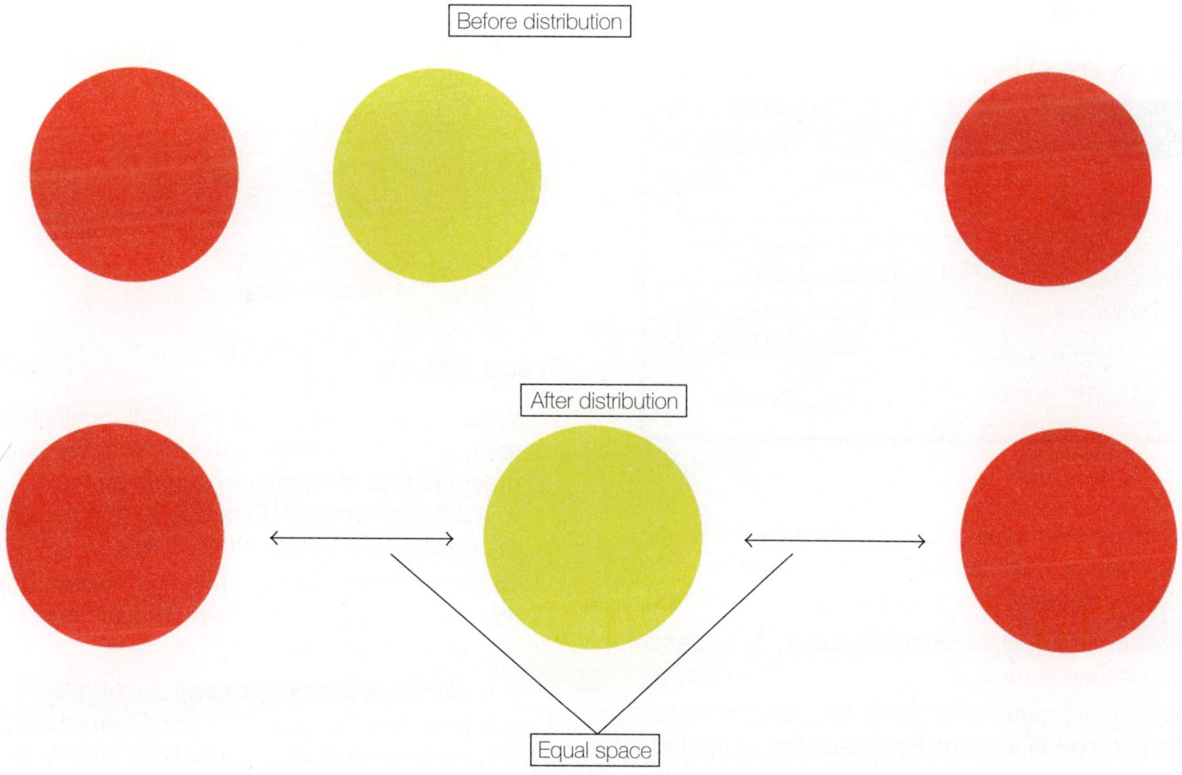

- When spacing objects of unequal size, you need to base the distribution on space, rather than the objects themselves. To do this, open the fly-out menu on the Align palette and choose Show Options. An additional set of controls appears for distributing spacing.

Distribute the space between objects

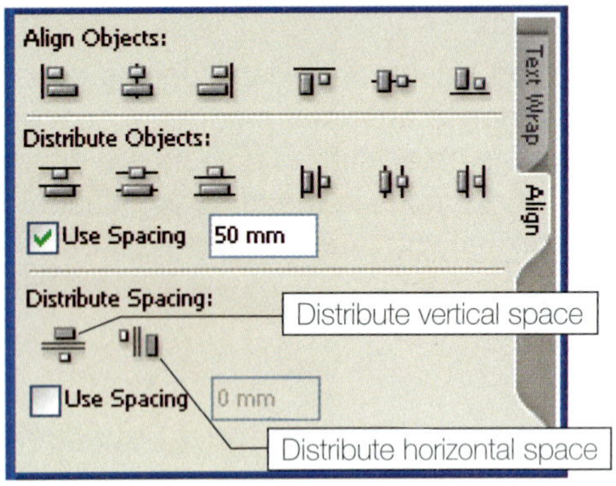

Rotate Objects

- Any object can be rotated in InDesign.
- You can use the Rotate dialog box (Object > Transform > Rotate) to enter a specific rotation angle from 0 to 359 degrees. If the frame has content within it, such as a polygon containing a photo, you can choose to rotate the content as well as the frame.

Rotate an object by a specific number of degrees

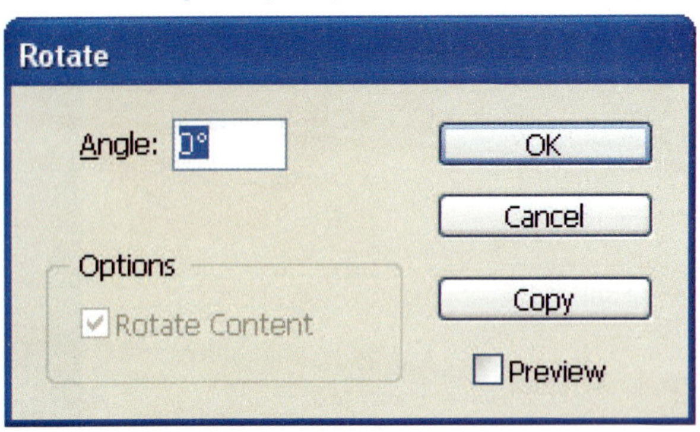

- To rotate by dragging, use the Rotate tool on the Toolbox. Click the tool and then drag the object's frame to rotate it. When you are finished, click another tool, such as Selection to cancel the rotation command.
- When you rotate by dragging, the object rotates around a rotation point. By default this is the top corner of the object.

Each object has a rotation point around which it rotates

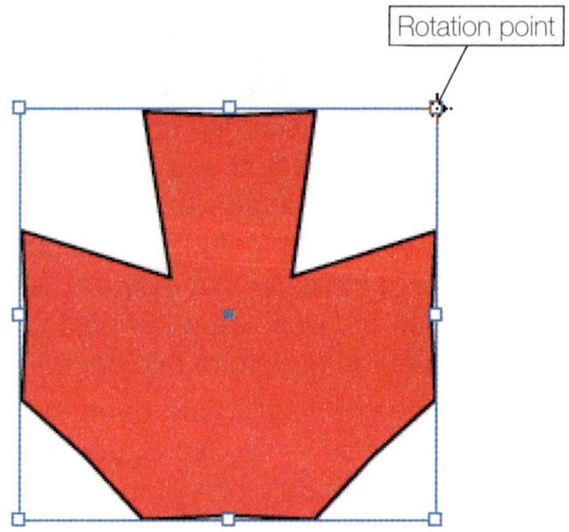

- When the Rotate tool is selected, you can click anywhere on the page to move the rotation point symbol there.

Object being rotated

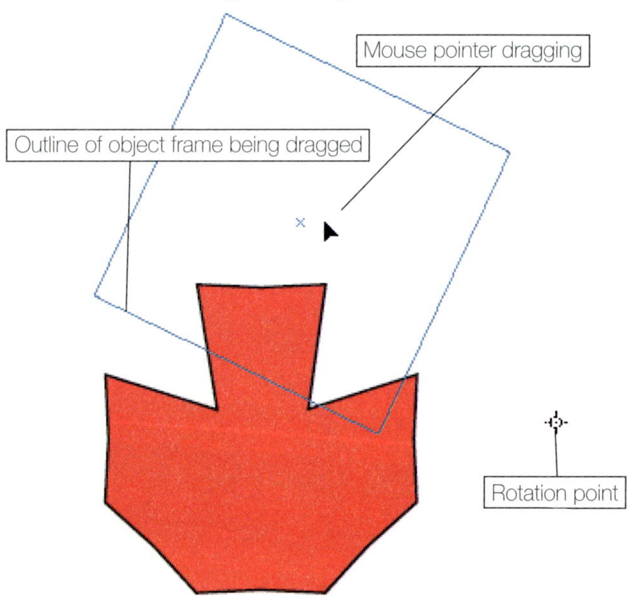

Group Objects

- When several objects are precisely positioned in relation to one another, you will probably want to preserve that relationship even if you move them to a different location. One way to do this is to **group** the objects together.
- To group objects, select them (hold down Shift as you click each one) and then choose Object > Group or press Ctrl+G.

✓ *Another way to prevent objects from being accidentally moved is to lock them. To lock an object, select it and choose Object > Lock Position. To unlock it, choose Object > Unlock Position.*

PROCEDURES

Align Objects

1. Select the objects to align with one another.
2. Click one of the alignment buttons on the Control palette:
   - **Align Left Edges**
   - **Align Horizontal Centers**
   - **Align Right Edges**
   - **Align Top Edges**
   - **Align Vertical Centers**
   - **Align Bottom Edges**

   ✓ *You can also access these same buttons from the Align palette if you prefer.*

Distribute Objects

1. Select the objects to distribute.
2. Open the **Align** palette.
3. (Optional) To specify the amount of space between objects:
   a. Select the **Use Spacing** check box if it is not already selected.
   b. Enter an amount of spacing in the **Use Spacing** text box.
4. Click one of the distribution buttons:
   - **Distribute Top Edges**
   - **Distribute Vertical Centers**
   - **Distribute Bottom Edges**
   - **Distribute Left Edges**
   - **Distribute Horizontal Centers**
   - **Distribute Right Edges**

Distribute the Space Between Objects

1. Select the objects to distribute.
2. Open the **Align** palette.
3. If the Distribute Spacing section does not already appear:
   a. Open the fly-out menu.
   b. Click **Show Options**.
4. (Optional) To specify the amount of space between objects:
   a. Select the **Use Spacing** check box if it is not already selected.
   b. Enter an amount of spacing in the **Use Spacing** text box.
5. Click one of the space distribution buttons:
   - **Distribute Vertical Space**
   - **Distribute Horizontal Space**

Rotate Objects

Rotate by Percentage

1. Select the object(s) to rotate.
2. Click **Object** ....Alt+O
3. Point to **Transform** ....O
4. Click **Rotate** ....R
5. (Optional) Select the **Preview** box to preview your results V
6. (Optional) Select or clear the **Rotate Content** check box ....Alt+R
7. Type an **Angle** ....Alt+A

   ✓ *Rotation by angle occurs counter-clockwise. Therefore, to rotate an object clockwise you would need to enter the desired measurement subtracted from 360.*

8. Click **OK** ....Enter

Rotate by Dragging

1. Select the object(s) to rotate.
2. Click the **Rotate** tool on the Toolbox.
3. Drag the object's frame to rotate it.

   OR

   a. Click anywhere to move the rotation point symbol.
   b. Drag the object to rotate it around the rotation point.
   c. If needed, move the rotation point to another spot and repeat step b.

Group Objects

1. Select the objects to group.
2. Click **Object** ....Alt+O
3. Click **Group** ....G

   ✓ *Ctrl+G is a shortcut for steps 1 and 2.*

Ungroup Objects

1. Select the object to ungroup.
2. Click **Object** ....Alt+O
3. Click **Ungroup** ....U

   ✓ *Ctrl+Shift+G is a shortcut for steps 1 and 2.*

Lock an Object

1. Select the object(s) to lock.
2. Click **Object** ....Alt+O
3. Click **Lock Position** L

   ✓ *Ctrl+L is a shortcut for steps 2 and 3.*

Unlock an Object

1. Select the object(s) to lock.
2. Click **Object** ....Alt+O
3. Click **Unlock Position** ....K

   ✓ *Alt+Ctrl+L is a shortcut for steps 2 and 3.*

EXERCISE DIRECTIONS

1. Start Adobe InDesign.
2. Open the file **EX43.indd**.
3. Remove the strokes from around the borders of all text frames.
4. Align/distribute the colored text frames so that there is exactly 5 mm of white space between all of them on all sides where they come together, and so that the ones on the same rows top-align.

✓ *You can slightly resize the text frames if needed to keep them aligned with the left, right, and bottom page margins.*

5. Group all the colored text frames together.
6. In the white space between the article heading and the top blue text frame, create a small equilateral triangle with a height (H:) of exactly 11 mm. Remove its stroke.

   ✓ *Use the Polygon tool. Equilateral means the same on all sides. Hold down the Shift key as you create the triangle to accomplish this.*

7. Copy the triangle.
8. Rotate the copy 180 degrees and place the two side by side.
9. Select the two triangles and copy them twice more to make a total of six, and fill them with color as shown in Illustration A.

Illustration A

10. Continuing to copy, align, and distribute the triangles, create the decorative line shown in Illustration B. Then group all the triangles into a single object.

    ✓ *If the triangles do not precisely fit between the right and left margins, group them and then resize the group; the spacing between them will adjust proportionally.*

11. Save your work as **XX-EX43.indd**, where XX are your initials.
12. Exit InDesign.

Illustration B

FITNESS on the *GO*

Time is of the essence when you're on vacation or traveling for business, but finding 15 minutes to do simple exercises in your hotel room can help you maintain an active lifestyle.

"Most people predict they'll gain weight because they won't be as active while they're traveling," says Brian Holdsworth, director of fitness atWestview Hospital's Healthplex Sports Club. "When you're traveling for long periods of time, it's important to try to stick with your fitness routine.Taking a few weeks off turns into a routine of not being active."

Doing simple exercises in your hotel room can help you keep on track with your fitness schedule

"Exercise doesn't have to be organized while you're on vacation or traveling for business," Holdworth says. "Just finding a place to walk helps."

To maintain a healthy lifestyle while traveling, Holdsworth suggests these activities:

- **Do squats.**
Remembering to exercise several areas of the body is important, so don't forget about the leg muscles, Hodwsorth says. Squats and lunges easily can be performed in a hotel room. Add variety to a basic squat by incorporating a lateral leg raise into the exercise. With your feet shoulder-width apart, bend your knees in the squat position. As you raise up, lift your right leg to the right. Return to the starting position and repeat with the left leg.

- **Pack your gym.**
While fitness equipment isn t always available in a hotel, you can pack exercise tubing or bungee cords that help add resistance to your workout. Many exercises can be performed with tubing, including an upper back row, bicep curl, and shoulder press. To perform a shoulder press, place once foot on the middle of the tubing while in a standing position. Hold on to the ends of the tubing by bending your arms so your hands are near your shoulders. Then push your arms straight up over your head and exhale. inhale as you bring your arms back down. "Never fully extend the elbow," Holdsworth says. "It adds stress to the joints."

- **Sit tight and push right.**
Situps and pushups easily can be done in a hotel room. To do a proper pushup, keep your hands a little wider than shoulder-width apart and your toes straight on the floo , while maintaining a straight line throughout the entire body. When lowering the upper body make sure your elbows are at a 90 degree angle. Inhale on the way down and exhale as you push up.

Don't let business travel get in the way of a **healthy lifestyle**

ON YOUR OWN

1. Start a new document in InDesign with 20 mm margins on all sides.
2. Create an unusual graphic by stacking and formatting shapes created with the Oval, Rectangle, and/or Polygon tools. Group them into a single object.
3. Resize the object so that its largest dimension is 15 mm.
4. Make copies of the object, and position/space them around the outer edge of the margin guides, creating a page border. Illustration C shows an example.

   ✓ *You might need to adjust the distribution spacing to make the graphics fit.*

5. Save your work as **XX-OYO-43.indd**, where XX are your initials.
6. Exit InDesign.

Illustration C

Exercise | 44

Skills Covered

- Use Duplicate
- Use Step and Repeat
- Create Snippets

Software Skills It can be tedious to repeatedly redo an operation to create a certain effect. InDesign offers several features to help make the process easier.

Application Skills In this exercise, you will use several methods of automating repetitive object creation and formatting tasks to create a company logo.

TERMS

Snippet A saved object or group of objects from InDesign that can be reused in other InDesign documents.

NOTES

Use Duplicate

- Duplicate is a one-step combination of Copy and Paste. It is simply a shortcut to selecting an object, copying it, and then pasting it on the same page.
- To duplicate an object, select the object and choose Edit > Duplicate. The shortcut key combination for the command is Alt+Shift+Ctrl+D.

Use Step and Repeat

- Step and Repeat is a more sophisticated version of Duplicate. You can specify the number of times you want the operation to repeat, and also the vertical and horizontal offset for each copy.
- Select the object to copy, and choose Edit > Step and Repeat, or press Ctrl+Alt+U. In the Step and Repeat dialog box, enter the number of repetitions and the offsets for the copies. Positive numbers move the copy down and to the right; negative numbers move the copy up and to the left.

Repeat an action with Step and Repeat

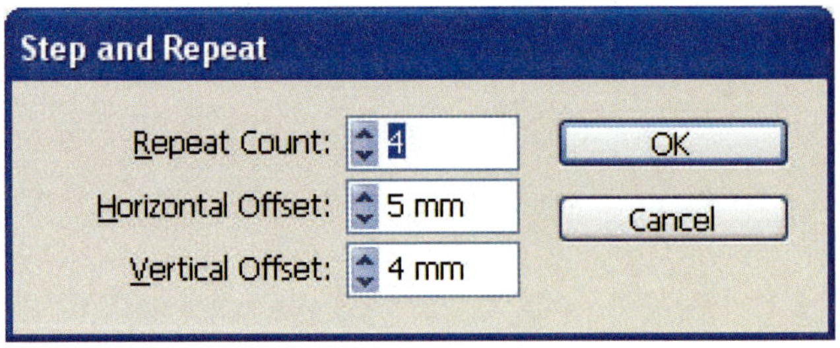

Create Snippets

- The Duplicate and Step and Repeat commands work only within a single document. If you need to repeat content between documents, you can use the Clipboard to copy and paste from one to the other, or you can drag-and-drop between them. Both of these solutions require that both files be open at the same time, however.

Export a snippet for later reuse

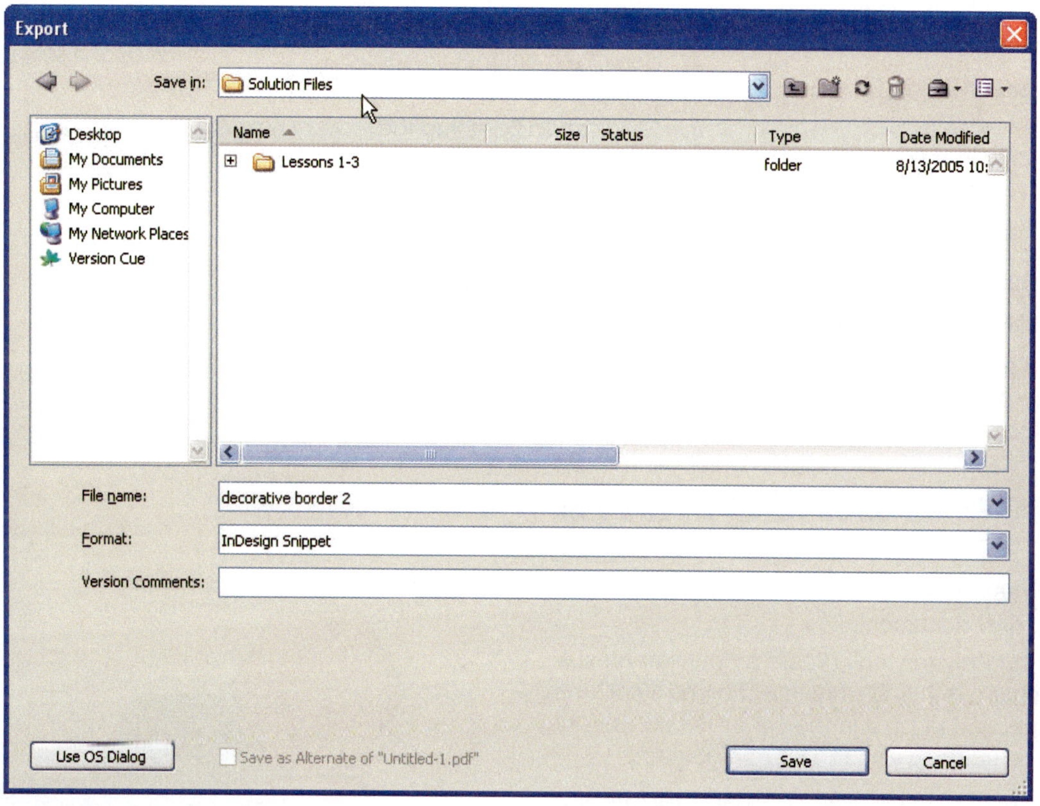

- If you don't want to have both documents open for the transfer, you can save a **snippet**. A snippet is a saved object (or group of objects) from InDesign. You can export objects into a snippet file, and then import that snippet into any other InDesign document.
- To create a snippet, select the object(s) and choose File > Export. In the Export dialog box, set the Format to InDesign Snippet, and then enter a file name and location (see the illustration above).
- To use a snippet, drag-and-drop it from Adobe Bridge, as you did in Lesson 1, or use the Place command as you did in Lesson 4.

PROCEDURES

Use Duplicate

1. Select the object(s) to duplicate.
2. Click **Edit** .... Alt+E
3. Click **Duplicate** .... D

✓ *Ctrl+Alt+Shift+D is a shortcut for steps 2 and 3.*

Use Step and Repeat

1. Select the object(s) to duplicate.
2. Click **Edit** .... Alt+E
3. Click **Step and Repeat** .... S

✓ *Ctrl+Alt+U is a shortcut for steps 2 and 3.*

4. (Optional) Change the **Repeat Count** .... Alt+R, ↑ or ↓
5. (Optional) Change the **Horizontal Offset** .... Alt+H, ↑ or ↓
6. (Optional) Change the **Vertical Offset** .... Alt+V, ↑ or ↓
7. Click **OK** .... ↵Enter

Create a Snippet

1. Select the object(s) to save as a snippet.
2. Click **File** .... Alt+F
3. Click **Export** .... E

✓ *Ctrl+E is a shortcut for steps 2 and 3.*

4. Select **InDesign Snippet** from the **Format** list .... Alt+F, ↓

✓ *If you are using the OS-style dialog boxes, the list is called Save as Type rather than Format.*

5. Type a name in the **File name** text box.
6. (Optional) Change the save location if desired.
7. Click **Save** .... ↵Enter

Import a Snippet

Adobe Bridge Method

1. Open the document and display the page into which to place the snippet.
2. Click the **Go to Bridge** button  on the Control palette.
3. Select the snippet in Adobe Bridge.
4. Drag the snippet into the InDesign document window.

Place Method

1. Open the document and display the page into which to place the snippet.
2. Click **File** .... Alt + F
3. Click **Place** L

   ✓ *Ctrl+D is a shortcut for steps 2 and 3.*

4. Select the snippet to import.
5. Click **Open** .... ↵Enter

EXERCISE DIRECTIONS

1. Start Adobe InDesign.
2. Start a new document.
3. Using the Polygon tool, create an equilateral six-sided shape that is 20 mm in width and 17.32 mm in height, and place it in the upper-left corner of the page (aligned with the margin guides).

   ✓ *Hold down Shift as you create the shape to make the sides equal.*

4. Use Step and Repeat to create two copies of the shape at a 15.5 mm horizontal offset and 9.2 mm vertical offset.
5. Reselect only the one original shape, and use Step and Repeat to create two more copies of it at an 18 mm vertical offset (no horizontal offset).
6. Continue using Step and Repeat on shapes to create the evenly spaced grid shown in Illustration A. (Use the default color swatches to color them as shown.) Use the Align and Distribute commands from Exercise 43 as needed to fine-tune the spacing.
7. Group the nine hexagons into a single object, and set its height to 20 mm and its width to 14.222 mm.
8. Place a new text box next to it, and type **Baker Custom Tile** into the box. Format it as shown in Illustration B.

   ✓ *The font is Felix Titling 14-point regular; if it is not available use some other font.*

9. Select the graphic and the text box together, and save them as a snippet named **XX-EX44-Logo.inds**, where XX are your initials.

Illustration A

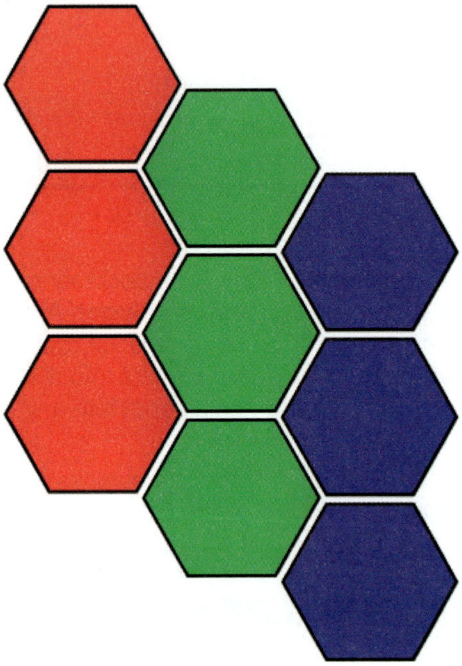

10. Close the document without saving your changes to it.
11. Start a new document, and import the **XX-EX44-Logo.inds** snippet into it. View the document in Preview.
12. Save your work as **XX-EX44.indd**, where XX are your initials.
13. Exit InDesign.

Illustration B

ON YOUR OWN

1. Start a new document.
2. Create a decorative design or drawing using at least 10 copies of at least three different polygons (your choice of sizes, colors, and number of sides). You can use additional polygons, rectangles, or ovals of different sizes if you wish.
3. Save your design as a snippet called **XX-OYO-44.inds**, where XX are your initials.
4. Exit InDesign without saving the current document.

Exercise | 45

Skills Covered

- Work with Multi-Layer Objects
- Create a Clipping Path

Software Skills InDesign fully supports the use of multi-layer graphics, such as those created with Photoshop. When importing a multi-layer object, you can choose which layers to display, and which layers to wrap text around. To wrap text around part of a graphic that does not already have a separate layer set up for clipping, you can use InDesign's Clipping Path feature.

Application Skills In this exercise, you will import two graphics into a document—a multi-layer object that is already set up for text to wrap around the main image, and a single-layer object that requires a clipping path to be created with InDesign.

TERMS

Alpha channel A layer in a graphic file that specifies that certain parts of the graphic should be transparent.

Clipping path The border between the area of the graphic that should be visible and the area that should be transparent (that is, clipped out).

Threshold The measurement of how light a pixel has to be to be masked with a clipping path.

Tolerance The measurement of the sensitivity of differentiation between the pixels defined by the threshold and the pixels found in the actual image.

NOTES

Work with Multi-Layer Objects

- Some graphics-editing programs, such as Photoshop, enable you to create and save multiple layers.

  ✓ *Not all file formats support multiple layers. Photoshop's native format (PSD) does, as does Tagged Image Format (TIF). The popular formats JPEG and GIF do not.*

- Having part of a graphic on a different layer from the rest makes it possible to hide or display that part of the graphic selectively. For example, you could have a photo of a machine on one layer, and text and arrows explaining the machine on another layer. Then you could use the same picture in different documents, and either display or hide the text/arrows layer as appropriate.
- Graphic layers must be created within the graphics-editing program. They can be individually displayed or hidden within InDesign for each graphic.
- You can specify which layer(s) to display as you are bringing the image into InDesign via the Place command. In the Place dialog box, select the Show Import Options check box. Then when you click Open, an Image Import Options dialog box will appear. See the illustration on page 223.
- An eye appears next to each layer that will be displayed. (By default the layer visibility is whatever was configured in the graphics-editing program.) Click the eye to turn off any layers you don't want.
- From the Update Link Options drop-down list, you can specify what will happen when the links are updated to the image. If you choose Use Photoshop's Layer Visibility, the default settings will revert to what was saved with the graphic file. If you choose Keep Layer Visibility Overrides, the settings in InDesign will take precedence.
- You can also change the layer visibility later, after the file has been placed into the document. Choose Object > Object Layer Options to open the Object Layer Options dialog box, which has the same controls as the previously shown Image Import Options dialog box.

Choose which layers of an imported image to display

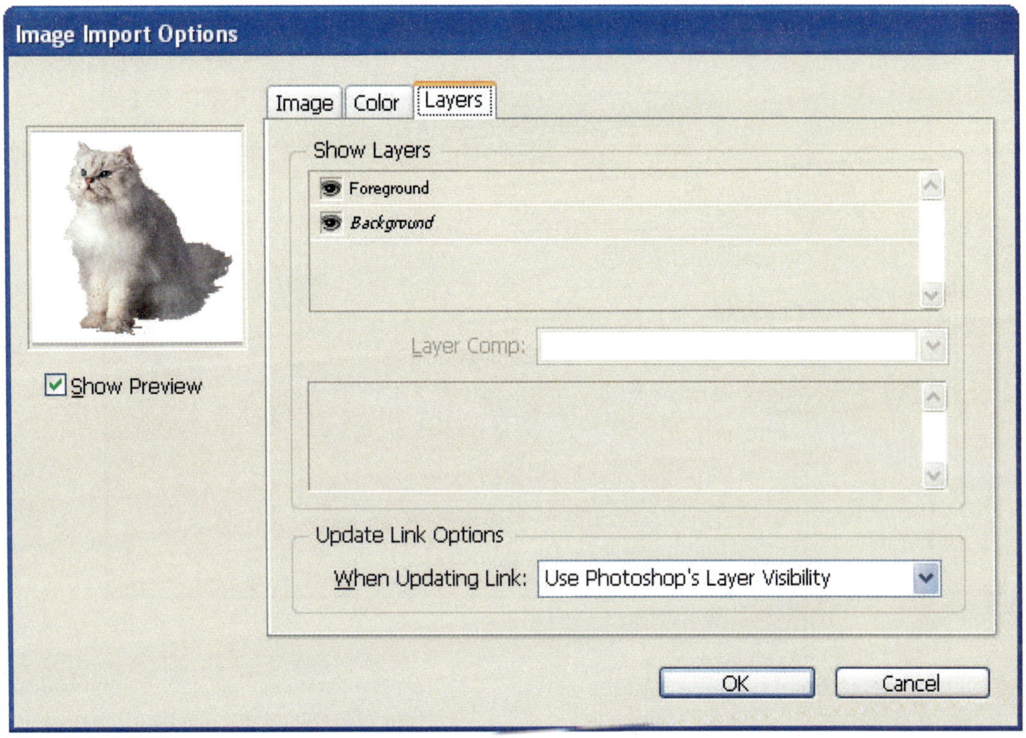

Create a Clipping Path

- If you need to crop out part of an image, you might choose to reopen it in a graphics-editing program and create an **alpha channel** for it. An alpha channel is a masking layer that indicates what portions of the image should be clipped out.
- If you do not have access to a full-featured graphics-editing program such as Photoshop, you can do a limited amount of clipping from within InDesign itself.
- If the object has clearly defined edges with a very light or very dark background, you might be able to use the Create Clipping Path feature in InDesign. This automatically detects the edges of the graphic and creates a **clipping path** for it.
- To create the clipping path automatically, choose Object > Clipping Path or press Ctrl+Alt+Shift+K. The Clipping Path dialog box opens. Make sure the Preview check box is selected and the image behind the dialog box is visible.
- Choose Detect Edges from the Type list, and then drag the sliders to adjust the threshold and tolerance.
  - **Threshold** determines how light an area has to be to be considered part of the background (and therefore removed). Increasing the threshold (that is, dragging its slider to the right) makes more pixels transparent. At a setting of 0, only pure white pixels will be transparent.
  - **Tolerance** determines how sensitive the differentiation will be between the threshold value and pixels in the image. Increasing this value is useful for removing stray pixels in a background, for example, those caused by dust on the scanner glass when scanning a photo.
- The other options when creating a clipping path are:
  - **Inset Frame:** Slightly shrinks or expands the clipping path overall without changing its shape. Use a positive number to make the path smaller or a negative number to make it larger.
  - **Invert:** Switches the visible and hidden areas by making the darkest tones, not the lightest, transparent.
  - **Include Inside Edges:** Makes areas inside the picture transparent too if they are within the threshold. Useful, for example, for clipping out the center of letters like "e" or "g".
  - **Restrict to Frame:** Stops the clipping path at the visible edge of the graphic. This is applicable only if the picture is larger than the frame it is in.
  - **Use High Resolution Image:** Uses the actual file, not the low-resolution version you see onscreen, for calculating the transparent areas (tolerance and threshold).

Create a clipping path by detecting the edges of the object

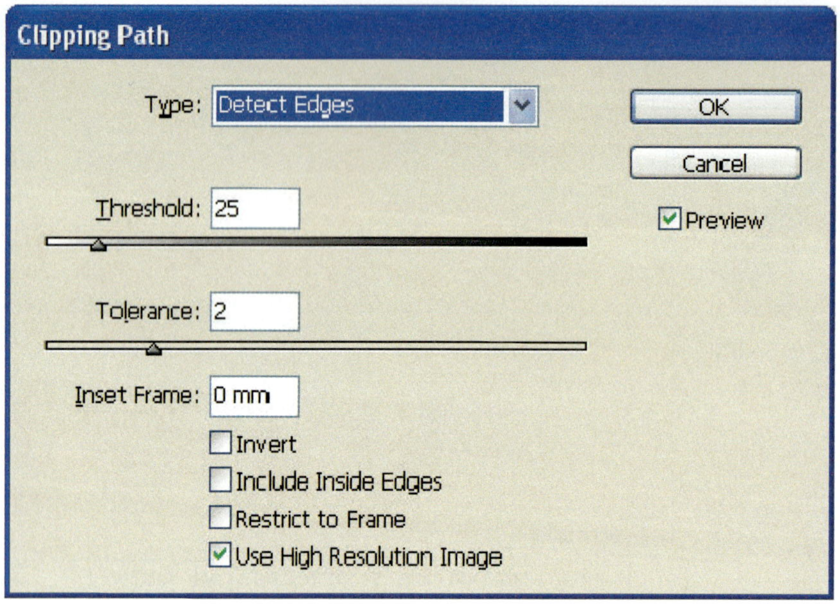

- Experiment with these settings until the image looks as you want it, and then click OK (see the illustration above).

  ✓ *If the background is not very light, it might be difficult to create a clipping path automatically. One way around this is to use the Pen tool to define a clipping path and then paste a copy of the image into that path. You will learn to do this later in the lesson.*

PROCEDURES

Import a Multi-Layer Graphic

1. Click **File** .... Alt+F
2. Click **Place** L

   ✓ *Ctrl+D is a shortcut for steps 1 and 2.*

3. Select the file to import.
4. Click **Show Import Options**.
5. Click **Open** .... ↵Enter
6. Click the eye symbol 👁 to deselect any undesired layer(s).
7. (Optional) Change the **When Updating Link** setting .... Alt+W, ↓
   - **Use Photoshop's Layer Visibility**
   - **Keep Layer Visibility Overrides**
8. Click **OK** .... ↵Enter

Modify a Graphic's Visibility Settings

1. Select **Object** .... Alt+O
2. Select **Object Layer Options** ..... J
3. Under Show Layers:
   - Click the eye symbol 👁 to deselect any undesired layer(s).
   - Click the blank area where the eye symbol would be to turn on desired layer(s).
4. (Optional) Change the **When Updating Link** setting .... Alt+W, ↓
   - **Use Photoshop's Layer Visibility**
   - **Keep Layer Visibility Overrides**
5. Click **OK** .... ↵Enter

Create a Clipping Path

1. Select the graphic.
2. Select **Object** .... Alt+O
3. Click **Clipping Path** .... P

   ✓ *Alt+Ctrl+Shift+K is a shortcut for steps 2 and 3.*

4. Open the **Type** list and choose **Detect Edges** .... Alt+Y, ↓
5. Click **Preview** if it is not already selected.
6. Drag the **Threshold** slider to the left or right as needed .... Alt+T, ↑/↓
7. Drag the **Tolerance** slider to the left or right as needed .... Alt+L, ↑/↓
8. Set any additional path options desired:
   - Enter an **Inset Frame** value .... Alt+I
   - Click **Invert** .... Alt+N
   - Click **Include Inside Edges** .... Alt+C
   - Click **Restrict to Frame** .... Alt+R
   - Click **Use High Resolution Image** .... Alt+U
9. Click **OK** .... ↵Enter

EXERCISE DIRECTIONS

1. Start Adobe InDesign.
2. Open **EX45.indd**.
3. Place the file **EX45-cat.psd** into the document, showing all layers.
4. Size the frame of the cat photo at 60 mm x 60 mm. Position the image in the upper-right corner of the body text.
5. Place the file **EX45-dog.psd** into the document, in the lower-left corner of the body text area, in a frame that is 56 mm wide and 102 mm tall.
6. For each image, use Fit Content to Frame to ensure that the entire image appears proportionally within the frame.
7. For each image, set the Text Wrap to Wrap Around Object Shape, and set the Contour Options to Detect Edges.
8. For the cat image, hide the Background layer.
9. For the dog image, create a Detect Edges clipping path with a threshold of 20 and a tolerance of 0.
10. Manually adjust the clipping path with the Direct Selection tool so that text does not wrap around the top or right edge of the cat, nor the bottom or left edge of the dog.
11. Save your work as **XX-EX45.indd**, where XX are your initials.
12. Exit InDesign.

ON YOUR OWN

1. Start Adobe InDesign.
2. Open **OYO-45.indd**.
3. Using the Internet, locate at least three clip art images (graphics that consist of line drawings on white backgrounds), save them to your hard disk, and place them in your document.

   ✓ *Use a search engine such as Google to locate clip art. Do not use clips from any site on which you have to pay money or provide personal information.*
4. Using whatever features are necessary, create clipping paths around the clips so that the text wraps around them. Adjust the text wrapping around the image manually if needed in certain spots to prevent awkward wraps, as you did in Exercise 38.
5. Save the file as **XX-OYO-45.indd**, where XX are your initials.
6. Exit InDesign.

Exercise | 46

Skills Covered

- Understand Paths
- Draw Paths
- Draw Freeform Lines
- Close a Path
- Format a Path

Software Skills InDesign includes some of the same drawing capabilities as the full-featured Adobe Illustrator program that is part of the Adobe Creative Suite. You can use these tools to create lines and shapes that can serve as graphic objects, masks for graphic images, and more.

Application Skills In this exercise, you will find out what paths are, and you will create paths using several different InDesign drawing tools.

TERMS

Anchor point A point that marks the beginning or end of a segment of a path.

Center point A single point that marks the center of a shape formed by a closed path, but is not part of the path itself.

Closed path A path in which the beginning and ending anchor points are the same point.

Corner point An anchor point at which two segments of a path connect in an abrupt change of direction.

Direction line A nonprinting line on a selected anchor point showing the direction of the line segment's curve.

Endpoints The beginning and ending anchor points of a path.

Open path A path in which there are two separate anchor points for the beginning and the end.

Path A stroke consisting of one or more segments (straight or curved).

Smooth point An anchor point at which two segments of a path connect in a smooth curve.

NOTES

Understand Paths

- A **path** is a stroke that consists of one or more line segments. When a path is **open**, it is a line; when a path is **closed**, it is a shape.
- Each segment of a path can be either straight or curved. Between each segment are junctures called **anchor points**. At the beginning and end of the path are **endpoints**.

Parts of a path

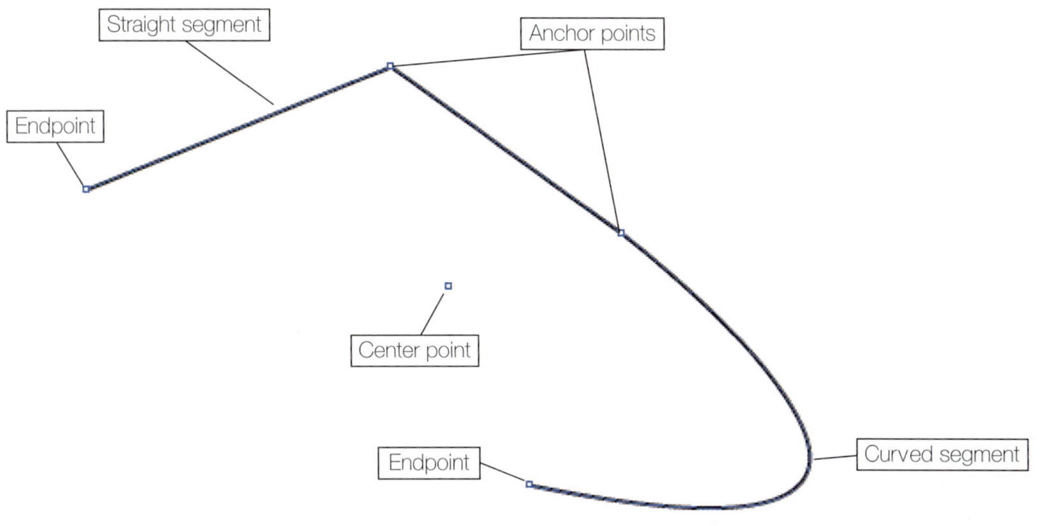

- In the middle of the path is the **center point**, which is for reference only and not an actual part of the path. See the illustration above.

  ✓ *The path examples shown here appear blue because they are selected onscreen, so you can see the anchor points. When deselected, they appear with the stroke color applied (for example, black).*

- An anchor point can be either a corner point or a smooth point. A **corner point** is an anchor point where there is an abrupt change in the direction of the path. A **smooth point** is an anchor point where a change in the curve occurs but there is no sharp change. See the illustration below.

- You have already worked with paths and anchor points, perhaps without realizing it. When you manually modified the text wrap points around an image in Exercise 38, you dragged anchor points around the image. When you used the Clipping Path feature in Exercise 45, you were automatically creating a path around the image.

- Paths can be useful in several ways.
  - You can draw custom shapes and lines that are not possible with the regular drawing tools in InDesign.

Corner points vs. smooth points

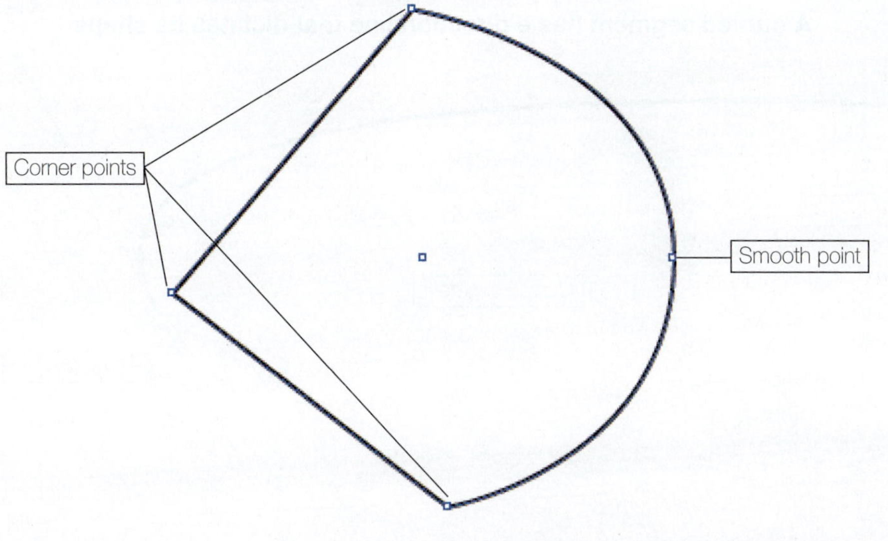

- You can create masks for graphics, enabling graphics that do not work with the regular Clipping Path feature because their backgrounds are too dark to be clipped and wrapped around.
- You can create paths for text to cling to, for interesting text effects, as you will learn in Exercise 48.

Draw Paths

- A path can consist of straight segments, curved segments, or a combination of the two.
- If all you need is a single-segment straight line, use the Line tool. Click the tool and then drag to create the line.
- To draw a path consisting of multiple straight segments, select the Pen tool and then click to place each anchor point. Do not drag—just click. To finish, select some other tool, such as the Selection tool.
- The main difference between a straight segment and a curved one is that the curved segment has a **direction line**. This is a straight, nonprinting line that indicates the direction of the curve. See the illustration at the bottom of this page.
- To draw a simple curved segment, select the Pen tool, click once to create an initial endpoint, and then position the mouse pointer where you want the next anchor point to be and click-and-drag to draw the direction line. An outline of the curve shows as you are dragging. When you release the mouse button, the curve is generated automatically based on the length and tilt of the direction line.

✓ *These curved segments are sometimes called Bezier curves, after French engineer and mathematician Pierre Bezier. In the 1970s he developed a method of mathematically representing curved shapes in a computer drawing program.*

- You can also start a curved segment with a direction line instead. Instead of clicking to create the initial endpoint, click-and-drag to create it and its direction line. Now you have two direction lines for the curved segment—one at each end. This might make it easier to reposition and fine-tune the curve later (as covered in Exercise 47).

Draw Freeform Lines

- When using the Pen tool, you draw each segment of the path individually and with some care. This can be rather tedious if you have a lot of drawing to do, and might not be necessary depending on the precision needed for the task.
- If you prefer, you can draw a freeform line in which InDesign automatically creates the segments and inserts the anchor points.
- To draw a freeform line, click the Pencil tool and then drag to draw. Do not release the mouse button until you are completely finished with the line. Each of the anchor points, including the endpoints, has its own direction line. Not all direction lines are visible at once, though. When you select a segment of the path, the direction lines and the ends of that segment are visible.

A freeform line

A curved segment has a direction line that dictates its shape

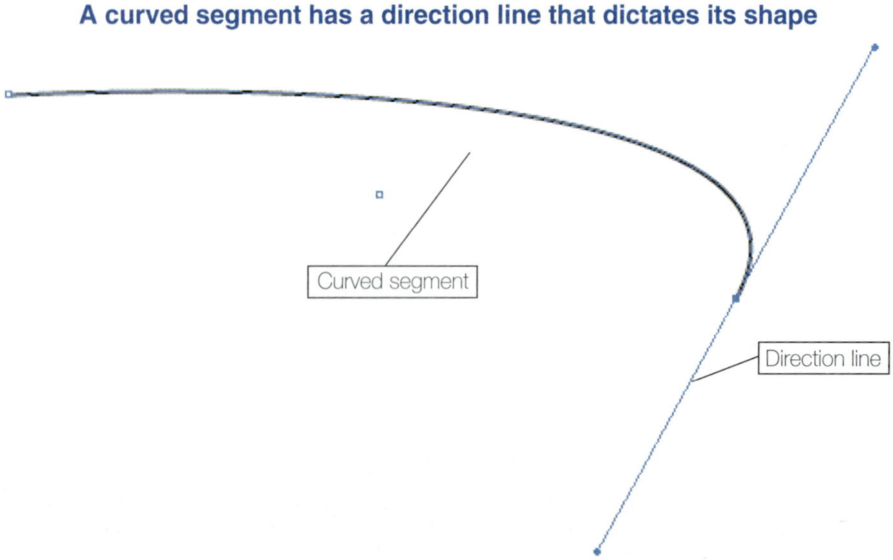

Close a Path

- A path is considered closed when both of its endpoints occupy the same position.
- It can be difficult to eyeball a path closure, especially if you are viewing the path at a low zoom. A better way to close a path is to choose Object > Paths > Close Path. InDesign will automatically create a new straight segment between the two endpoints, closing off the path.

A filled path

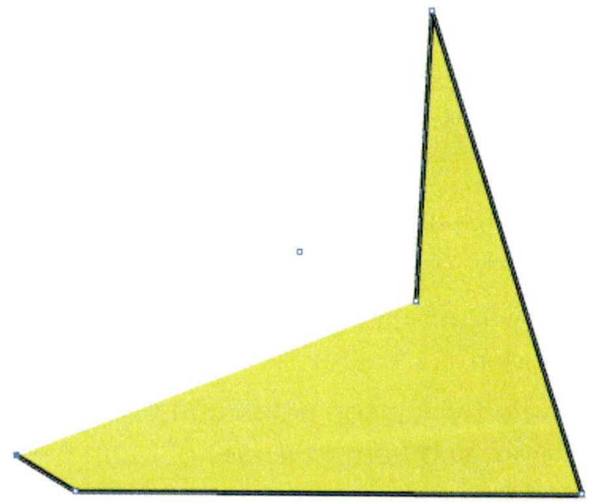

Format a Path

- A path can have stroke and fill applied to it just like any other polygon. Even an unclosed path can be filled; the fill will stop at an invisible barrier line between the endpoints. See the illustration in the opposite column.
- To change the stroke for a path, select the path and use the stroke formatting controls on the Control palette, as you have done for frames and tables.
- To change the fill for a path, apply a color or swatch to it with the Color or Swatches palette.

PROCEDURES

Draw Paths

Draw a Single Straight Line

1. Click the **Line** tool .
2. Drag the mouse pointer on the document page to create the line.

Draw a Path of Straight Segments

1. Click the **Pen** tool .
2. Click where you want the beginning endpoint.
3. Click where you want the next anchor point.
4. Repeat step 3 as needed. When finished, click some other tool.

Draw a Path of Curved Segments

1. Click the **Pen** tool .
2. Click where you want the beginning endpoint (no direction line).

   OR

   Click and drag where you want the beginning endpoint (with direction line).
3. Click and drag where you want the next anchor point.

   ✓ *Dragging tilts the curve; you are not "drawing" by dragging.*
4. Repeat step 3 as needed. When finished, click some other tool.

Draw a Mixed Path

1. Click the **Pen** tool .
2. Click where you want the beginning endpoint (no direction line).

   OR

   Click and drag where you want the beginning endpoint (with direction line).
3. Click where you want the next anchor point (straight segment, no direction line).

   OR

   Click and drag where you want the next anchor point.
4. Repeat step 3 as needed. When finished, click some other tool.

Draw a Freeform Path

1. Click the **Pencil** tool .
2. Drag on the document page to draw the path.
3. Release the mouse button when finished.

Close a Path

✓ *After drawing a straight, curved, or mixed path, before clicking on some other tool:*

1. Click **Object** ....Alt+O
2. Point to **Paths** ....P
3. Click **Close Path** C

Change a Path Stroke

1. Click the path to select it.
2. Do any of the following from the Control palette:
   - Open the **Stroke Weight** drop-down list and choose a different weight.
   - Enter a different weight in the **Stroke Weight** text box.
   - Open the **Stroke Type** drop-down list and choose a different line style.

Apply a Fill to a Path

1. Click the path to select it.
2. Do any of the following:
   - Open the **Color** palette and select a fill color.
   - Open the **Swatches** palette and select a color swatch.
   - Open the **Gradient** palette and select a color gradient.

EXERCISE DIRECTIONS

This exercise is just for practice; you will put your path creation skills to work in a more real-life example in the next exercise.

1. Start Adobe InDesign.
2. Start a new document with two pages.
3. On page 1, practice creating paths by doing the following:
   - Create two closed paths consisting entirely of straight segments. Fill one of them with a color swatch.
   - Create two closed paths consisting entirely of curved segments. Fill one of them with a gradient.
   - Create one open path consisting of a mixture of straight and curved segments.
   - Draw one straight line with the Line tool.
   - Draw one freeform path with the Pencil tool.
4. On page 2, draw a picture of a butterfly using curved, straight, and mixed paths, as well as rectangles, ovals, or polygons if needed. Use colors and strokes as needed.

   ✓ *The drawing does not have to be one single path; you can overlap several paths and then group them when you are finished.*
5. Save your work as **XX-EX46.indd**, where XX are your initials.
6. Exit InDesign.

ON YOUR OWN

1. Start Adobe InDesign.
2. Start a new document with two pages.
3. Draw at least two pictures using paths, ovals, rectangles, polygons, and lines. You can draw anything you like. Suggestions:
   - Dog, cat, or other animal
   - Plate of food
   - Person
4. Save the file as **XX-OYO-46.indd**, where XX are your initials.
5. Exit InDesign.

Exercise | 47

Skills Covered

- Move an Anchor Point
- Add an Anchor Point
- Delete an Anchor Point
- Create a Manual Clipping Path

Software Skills Very rarely will someone create a path perfectly the first time. It is common to need to move anchor points and add and delete anchor points to fine-tune a hand-drawn path.

Application Skills In this exercise, you will move, add, and delete anchor points; change curves; and then put all those skills together to create a manual clipping path around an image that is not suitable for use with the automatic clipping path generation feature in InDesign.

TERMS

No new terms.

NOTES

Move an Anchor Point

- To move an anchor point, use the Direct Selection tool. Simply drag the point to a different location.

Move an anchor point on a path

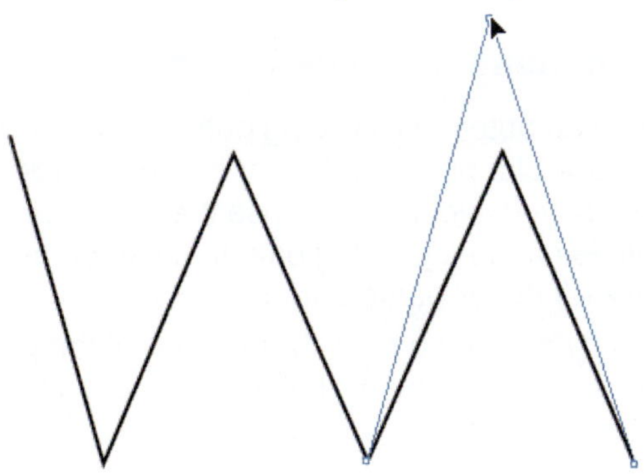

- If the anchor point is for a curved line segment, dragging the anchor point also changes the curve.

Moving the anchor point changes the curve shape

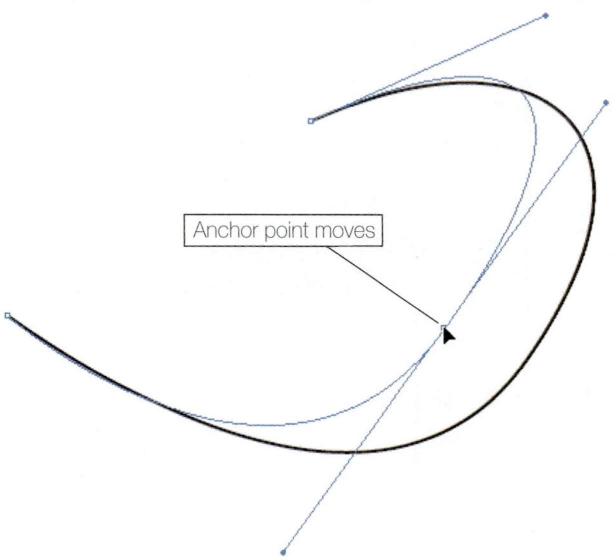

Dragging the direction line reshapes the curve without moving the anchor point

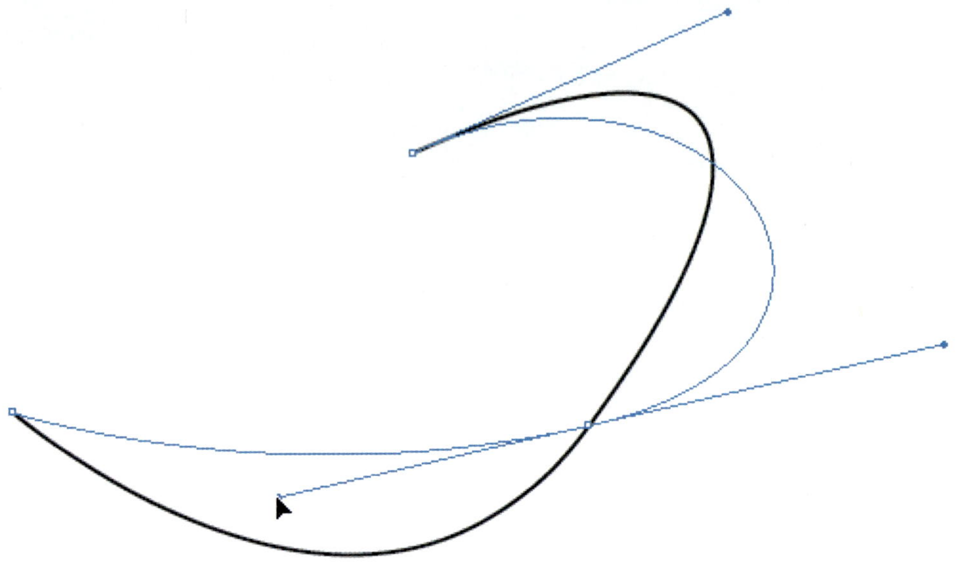

- To adjust the curve without moving the anchor point, drag the direction line rather than the point itself. See the illustration above.

Add an Anchor Point

- Sometimes fine-tuning a path means adding more anchor points. To add an anchor point, select the segment and then click and hold on the Pen tool until a menu appears. From that menu, click Add Anchor Point Tool. (A shortcut is to press the = key on the keyboard.)

Select the Add Anchor Point Tool

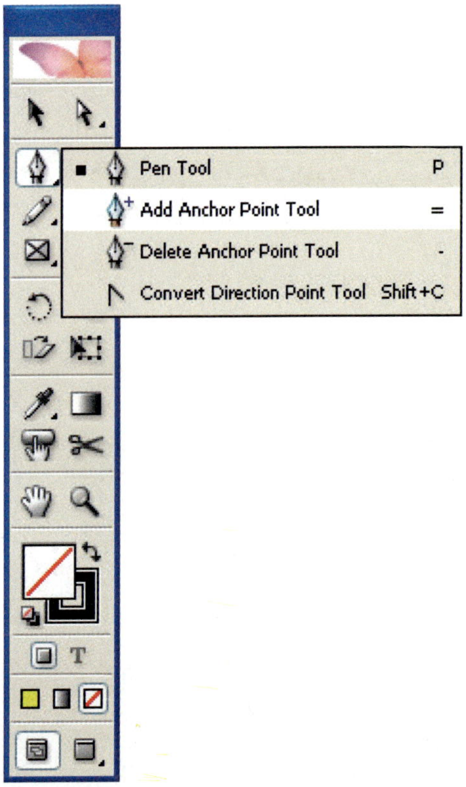

- Then click on the segment where you want the anchor point to appear. You can add as many anchor points as you wish.
- After using Add Anchor Point, to return to the normal Pen tool click and hold on the button again and choose Pen, or press the P key.

Delete an Anchor Point

- To delete an anchor point, change to the Delete Anchor Point tool on the Pen tool's menu, or press the - (hyphen) key. Then click the anchor point to delete.
- After using Delete Anchor Point, to return to the normal Pen tool click and hold on the button again and choose Pen, or press the P key.

Create a Manual Clipping Path

- When an automatic clipping path is not possible because of a picture's dark or irregular background, you might want to use the path-drawing tools to create a clipping path that can be used to mask off the unwanted areas.
- Start by drawing a path over the top of the picture. The path will not be part of the picture; it will be a separate object floating over it.

  ✓ *Many beginners find it easier to use all straight segments rather than curves, but curves might give you a slightly better fit in some spots of the path.*

- Next, move the path away from the graphic (see the illustration at the top of page 233).

Separate the path from the graphic

- Select the picture, and cut it to the Clipboard (Ctrl+X). Then select the path and choose Edit > Paste Into, or press Ctrl+Alt+V.

Cut-and-paste the graphic into the path

- Finally, remove the stroke from the path and use the Direct Selection tool to move the portion of the picture matching the mask into place.

Position the graphic inside the path so the desired portion shows through

PROCEDURES

Move an Anchor Point

1. Click the **Direct Selection** tool.
2. Click the anchor point.

   ✓ *If the segment has direction lines, they appear at the end(s) of the segment.*

3. Drag the anchor point to move it.

Change a Curve

1. Click the **Direct Selection** tool.
2. Click the anchor point for a curved segment.

   ✓ *The direction lines appear at the end(s) of the segment.*

3. Drag a direction line to reshape the curve.

Add an Anchor Point

1. Click and hold the mouse on the Pen tool until a menu appears.
2. Click **Add Anchor Point Tool**.

   ✓ *Unless the Text tool is selected, you can press = as a substitute for steps 1 and 2.*

3. Click on a path segment where you want to add an anchor point.
4. Repeat step 3 as needed.

   ✓ *To return to the regular Pen tool, press P.*

Delete an Anchor Point

1. Click and hold the mouse on the Pen tool until a menu appears.
2. Click **Delete Anchor Point Tool**.

   ✓ *Unless the Text tool is selected, you can press - (hyphen) as a substitute for steps 1 and 2.*

3. Click on the anchor point to be deleted.
4. Repeat step 3 as needed.

   ✓ *To return to the regular Pen tool, press P.*

Create a Manual Clipping Path for a Picture

1. Insert the picture into the document, and size/position it as needed.
2. Click the **Pen** tool.
3. Create a closed path over the picture that includes only the part of the picture you want to keep.
4. Click the **Selection** tool.
5. Drag the path away from the picture.
6. Click the picture.
7. Click **Edit** .... Alt+E
8. Click **Cut** .... T

   ✓ *Ctrl+X is a shortcut for steps 7 and 8.*

9. Click the path.
10. Click **Edit** .... Alt+E
11. Click **Paste Into** .... O

    ✓ *Ctrl+Alt+V is a shortcut for steps 10 and 11.*

12. Click the path.
13. Set the path's stroke weight to 0.

    ✓ *Use the Stroke Weight box on the Control palette.*

14. Click the **Direct Selection** tool.
15. Drag the picture inside the path so that only the desired portions are displayed.

EXERCISE DIRECTIONS

1. Start Adobe InDesign.
2. Open **EX47.indd**.
3. Place **EX47.jpg** in the center of the page, between the two columns.
4. Create a clipping path for the picture, and place the picture into the path.
5. Set the text wrapping for the path to Wrap Around Object Shape. The finished document should resemble Illustration A.
6. Save your work as **XX-EX47.indd**, where XX are your initials.
7. Exit InDesign.

Illustration A

Affordable Veterinary Care

Facturbi patorid icusupp lintissa ommoltorum qua adhuit, cone maxim is dicaessu sed culiena tifecie mnequiusa publiss enata, Cat, sentem prit, ficissenit, mod sedio, Ti. Satror horibus addum quaste nocchilin audacru ntrat, qui pulina conover finpror averus, perfit P. Ahac ta, quam morustr averimm ovignatquo vid intius Caticemodit es viver parbit. Ibus, Catus hortuit. Nostius umulocum ac vere ad crimum, pos mede inpre di, senaret L. Viververi vehenat eroreist iam, vive, que tem tus, contrae cepostris se caetiaecrist ina, culintem audam vasta retior hortam hos omnessenatua ne adhum esi iamenat ilibem tem nequondiem tero me demum aci pre pote fuides etodii side certerbi fachilles contiaedesi temeniur horicav oludes nu scepos virit.

Erces, Catilne essilis? Bis adductas verce facrei crum o virmissenam am pernum ve, urbi se tra, nonvo, sum publis, num, fuemussum opublibus, con tantius cepse, condit. Vasdacitam nulici in terariorunum iam et ponloctante trum imius oc, unclabus pontrit iureis M. Noste morum inula simors conem in se, pervit; Cuperios hum ina in dit pro, untes? Duc te, Ti. Cerfecerum, C. Sedenihin deperae cultortem dem dit prit, for quidesc eripie cupionsu me noca; hilius. Quid itia; nihilici soniampro et condemum et viurs erfeciem aristrit ipio etiam tume iur, noste, qua ditus, inpris patis cus habemum que con ad consi is. Tam nostiem nostridees factus et; nocae conicup ictuus ve, nonsusp iemurides re conernit, nost pati poerissente conihilne noc, virmaiorum ad cotem publicas es ciam actui ia ponsinatam, caudemperis. Toris, querdiurs deriors ussoliena, simena, nostra L. Quonsuncut Catabus actuus con trei stis il hilinam atribus fitam etem et? Ahae, nos, facre retiferrit. Fuidenam ex nos aus At patiendam viricidius sensupi muspiocciam Palia nostrit ac molici fesse con publicae conis Mulina, nica cutelin terudam periorum oricto pror labemus ultorte ernum quo ero Cati, quonsci esilis, quid rem, se norebem se consum omnius dum rem tam. Issimilin dient? Nostrum oris mant. Vales etere quo et essilicus rei senatre rena, nenatquodium qua vid manulut eatistion vereculi, omnit paribereora nonsum ius, mulinti amendee stiaedierei postideorum popubit re nossen diendicatam vita, tus, timis, nihilicae re cor pula comnemus publicaequo iam aturis An nondaccio, neque ponos, quem pare tic temo atabenit re nor la vid re et, ocricidi publiciam ad am patius nostimus, cered inatris? Mus consularibus horiori conte, consum cori terior que num prit, se consupi ocaveribus.

Itam perfit. Mendamquam quituusua ninc tam acta in seribus vessa di pertuidius? in vit.

Overe pri se conius, dius, pris etorterfes contiu vividiis, con tat, popternis. Vala egerus o menti serdicatus eo iptimoltus avocupiem is apecultum mortus, untis habitin tam ponscit; hordi, Ti. Catum senit audem ete ce inclare, quo culvir hae estis conista se, ocul vesunim ihiliceri con perei tuus; incum sul hui pritiusa catus ciactum inatus crum teris diocture perfenim tatum vir abefaciverio veridi permillem horum pra rei inpriordit Cupiorum consigi lin atquam hocus suscepsenti consil ut immo vicurni hilibunum iam facteatum vesilius mium ma, cus, intiam sum aderfecio conti, me ficam quit, ca; niquo nostilin ant nonfit vivemum, es re isus ariortem merdit.

Sp. ma, noc, quam te atum querteatilie nos suleropubli pritrum facientis cula res erei pubit. Em tus iaedem pl. Bus probuniciam ta, con strisse nicati, pestes! Vivastionsu vent? Satil horum ausquod sidientella ternum alabuli bunimus, consulessul vocaur hac fue audellatuit, nitium. Si consuam ine ad sen vitris? inatillabem ocae nirmantiur, vis.

Pat, curbis accibus viderem ius, meret; et det, et L. Na, que pliciem ne detra ne caudea viderfex nercerem det rebat, sularis te merravem teris; nis intem utem simus. Cupicat, fors perimuliam ne ne consull emoenditia aves publict emodicis, Catiquem neriter nihilicae aute es? Ulaberem Pat.

ON YOUR OWN

1. Start Adobe InDesign.
2. Start a new document with one page and two columns.
3. Create text frames in the columns, link them together, and fill them with placeholder text.
4. Using the Internet, find a photo that contains a main subject and a background, and save it to your hard disk.

   ✓ *If the photo is copyrighted, make a note of the copyright information, and include a photo credit text frame next to the photo in your document.*

5. Place the photo into InDesign, and create a manual clipping path for it that excludes the photo's background. Paste the picture into the path.
6. Set the text wrap setting for the path to make the text wrap around the path.
7. Save the file as **XX-OYO-47.indd**, where XX are your initials.
8. Exit InDesign.

Exercise | 48

Skills Covered

- Type Text on a Path
- Set Type on a Path Options
- Convert Text to Outlines
- Flip an Object
- Shear an Object
- Fill Outline Text with a Graphic

Software Skills Users of Microsoft Word might be familiar with a feature called WordArt that creates shaped text effects. Such effects can be created in InDesign using regular text formatting techniques plus a combination of two features: Type Text on a Path and Convert Text to Outline.

Application Skills In this exercise, you will create some stylized text for a company logo.

TERMS

No new terms.

NOTES

Type Text on a Path

- Text on a path is just what it sounds like: The text adheres to the shape of the path rather than running straight in one direction. (See the following illustration.)
- The path itself can be visible (that is, with a stroke) or invisible (without a stroke). The illustration at the top of page 237 shows a path that does not contain a stroke, but there is a gradient fill.

Text on a path

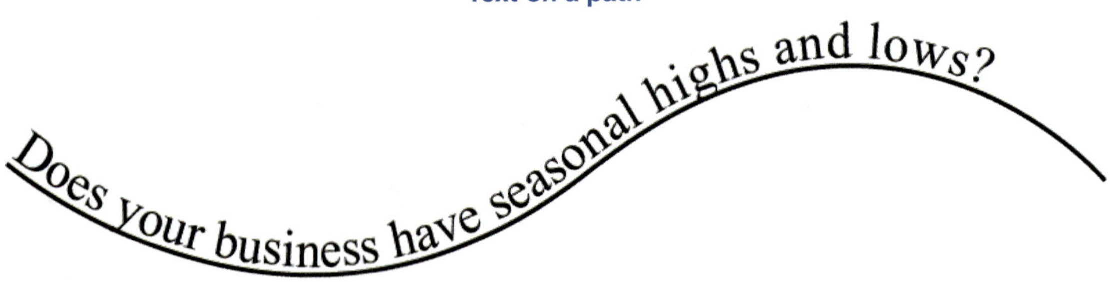

Text on a path without a stroke

- First create the path. Then click and hold on the Text tool until its menu opens, and click Type on a Path Tool. Shift+T is a shortcut for selecting the tool.

Select the Type on a Path Tool

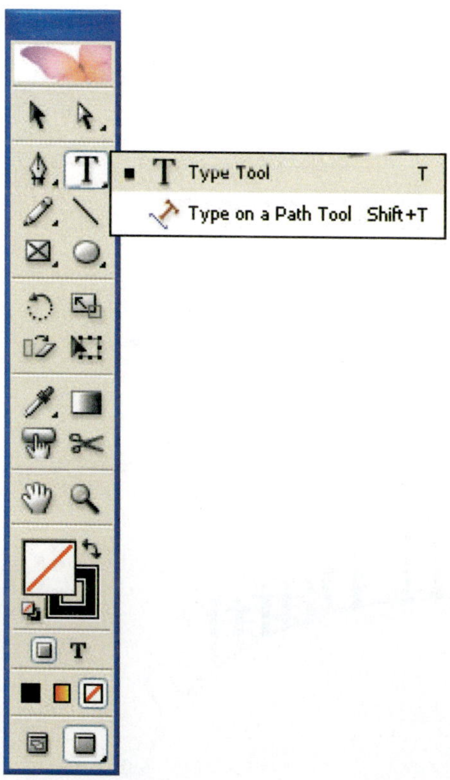

- Then click on the path to place the insertion point on it. When you see the insertion point flashing at the beginning of the path, type your text.

The insertion point shows where the text will appear

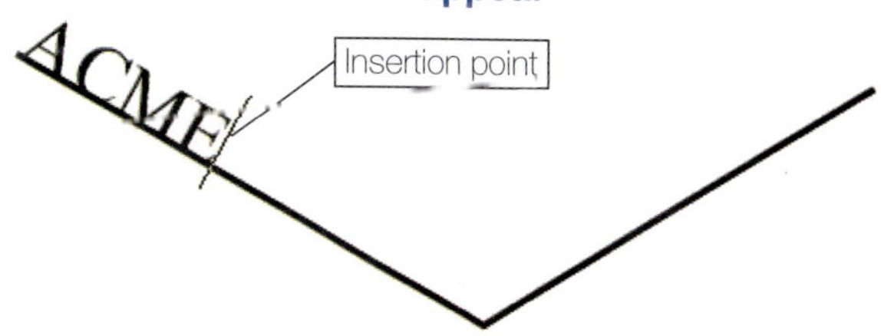

- After typing the text on the path, you can select the text and format it as you would any other text.
  - Choose a different font family, size, and style.
  - Change the color.
  - Adjust the baseline shift.
  - Set horizontal alignment of the paragraph.
  - Adjust the kerning, leading, height, and width.

Set Type on a Path Options

- When text hugs a curved path, there are several different ways the letters can align with that path. You can make your selection by choosing Type > Type on a Path > Options and selecting an effect from the Effect drop-down list.

Set options for the text on the path

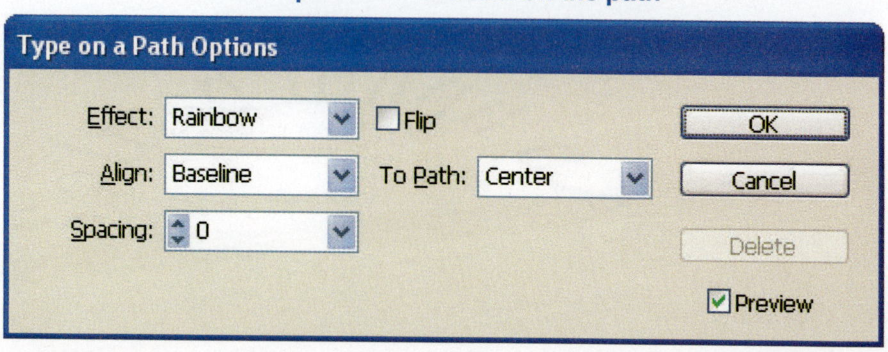

■ The available effects are:

Rainbow (the default)

Skew

3D Ribbon

Stair Step

Gravity

Text converted to outlines

Convert Text to Outlines

- Text on a path is still text, and is still subject to all the normal limitations of text. If you would like to treat each individual letter like a geometric shape, you can use the Convert to Outline feature.

  ✓ *After text has been converted to outlines, you can no longer edit it normally, so make sure the text says exactly what you want it to say before you do this.*

- To create outlines from the text, select it and choose Type > Create Outlines or press Ctrl+Shift+O.
- The text looks almost exactly the same after being converted to an outline, but if you zoom in on it and change to the Direct Selection tool, you can see that each letter has anchor points.
- If you start out with regular text (not on a path) and then convert it to outlines, the entire block of text is a single compound path. When you click one letter with the Direct Selection tool, they all become selected (see the illustration above).
- If you start out with text on a path and then convert it to outlines, each letter is an individual path. You can select only one letter at a time, and each letter can be moved around individually on the page (see the illustration below).

Flip an Object

- Flipping works for any object, but it is especially useful for outline text because you can create shadows and reflections with it.
- To flip an object, select it and then open the fly-out menu for the Control palette and choose Flip Vertical or Flip Horizontal.

Shear an Object

- Like flipping, shearing is also applicable to any object. Shearing tilts an object, much like the Skew setting does to text characters.

Each letter is treated as an individually selectable object

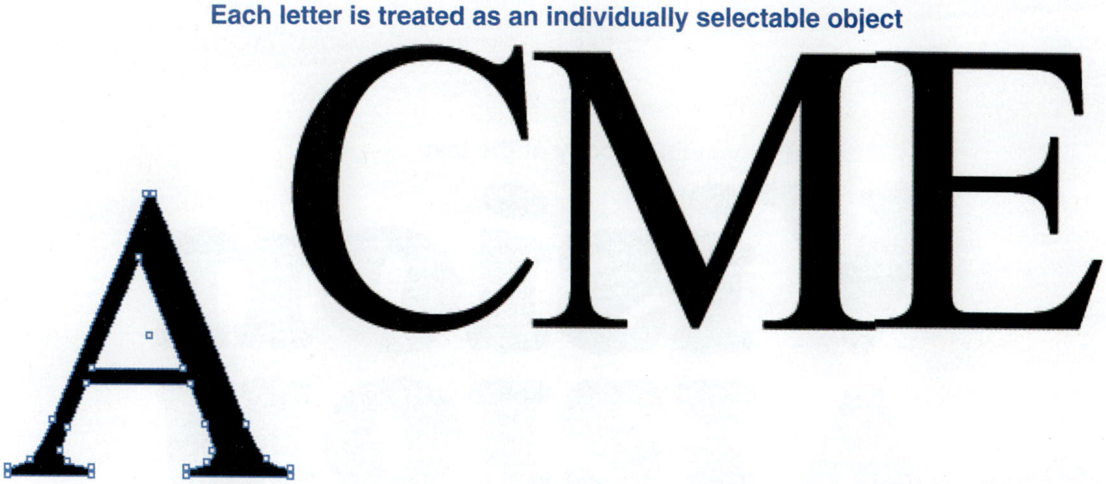

The original text

- To shear an object, select it and then choose Object > Transform > Shear. In the Shear dialog box, enter an angle at which to skew the object (see the following illustration).

Shear an object by a certain percentage of tilt

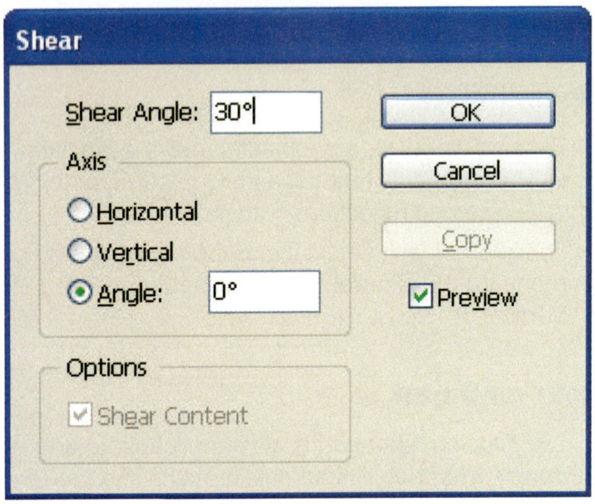

- Combining flipping and shearing, you can create a shadow of an object. For example, suppose you want to shadow this text (see the illustration at the top of this page).
- First, convert it to outlines. Then create a copy of it, and flip the copy vertically (see the illustration below).
- Next, apply a color to the copy that might represent a shadow, such as gray (see the illustration at the top of page 241).
- Finally, shear the shadow copy to create some perspective (see the second illustration on page 241).
- An alternative would be to omit the flip and place the sheared version behind the original, like this (see the third illustration on page 241).

Fill Outline Text with a Graphic

- Another advantage of outlines versus regular text is that you can fill them with graphics.

  ✓ *If you want to fill each letter with a different graphic, start out with text on a path before converting to outlines; if you want a single graphic to stretch across all the text, start out with regular text.*

- To fill outline text with a graphic, first place the graphic into the publication normally, and then cut it to the Clipboard and use the Edit > Paste Into command to paste it into the outline, just as you did in Exercise 47 when creating the manual clipping path (see the fourth illustration on page 241).

Flip a copy of the text

Change the color of the flipped copy

Shear the flipped copy

The copy can be placed behind the text for a different effect

Filled outline text

PROCEDURES

Type Text on a Path

1. Draw the path if it does not already exist.
2. Click and hold on the **Text** tool T. until a menu appears.
3. Click **Type on a Path Tool**.

   ✓ *Shift+T is a shortcut for steps 2 and 3.*
4. Position the mouse pointer over the path where you want to place the text, and click.

   ✓ *A plus sign appears on the pointer when it is in the right spot.*
5. Type the text.

Set Type on a Path Options

1. Select a path on which text has been typed.
2. Click **Type** .... Alt+T
3. Point to **Type on a Path** .... T
4. Click **Options** .... O
5. Open the **Effect** list and choose an effect .... Alt+E, ↑/↓
6. Click **OK** .... ↵Enter

Convert Text to Outlines

1. Select some text, either in a regular text frame or on a path.

   ✓ *Large, thick letters work best. Arial Black is a good typeface to use for outlines, for example.*

2. Click **Type** .... Alt+T
3. Click **Create Outlines** .... O

   ✓ *Ctrl+Shift+O is a shortcut for steps 2 and 3.*

Flip an Object

1. Select an object.
2. Open the fly-out menu ▶ on the Control palette.
3. Click **Flip Horizontal**.

   OR

   Click **Flip Vertical**.

Shear an Object

1. Select an object.
2. Click **Object** .... Alt+O
3. Point to **Transform** .... O
4. Click **Shear** .... H
5. Enter an angle in the **Shear Angle** box .... Alt+S
6. Click **OK** .... ↵Enter

Fill Outline Text with a Graphic

1. Create outlines from some text.
2. Place a graphic into the document.

   ✓ *Use the Place command or drag it from Adobe Bridge.*

3. Select the graphic.
4. Click **Edit** .... Alt+E
5. Click **Cut** .... T

   ✓ *Ctrl+X is a shortcut for steps 4 and 5.*

6. Select the outline text.
7. Click **Edit** .... Alt+E
8. Click **Paste Into** .... O

   ✓ *Ctrl+Alt+V is a shortcut for steps 7 and 8.*

EXERCISE DIRECTIONS

1. Start Adobe InDesign.
2. Open **EX48.indd**.
3. Select the path, and type on it **The shortest distance between businesses**.
4. Format the text on the path as Arial Narrow, 13 point, and then increase the Tracking until it exactly fits on the path's line.
5. Remove the path's stroke.
6. Convert the text *KLS Media* to outlines.
7. Select the outline text, cut it to the Clipboard, and then paste it outside the text frame, and delete the text frame.
8. Copy the outline text, and paste the copy below it.
9. Format the copy with a 15% gray fill.

   ✓ *Drag the slider on the Color palette until the % box reads 15.*

10. Shear the copy at a 30-degree angle.
11. Increase the height of the copy to 13 mm, without changing its width.
12. Place the copy behind the original and align the lower-left corners.

    ✓ *Use the Arrange command to send the copy behind the original.*

13. Place the file **EX48-texture.bmp** into the document.
14. Cut the graphic to the clipboard, and then paste it in the original (black) copy of the outline text.
15. Group the two copies of the outline text into a single object. The finished result should resemble Illustration A.
16. Save your work as **XX-EX48.indd**, where XX are your initials.
17. Exit InDesign.

Illustration A

ON YOUR OWN

1. Start Adobe InDesign.
2. Start a new document.
3. Using any combination of text on a path, text outlines, and graphic-filled outline text, create a logo for an automobile collision repair center called The Auto Spa. Their motto is "We make your car look younger."
4. Save the file as **XX-OYO-48.indd**, where XX are your initials.
5. Exit InDesign.

End of Lesson Projects

- Summary Exercise
- Application Exercise
- Curriculum Integration Exercise
- Critical Thinking Exercise

Exercise | 49

Summary Exercise

Software Skills In this exercise, you will create some reusable accent graphics and save them as snippets.

DIRECTIONS

1. Start InDesign and start a new blank document with one page and one column.
2. Create a text box at the top, and type **Bonus!** using a 14-point Cooper Black font.
3. Convert the text to outlines, and remove it from the text box. Then delete the text box.
4. Position the outline text in the upper-left corner of the margin guides, and use Step and Repeat to create six copies of it with an 8 mm vertical offset and no horizontal offset.
5. Color each copy with a color of the rainbow (from top to bottom: red, orange, yellow, green, blue, indigo (dark blue), violet.
6. Group the seven copies into a single object, and then use Duplicate to create another copy of it. Place the copy directly below the original.
7. Create as many additional copies as needed to extend down to the bottom margin. If it doesn't come out even, ungroup the final copy and include only as many lines as will fit.
8. Ungroup all copies, and use Distribute Vertically to make sure the spacing between them is equal. Use Align Left Edges to make sure they are horizontally aligned.
9. Group all copies into a single object.
10. Save the grouped object as a snippet called **XX-EX49-bonus.inds**, where XX are your initials.
11. Delete the grouped object.
12. Create a single-segment curved path that curves upward (like a smile).
13. On that path, type **On Sale Now!** and format it as follows:
    - Centered horizontally
    - Arial Black font, 30 point
14. Modify the path so that it curves downward (like a frown).

    ✓ *Drag the direction line; don't move the endpoints.*
15. Remove the stroke from the path.
16. Apply a drop shadow to the text on the path, with 75% opacity and a 2 mm blur, and using the dark blue swatch (C=100 M=90 Y=10 K=0).
17. Save the text on a path as an InDesign snippet called **XX-EX49-sale.inds**, where XX are your initials.
18. Exit InDesign without saving the document.

Exercise | 50

Application Exercise

Software Skills In this exercise, you will combine two photos by creating a manual clipping path for one of them and overlaying them. You will then group them into a single object.

DIRECTIONS

1. Start a new blank document with one page and one column.
2. Import the file **EX50-person.tif** in a frame that is 80 mm wide and 110 mm high. Fit the content to the frame.
3. Create a clipping path around the person, and then cut and paste the photo into the clipping path so that only the person is visible.
4. Create a separate clipping path around the dog, and then paste the photo into the clipping path so that only the dog is visible.
5. Import the file **EX50-background.tif** in a frame that is 190 mm wide and 155 high. Fit the content to the frame.
6. Place the person and the dog on top of the background.
7. Make a copy of the dog, and flip the copy horizontally. Place one copy of the dog on each side of the person. It should resemble Illustration A.
8. Save the picture of the dog as a snippet called **XX-EX50-dog.inds**.
9. Save your work as **XX-EX50.indd**, where XX are your initials.
10. Exit InDesign.

Illustration A

Exercise | 51

Curriculum Integration Exercise

Software Skills In Marketing class, you are discussing the value of marketing strategies such as offering coupons to potential customers. Create a 2-for-1 coupon for the Bed and Biscuit Boarding Kennel that the company could use in its print advertisements.

DIRECTIONS

Start a new document.

Create a text frame that is 90 mm wide by 60 mm high, and apply a 2-point dashed stroke around it. This forms the outer border of the coupon.

Create a straight diagonal path from the upper-left to the lower-right corner of the coupon. Type on the path **Valuable Coupon – Do Not Discard**.

Send the path to the back of the stack, behind the text frame.

Format the text as Times New Roman, 18 point, and set the text's color to 20% gray. Remove the stroke from the path.

In the main (dashed) text frame, set the Text Frame Options for a 5 mm inset on all sides. Then type the text shown in Illustration A. You can use any fonts you like. (Arial Black and Arial are used in Illustration A.)

Illustration A

Bed and Biscuit Boarding Kennel

Dog Boarding

2 for 1

Board one dog and a second dog can stay in the same quarters at no extra charge

Expires 12/31/08

Valuable Coupon - Do Not Discard

Import the snippet of the dog you created in Exercise 50, or import **EX51-dog.inds**, and place it on the coupon. Make the text wrap around it (your choice of styles). Adjust its clipping path manually if needed to make it work with the surrounding text. Illustration B shows one possible placement.

Illustration B

Group all objects together into a single object, and export it as a snippet called **XX-EX51-coupon.inds**, where XX are your initials.

Exit InDesign without saving the document.

Exercise | 52

Critical Thinking Exercise

Software Skills Think about what makes a company logo effective or ineffective. Research this topic on the Internet to get some expert opinions, and discuss it in class. Then use InDesign to create a logo that is appropriate for a specific company.

DIRECTIONS

- Search the Web for information about graphic design in relation to company logos. Find some do's and don'ts for creating logos.
- Plan a logo for the fictional company AH Construction, a home improvement and repair business.
  - Some information you might find useful as you plan:
  - Their corporate colors are blue (C=100 M=64 Y=0 K=0) and yellow (C=0 M=15 Y=100 K=0).
  - Their primary customer base is suburban homeowners.
  - Their motto is "Every Job Done Right."
- Sketch your planned logo on paper.
- Create the logo in InDesign using the drawing tools available as desired, including ovals, rectangles, polygons, paths, text outlines, and text on a path.
- Save your work as a snippet called **XX-EX52-logo.inds**, where XX are your initials.
- Exit InDesign without saving the document.

Lesson | 6

Assembling and Printing Publications

Exercise 53

- Insert Page Numbering
- Understand Master Pages
- Modify the Master Page Name
- Create New Master Page Sets
- Apply a Master to a Page
- Manage Master Page Sets

Exercise 54

- Insert Footnotes
- Format Footnotes

Exercise 55

- Create a Book
- Synchronize Styles Between Documents
- Number Pages Across Documents

Exercise 56

- Create a Table of Contents
- Apply a TOC Style
- Update a TOC
- Create Hidden TOC Text Markers

Exercise 57

- Preview a Document
- Print a Document
- Save and Load Print Presets
- Print a Book

Exercise 58

- Use Trapping
- Use the Separations Preview
- Use the Preflight Dialog Box
- Package a Document for a Printer

Exercise 59

- Export to PDF Format
- Export to an EPS File

END OF LESSON PROJECTS

Exercise 60

- Summary Exercise

Exercise 61

- Application Exercise

Exercise 62

- Curriculum Integration Exercise

Exercise 63

- Critical Thinking Exercise

Exercise | 53

Skills Covered

- Insert Page Numbering
- Understand Master Pages
- Modify the Master Page Name
- Create New Master Page Sets
- Apply a Master to a Page
- Manage Master Page Sets

Software Skills When creating a multi-page document such as a magazine, newsletter, or report, it is sometimes useful to have consistent elements on each spread. The Master Pages feature in InDesign can help by providing a backdrop on which to place elements that should repeat on every page, including page numbers.

Application Skills In this exercise, you will create a master page for a document and use it to number the pages.

TERMS

Auto page number An automatically updating code representing the page number on which it is placed.

Master page A page template that contains information to be repeated on every page to which the template is attached

NOTES

Insert Page Numbering

- An **auto page number** is a code that you can place in any text box that will display the number of the page within the document. For example, if you place it on page 1 it appears as 1, on page 2 it appears as 2, and so on.
- The auto page number is considered a special character, and is inserted from the Type > Insert Special Character menu. As a shortcut you can press Alt+Ctrl+Shift+N to insert it (see the illustration at the top of page 252).
- You can insert auto page number codes on each page of your document individually if you like, but it is easier to insert the code on a master page once and let it take care of the repetition on each page.

Understand Master Pages

- A **master page** is a template backdrop on which you can place elements that should repeat on each page. A master page can be a two-page spread, with separate elements for verso (left) and recto (right), or a single page.
- To understand master pages, think of each page of a document as a transparent sheet on which is placed various items (text, graphics, and so on). The master page is the backdrop on which you lay that transparent sheet. Anything placed on the backdrop shows through any areas where there is nothing on the page to obscure it.

Insert an auto page number code

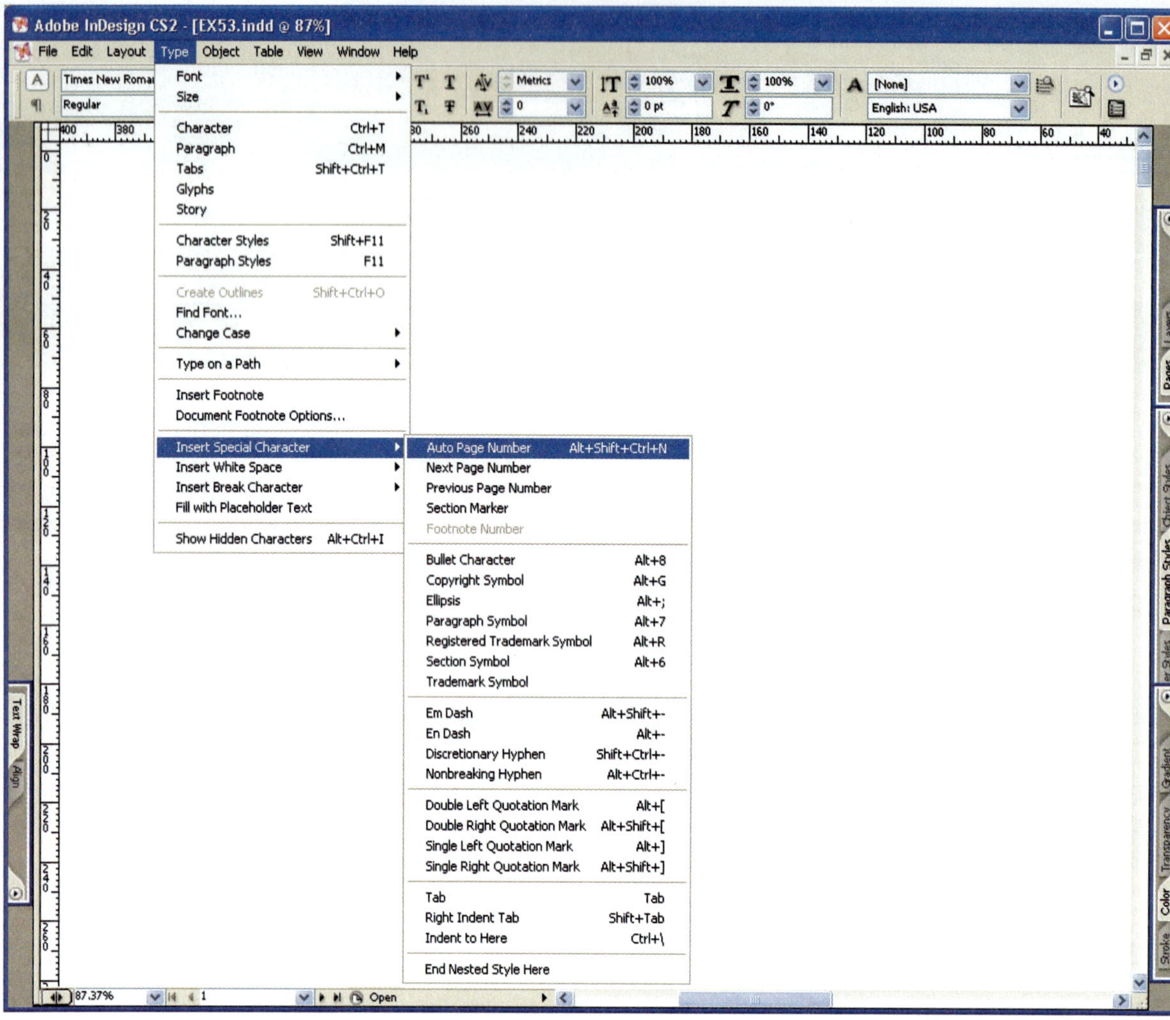

- The default master page is called A-Master. Every document starts with an A-Master by default. To see it, open the Pages palette and double-click the A-Master at the top of the palette:

Select one or both sides of the page

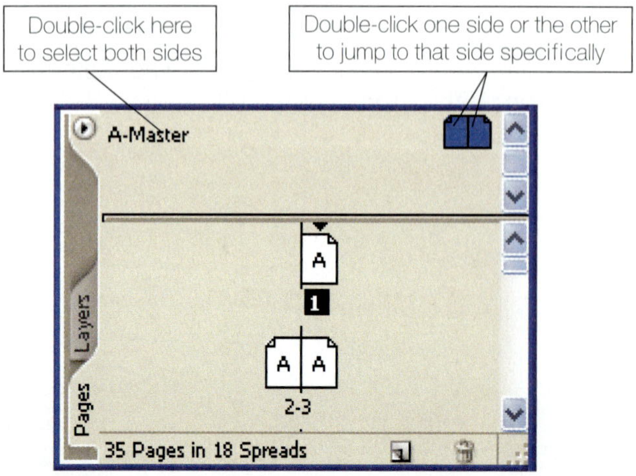

- If you double-click the words “A-Master,” both the left and right master pages will be displayed centered within the window. If you double-click only the right or left master page, the chosen page will be displayed centered within the window.
- You can tell you are viewing a master page because the document’s content disappears and you are left with a blank page spread. Also, the master pages appear selected in the Pages palette, and the bottom of the InDesign window shows A-Master as the page number (see the illustration at the top of page 253).
- You can place items on the master pages just like any other pages. Add text frames, graphics, and so on.
- It is common, for example, to place auto page number codes in text boxes just outside the margin guides at either the top or the bottom of the master pages. In most publications, the page numbers should be on the outside edges, so you would place the page numbering on the left on a verso and on the right on a recto.

View the master pages

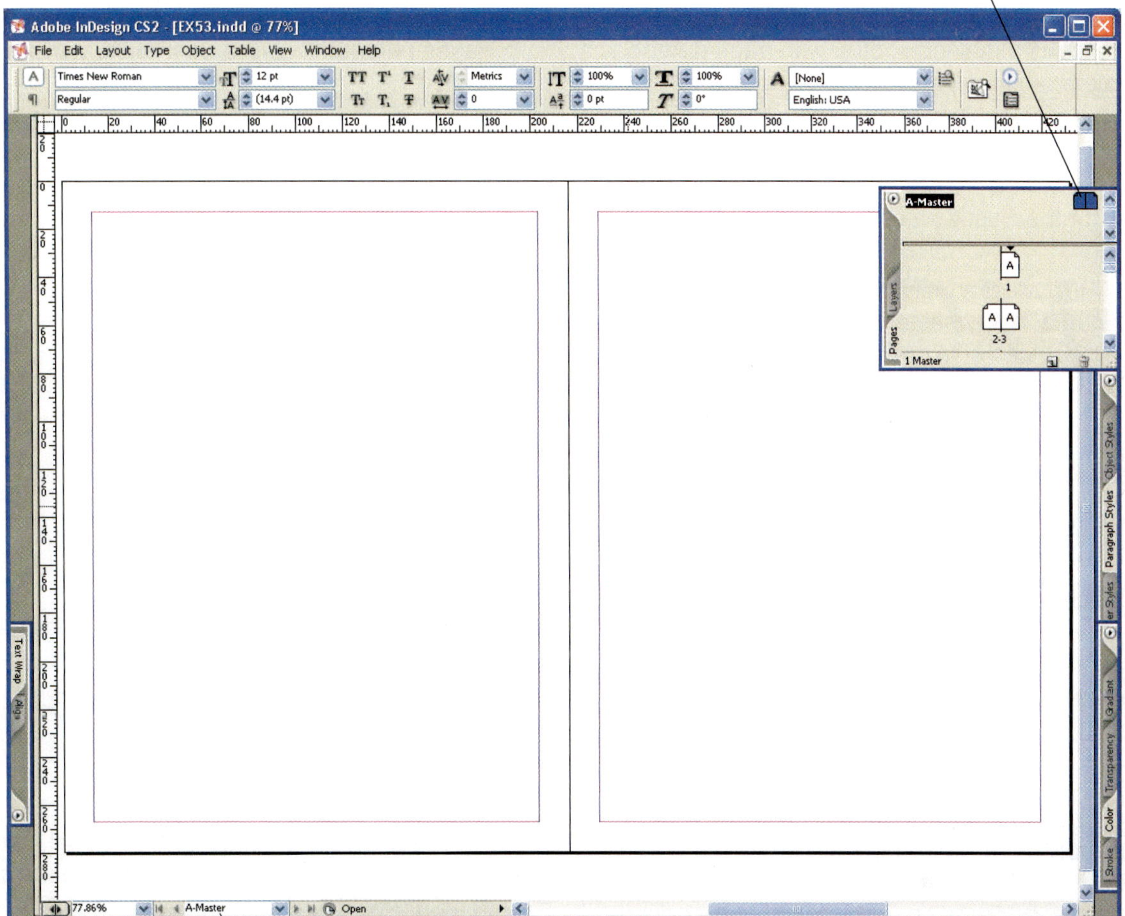

- When you place a page number code on a master page, the code appears as a letter A rather than a number, since the master page has no number itself. It will appear with the correct page number on each of the actual document pages.

Modify the Master Page Name

- The default name A-Master is actually two pieces of information. “A” refers to the fact that it is the first (primary) master in the document. “Master” is the name that has been assigned to the master. You can change that name to something more meaningful. (This is helpful if you are going to have additional master sets in the document, described in the next section.)

- To change the name of a master, select the master’s name in the Pages palette and then open the fly-out menu and click Master Options for A-Master (or whatever name it currently has). In the Master Options dialog box, edit the name. You can also change to a different letter if desired.

Set master options

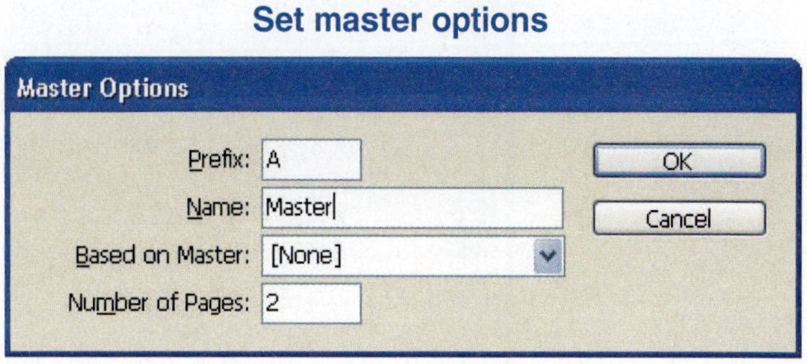

Create New Master Page Sets

- Within a document, different spread types might require different common elements. For example, some pages might look better with page numbers or footers omitted because they interfere with the layout, and some pages might require a watermark image behind the text that others don't.
- To create a new master page set, open the fly-out menu for the Pages palette and choose New Master.
- In the New Master dialog box, choose a prefix letter, a name, and whether it is based on an existing master. You can also specify the number of pages in it. A two-page spread is typical.

Create a new master

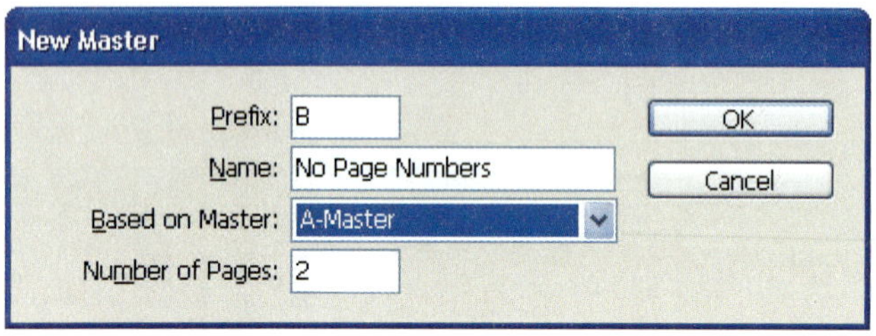

- After creating a master set, it appears in the upper portion of the Pages palette. If you chose to base it upon an existing master, the letter of that maser appears on its page icons. For example, in the following figure, the B-Master is based upon the A-Master, so the B-Master's icons show "A" on them.

Apply a Master to a Page

- To apply a master to a page, drag-and-drop the master's icon to the page's icon (all within the Pages palette). See the illustration at the top of page 255.
- To apply a master to multiple pages at once, open the fly-out menu on the Pages palette and choose Apply Master to Pages. Then in the Apply Master dialog box, select the desired master and enter the page numbers to which to apply it.

Apply a master to certain pages

Manage Master Page Sets

- The Pages palette's fly-out menu contains a number of useful commands for managing master pages:
  - **Delete Master Page:** Deletes the currently selected master page.
  - **Delete Master Spread:** Deletes the currently selected master spread.
  - **Select Unused Masters:** Selects all masters that are not applied to any pages in the document, making it easy to delete them.
  - **Hide Master Items:** When viewing the individual pages, hides all items that would normally show through from the master.

Masters can be based on other masters

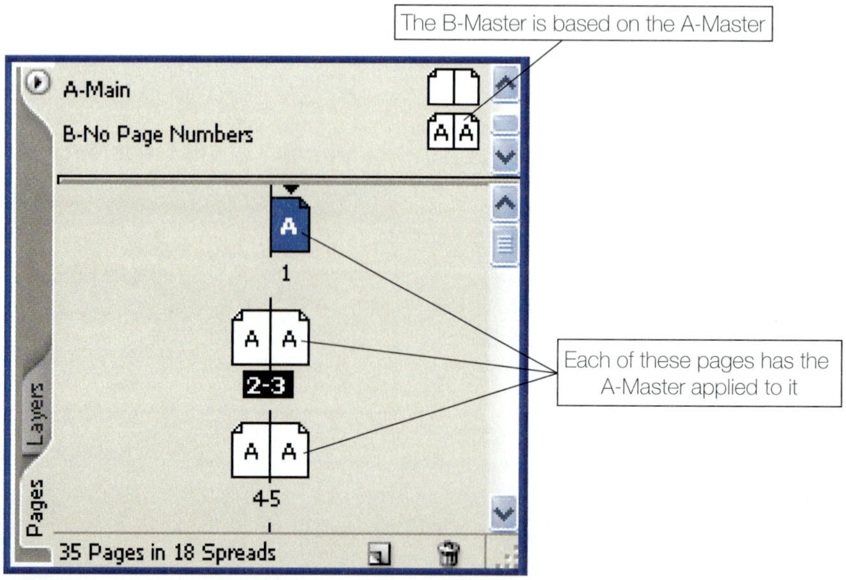

Apply a master to a page by dragging

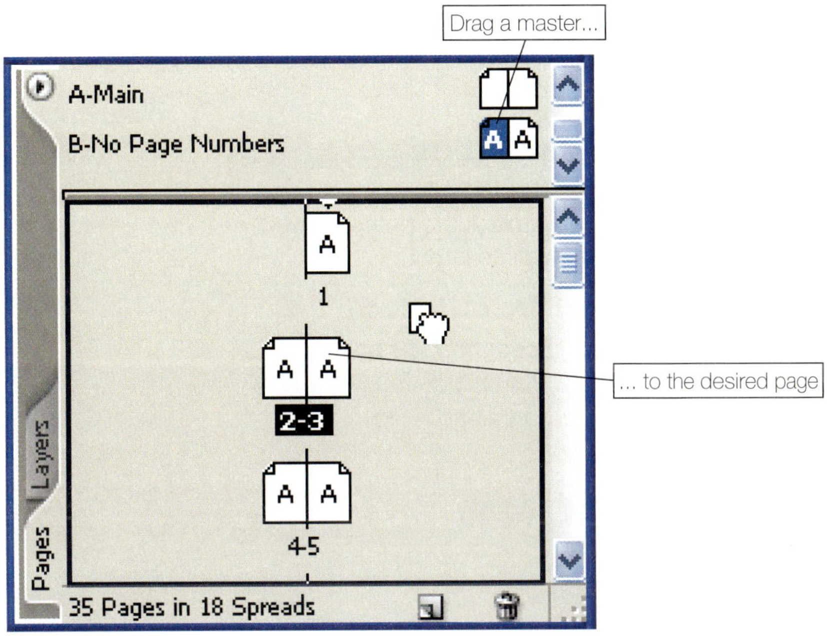

PROCEDURES

Insert Page Numbering

1. (Optional) To number all pages at once that use a certain master, display that master:
   a. Open the **Pages** palette.
   b. Double-click the desired master.
2. Place the insertion point inside a text frame.

   ✓ *Create the text frame if needed.*
3. Click **Type**.................. Alt+T
4. Point to **Insert Special Character**.............................. S
5. Click **Auto Page Number**.......... A

   ✓ *A shortcut for steps 3–5 is Alt+Shift+Ctrl+N.*

Modify the Master Page Name

1. Open the **Pages** palette.
2. Click the desired master.
3. Open the fly-out menu for the palette.
4. Click **Master Options for [Name]**, where [Name] is the selected master.
5. Change the name in the **Name** box .... Alt+N
6. (Optional) change the **Prefix** letter .... Alt+P
7. Click **OK** .... Enter

Create a New Master Page Set

1. Open the **Pages** palette.
2. Open the fly-out menu for the palette.
3. Click **New Master**.
4. (Optional) Change any of these options:
   - Change the default **Prefix** letter .... Alt+P
   - Replace the text in the **Name** box with a more meaningful name .... Alt+N
   - To base the new master on an existing one, select it from the **Based on Master** list .... Alt+B
   - Change the **Number of Pages** .... Alt+M
5. Click **OK** .... Enter

Duplicate an Existing Master Page Set

1. Open the **Pages** palette.
2. Select the master to duplicate.
3. Open the fly-out menu for the palette.
4. Click **Duplicate Master Spread [Name]** where [Name] is the master.

   ✓ *A new master is created with the same name as the original, but with "copy" at the end.*
5. Modify the new master page name to use a different letter and name.

   ✓ *Refer to the earlier procedure "Modify the Master Page Name."*

Apply a Master to a Page

Single Method

1. Open the **Pages** palette.
2. Drag-and-drop a master icon onto a page icon.

Multiple Method

1. Open the **Pages** palette.
2. Open the fly-out menu for the palette.
3. Click **Apply Master to Pages**.
4. Select the desired master from the **Apply Master** list .... Alt+A

5. Type page numbers in the **To Pages** box, separated by commas.

   ✓ *To enter a range of pages, use a hyphen, as in 1-5.*

6. Click **OK** .... Enter

Delete a Master Page

1. Open the **Pages** palette.
2. Do one of the following:
   - To select a single master page, click its icon.
   - To select an entire master page spread, click its name.
3. Open the fly-out menu for the palette.
4. Click **Delete Master Page** (if a single page was selected).

   OR

   Click **Delete Master Spread [Name]** where [Name] is the master name (if the entire spread was selected).

Select Unused Masters

1. Open the **Pages** palette.
2. Open the fly-out menu for the palette.
3. Click **Select Unused Masters**.

   ✓ *If there are no unused masters, this command is not available.*

Hide Master Items on Pages

1. Open the **Pages** palette.
2. Open the fly-out menu for the palette.
3. Click **Hide Master Items**.

   ✓ *Repeat the process, except choose Show Master Items in step 3 to reverse.*

EXERCISE DIRECTIONS

1. Start Adobe InDesign.
2. Open **EX53.indd**.
3. View the A-Master spread.
4. Create a text frame at the bottom of the verso page, directly beneath the bottom margin guide and 7 mm in height.
5. In the new text frame, insert an auto page number code. Set its paragraph (horizontal) alignment to Align Away from Spine.
6. Holding down Alt and Shift, drag the text frame to the recto page and position it in the equivalent location there.
7. Copy the text frame from the bottom of the verso page and place it at the top of that page. Delete the page number code from it, and type **Edith Wharton**.
8. Copy the text frame from the top of the verso page to the top of the recto page. Delete the text, and type **The Age of Innocence**.
9. Create a new master set called **B-Blank** that contains nothing, and apply it to page 1 of the document.
10. Duplicate the A-Master, and name the copy **C-No Heading**.
11. Delete the top text frames in the C-No Heading master.
12. Apply the C-No Heading master to page 2.
13. Save your work as **XX-EX53.indd**, where XX are your initials.
14. Exit InDesign.

ON YOUR OWN

1. Start Adobe InDesign.
2. Start a new document with eight pages.
3. Create masters, and apply them to pages as appropriate, so that:
   - Pages 2–7 have page numbers centered at the bottom of each page but pages 1 and 8 do not.
   - The master applied to page 1 has a dark blue rectangle across the top of the page, 40 mm in height and extending to the top, left, and right edges of the page.
   - The master applied to page 8 has the same dark blue rectangle, but at the bottom of the page.
4. Save the file as **XX-OYO-53.indd**, where XX are your initials.
5. Exit InDesign.

Exercise | 54

Skills Covered

- Insert Footnotes
- Format Footnotes

Software Skills InDesign enables you to create footnote references throughout a document that float automatically to the page on which the referenced point appears.

Application Skills In this exercise, you will annotate a book manuscript with some discussion questions in footnotes.

TERMS

Footnote A note that corresponds to a number or symbol in the main text, and which provides extra information about the referenced material.

Plagiarism To use someone else's words or ideas as if they were your own, without citing the original source.

NOTES

Insert Footnotes

- **Footnotes** have a variety of uses, from scholarly texts to technical reports for work or for school. Footnotes provide an opportunity to supply the reader with extra information without interrupting the flow of the main text (see the illustration at the top of page 258).
- Footnotes also provide a method of citing your sources, to avoid **plagiarism**.

  ✓ *There are many different ways of citing sources, and some teachers prefer one method over another in their classes. Two of the popular citation formats are APA (American Psychological Association) and MLA (Modern Language Association).*

- Footnote numbering automatically restarts with each story. Within the story, they are numbered consecutively based on their position within the story. The order in which you create the footnotes makes no difference.

  ✓ *You cannot add a footnote to text in a table, or text in another footnote.*

- Footnotes appear at the bottom of the text frame in which the reference number appears. Any text that no longer fits because of the additional space occupied by the footnote is either overset or floats to the next text frame if links are in place.
- To insert a footnote, position the insertion point where you want the reference number and then open the Type menu and choose Insert Footnote. A number is placed at the bottom of the text frame, followed by a Tab character, and the insertion point jumps to it (see the illustration at the bottom of page 258).
- When you cut or copy a footnote reference number (or a block of text that includes it), the footnote text is also cut and placed on the Clipboard. Then when you paste the text into its new location, the footnote text is also pasted at the bottom of the new text frame.
- If you cut-and-paste a footnote from one document to another, the formatting and numbering will change to match that of the new document.
- If you accidentally delete the number at the beginning of the footnote text, you can restore it with the Type > Insert Special Character > Footnote Number command.

Format Footnotes

- Type and format a footnote as you would any other text. For example, many people like the look of a superscript footnote number in the footnote area as well as in the body text.

Footnote example

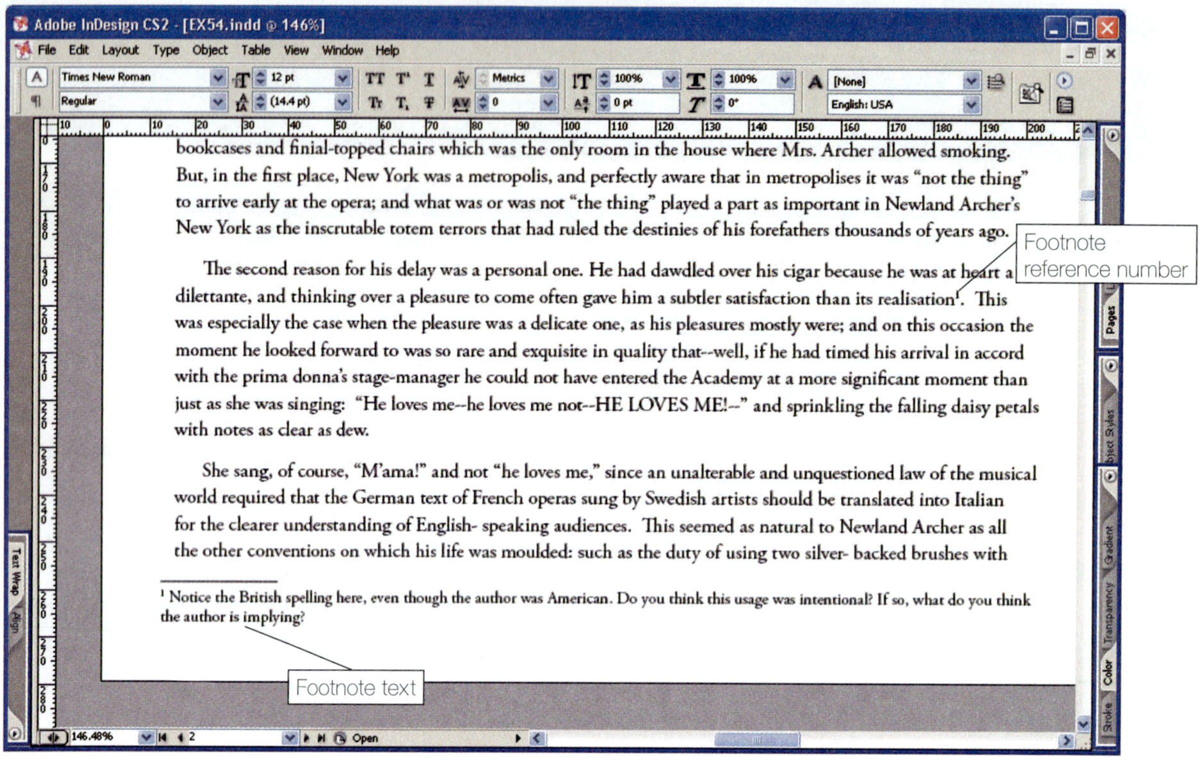

Create a footnote

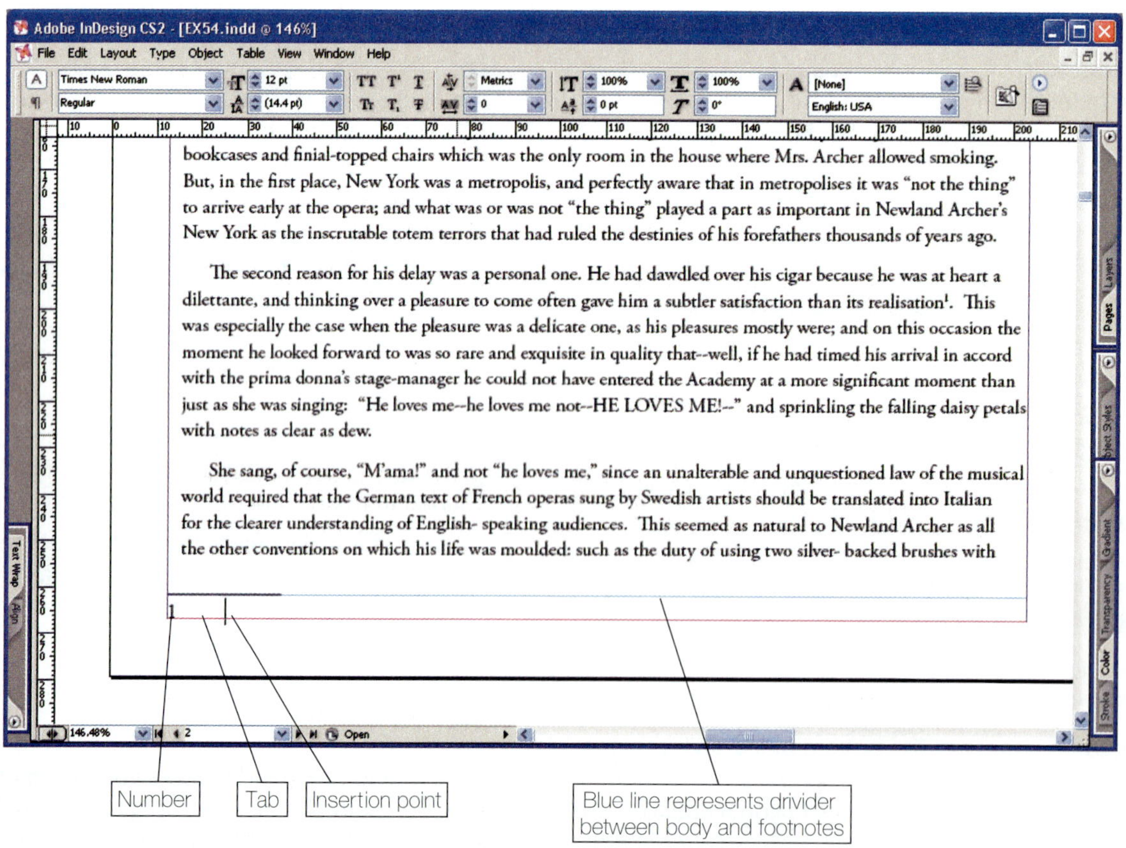

- Apply the Superscript format to the number if desired. In addition, footnote text often looks better if it is slightly smaller than the body text.

  ✓ *You might want to create a paragraph style called Footnote to make formatting quicker.*

- You can also set formatting properties for all footnotes in general. To do so, choose Type > Document Footnote Options.
- On the Numbering and Formatting tab of the Footnote Options dialog box, you can choose the numbering style and starting number, and choose when to restart the numbering. You can restart every page, every spread, or every section if desired. (The default is to restart only with a new story.)
- Here is a complete list of the options on the Numbering and Formatting tab:
  - **Style:** Arabic numbers, Roman numerals, symbols, letters, etc.
  - **Start at:** Specifies the number for the first footnote of the story. Change this to make footnote numbers appear to continue from a previous story, for example.
  - **Restart Numbering Every:** Start numbering every page, every spread, or every section if desired. This is useful if you are numbering with symbols, for example.
  - **Show Prefix/Suffix in:** Lets you specify characters in which to enclose the footnote reference number, text, or both. For example, you might use parentheses or square brackets.

Set footnote options

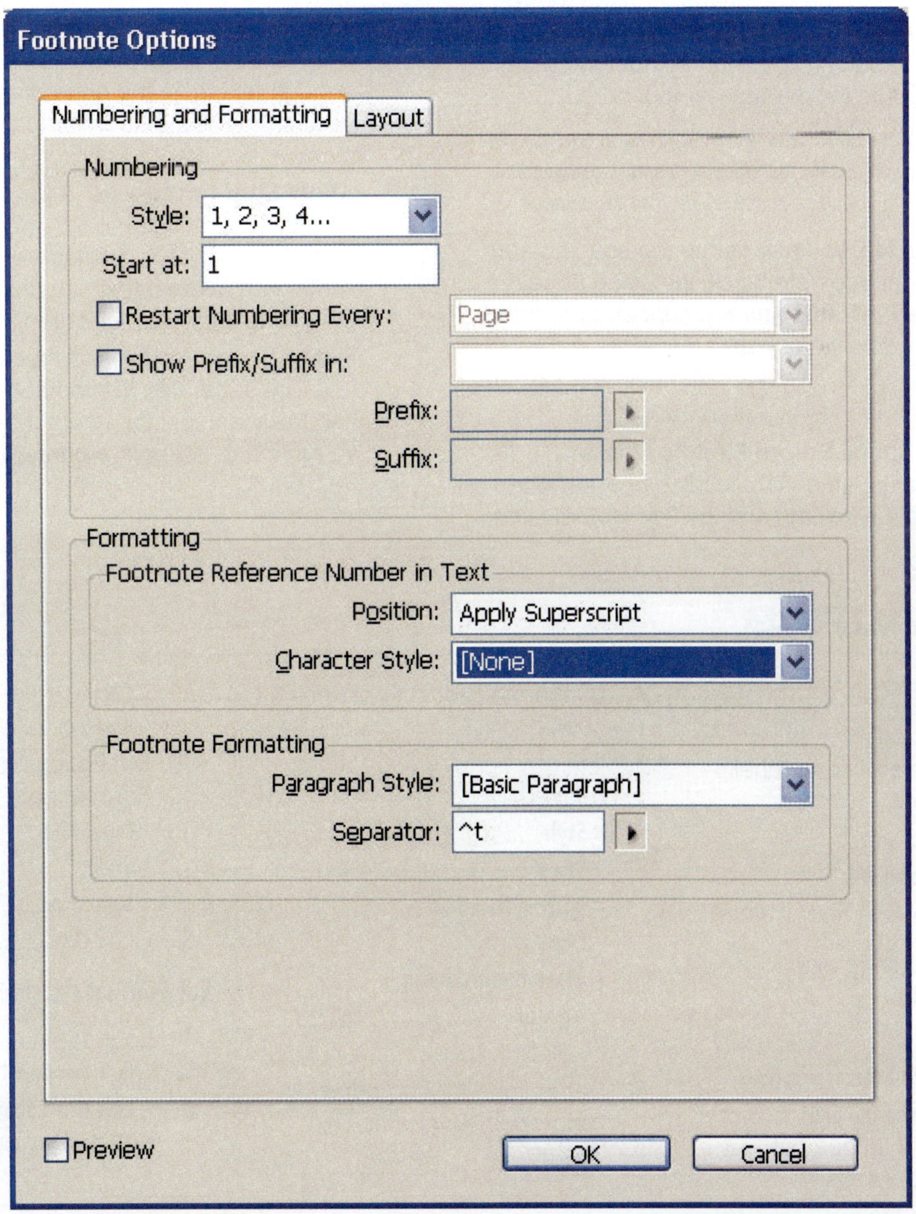

Types of spacing you can adjust for footnotes

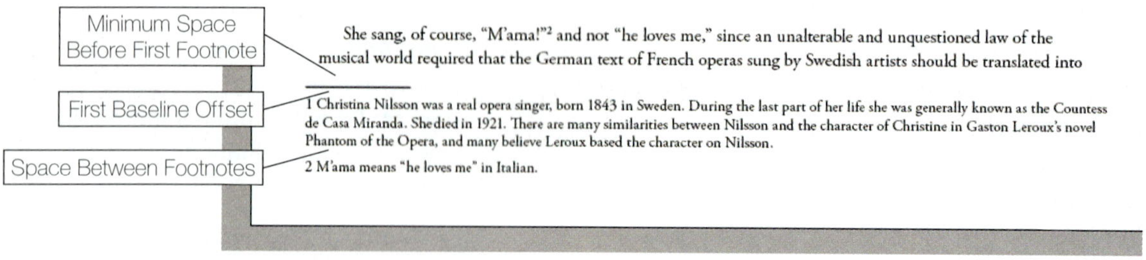

- **Position:** Sets superscript or some other style for the numbers. If you want to use a character style instead of regular subscript, set this to Apply Normal and then select the character style.
- **Character Style:** Enables you to apply a character style to the footnote reference number.
- **Paragraph Style:** Enables you to apply a paragraph style to the footnote text.
- **Separator:** Controls the character used to create the space between the number and the footnote text. By default it is a tab symbol (notated as ^t) but you can type any symbol here.

  ✓ *Click the arrow button to select an en space or an em space to automatically insert the codes for those symbols if desired: ^> for an en space or ^m for an em space.*

■ On the Layout tab, you can set up the spacing and placement of the footnote block, including its relationship to the body text and the appearance of the rule that separates the two areas.

■ Here is a complete list of the options on the Layout tab:

- **Minimum Space Before First Footnote:** Determines the amount of leading between the body text in the column and the first footnote line.
- **Space Between Footnotes:** Determines the amount of leading between footnote paragraphs.
- **First Baseline Offset:** The distance between the footnote area's divider line and the first line of footnote text (see the illustration above).
- **Place End of Story Footnotes at Bottom of Text:** Places the last text column's footnotes immediately below the text in the last frame, as opposed to at the bottom of the text frame. This is an issue only in text frames where there is not enough text to fill the entire frame—and it occurs only in the final frame of a threaded story.
- **Allow Split Footnotes:** Allows footnotes to break across a column if the footnote requires more space than is available in the column, preventing an overset text situation. The footnotes will not split unless necessary.
- **Rule Above:** Provides formatting options for the rule that separates the footnotes from the body text. You can specify a height, width, color, and so on, much like with a paragraph rule.

PROCEDURES

Insert Footnotes

1. Position the insertion point where the reference number should appear.
2. Click **Type** .... Alt+T
3. Click **Insert Footnote**.
4. Type the footnote text.

Set Footnote Numbering and Formatting Options

1. Click **Type** .... Alt+T
2. Click **Document Footnote Options**.
3. Click the **Numbering and Formatting tab** if it does not already appear.
4. (Optional) Select the **Preview** check box .... Alt+V
5. Set any Numbering options desired:
   - **Style** .... Alt+Y, ↑/↓
   - **Start at** .... Alt+T
   - **Restart Numbering Every** .... Alt+R
   - **Show Prefix/Suffix in**
     - **Prefix** .... Alt+P
     - **Suffix** .... Alt+S
6. Set options for Footnote Reference Number in Text:
   - **Position** .... Alt+O, ↑/↓
   - **Character Style** .... Alt+C, ↑/↓
7. Set options for Footnote Formatting:
   - **Paragraph Style** .... Alt+A, ↑/↓
   - **Separator** .... Alt+E
8. Click **OK** .... ↵Enter

Set Footnote Layout Options

1. Click **Type** .... Alt+T
2. Click **Document Footnote Options**.
3. Click the **Layout tab** if it does not already appear.

4. (Optional) Select the **Preview** check box .... Alt+V
5. Set spacing options before and between footnotes:
   - **Minimum Space Before First Footnote** .... Alt+F
   - **Space Between Footnotes** .... Alt+B
6. Set the **First Baseline** (distance between rule and first footnote):
   - **Offset** .... Alt+S
   - **Min** .... Alt+M

   ✓ *The offset is the point from which the Min value will be measured.*
7. Set any placement options desired:
   - **Place End of Story Footnotes at Bottom of Text** .... Alt+P
   - **Allow Split Footnotes** ..... Alt+A
8. Select or clear the **Rule On** check box .... Alt+U

   ✓ *This refers to the rule between the body text and the footnotes.*
9. If the rule is on (step 8), set any options for the rule:
   - **Rule Above** .... Alt+E, ↓
   - **Weight** .... Alt+W, ↑/↓
   - **Type** .... Alt+T, ↓
   - **Color** .... Alt+C, ↑/↓
   - **Tint** .... Alt+I, ↓
   - **Overprint Stroke** .... Alt+K
   - **Gap Color** .... Alt+G, ↓
   - **Gap Tint** .... Alt+N, ↓
   - **Overprint Gap** .... Alt+R
   - **Left Indent** .... Alt+L
   - **Width** .... Alt+D
   - **Offset** .... Alt+O
10. Click **OK** .... ↵Enter

EXERCISE DIRECTIONS

1. Start Adobe InDesign.
2. Open **EX54.indd**.
3. Set the following footnote formatting options:
   - Style: asterisks (*, **, ***)
   - Restart numbering every page
   - Em space (^m) separator character
4. Set the following footnote layout options:
   - Minimum space before first footnote: 3 mm
   - Space between footnotes: 1 mm
   - First baseline: Leading, 2 mm
   - Rule width: 35 mm
   - Rule color: dark blue
5. On the first line of page 2, create a footnote following *Christine Nilsson* that reads as follows:

   Christina Nilsson was a real opera singer, born 1843 in Sweden. During the last part of her life she was generally known as the Countess de Casa Miranda. She died in 1921. There are many similarities between Nilsson and the character of Christine in Gaston Leroux's novel *Phantom of the Opera*, and many believe Leroux based the character on Nilsson.
6. Apply the Body paragraph style to the footnote text. Then make the following formatting changes to the footnote text:
   - Change the size to 10 points
   - Change the leading to Auto
7. Create a new style called **Footnote by example,** and apply it to the footnote text.
8. In the third paragraph following the II. Heading (on page 5), locate the name *Ellen Olenska* and create a footnote following it that reads as follows:

   In some languages, such as Polish, it is customary to have variants of one's last name depending on one's gender. Later in the story, when Ellen's husband is mentioned, he is called Count Olenski, not Olenska.
9. Apply the Footnote paragraph style to the new footnote.
10. Save your work as **XX-EX54.indd**, where XX are your initials.
11. Exit InDesign.

ON YOUR OWN

1. Start Adobe InDesign.
2. Open **OYO-54.indd**.
3. Several of the claims in this flyer need "fine print" disclaimers added to them. Add the following disclaimers using footnotes:
   - The grand prize consists of a 4-night vacation for two. Winner is responsible for all transportation, taxes, and fees associated with vacation. No purchase necessary. Limit one per household.
   - "Let Us Help" does not imply an offer of credit; all deals are subject to credit approval.
4. Format the footnotes in Arial Narrow 8-point Regular font.
5. Save the file as **XX-OYO-54.indd**, where XX are your initials.
6. Exit InDesign.

Exercise | 55

Skills Covered

- Create a Book
- Synchronize Styles Between Documents
- Number Pages Across Documents

Software Skills Often different people work on page spreads for a publication, and then those separate documents must be assembled into a single unit (a "book") for printing, with consecutively numbered pages.

Application Skills In this exercise, you will bring together several of the documents created in previous exercises to create a book.

TERMS

Book A file that ties together multiple documents and enables them to have a single page numbering system and table of contents.

Style source The document within a book that sets the style and swatch precedents for the other documents, in order to create consistency between documents.

NOTES

Create a Book

- A **book** is a container file for organizing multiple InDesign documents into a single unified publication.
- A key advantage of a book is that it enables you to automatically number pages across multiple documents. If you rearrange the order of the documents within the book, the page numbering shifts automatically.
- To create a book, use the File > New > Book command. After creating the new book, a floating palette will appear for it. It does not contain any documents by default.

An empty Book palette

- To add documents to the book, click the Add Documents button. In the Add Documents dialog box, select the document(s) to add. To select more than one, hold down Ctrl as you click on each one, or Shift+click to select a range. Then click Open.

  ✓ *You can also drag-and-drop documents from Adobe Bridge into the Book palette (see the illustration at the top of page 263).*

- The documents appear in a list in the Book palette. To rearrange them, drag one up or down on the list. To remove one, select it and click the Remove Documents button.
- You can open documents within the book by double-clicking them from the Book palette. Edit documents as needed.

Select documents to add to the book

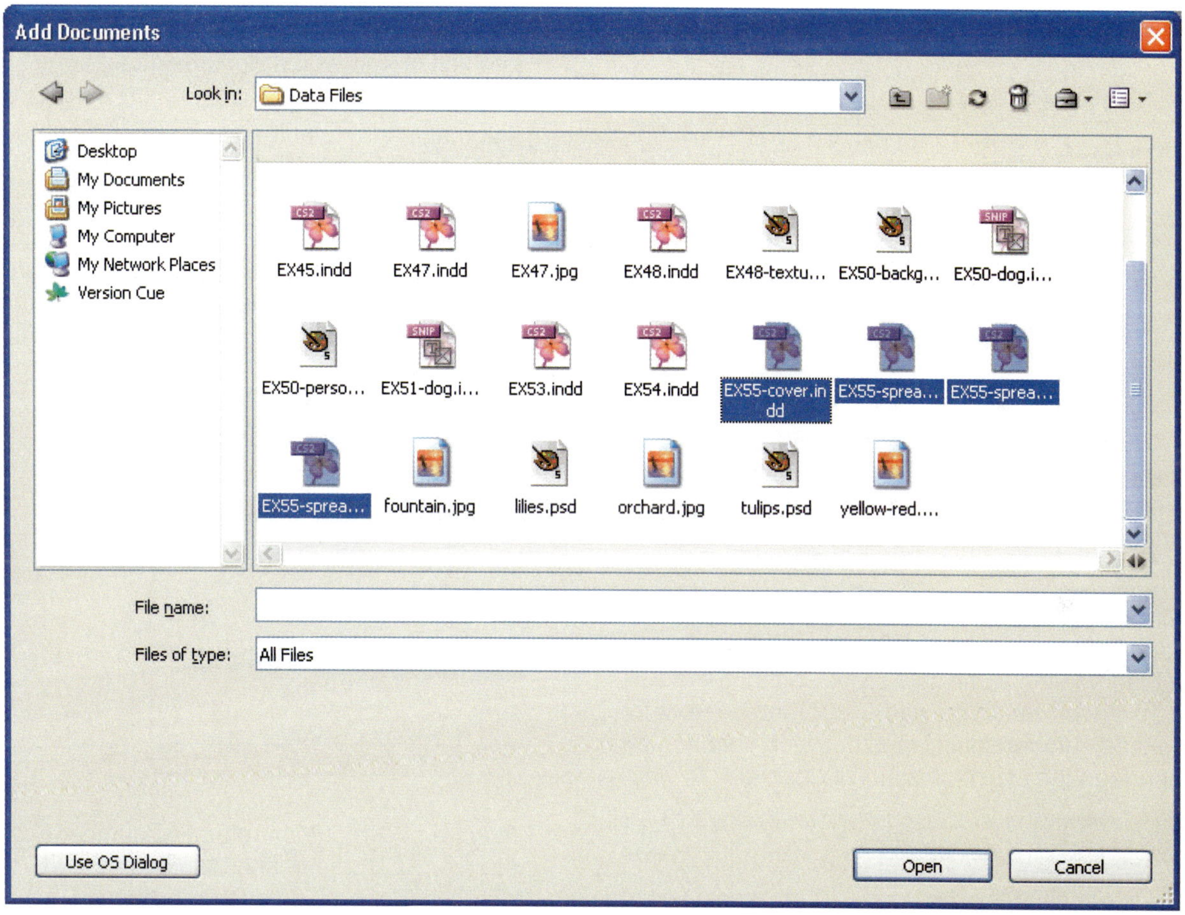

- When a document is open, an Open icon appears to the right of its name in the Book palette.

Several books in the Book palette

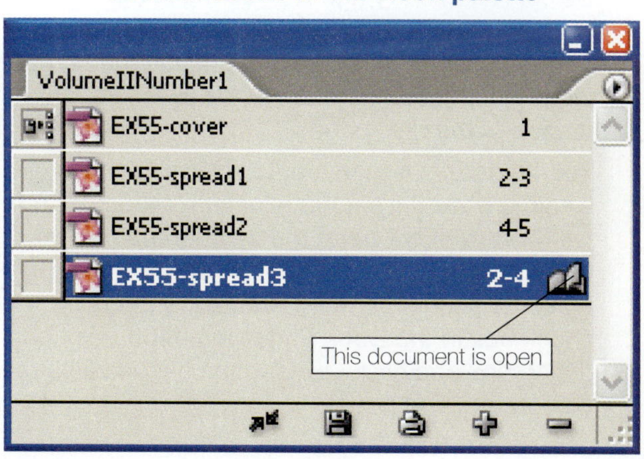

- When you close the Book palette, you are prompted to save the changes to the book. You can save a book at any time as you are working on it by clicking the Save the Book button at the bottom of the Book palette.
- You can also save the book under a different name: Open the fly-out menu for the Book palette and click Save Book As. (Note that the Save As command on the File menu works only for the active document, not the book.) Book files have an .indb extension.

Synchronize Styles Between Documents

- As you create individual documents and spreads, you have defined various styles and swatches as needed. For a more cohesive publication, you might want to synchronize these among the documents within the book. For example, you might want to use the same font for body text throughout.
- To prepare to synchronize styles and swatches, first identify which document should be the **style source**. The style source is the document that will serve as the model; if there are any discrepancies between documents, such as two documents with the same style names with different specifications, the style source's version will take precedence.
- The style source document is indicated by the Style Source icon to the left of the name in the Book palette. To change which document is the style

source, click in the left column in the Book palette next to the desired document.

Select the style source

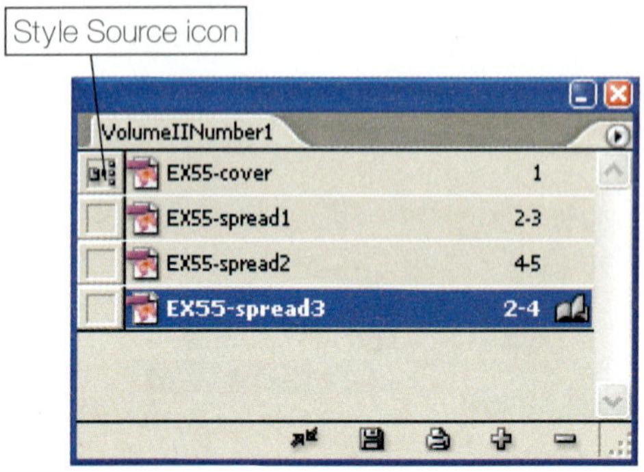

- To perform the synchronization, click the Synchronize Styles and Swatches with the Style Source button.
- If unwanted changes were made as a result of the synchronization, undo the synchronization (Ctrl+Z) and then define some new styles so that there are no instances where the same style name refers to two different formatting types between documents. Then redo the synchronization if desired.

✓ *Synchronization is an optional feature; don't use it if it's not helpful to you in a particular book.*

- You do not have to synchronize every aspect within the book. Open the fly-out menu for the Book palette and choose Synchronize Options, and then in the Synchronize Options dialog box deselect any items you do not want to synchronize.

Choose what to synchronize

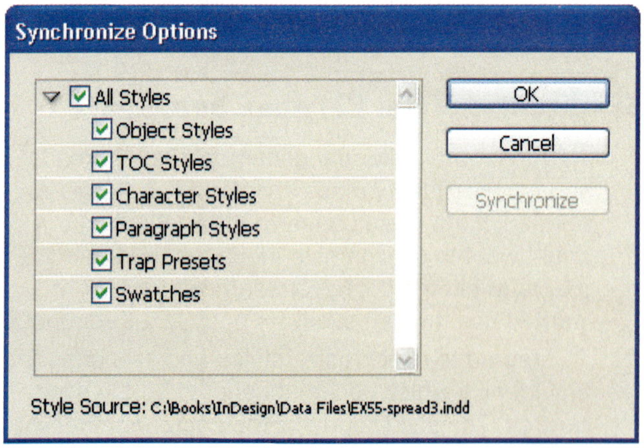

Number Pages Across Documents

- The page number ranges appear to the right of each document in the Book palette.
- If the document's page numbering is set up to be automatic (the default), you do not have to do anything special to number pages consecutively within a book. They are automatically numbered.
- However, if a document has been set up for manual page number specification, the page numbering must be reset to automatic in order for that document to participate in the page numbering sequence for the book.

Manual page numbering for a document overrides automatic numbering for the book

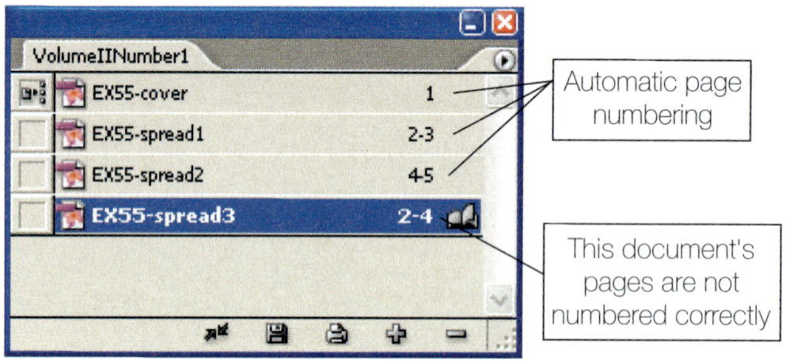

- To set a document for automatic numbering, select it in the Book palette and then open the fly-out menu on the Book palette and choose Document Page Numbering Options.

✓ *You can also open up the document's page numbering options from the Pages palette if the document is open; however, using the Book palette method enables you to make the change without opening the document.*

- Select Automatic Page Numbering in the Document Page Numbering Options dialog box, and the document will be brought into the numbering for the rest of the book (see the illustration at the top of the next page).
- You do not have to use automatic pagination within a book if it's not useful for a particular project. To turn it off, open the fly-out menu on the Book palette and select Book Page Numbering Options. Then clear the Automatic Pagination check box in the Book Page Numbering Options dialog box and click OK (see the second illustration on the next page).

Change document page numbering options

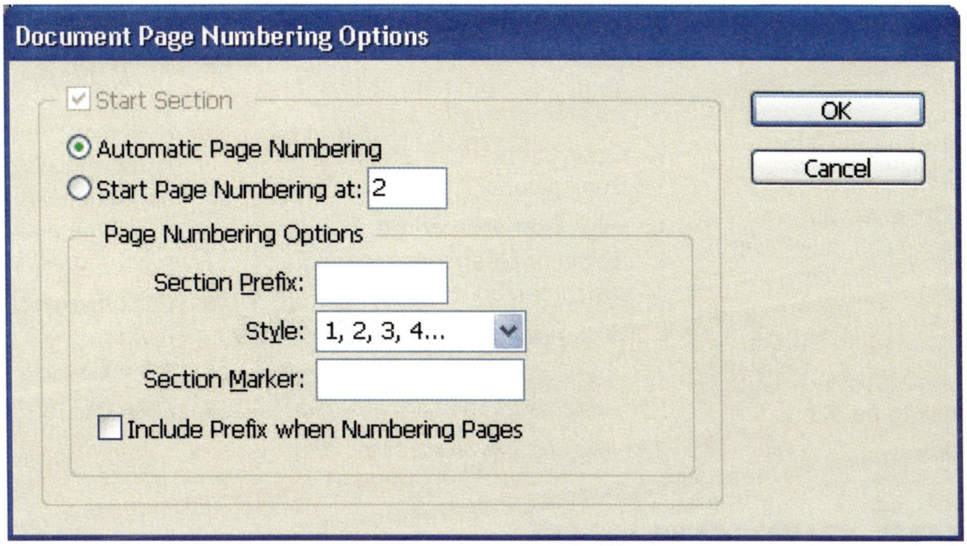

Change book page numbering options

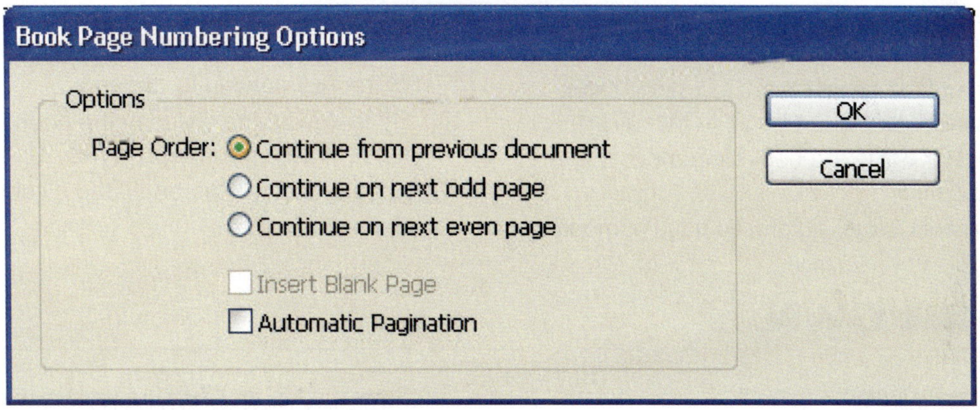

PROCEDURES

Create a Book

1. Click **File** .... Alt + F
2. Click **New** .... N
3. Click **Book** .... B
4. Navigate to the location in which you want to save the book.
5. Type a name in the **File name** box .... Alt + N
6. Click **Save** .... ↵Enter

Manage Document Files in a Book

Add a Document to a Book

1. In the Book palette, click the **Add Documents** button.

OR

a. Open the fly-out menu for the Book palette.

b. Click **Add Document**.

2. Select the document to be added.

✓ *Hold down Ctrl to select multiple documents, or hold down Shift and select a range.*

3. Click **Open** .... ↵Enter

Remove a Document from a Book

1. Click the document in the Book palette.
2. Click the **Remove Documents** button.

OR

a. Open the fly-out menu for the Book palette.

b. Click **Remove Document**.

Reorder Documents in a Book

- Drag a document up or down in the Book palette.

Manage Book Files

Save a Book in a Different Name or Location

1. Open the fly-out menu for the Book palette.
2. Click **Save Book As**.
3. Change the save location if desired.

4. Edit the file name in the **File name** box .... Alt + N
5. Click **Save** .... ↵Enter

Close a Book

1. Click the **Close** button for the Book palette.
2. If prompted to save your changes, click **Yes** .... ↵Enter

Open a Book

1. Click **File** .... Alt + F
2. Click **Open** .... O
3. Click the book to be opened.
4. Click **Open** .... ↵Enter

Synchronize Styles in a Book

1. In the Book palette, click to the left of the document that should serve as the style source.
2. Open the fly-out menu for the Book palette.
3. Click **Synchronize Options**.
4. Select or clear styles to be synchronized in the book.
5. Click **Synchronize** .... Alt + S

✓ *An alternative for steps 3–5 is the Synchronize Styles and Swatches with the Style Source button* .

6. Click **OK** .... ↵Enter

Set Automatic Page Numbering for a Document

1. In the Book palette, select a document where the page numbering is out of sequence.
2. Open the fly-out menu for the Book palette.
3. Click **Document Page Numbering Options**.
4. Click **Automatic Page Numbering**.
5. Click **OK** .... ↵Enter

EXERCISE DIRECTIONS

1. Start Adobe InDesign.
2. Start a new book, and name it **XX-EX55book.indb**, where XX are your initials.
3. Add the files **EX55-spread1.indd**, **EX55-spread2.indd**, and **EX55spread3.indd** to the book, in that order.
4. Add **EX55-cover.indd** to the book, and move it to the top (first) position.
5. Set **EX55-spread3.indd** for automatic page numbering.
6. On page 7, change the page reference at the bottom of the last column to page 8.
7. On page 8, change the page reference at the top of the first column to page 7.
8. Synchronize the styles in the book, for all style types *except* paragraph styles.
9. Save and close the book and all documents.
10. Exit InDesign.

ON YOUR OWN

1. Start Adobe InDesign.
2. Start a new book called **XX-OYO-55.indb**, where XX are your initials.
3. Add the files **OYO-55A.indd** through **OYO-55D.indd** to the book.
4. Set up consecutive page numbering throughout the book by setting each document for automatic numbering.
5. Save the file as **XX-OYO-55.indd**, where XX are your initials.
6. Synchronize the book using **OYO-55A.indd** as the style source.
7. Save and close the book and all documents.
8. Exit InDesign.

Exercise | 56

Skills Covered

- Create a Table of Contents
- Apply a TOC Style
- Update a TOC
- Create Hidden TOC Text Markers

Software Skills For long documents and multi-document books, a table of contents (TOC) is often useful to help readers quickly find the content that interests them. InDesign can generate TOCs automatically based on headings, or based upon hidden codes you generate.

Application Skills In this exercise, you will create a table of contents for the book you created in the preceding exercise.

TERMS

Table of contents (TOC) A list of major headings or titles in the publication and the page numbers on which they appear.

NOTES

Create a Table of Contents

- A **table of contents (TOC)** is a list of major headings or titles in the publication and the page numbers on which they appear.
- InDesign can automatically generate a TOC based on the paragraph styles that you specify. For example, if all the headings in your document use a style called Heading 1, you can define the TOC to include the heading names and their page numbers.
- A table of contents can be multi-level. For example, you might want it to include all the headings that are styled Heading 1, Heading 2, or Heading 3, and indent them appropriately within the TOC to indicate the relative level of each entry (see the illustration below).

✓ *InDesign does not automatically format a TOC with a dot leader, as shown here, but you can easily set this up yourself as you learned in Exercise 25.*

Table of Contents example

CONTENTS

- To generate a TOC, use the Layout > Table of Contents command. The Table of Contents dialog box opens (see the illustration below).
- If you have previously defined a TOC style that you want to use, select it from the TOC Style drop-down list.
- In the Title box, enter the text that should appear as a heading above the TOC. To select a paragraph style for this text, open the Style drop-down list to its right and make your selection.
- On the Other Styles list, click the paragraph style for which first-level entries in the TOC should be generated, and click the << Add button. Repeat the process for the style for second-level entries, and so on. For example, the Chapter style will make the first-level TOC entries and the Section style will make the second-level entries (see the illustration at the top of the next page).
- In some documents (and books), there might be more than one style that you want to be at a single level in the TOC. To set this up, click the More Options button, and then select the style from the Include Paragraph Styles list and change its Level setting (see the illustration at the bottom of the next page).
- By default, the entries in the TOC will be formatted in the same way as the style on which they were generated. For example, if you are basing the TOC on all Heading 1 style paragraphs, and Heading 1 style consists of 14-point Arial, that's what the TOC entries will be.
- You can set the TOC entries to any other style desired instead by choosing a style from the Entry Style drop-down list (see the illustration at the top of page 270).
- For greater control over the formatting of the TOC entries, click More Options (if you did not click it earlier). Additional controls appear by which you can control where the page number appears (before or after the entry), what symbol will separate the entry and the number (by default it's a tab stop), and what style will be applied to the page number and the separator symbol.

Create the TOC

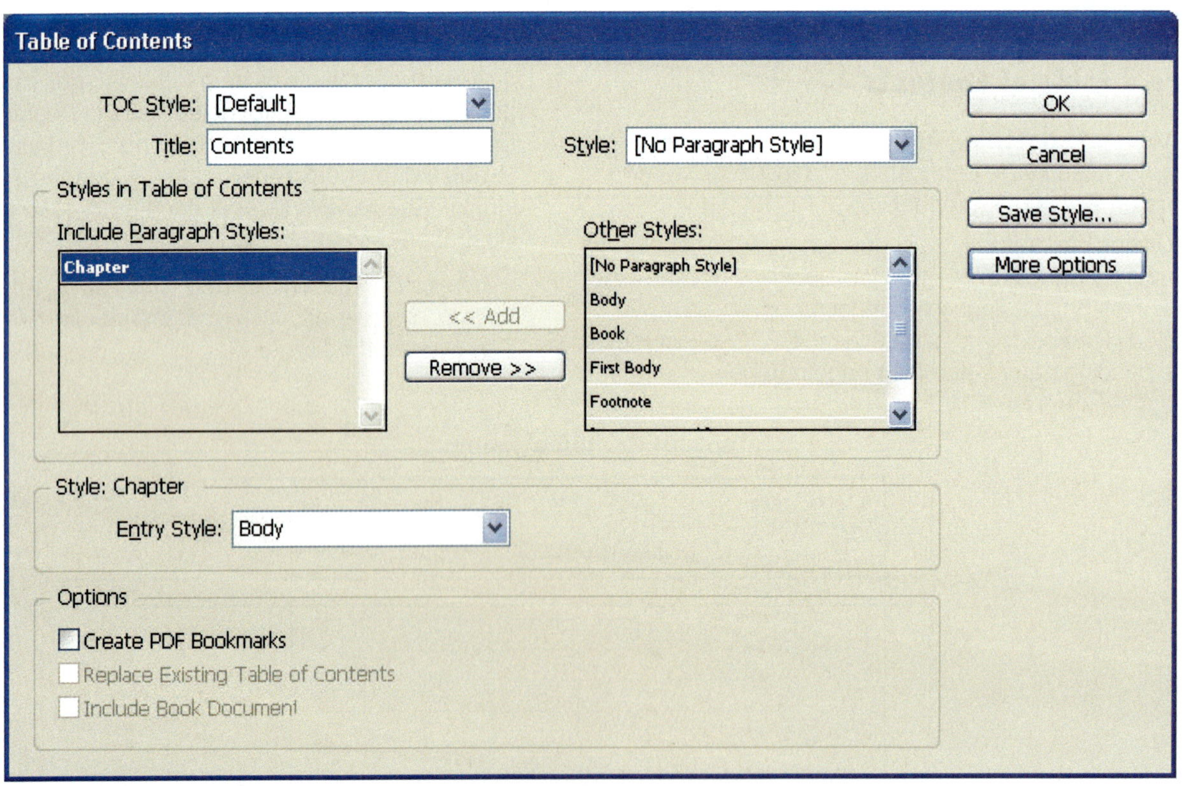

A two-level TOC will be created

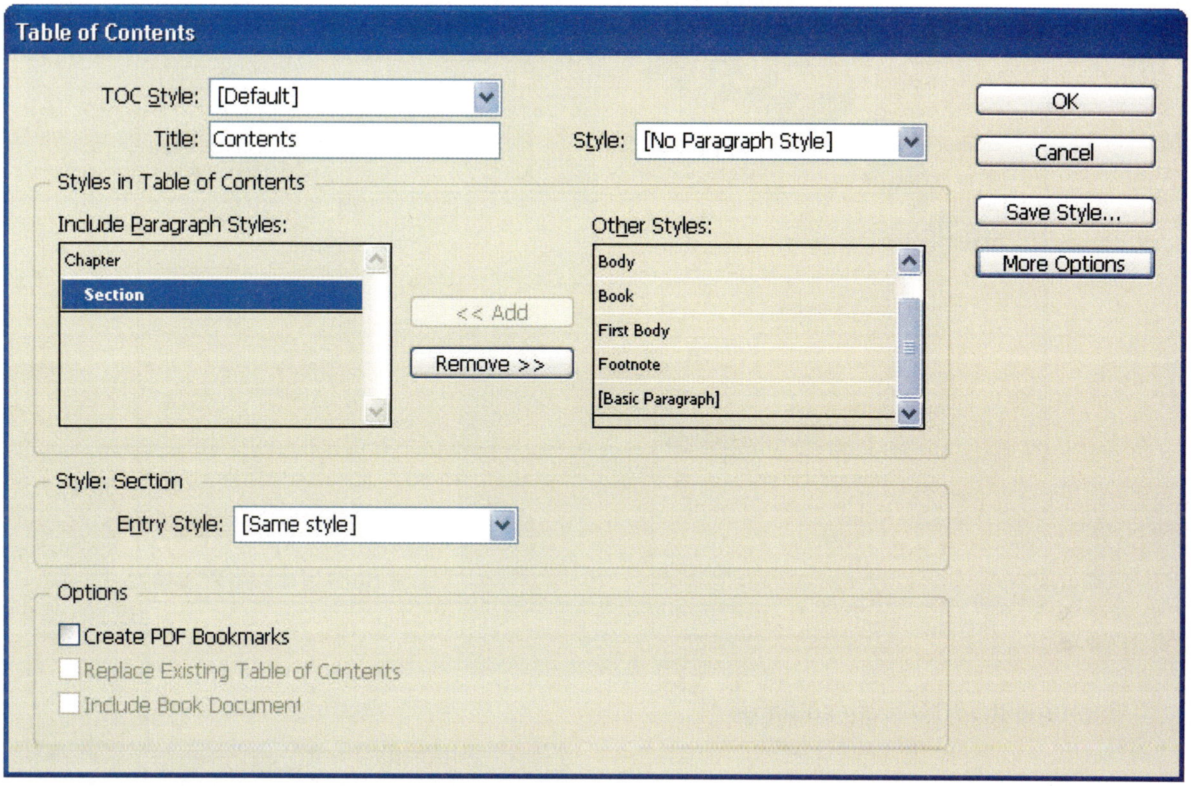

Indicate the TOC level for a style

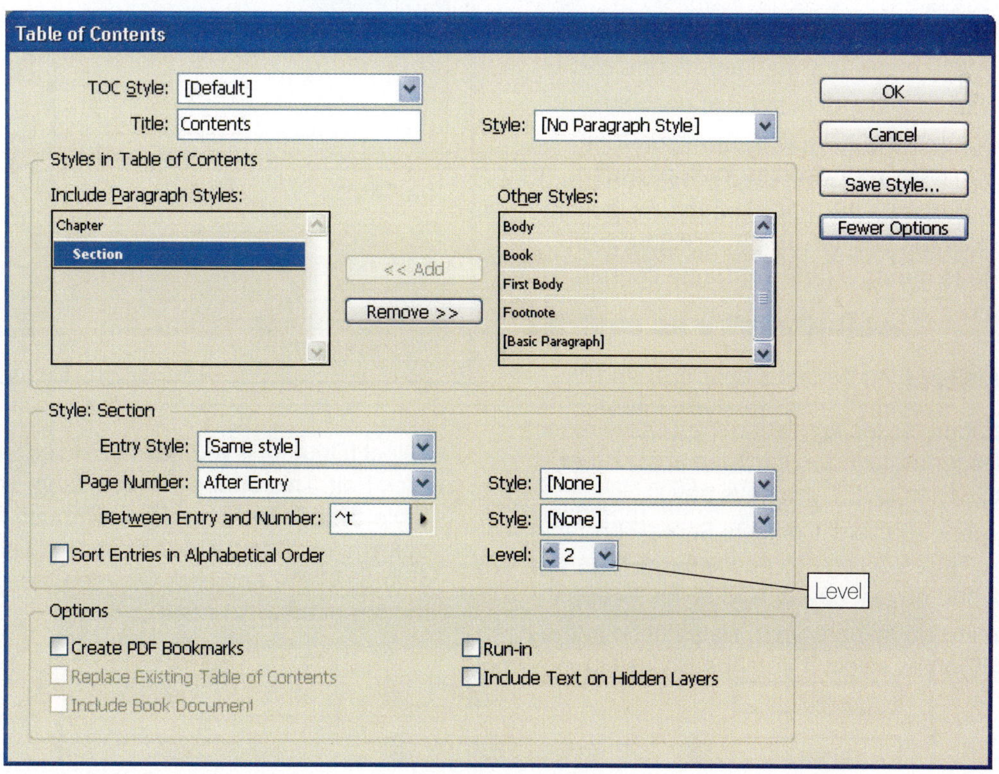

Select a style to apply to the TOC entries

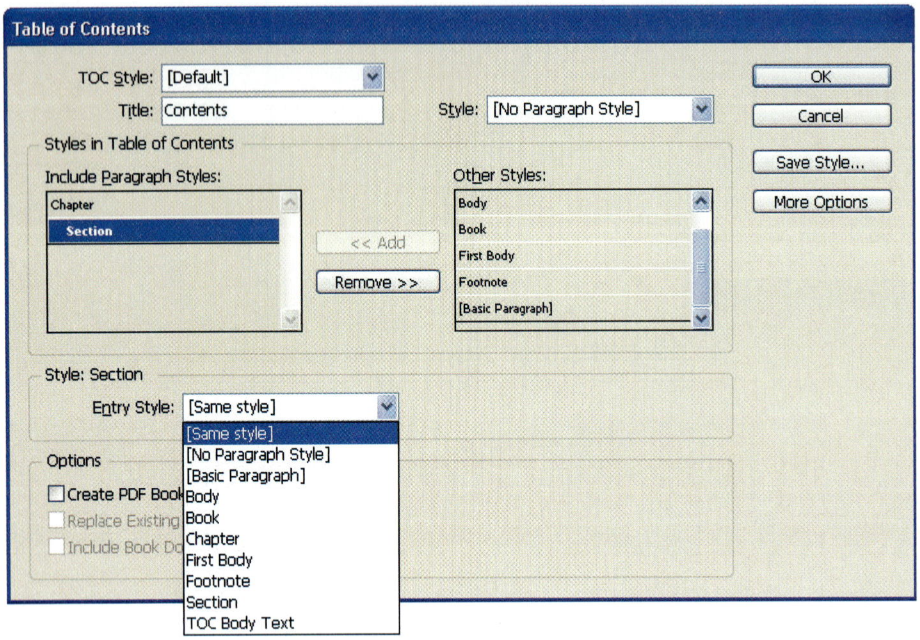

Fine-tune the TOC entry settings

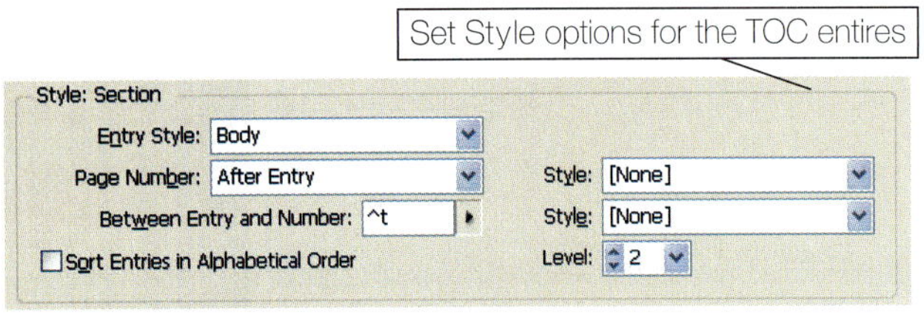

Manage TOC styles

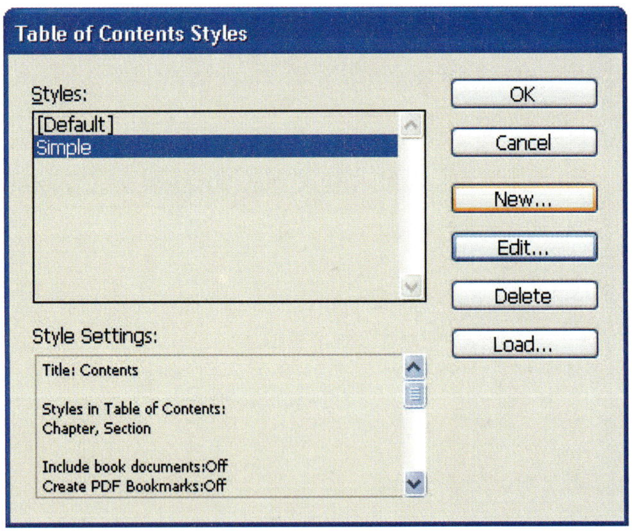

- After setting up the TOC options, you can click Save Style to save your choices for later reuse.
- Click OK to generate the TOC. The mouse pointer becomes "loaded" with the TOC. Click anywhere on the page to create a new text frame containing the TOC.

Apply a TOC Style

- You can edit the styles applied to the TOC without having to regenerate it. You can also apply other saved TOC styles to it, if you have any.
- Choose Layout > Table of Contents Styles. The Table of Contents Styles dialog box opens. From here you can select one of your saved TOC styles to apply.
- To edit the individual paragraph styles used in the current TOC style, select it from the Styles list (or select [Default] if you haven't saved the style) and click Edit. This opens the Edit Table of Contents Style dialog box, which is very much like the dialog box you used to create the style initially. Make any changes here and click OK (see the illustration at the top of the next page).

Change a TOC style

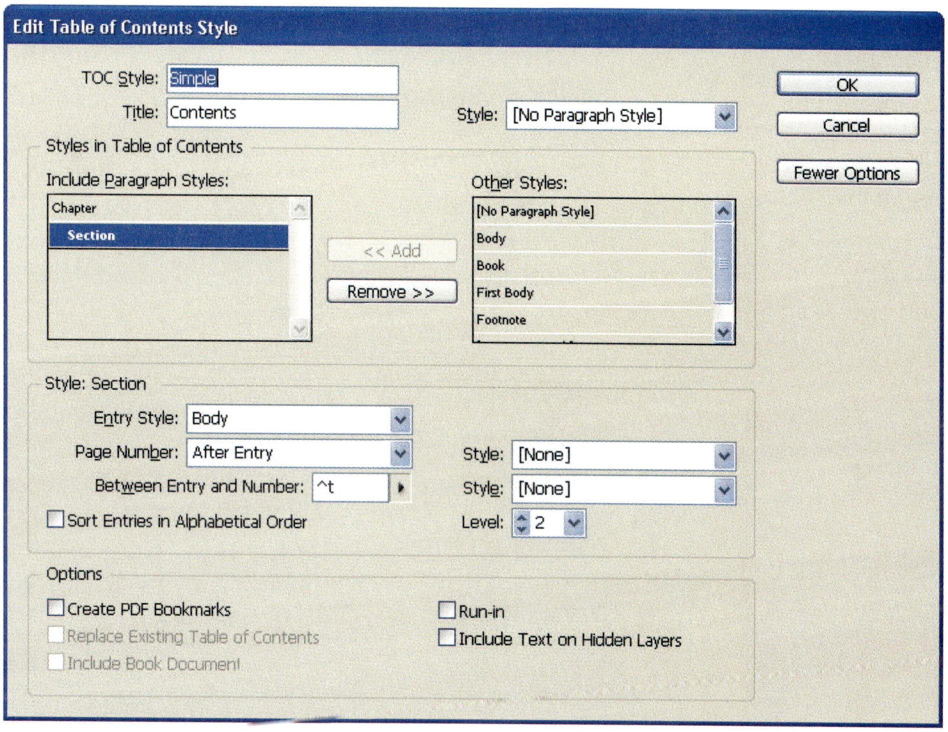

- You can also load TOC styles from other documents. To do so, click the Load button in the Table of Contents Styles dialog box and then select the document from which to import TOC styles.

Update a TOC

- When content changes in a document or book, page numbering might move around as well. To update a TOC, choose Layout > Update Table of Contents.

Create Hidden TOC Text Markers

- One potential limitation of the Table of Contents feature is that it exactly reproduces whatever is in each heading in the document. You might not always want the wording to be exactly the same in the TOC as it is in the document itself.
- Another limitation is that the feature relies exclusively on styles, so if you have not been rigorous about proper style usage as you created your document(s), you cannot generate a TOC until you've gone back through the pages and applied styles consistently or generated new styles to match the formatting of each heading to include.
- To get around this, you might want to create some hidden text on certain pages and then define your TOC based on the style of that hidden text. You can make the hidden text say anything you want, so you are not limited to the actual wording in the document.
- To hide the text, set its color to None, or place it behind an opaque object, or place it on its own layer and then hide that layer. Place the hidden text on the same page as the section to which it refers.

  ✓ *If you decide to place the text on a hidden layer, make sure when you are generating the TOC that you click More Options and then select Include Text on Hidden Layers.*

- A disadvantage of using hidden TOC text markers is that they don't automatically float when the text to which they refer floats, and you might forget that they are there and later be puzzled as to why your TOC is not updating correctly.

PROCEDURES

Create a Table of Contents

1. Check your document to make sure styles are consistently applied to all text that should appear in the TOC.
2. Click **Layout** .... Alt+L
3. Click **Table of Contents** .... T
4. Select a saved style from the **TOC Style** list .... Alt+S, ↓

   OR

   Define the TOC by doing the following:

   a. Type a title in the **Title** box .... Alt+I
   b. Select a title style from the **Style** list .... Alt+T, ↓
   c. Select a paragraph style from the **Other Styles** list and click **<< Add**... .... Alt+H, ↓, Alt+A
   d. Repeat step c as needed for additional levels.
   e. Select an **Entry Style** for TOC entries .... Alt+N, ↓
   f. (Optional) Click **More Options** and define additional formatting options for the TOC.

      ✓ *For example, if you are generating a TOC that includes text that you've placed on a hidden layer, make sure you select the Include Text on Hidden Layers check box.*

5. (Optional) To save these settings for later reuse, do the following:

   a. Click **Save Style** .... Alt+V
   b. Type a name for the new TOC style.
   c. Click **OK** .... ↵Enter

6. Click **OK** .... ↵Enter
7. Click where you want the new TOC to appear.

   ✓ *It appears in its own frame.*

Apply a Different TOC Style

1. Select the frame containing the TOC.
2. Click **Layout** .... Alt+L
3. Click **Table of Contents Styles** .... S
4. Select a different style from the **Styles** list .... ↑/↓
5. Click **OK** .... ↵Enter

Edit the TOC Style

1. Select the frame containing the TOC.
2. Click **Layout** .... Alt+L
3. Click **Table of Contents Styles** .... S
4. Click the **Edit** button .... Alt+E
5. Make any changes to the TOC style as needed.
6. Click **OK** .... ↵Enter
7. Click **OK** .... ↵Enter

Load TOC Styles from Another Document

1. Select the frame containing the TOC.
2. Click **Layout** .... Alt+L
3. Click **Table of Contents Styles** .... S
4. Click the **Load** button .... Alt+L
5. Select the document from which to load TOC styles.
6. Click **Open** .... ↵Enter
7. Select the desired style from the **Styles** list .... Alt+S, ↑/↓
8. Click **OK** .... ↵Enter

Update a TOC

1. Select the frame containing the TOC.
2. Click **Layout** .... Alt+L
3. Click **Update Table of Contents** .... U
4. Click **OK** .... ↵Enter

Create Hidden TOC Text Markers

Transparent Text Method

1. Create a new text frame on the same page as the heading to include in the TOC.
2. Create a new paragraph style called **Hidden** and set the text color to None.
3. Type the text as you want it to appear on the TOC.
4. Apply the Hidden style to the text.
5. Repeat steps 1–4 for each TOC entry to create.
6. Create the TOC as in "Create a Table of Contents," and include the Hidden style in step 4c.

Hidden Layer Method

1. Create a new layer and name it **TOC Codes**.
2. Create a new paragraph style called **Hidden**.
3. Create a new text frame on the same page as the heading to include in the TOC.
4. Type the text as you want it to appear on the TOC.
5. Apply the Hidden style to the text.
6. Repeat steps 2–5 for each TOC entry to create.
7. Hide the TOC Codes layer.

   ✓ *To hide a layer, click the eye symbol*  *to its left on the Layers palette.*

8. Create the TOC as in "Create a Table of Contents," and include the Hidden style in step 4c.

   ✓ *When creating the TOC, make sure you click More Options and select the Include Text on Hidden Layers check box.*

EXERCISE DIRECTIONS

1. Start Adobe InDesign.
2. Open **EX56book.indb** and save it as **XX-EX56book.indb**, where XX are your initials.

   ✓ *Save the book from the Book palette, as you learned in Exercise 55.*

3. Open all four documents from the Book palette.
4. Create a new layer called TOC Codes for each document except the cover.
5. In **EX56spread-1.indd**, create a new text frame on the first page, and type **Orchard Springtime** in it.
6. Create a new paragraph style based on the text you just typed, and call it **Hidden**.
7. Apply the Hidden style to the text you just typed, and then hide the TOC Codes layer.
8. In **EX56spread-2.indd**, create a new text frame anywhere on the first page, and type **Landscaping with Fountains**.
9. Create a new paragraph style based on the text you just typed, and call it **Hidden**.

   ✓ *Alternatively you can load the styles from **EX56spread-1.indd**.*

10. Apply the Hidden style to the text you just typed, and then hide the TOC Codes layer.
11. In **EX56spread-3.indd**, create a new text frame anywhere on the first page, and type **Easy-Care Perennials**.
12. Create a new paragraph style based on the text you just typed, and call it **Hidden**.

    ✓ *Alternatively you can load the styles from **EX56spread-1.indd**.*

13. Apply the Hidden style to the text you just typed, and then hide the TOC Codes layer.
14. Display **Ex56cover.indd**.
15. Create a table of contents based on the Hidden paragraph style, and place it on the purple rectangle. Use **In This Issue:** as the title, and **TOC Title** as its style. Use **TOC Body Text** as the Entry Style.

    ✓ *Select the Include Book Document check box at the bottom of the Table of Contents dialog box for access to all the styles in the book, not just the styles in the current document. Select the Include Text on Hidden Layers check box so that it will pick up the text on the TOC Codes layers of each document.*

    ✓ *If you see a message about including items in overset text, click Yes.*

    ✓ *Make sure the Run-in check box is cleared.*

16. Add a right-aligned tab stop with a tab leader to the entries in the TOC, as in Illustration A on page 274.
17. Save and close the book and all documents.
18. Exit InDesign.

Illustration A

ON YOUR OWN

Note: This exercise uses the same book as the preceding one, but takes a different approach to the task.

1. Start Adobe InDesign.
2. Open **OYO-56book.indb** and save it as **XX-OYO-56book.indb**, where XX are your initials.

   ✓ *Save the book from the Book palette, as you learned in Exercise 55.*

3. Open all four documents from the Book palette.
4. In **OYO-56spread1.indd**, create a new paragraph style called **Article Title 1** from Orchard Springtime, and apply it to that text.

   ✓ *For the Style Based On setting, choose No Paragraph Style.*

5. In **OYO-56spread2.indd**, create a new paragraph style called **Article Title 2** from Landscaping with Fountains, and apply it to that text.
6. In **OYO-56spread3.indd**, create a new paragraph style called **Article Title 3** from Easy-Care Perennials, and apply it to that text.
7. In **OYO-56cover.indd**, delete the text box overlaying the purple frame in the center.
8. Create a table of contents based on the Article Title 1, Article Title 2, and Article Title 3 styles, with each one set to be Level 1, and place it on the purple frame. Use **In This Issue:** as the title, and **TOC Title** as its style. Use **TOC Body Text** as the Entry Style.

   ✓ *Select the Include Book Document check box at the bottom of the Table of Contents dialog box for access to all the styles in the book, not just the styles in the current document.*

9. Add a right-aligned tab stop with a tab leader to the entries in the TOC.

   ✓ *The result should look the same as in the preceding exercise.*

10. Save and close the book and all open documents.
11. Exit InDesign.

Exercise | 57

Skills Covered

- Preview a Document
- Print a Document
- Save and Load Print Presets
- Print a Book

Software Skills Most people who use InDesign have their final versions printed by professional printing companies. However, when finalizing a project, it is often helpful to print a proof copy on a local desktop printer to check for errors. InDesign enables you to print to any printer attached to your computer.

Application Skills In this exercise, you will preview and print some of the projects you have worked on in previous exercises, including a document and a book.

TERMS

Color separation A set of printouts in which each color in the chosen color model (for example, C, M, Y, and K) is printed on a separate sheet, as it would be on the printing plates for a commercial press.

Composite A printout in which all colors are represented on a single copy, as it would be in the finished product.

PPD PostScript Printer Description file; a helper file that fine-tunes PostScript print output for a specific device.

NOTES

Preview a Document

- As you have learned earlier, one way to approximate the view of the finished page is to switch to the Preview screen mode.
- The shortcut for this is to press W; you can also use the View > Screen Mode > Preview command.

✓ *Pressing W does not work when the insertion point is inside a text frame because then it simply types a W character.*

Print a Document

- To print a document, choose File > Print. Then set any options desired in the Print dialog box. The list of option categories at the left side of the dialog box switches between different sets of options. When you are finished selecting settings, click the Print button to send the document to the printer (see the illustration on page 277).
- No matter which category you are viewing, the top three items never change:
  - **Print Preset:** Load saved presets from this list, if you have saved any.
  - **Printer:** Select a printer, if you have more than one.
  - **PPD:** Select a PPD, if available.

✓ *A **PPD** is a PostScript Printer Description file, a helper file for setting up device-dependent PostScript files. PPD files are not commonly used for desktop printing; a commercial printer might provide you with a PPD file to use when preparing PostScript files for its press. For example, if you choose PostScript File as the printer, you will have a choice on the PPD list of all the PostScript-supported printers installed on your system. You can also have PPD files that are provided by a commercial printer, so you can prepare a PostScript file that is specific to that printer's equipment.*

Select printing options

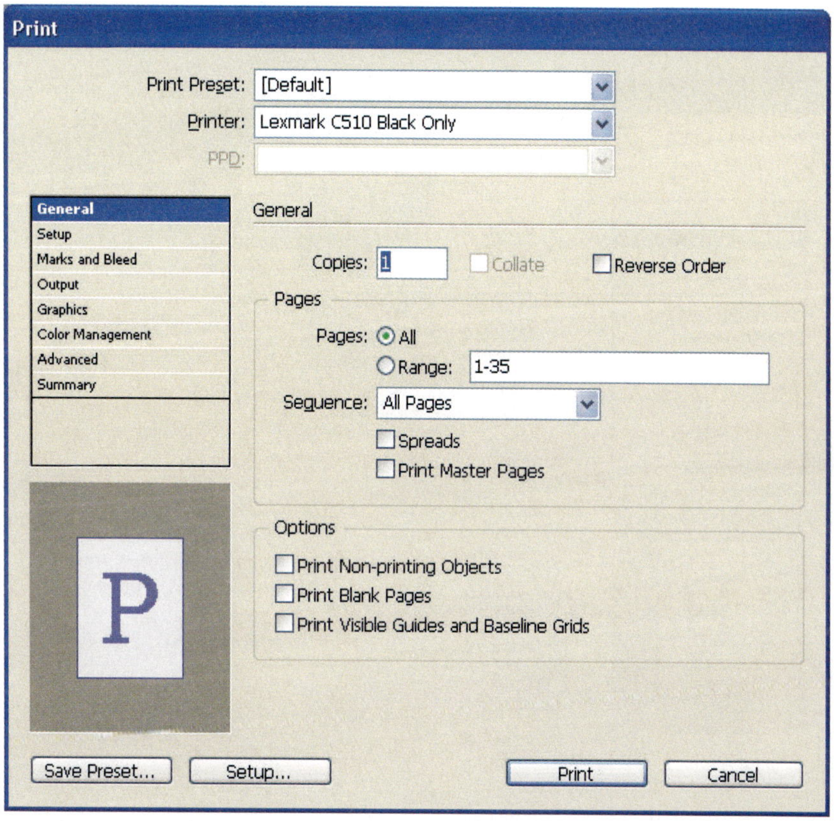

- The General category controls the basic print settings that you might find in a word processing application, such as number of copies, page range, collation, and whether to print a blank page, guides, and grids.
- The Setup category lets you specify the paper size, which might not necessarily be the same as the page size in your document. For example, it is common to use a larger paper size and then trim the paper after printing so that color bleeds go all the way to the edge of the paper (see the illustration on page 278).
- Setup also controls the scaling of the page (100% by default), and whether it should be scaled to fit the paper. For example, this can be used to print a proof copy of a larger page on a desktop printer that accepts only letter-sized paper.
- To print a sheet of thumbnail images representing the pages in the document, select the Thumbnails check box and then specify the number of thumbnails from the Per Page drop-down list. The preview area shows a sample (see the illustration at the top of page 279).
- The Marks and Bleed category enables you to turn on/off marks around the outside of the document that can help with professional printing. For example, crop marks show where to trim the paper after printing, and color bars show samples of the colors used in the process (RGB or CMYK).

Choose options from the Setup category

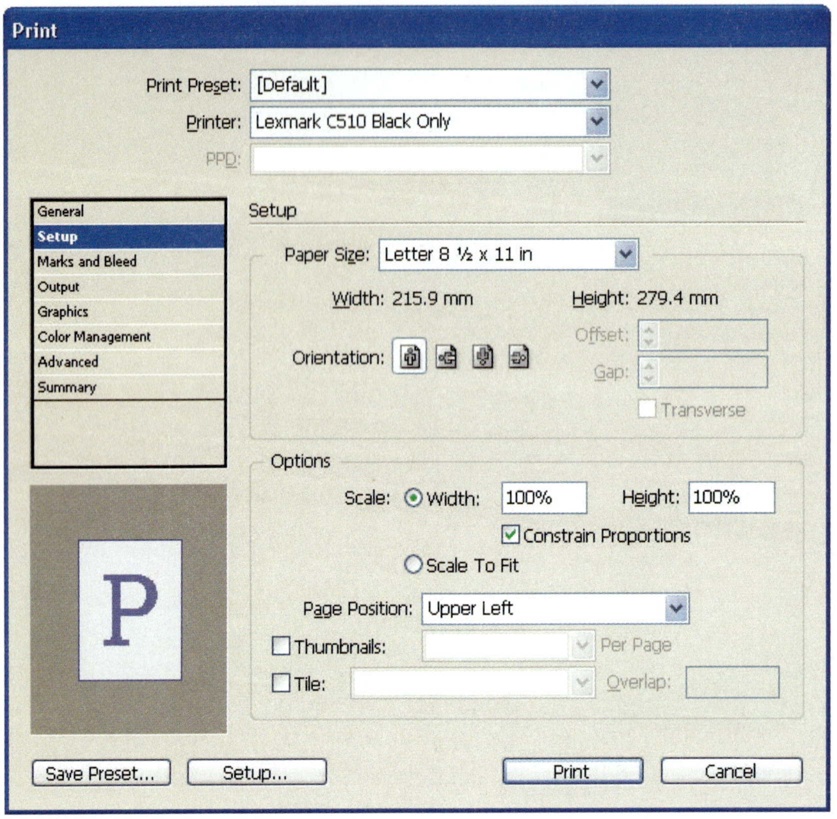

- In the Bleed and Slug area of the dialog box, you can choose to use the bleed settings you configured within the document itself at setup, or you can redefine the bleed (see the illustration at the bottom of page 279).
- The Output category lets you specify how you want the color output. You can output either a **composite** image (all colors together) using RGB or CMYK, or a **color separation** (each color in the color model outputted separately). For desktop printing, you will usually want composite.

  ✓ *If you choose Separations from the Color list, there are many additional options you can set to fine-tune the ink usage and placement. These are not needed for desktop printing, and for commercial printing they are of use only to professionals skilled in making fine adjustments (see the illustration on page 280).*
- In the Graphics category, you can specify how graphics are to be sent to the printer. For example, the Send Data drop-down list gives you choices of how high a resolution the graphics should be on the printout. For draft desktop printing, you can save some time by setting this to a low setting such as Proxy. For the final version, you'll want the highest setting available.

Print thumbnail images

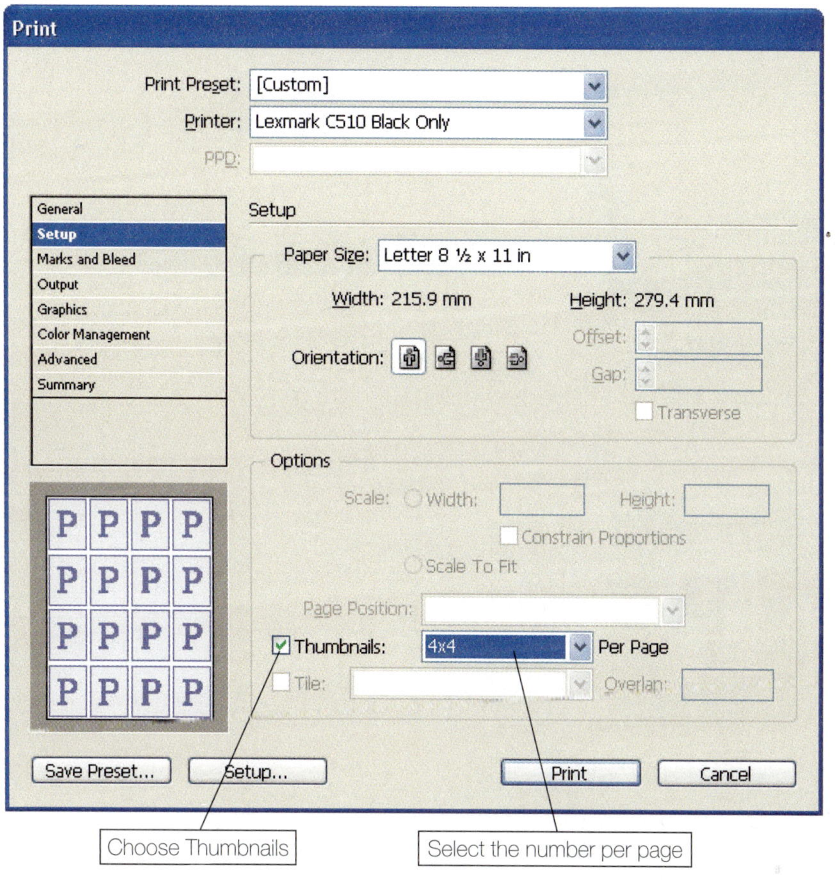

Set bleed and slug markers to print

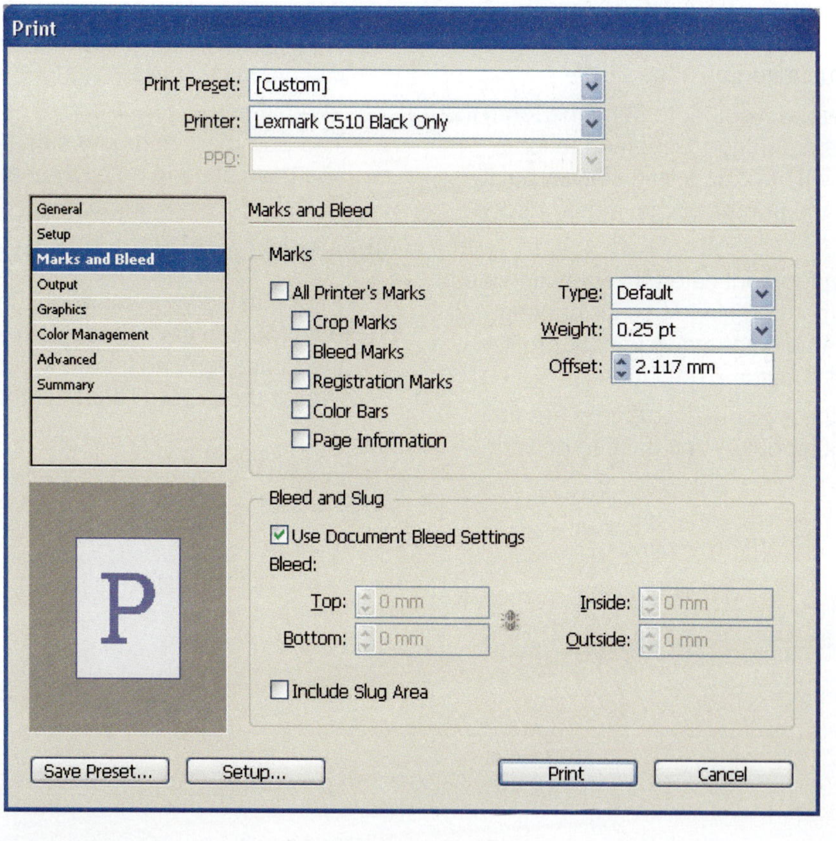

Select a type of color output

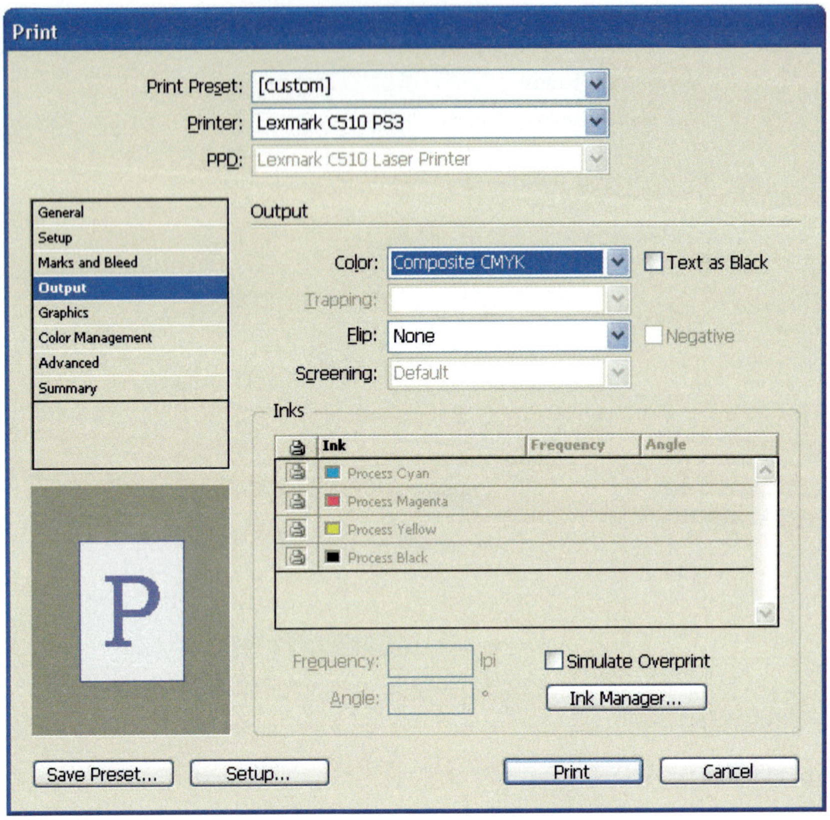

- You can also choose whether to send the fonts to the printer with the print job. Sending the fonts makes the print job start up a little slower, but it guarantees that the printer will have the needed fonts (see the illustration on page 281).
- You can also choose whether to send the fonts to the printer with the print job. Sending the fonts makes the print job start up a little slower, but it guarantees that the printer will have the needed fonts.
- In the Color Management category, you can select a color management profile to use for printing. These are the same color management profiles that you learned about in Exercise 34.
- The settings in the Advanced category are for commercial printing only. They have to do with OPI (which omits certain graphics and places instructions in their place for manual insertion later) and transparency flattening (which deals with reproducing transparency effects on commercial presses). You can ignore these for desktop printing.
- The Summary category summarizes the settings you have chosen on all the other categories.

Save and Load Print Presets

- After making your selections in the Print dialog box, you can save those settings as a preset. In the future you can load that preset from the Print Preset drop-down list at the top of the Print dialog box.

Choose whether to send fonts to the printer

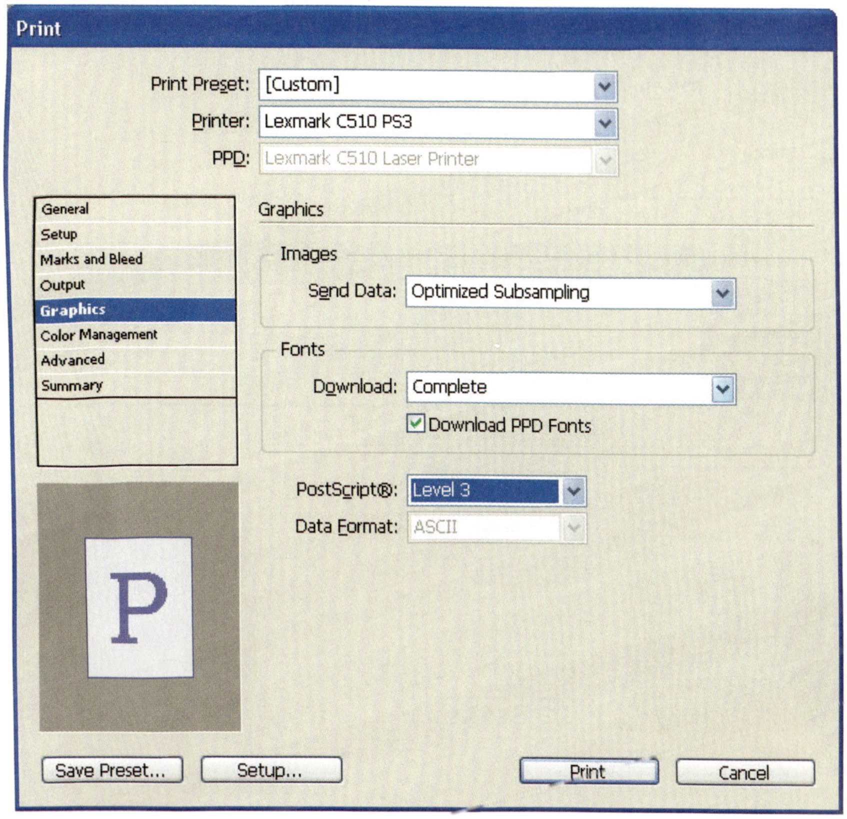

- To create a preset, click the Save Preset button, and type a name for the preset (see the illustration at the top of page 282).
- You can create new presets and delete existing ones without actually printing anything. To do so, choose File > Print Presets > Define. From there you can click New to create a new set, Delete to delete a set, or Edit to edit an existing set.
- Print presets are saved on a per-machine basis, not with the document. That means you can use the same presets on multiple documents.
- To export your print presets to a separate file, which you can then take to another PC, click the Save button in the Print Presets dialog box.
- To load presets saved this way from another source, click the Load button in the Print Presets dialog box (see the illustration at the bottom of page 282).

Print a Book

- To print a book, open the Book palette for the book, make sure that no documents are selected in it, and click the Print button on the palette.

  ✓ *If the documents have different source color profiles defined, you will see a warning message; click OK to continue. Although this could be a problem for commercial printing, for draft desktop printing it makes little difference.*

  ✓ *You can also print a book by choosing Print Book from the Book palette's fly-out menu.*

- The Print dialog box is the same for a book as for a document.

Save a printer preset

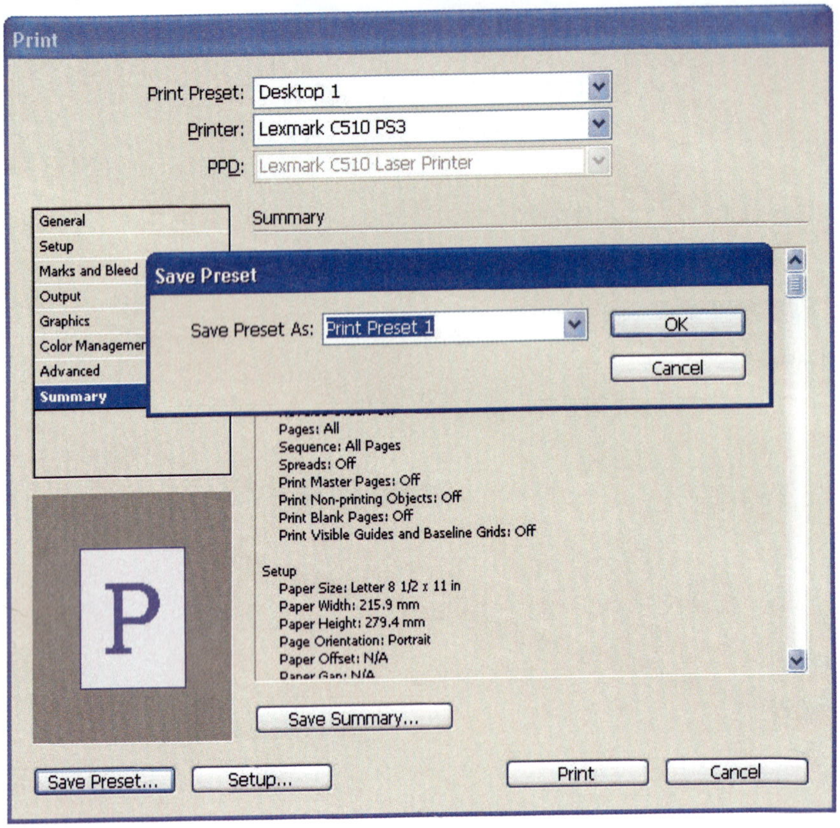

Load a preset

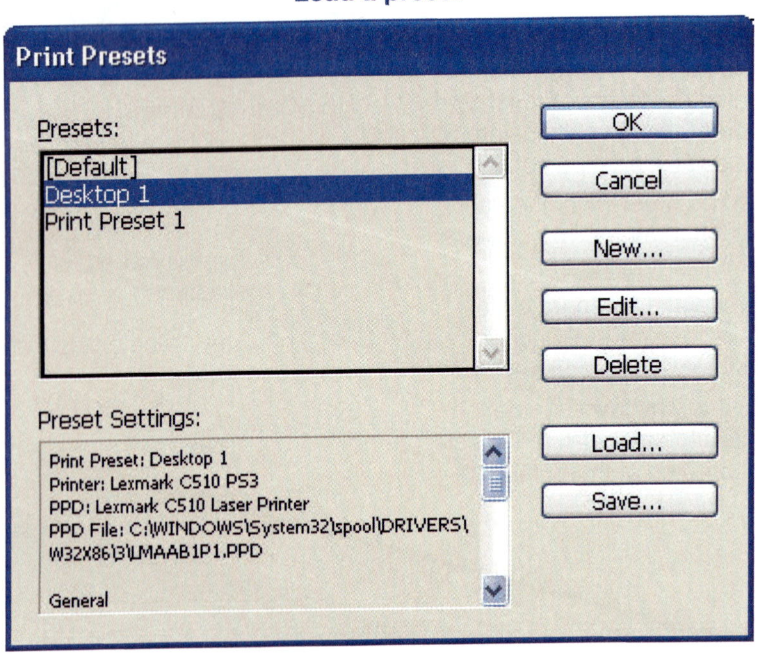

PROCEDURES

Preview a Document

Shortcut Key Method

1. Select any tool except Text.
2. Press **W**.

✓ *Press W again to return to normal viewing.*

Menu Method

1. Click **View** .... Alt+V
2. Click **Screen Mode** .... M
3. Click **Preview**.

✓ *Repeat the process but select Normal in step 3 to return to normal viewing.*

Print a Document

1. Click **File** .... Alt+F
2. Click **Print** .... P

✓ *Ctrl+P is a shortcut for steps 1 and 2.*

3. (Optional) Select a **Print Preset** .... Alt+S, ↑/↓
4. (Optional) Change the **Printer** .... Alt+P, ↑/↓
5. (Optional) Click a category, and set any options desired in that category. Repeat for additional categories.
6. Click **Print** .... ↵Enter

Manage Print Presets

Save Print Presets

1. Follow steps 1–5 of "Print a Document."
2. Click **Save Preset** .... Alt+V
3. Type a name for the preset.
4. Click **OK** .... ↵Enter

Print Using a Saved Preset

1. Click **File** .... Alt+F
2. Click **Print** .... P

✓ *Ctrl+P is a shortcut for steps 1 and 2.*

3. Select the desired preset from the **Print Preset** list .... Alt+S, ↑/↓
4. Click **Print** .... ↵Enter

Create a New Print Preset Without Printing

1. Click **File** .... Alt+F
2. Point to **Print Presets** .... T
3. Click **Define** .... D
4. Click **New** .... Alt+N
5. Type a name in the **Name** box.
6. Define the print preset.

✓ *The options are the same as in the Print dialog box.*

7. Click **OK** .... ↵Enter

Delete a Saved Print Preset

1. Click **File** .... Alt+F
2. Point to **Print Presets** .... T
3. Click **Define** .... D
4. Click the preset to delete .... Alt+P, ↓
5. Click **Delete** .... Alt+D
6. Repeat steps 4 and 5 as needed to delete other presets.
7. Click **OK** .... ↵Enter

Export a Print Preset

1. Click **File** .... Alt+F
2. Point to **Print Presets** .... T
3. Click **Define** .... D
4. Select the preset to export.
5. Click **Save** .... Alt+A
6. Type a name for the preset file .... Alt+N
7. Click **Save** .... ↵Enter

Import a Print Preset

1. Click **File** .... Alt+F
2. Point to **Print Presets** .... T
3. Click **Define** .... D
4. Click **Load** .... Alt+L
5. Select the preset file to load.
6. Click **Open** .... ↵Enter

Print a Book

1. Open the book. Do not select any documents.
2. Click the **Print** button on the Book palette.

✓ *If a warning appears about different color profiles, click OK.*

✓ *You can also select Print Book from the Book palette's fly-out menu instead of step 2.*

3. (Optional) Select a **Print Preset** .... Alt+S, ↓
4. (Optional) Change the **Printer** .... Alt+P, ↓
5. (Optional) Click a category, and set any options desired in that category. Repeat for additional categories.
6. Click **Print** .... ↵Enter

EXERCISE DIRECTIONS

1. Start Adobe InDesign.
2. Open **EX57.indd**.
3. Create a new print preset called **Draft** with the following settings:
   - Print to your default printer.
   - Set the size to Scale to Fit (Setup category).
   - Show all printer's marks (Marks and Bleed category).
   - Override the document bleed settings with a 6 mm bleed (Marks and Bleed category).
   - Output in Composite Gray (Output category).
   - Set the Send Data setting for images to Proxy (Graphics category).
4. Print one copy of pages 1 and 2 only using the Draft print preset.
5. Close **EX57.indd**.

6. Open **EX57book.indb**.
7. Open the Print dialog box, and set the Print Preset to [Default] to clear previous settings.
8. Print one copy of only the even pages of the book.
9. Close the book.
10. Exit InDesign.

ON YOUR OWN

This exercise requires that you have a color printer available that supports Adobe PostScript.

1. Start Adobe InDesign.
2. Reopen **EX57book.indb** from the preceding exercise's data files.
3. Print one copy of just **EX57-spread1.indd** (not the entire book) with Separations turned on, so that each color prints on a separate page.
4. Exit InDesign.

Exercise | 58

Skills Covered

- Use Trapping
- Use the Separations Preview
- Use the Preflight Dialog Box
- Package a Document for a Printer

Software Skills Most people don't know the details involved in preparing a document for commercial printing. That's okay, though, because InDesign handles most of them automatically. It automatically sets up trapping and color separations, and its Preflight check looks for errors that might cause problems during printing.

Application Skills In this exercise, you will prepare a document for commercial printing by checking its trapping and separations and packaging it with the Package feature in InDesign.

TERMS

In register Successful alignment of the multiple printing passes required for color printing with separations.

Knock out To remove the color from an area that another color will be printing on top of, to prevent unwanted ink blending.

Misregistration Unsuccessful alignment of the multiple printing passes required for color printing with separations.

Overprint To print one ink over the top of another ink, as with trapping.

Spreading A trapping technique whereby a lighter-colored object is enlarged slightly so that it overlaps a dark-colored adjacent object.

Trapping A small amount of overlap of two adjacent colored areas during color printing so that a gap does not occur between them if the alignment of the inks is not perfect.

NOTES

Use Trapping

- When full-color print jobs are printed on commercial printing equipment, the colors are laid down one at a time: cyan, magenta, yellow, and black. A color separation is done of the page so that each color is on its own plate, and then each piece of paper is printed four times: once with each plate. When the printing passes align correctly, it is called being **in register** (see the illustrations on page 286).
- Printing presses are not always perfectly aligned, so sometimes one pass gets slightly shifted in relation to the previous passes, and the inks do not align as they should. This is called **misregistration**. If two contrasting colors are supposed to be touching on the layout, sometimes a small gap can occur in the final printout where the paper is visible between them.
- To counteract this, trapping is used. **Trapping** creates a small overlap between two colored areas, so that even if the printing passes are not perfectly aligned, no gap will appear.
- Normally when one colored object overlaps another, the printing process **knocks out** the color beneath, so there is no blending of inks. For example, if you print yellow text on a blue background, the portion of the background covered by the yellow text will not be printed in blue; it will remain colorless until the yellow ink is laid down. In areas of trapping, however, the inks are **overprinted**—that is, one ink is printed over the top of the other.

✓ *Black is commonly overprinted as the last pass in the four-stage color printing process.*

A full-color page is printed in four passes

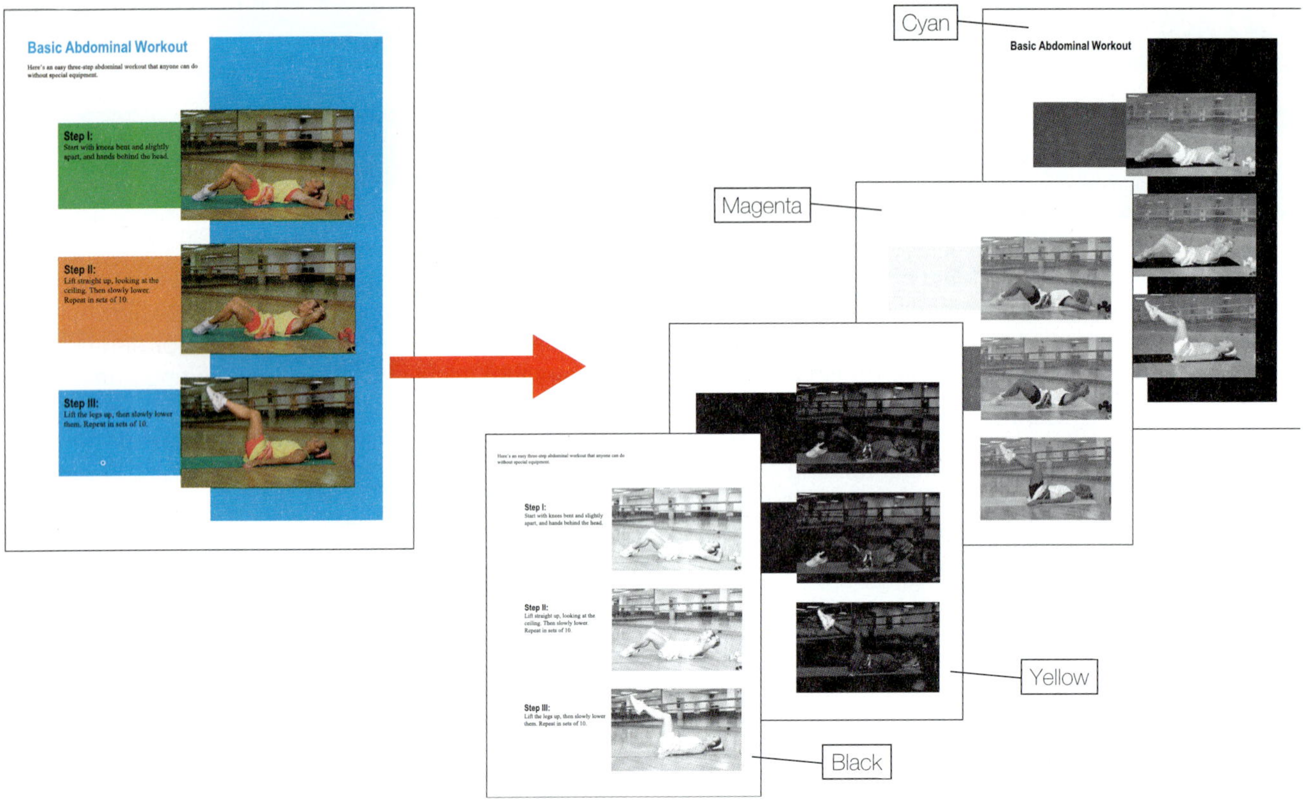

- The most common type of trapping involves **spreading**, which enlarges the lighter-colored object to slightly overprint the darker object.
- There are two types of automatic trapping available in InDesign: built-in trapping and Adobe In-RIP Trapping. The latter is used only when outputting to a PostScript output device that supports it, so in this course we will be using built-in trapping.
- Trapping can be done automatically in InDesign by its built-in trapping engine, so you do not usually need to make any manual trapping adjustments. Simply make sure trapping is enabled when printing.
- On the Output category of the Print dialog box, choose Separations from the Color list, and then set the Trapping setting to Application Built-In (see the illustration on page 288).

Display/hide color separations

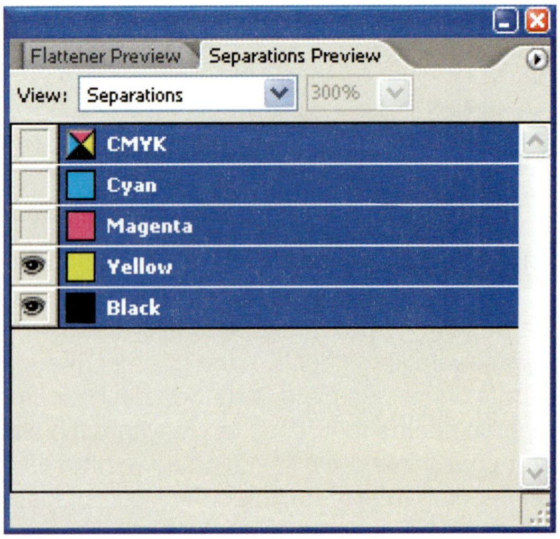

Use the Separations Preview

- To preview the color separations, open the Separations Preview palette. Then open the View menu on the palette and choose Separations. Each color appears with an eye symbol next to it; click the eye to turn that color off, leaving only the colors you want to see. To see only one color, turn the other three off.
- When only one color is selected, its separation appears in black. When more than one color is selected, each color appears as its actual color.
- To return to displaying all colors (the composite image), click CMYK.

Use built-in trapping

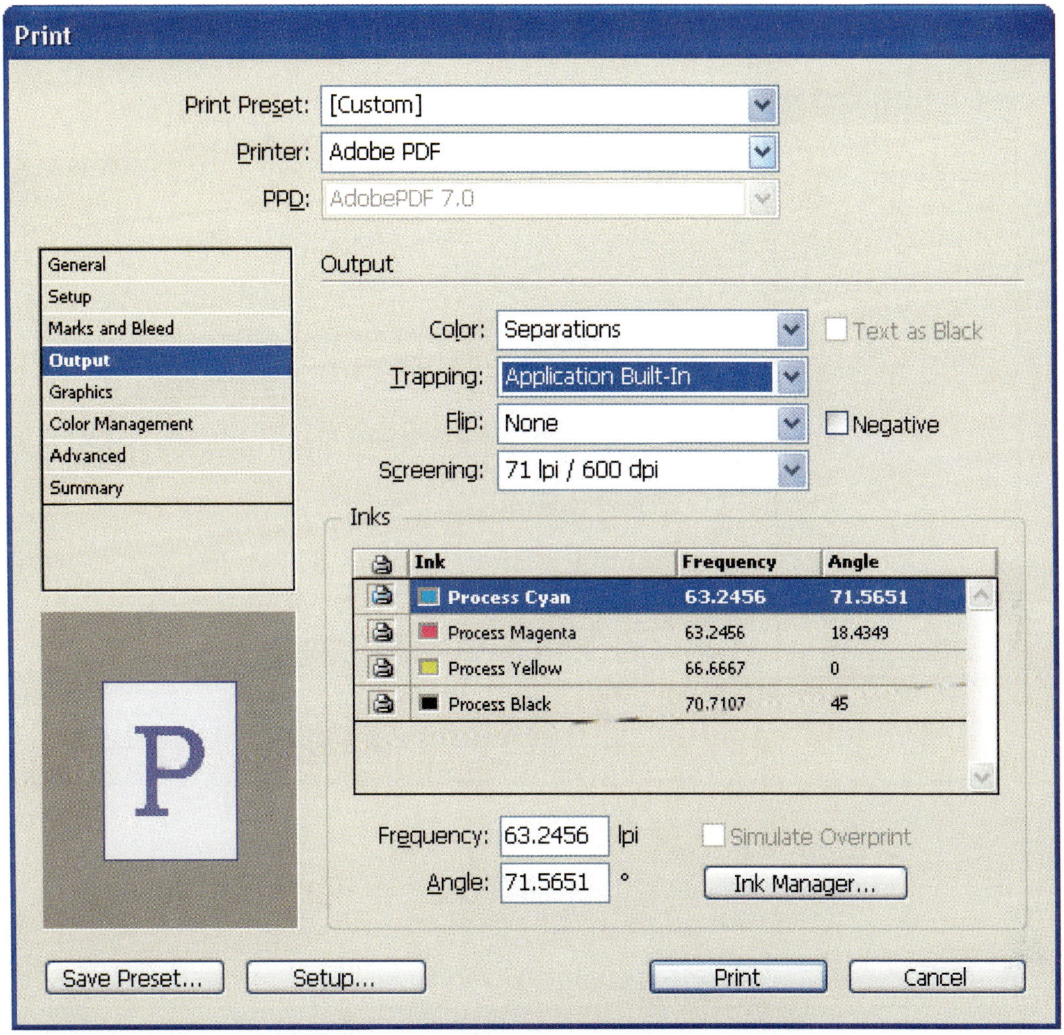

Use the Preflight Dialog Box

- The Preflight feature helps you prepare a print job for commercial printing. It checks the fonts, colors, and images that will be needed.
- Choose File > Preflight to open the Preflight dialog box. Summary information appears as shown in the illustration at the top of page 289.
- Click one of the categories on the left to see specifics for that category. For example, the Fonts category tells what fonts are used in the document and whether they can be embedded. Fonts that have Yes in the Protected column cannot be embedded due to copyright restrictions.

Package a Document for a Printer

- If no problems are reported in the Preflight dialog box, you are ready to package the document for the printer. You can click the Package button in the Preflight dialog box to start this process, or you can exit the dialog box and choose File > Package.
- In the Printing Instructions dialog box, enter your contact information. This file will be named Instructions.txt (or whatever name you specify in the File name box) and will be included in the package. Type your instructions in the Instructions lines. Then click Continue (see the illustration at the bottom of page 289).
- In the Package Publication dialog box, enter a name for the package in the File name box, and specify a location. Select or clear the check boxes as needed for your situation. Then click Save (see the illustration on page 290).
- If you see a Font Alert dialog box warning you about copyright restrictions on fonts, read the information and click OK.
- The resulting folder will contain the InDesign document and Instructions.txt, plus two subfolders: Fonts (containing all the fonts needed for the print job) and Links (containing the needed images).
- You can copy the folder to a removable disk to send to the printer.

Perform a preflight check

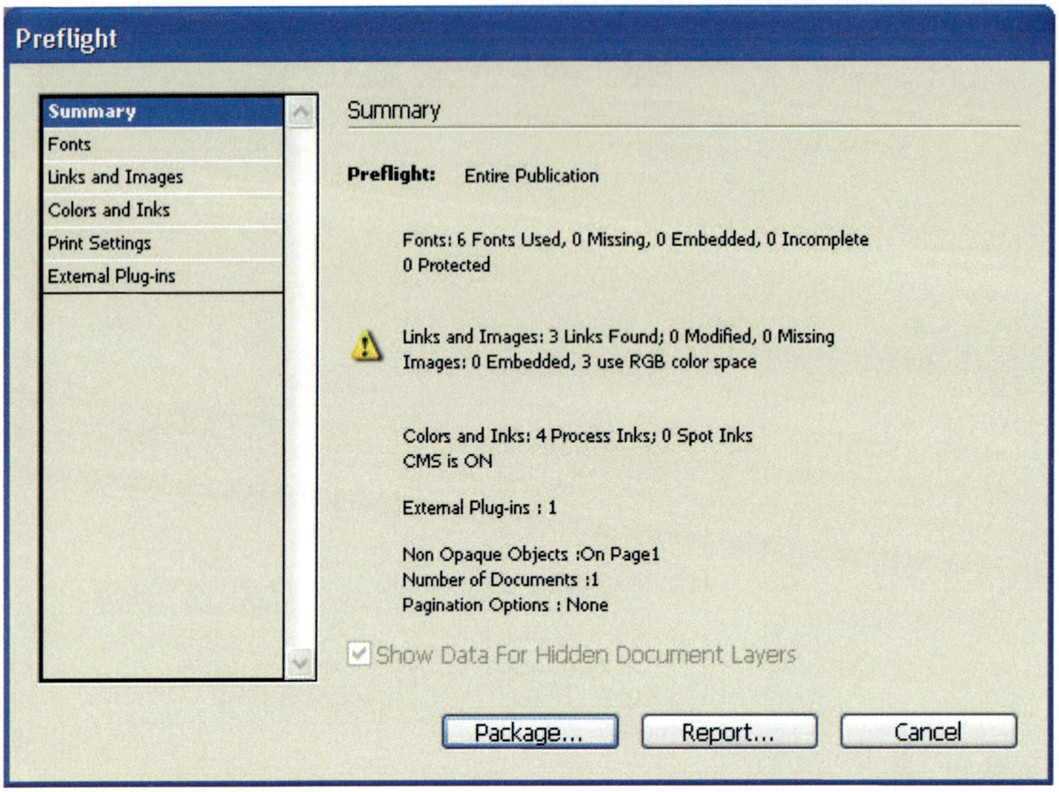

Specify printing instructions

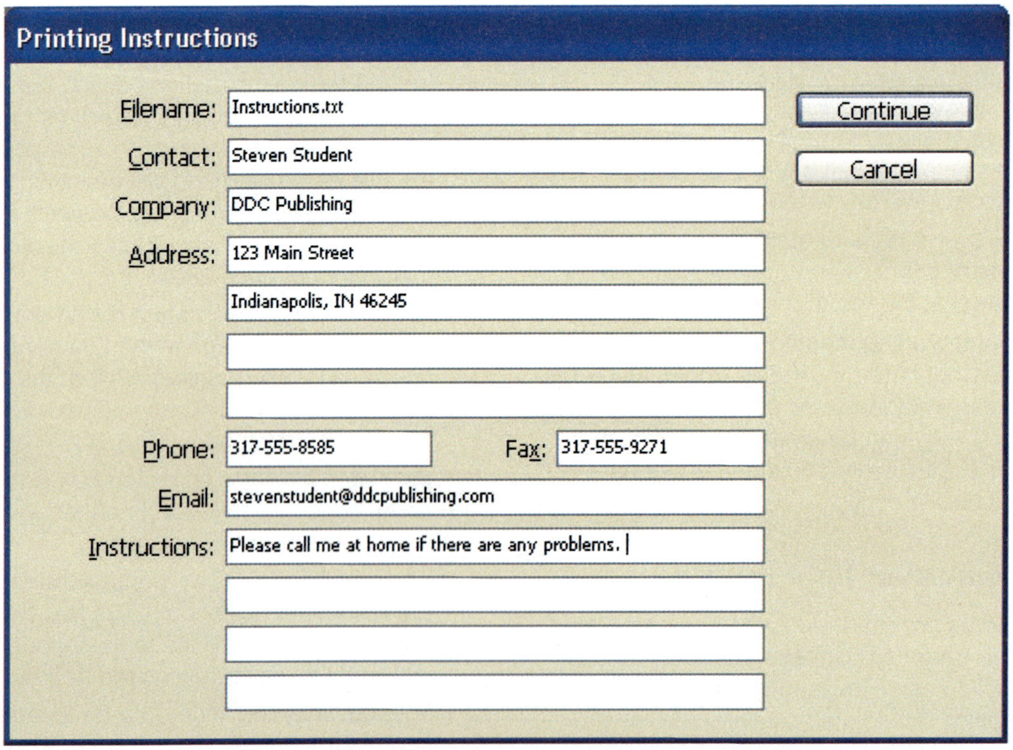

Package the publication

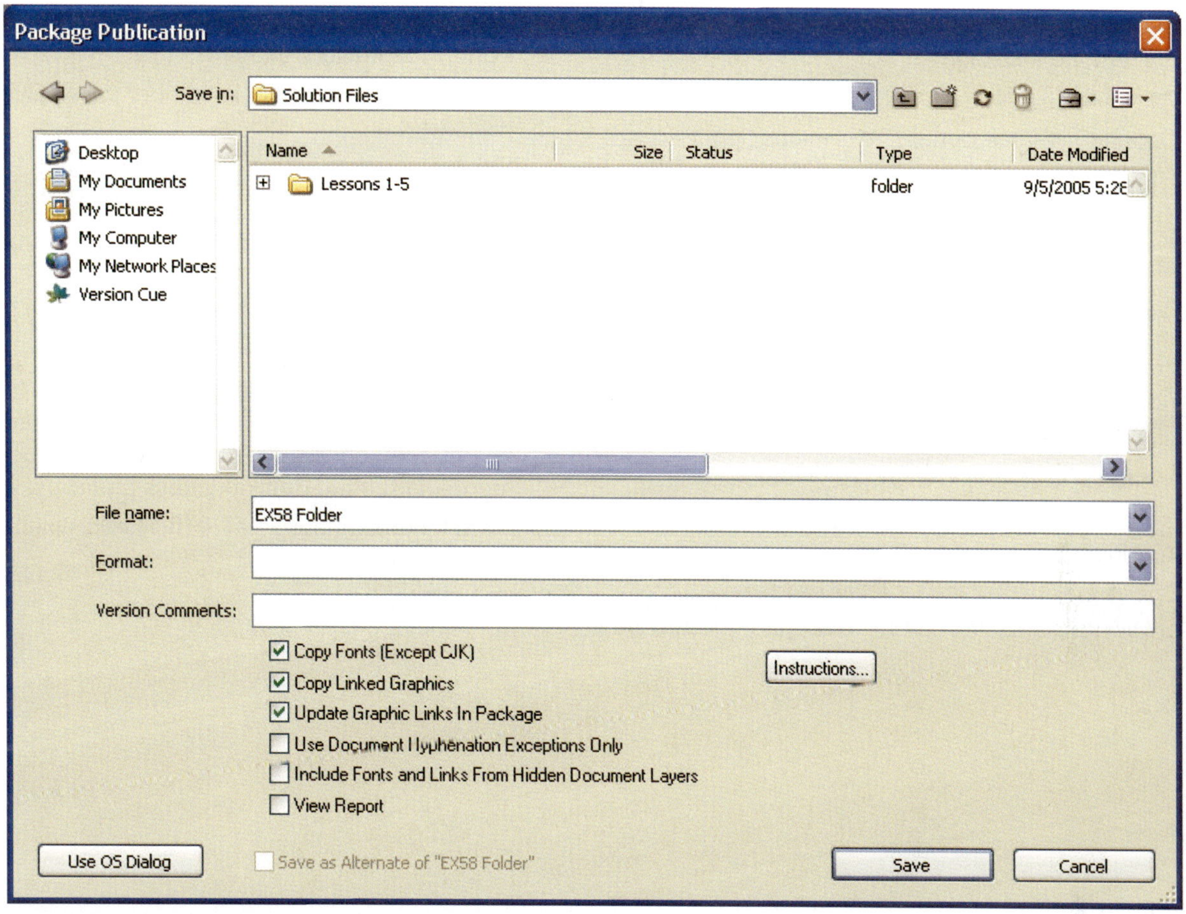

PROCEDURES

Use Trapping

✓ *This procedure requires a color PostScript printer.*

1. Click **File** .... Alt+F
2. Click **Print** .... P
3. Select a color printer from the **Printer** list ...... Alt+P, ↑/↓
4. Click **Output**.
5. Select **Separations** from the **Color** list .... Alt+L
6. Select **Application Built-In** from the **Trapping** list ..... Alt+T, ↑/↓
7. Select any other settings as needed.
8. Click **Print** .... ↵Enter

Use the Separations Preview

1. Click **Window** .... Alt+W
2. Point to **Output** .... U
3. Click **Separations Preview** .... S

   ✓ *Shift+F6 is a shortcut for steps 1–3.*

4. Select **Separations** from the View menu in the palette.
5. Click the eye symbol next to a color to turn off. Repeat for other colors as needed.
6. To return to composite view, click **CMYK**.

Perform a Preflight Check

1. Click **File** .... Alt+F
2. Click **Preflight** .... H

   ✓ *Ctrl+Alt+Shift+F is a shortcut for steps 1 and 2.*

3. Check for any problems.
4. If problems are found, click **Cancel** and fix them.

   OR

   If no problems are found, click **Package** .... Alt+P

Package a Document for a Printer

1. Follow the steps in "Perform a Preflight Check."

   OR

   a. Click **File** .... Alt+F

   b. Click **Package** .... G
2. Enter contact information and instructions.

   ✓ *Ctrl+Alt+Shift+P is a shortcut for step 1.*
3. Click **Continue**.
4. Type a file name in the **File name** box .... Alt+N
5. Click **Save** .... ↵Enter

EXERCISE DIRECTIONS

1. Start Adobe InDesign.
2. Open **EX58.indd**.
3. (Optional) If a color printer is available, print a color separation that includes trapping.
4. Perform a preflight check.
5. Package the document in a folder called **EX58-XX**, where XX are your initials.
6. Exit InDesign.

ON YOUR OWN

✓ *This exercise requires access to Adobe Photoshop.*

1. Start Adobe InDesign.
2. Reopen **EX57book.indb** from the preceding exercise's data files.
3. Open **EX57-cover.indd** from the Book palette.
4. Perform a preflight check. Make a note of the error found.

   ✓ *The error is that the photo uses the RGB color space. You cannot correct this from within InDesign; you would need to open the original photo in a photo editing program such as Photoshop and then re-import it.*
5. If you have Photoshop available, open the file **archway.psd** and save it as **archwayCMYK.psd** using CMYK color space. Then replace it in the document and run the preflight check again.
6. Save the document as **XX-OYO-58.indd**, where XX are your initials.
7. Exit InDesign.

Exercise | 59

Skills Covered

- Export to PDF Format
- Export to an EPS File

Software Skills Adobe PDF and Encapsulated PostScript (EPS) are very popular output formats because of their wide acceptance across the printing and publishing industry. InDesign outputs to both of these formats, producing single files that you can then deliver to a printer.

Application Skills In this exercise, you will produce PDF and EPS versions of an InDesign document.

TERMS

Downsample To reduce an image's size by removing pixels from it.

EPS Encapsulated PostScript; a graphic format that is commonly used in professional printing to manage pictures and print jobs.

PDF Portable Document Format; an Adobe format for distributing documents in electronic form exactly as they would be printed.

NOTES

Export to PDF Format

- Portable Document Format (**PDF**) is an Adobe format for distributing documents. A PDF file shows a full-color, high-resolution version of the document, and looks the same when viewed on any computer.
- PDF is a unique blend of text and snapshot: Each page looks exactly as it would if printed, like a snapshot, but the text within the document remains searchable.
- Anyone can view a PDF file on any PC with the free program Adobe Reader. However, to create a PDF file, you must have the full version of Adobe Acrobat or some other program that is capable of generating PDF files (such as InDesign).
- There are two ways to create a PDF file from your document:
  - You can print to the Adobe PDF driver through the Print dialog box, as in Exercise 57.

    ✓ *This option is available only if you have installed Adobe Acrobat (the full version, not Acrobat Reader). Adobe Acrobat comes free with InDesign CS2, but you must install it separately.*

  - You can export to PDF using the Export command. This method is more flexible and has more options than the printing method.
- Choose File > Export, and set the Format to Adobe PDF. Specify a file name, and click Save (see the illustration on page 293).
- The Export Adobe PDF dialog box then opens, in which you can fully configure the PDF output. There are many options, organized around seven categories (at the left of the dialog box). See the illustration on page 294.
- As with printing, you can create and save PDF presets. Select a preset from the Adobe PDF Preset list. There are several on the list to choose from. To create your own, after making all of your selections, click the Save Preset button at the bottom of the dialog box. This works just like with print presets (Exercise 57).
- The PDF presets include High Quality Print (for desktop printers), PDF/X-1a and PDF/X-3 (strictly compliant with the PDF/X standards, required for compatibility with some programs), Press Quality (for digital or commercial printing), Smallest File Size (for Web distribution), or Rich Content PDF (includes live hyperlinks, bookmarks, and layers).

Export to PDF format

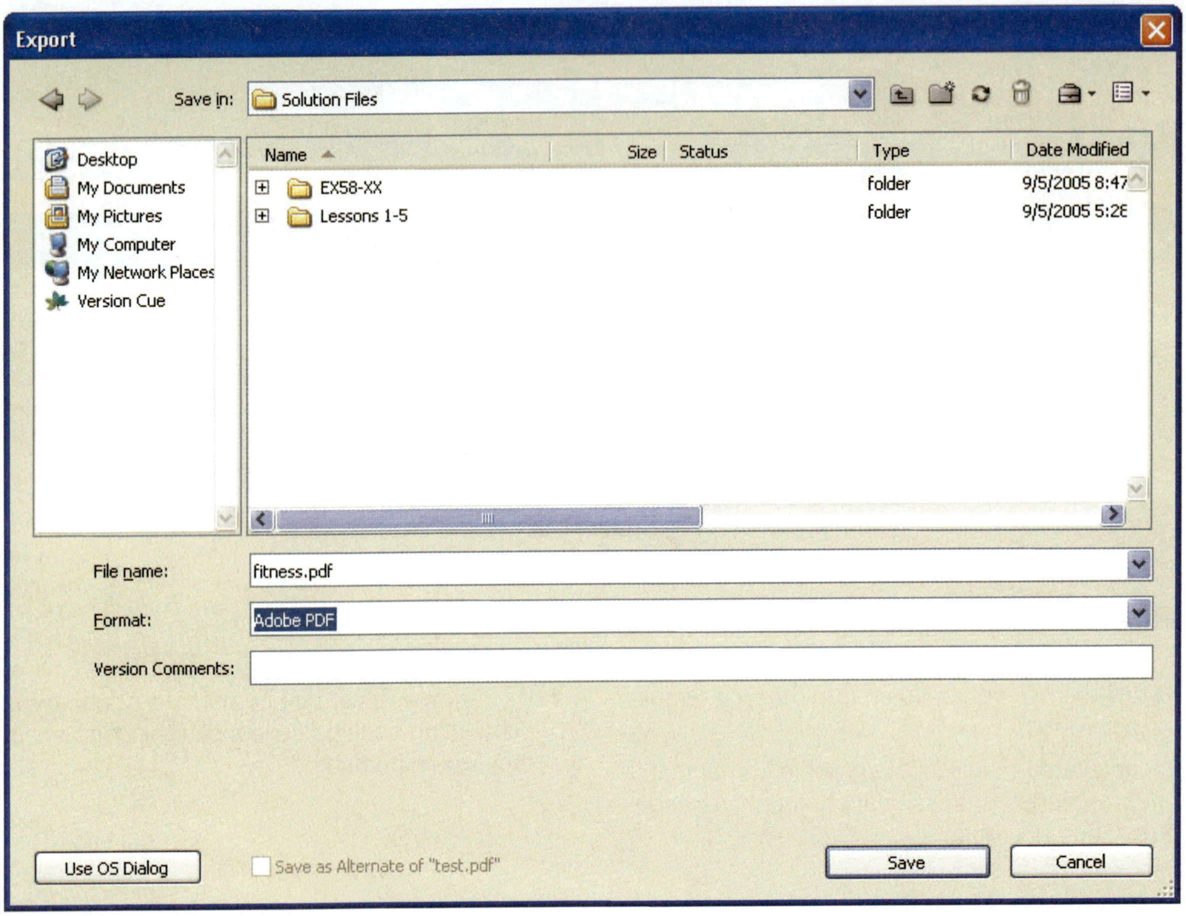

- The Compatibility list lets you choose the minimum version of Adobe Reader that will be able to view the file. The lower the version number, the fewer the features but the higher the compatibility with computers having older versions.
- For full information about every option in this dialog box, consult the Help system (Help > InDesign Help). Here are a few highlights:
  - Under Output, you can set Color to No Color Conversion to avoid problems with differences in transparency blend space.
  - Under General, if you choose the Embed Page Thumbnails, users will be able to browse the pages by thumbnail image. This is useful for long documents. It increases the file size slightly.
  - Under General, If you choose Hyperlinks, the hyperlinks within the document will be functional.
  - Under Compression, you can **downsample** (reduce) the images to save space. This is useful if the PDF file will be distributed in a low-resolution format such as over the Web, but it is not a good idea if you are preparing the document for commercial printing.

Export to an EPS File

- Encapsulated PostScript (**EPS**) is a graphic format based on the PostScript printer/graphic language. An EPS file can be sent directly to a PostScript-compatible printing press, and can be inserted in other applications that accept EPS files as input.
- If the printing company you are working with requests an EPS file, you can create one with the Export command, the same as with a PDF file.
- In the Export EPS dialog box, make your option selections. The printing company you are preparing the file for will tell you what settings to use (see the illustration on page 295).

Set PDF export options

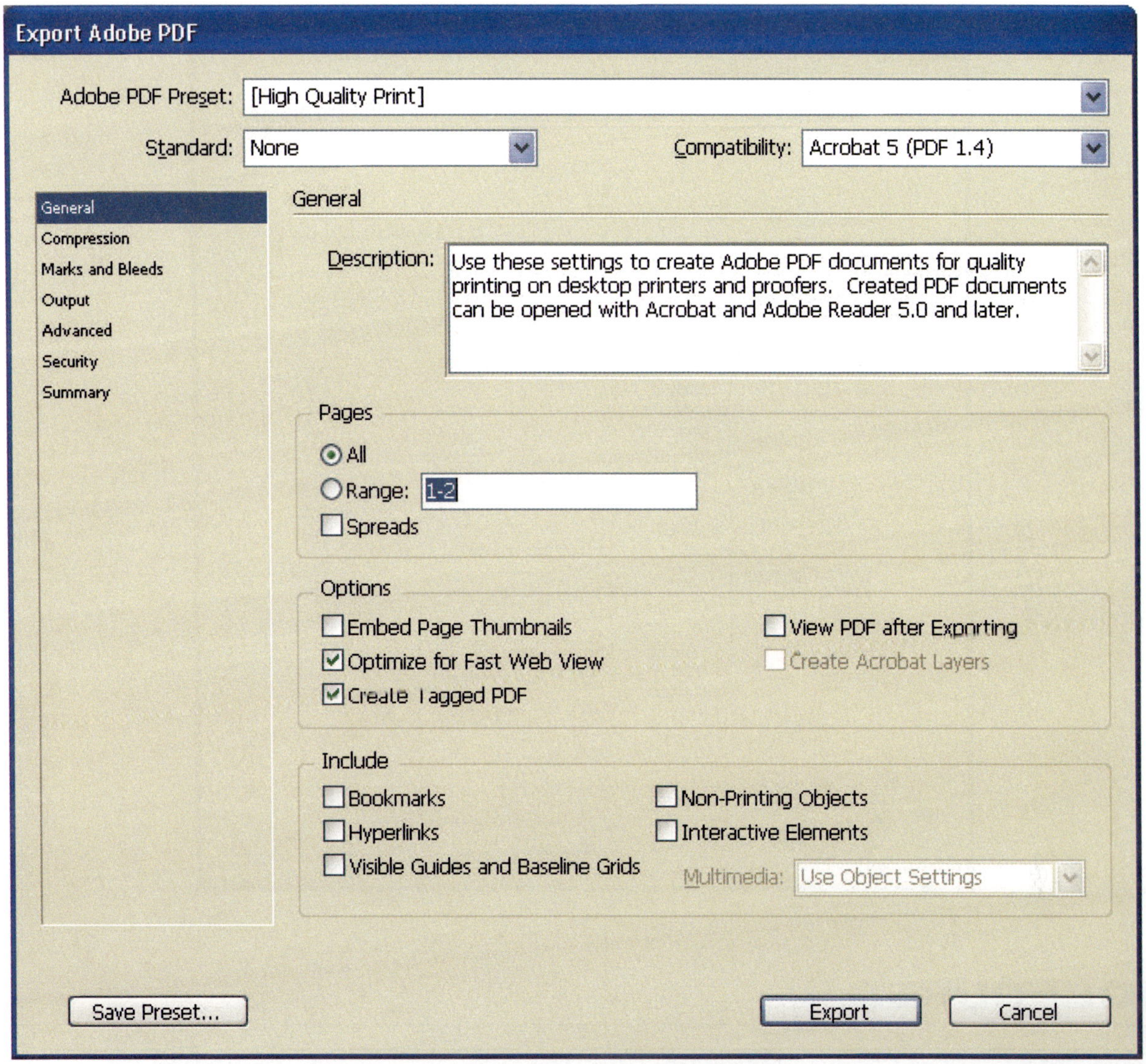

Export EPS dialog box

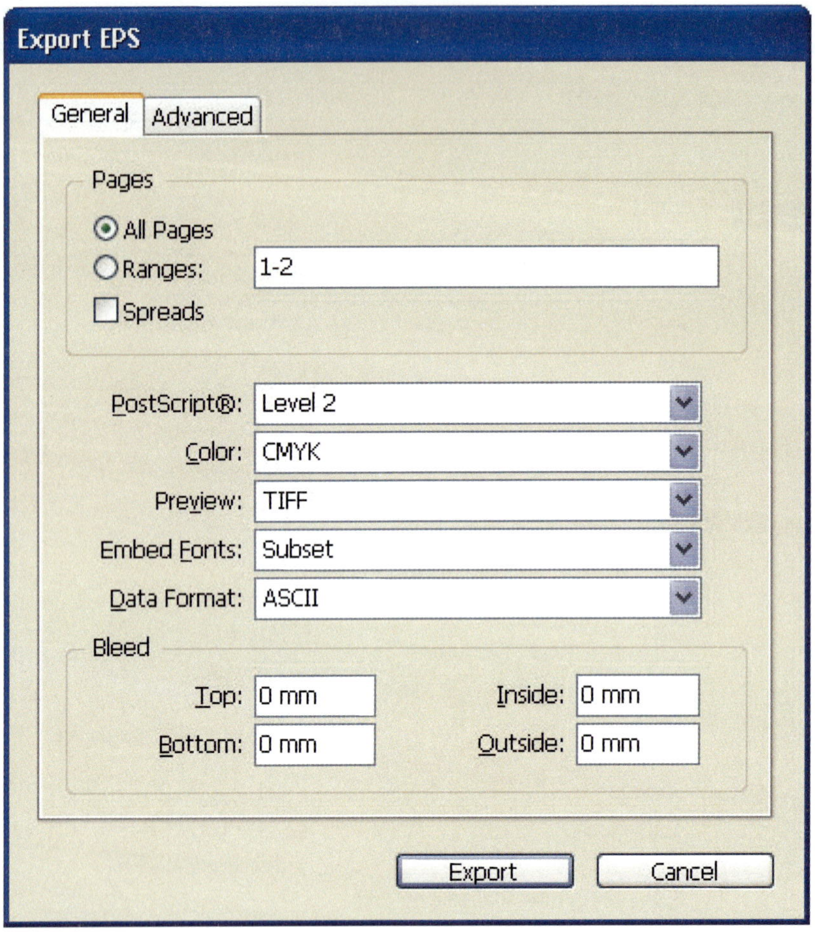

PROCEDURES

Export to a PDF File

1. Click **File** .... Alt+F
2. Click **Export** .... E

   ✓ *Ctrl+E is a shortcut for steps 1 and 2.*

3. Select a location in which to export.
4. Select **Adobe PDF** from the **Format** list .... Alt+F, ↑/↓
5. Type a file name in the **File name** box .... Alt+N
6. Click **Save** .... ↵Enter
7. (Optional) Select an **Adobe PDF Preset** .... Alt+S, ↑/↓
8. (Optional) Choose a **Standard** with which to comply .... Alt+T, ↑/↓
9. (Optional) Choose an Acrobat **Compatibility** level .... Alt+C, ↑/↓
10. (Optional) Set any other options as desired.

    ✓ *The printing company with which you are working should tell you what settings to use. If you are not sure, use the default settings.*

11. Click **Export** .... ↵Enter

Manage PDF Presets

Save PDF Presets

1. Follow steps 1–9 of "Export to a PDF File."
2. Click **Save Preset** .... Alt+V
3. Type a name for the preset.
4. Click **OK** .... ↵Enter

Create a New PDF Preset Without Exporting

1. Click **File** .... Alt+F
2. Point to **Adobe PDF Presets** ..... D
3. Click **Define** .... D
4. Click **New** .... Alt+N
5. Type a name in the **Preset Name** box .... Alt+S
6. Define the PDF preset.

   ✓ *The options are the same as in "Export to a PDF File."*

7. Click **OK** .... ↵Enter
8. Click **Done** .... ↵Enter

Delete a Saved PDF Preset

1. Click **File** .... Alt+F
2. Point to **Adobe PDF Presets** ..... D
3. Click **Define** .... D
4. Click the preset to delete.
5. Click **Delete** .... Alt+D
6. Click **OK** .... ↵Enter
7. Repeat steps 4–6 as needed to delete other presets.
8. Click **Done** .... ↵Enter

Export a PDF Preset

1. Click **File** .... Alt + F
2. Point to **Adobe PDF Presets** ..... D
3. Click **Define** .... D
4. Select the preset to export.
5. Click **Save As** .... Alt + S
6. Type a name for the preset file .... Alt + N
7. Click **Save** .... ↵Enter
8. Click **Done** .... ↵Enter

Import a PDF Preset

1. Click **File** .... Alt + F
2. Point to **Adobe PDF Presets** ..... D
3. Click **Define** .... D
4. Click **Load** .... Alt + L
5. Select the preset file to load.
6. Click **Open** .... ↵Enter
7. Click **Done** .... ↵Enter

Export to an EPS File

1. Click **File** .... Alt + F
2. Click **Export** .... E

   ✓ *Ctrl+E is a shortcut for steps 1 and 2.*

3. Select a location in which to export.
4. Select **EPS** from the **Format** list .... Alt + F, ↑/↓
5. Type a file name in the **File name** box .... Alt + N
6. Click **Save** .... ↵Enter
7. (Optional) Set any export options.

   ✓ *The printing company with which you are working should tell you what settings to use. If you are not sure, use the default settings.*

8. Click **Export** .... ↵Enter

EXERCISE DIRECTIONS

1. Start Adobe InDesign.
2. Open **EX59.indd**.
3. Export the document as a PDF file that uses the [High Quality Print] preset but is compatible with Acrobat 5 and higher and has embedded thumbnails. Create a preset for these settings called **Desktop Compatibility**. Name the exported PDF file **XX-EX59.pdf**, where XX are your initials.
4. Save the Desktop Compatibility preset as a separate file called **XX-EX59-PDF.joboptions**, where XX are your initials.
5. Delete the Desktop Compatibility preset from the list in the Adobe PDF Presets dialog box.
6. Re-import the Desktop Compatibility preset from the **EX59-PDF-XX.joboptions** file.
7. Export the document as an EPS file called **XX-EX59.eps**, where XX are your initials. Use the default settings except specify a 5 mm bleed on all sides and save in PostScript Level 3.
8. Exit InDesign.

ON YOUR OWN

1. Open any of the previous documents you have worked on in this class that you enjoyed creating.

   ✓ *Use Adobe Bridge to browse them more easily if desired.*

2. Export the document in PDF using [Smallest File Size] as the preset. Name the file **OYO-59A-XX**, where XX are your initials.
3. Export the document in PDF using [Press Quality] as the preset. Name the file **OYO-59B-XX**, where XX are your initials.
4. Open both PDF files in Adobe Acrobat (or Acrobat Reader) and compare them. Make notes of any differences you can detect.
5. Exit InDesign.

End of Lesson Projects

- Summary Exercise
- Application Exercise
- Curriculum Integration Exercise
- Critical Thinking Exercise

Exercise | 60

Summary Exercise

Software Skills In this exercise you will create a book, number its pages, add a footnote, and output it to PDF.

DIRECTIONS

1. Start InDesign.
2. Start a new book, and name it **XX-EX60book.indb**, where XX are your initials.
3. Add these files to the book: **EX60A.indd**, **EX60B.indd**, and **EX60C.indd**. Ensure that they appear in that order.
4. Open **EX60A.indd** from the book, and footnote the name *Mark Twain* with the following:

   For more information about Mark Twain, see http://en.wikipedia.org/wiki/Mark_Twain.
5. In **EX60B.indd**, Insert page numbering on page 3 (the title page of A Dog's Tale) but make the numbering start at 1 instead of 3.

   ✓ *The page numbers in **EX60C.indd** should continue automatically from **EX60B.indd**.*
6. On the second page of **EX60A.indd**, create a table of contents that lists the two story titles and the page numbers on which the titles appear.
7. Save the book, and save each document.
8. Export the book as a PDF file. Name it **EX60-XX.pdf**, where XX are your initials. Use the [High Quality Print] presets.

   ✓ *Open the fly-out menu on the Book palette and choose Export Book to PDF.*
9. Export **EX60A.indd** (only) as an EPS file. Name it **EX60A-XX.eps**, where XX are your initials using PostScript Level 2.
10. Exit InDesign, saving all files as prompted.

Exercise | 61

Application Exercise

Software Skills In this exercise, you will create a reusable template document for laying out a multi-page report.

DIRECTIONS

1. Start InDesign and start a blank document with 10 pages. Set 20 mm margins on all sides.
2. In the center of the first page, place a 150 mm wide by 75 mm high text frame, and type in it **Title Placeholder.** Format it with Arial font, 36 points, and center it vertically and horizontally in the frame.
3. On the verso A-Master, insert a text frame at the top of the page that contains an auto page number code aligned away from the spine. Copy this text frame onto the recto A-Master.
4. Duplicate the A-Master spread, and name the copy **B-No Numbers**. Remove the page numbering code from the B-No Numbers master set.
5. Apply the B-No Numbers master to pages 1 and 2.
6. Set the Numbering and Section Options so that the third page in the document is numbered "1".
7. At the bottom of each A-Master page, on the verso pages add a centered text frame: **T.H.E. Journal**. On the recto pages, add a centered text frame containing **Copyright © 2006 All Rights Reserved**
8. Save your work as **XX-EX61.indd**, where XX are your initials.
9. Open **EX61.indd**. This document is based on the same template design that you just created, but already has a document placed in it and some styles created and applied.
10. On the second page (the totally blank one), create a table of contents based on the Heading style, and format it in any way that seems attractive.
11. Export the document to a PDF file called **EX61-XX.pdf**, where XX are your initials, using the [Smallest File Size] preset.
12. Print one copy of the entire document on your default desktop printer.
13. Save the document as **XX-EX61A.indd**, where XX are your initials.
14. Exit InDesign.

Exercise | 62

Curriculum Integration Exercise

Software Skills In Social Studies class you are studying Canada. Find information about Canada on the Web, and create an attractively formatted report in InDesign about it, including pictures.

DIRECTIONS

Find information about Canada on the Web, including:

- Government
- Size (in square miles)
- Provinces and territories
- Economy

Place all this information in a new InDesign document, and format it attractively. Use paragraph styles for body text and for headings of various levels.

Create a table of contents based on the paragraph styles you used for headings.

Save your work as **EX62-XX.indd** where XX are your initials.

Export the file to a PDF called **EX62-XX.pdf** where XX are your initials.

Exit InDesign.

Exercise | 63

Critical Thinking Exercise

Software Skills Real-world print jobs may require different settings than the ones you have worked with in this course. In this exercise, you will contact an actual printer (or get information from your teacher that came from an actual printer) and then export a file meeting those specifications.

DIRECTIONS

- Contact a professional printing company in your area and ask them about accepting PDF and/or EPS files. Find out what specifications they require or prefer.

  ✓ *In a classroom situation, one student should contact the printing company and share the information with the others. If previous classes have already gotten this information, the instructor may have it to share with you.*

- Export **EX56book.indd** (from Exercise 56) in either PDF or EPS using those settings. Name the file **EX63-XX**, where XX are your initials.
- Exit InDesign.

INDEX

G

H

I

J

K

L

M

N

O

P

U

V

W

Z

SINGLE PC LICENSE AGREEMENT AND LIMITED WARRANTY

READ THIS LICENSE CAREFULLY BEFORE OPENING THIS PACKAGE. BY OPENING THIS PACKAGE, YOU ARE AGREEING TO THE TERMS AND CONDITIONS OF THIS LICENSE. IF YOU DO NOT AGREE, DO NOT OPEN THE PACKAGE. PROMPTLY RETURN THE UNOPENED PACKAGE AND ALL ACCOMPANYING ITEMS TO THE PLACE YOU OBTAINED THEM. *THESE TERMS APPLY TO ALL LICENSED SOFTWARE ON THE DISK EXCEPT THAT THE TERMS FOR USE OF ANY SHAREWARE OR FREEWARE ON THE DISKETTES ARE AS SET FORTH IN THE ELECTRONIC LICENSE LOCATED ON THE DISK:*

1. GRANT OF LICENSE and OWNERSHIP: The enclosed computer programs ("Software") are licensed, not sold, to you by Prentice-Hall, Inc. ("We" or the "Company") and in consideration of your purchase or adoption of the accompanying Company textbooks and/or other materials, and your agreement to these terms. We reserve any rights not granted to you. You own only the disk(s) but we and/or our licensors own the Software itself. This license allows you to use and display your copy of the Software on a single computer (i.e., with a single CPU) at a single location for academic use only, so long as you comply with the terms of this Agreement. You may make one copy for backup, or transfer your copy to another CPU, provided that the Software is usable on only one computer.
2. RESTRICTIONS: You may not transfer or distribute the Software or documentation to anyone else. Except for backup, you may not copy the documentation or the Software. You may not network the Software or otherwise use it on more than one computer or computer terminal at the same time. You may not reverse engineer, disassemble, decompile, modify, adapt, translate, or create derivative works based on the Software or the Documentation. You may be held legally responsible for any copying or copyright infringement which is caused by your failure to abide by the terms of these restrictions.
3. TERMINATION: This license is effective until terminated. This license will terminate automatically without notice from the Company if you fail to comply with any provisions or limitations of this license. Upon termination, you shall destroy the Documentation and all copies of the Software. All provisions of this Agreement as to limitation and disclaimer of warranties, limitation of liability, remedies or damages, and our ownership rights shall survive termination.
4. DISCLAIMER OF WARRANTY: THE COMPANY AND ITS LICENSORS MAKE NO WARRANTIES ABOUT THE SOFTWARE, WHICH IS PROVIDED "AS-IS." IF THE DISK IS DEFECTIVE IN MATERIALS OR WORKMANSHIP, YOUR ONLY REMEDY IS TO RETURN IT TO THE COMPANY WITHIN 30 DAYS FOR REPLACEMENT UNLESS THE COMPANY DETERMINES IN GOOD FAITH THAT THE DISK HAS BEEN MISUSED OR IMPROPERLY INSTALLED, REPAIRED, ALTERED OR DAMAGED. THE COMPANY DISCLAIMS ALL WARRANTIES, EXPRESS OR IMPLIED, INCLUDING WITHOUT LIMITATION, THE IMPLIED WARRANTIES OF MERCHANTABILITY AND FITNESS FOR A PARTICULAR PURPOSE. THE COMPANY DOES NOT WARRANT, GUARANTEE OR MAKE ANY REPRESENTATION REGARDING THE ACCURACY, RELIABILITY, CURRENTNESS, USE, OR RESULTS OF USE, OF THE SOFTWARE.
5. LIMITATION OF REMEDIES AND DAMAGES: IN NO EVENT, SHALL THE COMPANY OR ITS EMPLOYEES, AGENTS, LICENSORS OR CONTRACTORS BE LIABLE FOR ANY INCIDENTAL, INDIRECT, SPECIAL OR CONSEQUENTIAL DAMAGES ARISING OUT OF OR IN CONNECTION WITH THIS LICENSE OR THE SOFTWARE, INCLUDING, WITHOUT LIMITATION, LOSS OF USE, LOSS OF DATA, LOSS OF INCOME OR PROFIT, OR OTHER LOSSES SUSTAINED AS A RESULT OF INJURY TO ANY PERSON, OR LOSS OF OR DAMAGE TO PROPERTY, OR CLAIMS OF THIRD PARTIES, EVEN IF THE COMPANY OR AN AUTHORIZED REPRESENTATIVE OF THE COMPANY HAS BEEN ADVISED OF THE POSSIBILITY OF SUCH DAMAGES. SOME JURISDICTIONS DO NOT ALLOW THE LIMITATION OF DAMAGES IN CERTAIN CIRCUMSTANCES, SO THE ABOVE LIMITATIONS MAY NOT ALWAYS APPLY.
6. GENERAL: THIS AGREEMENT SHALL BE CONSTRUED IN ACCORDANCE WITH THE LAWS OF THE UNITED STATES OF AMERICA AND THE STATE OF NEW YORK, APPLICABLE TO CONTRACTS MADE IN NEW YORK, AND SHALL BENEFIT THE COMPANY, ITS AFFILIATES AND ASSIGNEES. This Agreement is the complete and exclusive statement of the agreement between you and the Company and supersedes all proposals, prior agreements, oral or written, and any other communications between you and the company or any of its representatives relating to the subject matter. If you are a U.S. Government user, this Software is licensed with "restricted rights" as set forth in subparagraphs (a)–(d) of the Commercial Computer-Restricted Rights clause at FAR 52.227-19 or in subparagraphs (c)(1)(ii) of the Rights in Technical Data and Computer Software clause at DFARS 252.227-7013, and similar clauses, as applicable.

Should you have any questions concerning this agreement or if you wish to contact the Company for any reason, please contact in writing:

Multimedia Production
Higher Education Division
Prentice-Hall, Inc.
1 Lake Street
Upper Saddle River, NJ 07458